THE POLITICS OF POSTSECULAR RELIGION

INSURRECTIONS:
CRITICAL STUDIES IN RELIGION, POLITICS, AND CULTURE

Insurrections: Critical Studies in Religion, Politics, and Culture
Slavoj Žižek, Clayton Crockett, Creston Davis, Jeffrey W. Robbins, editors

The intersection of religion, politics, and culture is one of the most discussed areas in theory today. It also has the deepest and most wide-ranging impact on the world. Insurrections: Critical Studies in Religion, Politics, and Culture will bring the tools of philosophy and critical theory to the political implications of the religious turn. The series will address a range of religious traditions and political viewpoints in the United States, Europe, and other parts of the world. Without advocating any specific religious or theological stance, the series aims nonetheless to be faithful to the radical emancipatory potential of religion.

After the Death of God   John D. Caputo and Gianni Vattimo, edited by Jeffrey W. Robbins

THE POLITICS OF

POSTSECULAR RELIGION

Mourning Secular Futures

Ananda Abeysekara

Columbia University Press   New York

Columbia University Press

Publishers Since 1893

New York   Chichester, West Sussex

Library of Congress Cataloging-in-Publication Data

Abeysekara, Ananda, 1968–

    The politics of postsecular religion : mourning secular futures / Ananda Abeysekara.

        p. cm. — (Insurrections)

    Includes bibliographical references and index.

    ISBN 978-0-231-14290-8 (cloth : alk. paper) — ISBN 978-0-231-51267-1 (e-book)

I. Religion.   2. Secularism.   3. Democracy.   I. Title.   II. Series.

    BL51.A33 2008

    201'.72—dc22

                                                            2007045831

∞

Casebound editions of

Columbia University Press books are printed on

permanent and durable acid-free paper.

Printed in the United States of America

c 10 9 8 7 6 5 4 3 2

p 10 9 8 7 6 5 4 3 2 1

For Gunjan

Contents

Acknowledgments

"Acknowledgments"—yes, they are indeed a pleasure to do. Yet skulking behind the façade of such acknowledgments is a "peril-less peril," not in the luxury of self-gratification that acknowledging affords, but in the deluded comfort of completing the task, thereby exorcising, eventually forgetting, and perhaps even foregoing those who are acknowledged. How then to acknowledge the peril of the un-acknowledgeable?

Too many figures whose rigor of mind, boldness of thinking, and novelty of imagination—way too many of them to be really acknowledged—have been absent-present in helping me meditate on the ideas in this book. I can think of them only in terms of absent-present, because there was not a moment when I could escape from fear and anxiety about what they would think of every sentence I wrote. Among them Jacques Derrida haunts my thinking. Quite simply, without his work I could not have conceived and completed the book. And then, of course, who can ever forget Nietzsche? If I have learnt anything from these two dead-living figures—this is the only way to speak of them—it is that a life without mourning and un-inheriting is a life that is quite simply im-possible to live. I do not know how to express any gratitude to them except through imagining this im-possibility, which must and will always remain an im-possibility. In one, another, or some other way—and let's not be seduced into reducing it to some self-serving empirical example—I think we all live with the monstrosity of this im-possibility. There can be no democracy, no politics, no responsibility, no ethics, no nonracist future without imagining the im-possibility of un-inheriting. To this endeavor here the works of Talal Asad, Dipesh Chakrabarty, and William Connolly were also critical sources of muse.

Over the years many others have pressed me hard to think the question of the political, demanding me to risk the futureless future of colonialist area studies, barricaded within the liberal-humanist disciplines of Euro-American academia. To that extent the examples of Qadri Ismail and Pradeep Jeganathan have been indispensable. Try though I do, I can hardly reach the bar they have raised in terms of their steadfast commitment to thinking the questions of politics, peace, and nonracist futures in Sri Lanka. My conversations with them, in ways to which they cannot perhaps attest, have taught me that one can no longer produce disquisitions about a subject like religion, history, and heritage in Sri Lanka, or anywhere else for that matter, without a view toward undermining the very disciplinary *and* political possibilities of such exercises. This is, of course, bound to threaten area studies career professionals who continue to write about "others" and their worlds of religion, politics, and even violence, always comforted by the belief that, at the end of the day, the semester, the fieldresearch or the book project, they can, as Dipesh Chakrabarty reminds us, always say, "Yes, I respect your beliefs, but they are not mine." In that sense all our liberal-humanist disciplinary projects—yes, I say "all"—laboring to give the natives back their histories and whatnot, are indeed works of respectful acknowledgment of (always visible) others, but of course with no conceptual, never mind ethical-political, risks ever taken. No, no, simply producing critiques of nationalism, xenophobia, or even capitalism does not amount to taking such risks. But would there be a future where the others are not simply acknowledged, recognized, and respected but also engaged to the point of risking, as Judith Butler might say, the unrecognizability of oneself, if not others? How would our empiricist disciplines write about "such" unrecognizability and think of the question of the political in relation to it? That would be a challenge to be acknowledged.

If there is at least a bit of such challenge undertaken here, it was also challenged by the questions and comments of several friends and colleagues. Brian Britt—who perhaps grasps postcoloniality better than most of the postcolonialists springing up everywhere these days as the season seems to be right and ripe—heard me think out loud many moves that I have made in this book. He took time to read and comment on several chapters in their previous apparitions. A scholar of Brian's caliber—and they are rare—makes me believe that religious studies, dominated by area studies, might still have a future other than the one that is already designed for the field by the powers that be. My new colleague and friend from political science Antonio Y. Vazquez Arroyo argued with me about Derrida, politics, and much more, all the while keeping it real, always cautioning me against the trap of do-nothing, agree-to-disagree, sterilized professionalism that affords scholars the pretense of interest in questions of politics. Needless to say, I have profited from our many uncommonly candid and unpretentiously heated discussions about the notions of responsibility and catastrophe that form the subject of Antonio's own up-and-coming work. Jerome Copulsky kindly read two chapters and cavalierly dismissed Derrida for his supposed lack of a political vision. Mangalika de Silva and Kanchana N. Ruwanpura read parts of the book carefully and challenged me on several points, helping me impose clarity and rigor on some of my arguments. Sally Serafim and Susan Pensak, too, read the manuscript and made many valuable corrections. Now I would be remiss if I did not mention my friend Premakumara De Silva, whose support for this project cannot be adequately stated. Both in Colombo and in Edinburgh, on many occasions of good beer and occasionally good food, I learned enormously from his breadth of vision for the future of Sri Lankanist anthropology and Sri Lankan politics. And, then, at different stages of writing and rewriting, upon my slightest request, as usual Joseph Walser put aside his own work to read and engage several chapters. Others whose intellectual support or friendship continues to be important to me are George D. Bond, Robert Launay, Kumari Jayawardena, Gananath Obeyesekere, C. B. Disanayaka, Indrani and H. L. Seneviratne, Chandrika and Abey Bandara, Nirmala Salgado, Tim Luke, Chris Clement, Paulo S. Polanah, Malory Nye, Steve Berkwitz, Karl Precoda, and Marian Mollin.

At Columbia University Press, Wendy Lochner, one of the best editors around, has unstintingly backed the project ever since I proposed the idea to her in a slightly varyied form several years ago. She saw its promise from the inception and never gave up on it, prodding and counseling me over the years to complete it. Indeed, I doubt that I could have even carried out the project without her unflinching belief in its potential. Needless to say, I consider it my chance-fortune to have been able to work with an editor of her expertise and patience. Insightful comments by the reviewers of the manuscript for the press and pointed questions about history and heritage by a reviewer at the press helped me spell out some of these ideas more clearly. I hope that T. David Brent at the University of Chicago Press, whose firm support for the manuscript kept my hopes alive, understands my decision to go with Columbia. I read parts of these chapters at numerous venues, including the International Center for Ethnic Studies, Oxford University, University of Amsterdam, University of Toronto, University of Colombo, Washington University, Vanderbilt University, University of North Carolina at Chapel Hill, Virginia Tech, Tufts University, and Macalester College. Among those who helped to organize these occasions and commented on my work, I would like to single out Jonathan Spencer, Raphael Sanchez, John Bowen, Mangalika de Silva, David Gellner, Premakumara De Silva, Nimanthi Perera-Rajasingham, Joseph Walser, Steven Berkwitz, and P. Thambiraja. Portions of the book appeared in different form in the following journals: *Journal of the American Academy of Religion* 72(4): 973–1000 and *Culture and Religion* 7(3): 205–243 (http://www.tandf.co.uk/journals).

There is no way passably to avow and testify to the care of love and friendship Gunjan Pant extends toward me. She has taught me everything I could possibly know—or cannot ever know—about the impossibility of chance and life. Her critical input and counsel made this, without doubt, a better book. To her, I dedicate the book. And Arjun, the "joker" and the smart one in our adventure, brought humor to my thinking without ever humanizing it. I could not cogitate about the im-possibilities of surviving, living-on, and un-inheriting without often thinking of Arjun and the futures he might un-inherit.

And, finally, what would acknowledgments amount to without acknowledging what is often un-acknowledged or un-acknowledgeable in our academia? And what gives me the propitious (or perhaps the un-propitious) opportunity to do so is the book's being published in the promising new series Insurrections: Critical Studies in Religion, Politics, and Culture. The editors who wanted the book for the series and other readers will, I hope, find, at the least, moments of insurrectionary thinking in this work. This is important because, if I may say so callously, these days very little if any insurrectionary thinking takes place within the garrisons of our liberal disciplines (including religious studies) where a system of patronage overshadows any possibility of what was once called—perhaps in the simplest Marxist sense of the term—radical thinking. What we inherit under this system—prevalent not just in academia but in the mainstream public as well—is a capitalist and humanist culture of "being nice" that today passes for a progressive sense of politics, responsibility, and even nonracism. (After all, when one is armored with the virtue of being nice, all that is left to do is to make oneself less immune to possible charges of racism. If this virtue counts for a twenty-first century sense of political progress, that progress can always remain progressive! And, might I remind my readers that the most welcoming hosts of this virtue are the departments of liberal arts, whose topography of racial "diversity" today—certainly in America—is exemplified by the token, rare one or two nonwhite colleagues whose expertise in non-Western area studies, by the very imperialist politics of definition, assigns them a priori to a politically "safe" location within the disciplines.) The guise of this progressive civility in our humanist academia, which does not demand of ourselves or our students, never mind the public, any hard *labor of thinking*, barely masks a hierarchy of power, control, and conformity in terms of who gets hired and retained and what gets funded, researched, and published within what fields. All our talk about constantly critiquing and *improving* our existing problems of capitalism, inequality, nationalism, racism, and whatnot operates in the name of this progressive culture. Such talk, of course, does not really think about deracinating the problems of racism, which, as I argue in the book, demands not a mere critique but a wholly other labor. To that extent, I would like to assure misguided conservatives who tirelessly bemoan the supposed radicalizing of academia that their interests and agendas are hardly under attack from the sentinels of the liberal disciplines.

OK, OK (I can already imagine some shaking their heads now), the purpose of these seemingly *generalizing* claims is not to acknowledge a problem that we can easily mock, a problem that we perhaps all know about, but rather to make a different point that has deeper ethical-political implications. That is, I suspect that those who (probably never heard of what is called strategic essentialism and) preach the virtue of attention to the *particular* will write off or carp at the above claims as baseless. After all, there are some, if not many, scholars who challenge the corporate culture of civility in academia and refuse fidelity to it. I too suspect that such persons might exist, even if they may not be able to put a damaging enough dent in its system. All the same, the rush to appeal to the *particular*—whose echo these days can be heard in the ubiquitous self-congratulatory cries of "we are not all the same" or "we all do not do the same thing" or some other variation thereof—indeed risks, if it can ever be a risk at all, promoting the racist system. Surely one cannot disavow any generalization without resorting to the same logic of generalization one is disavowing. But my point here is not that. Rather, when one appeals to the virtue of the particular, one privileges and invokes the treacherous humanist figure of the "I-witness." To insist on the particular is always to insist on an I-witness who can testify to the "presence" of the particular. This figure of the I-witness can, of course, be (and often is) oneself or someone else who acts as a witness to the particular.

Without being able to subject this concept to the kind of interrogation that it rightfully deserves, all I can say here is that the figure of the I-witness, whose parasitical host always remains the evasive domain of the "courthouse," that is, the domain of the juridical, the space of modern justice, or democracy itself, is the figure of a double contradiction that does more harm than good. To witness is not to witness. Even better, witnessing is always a form of un-witnessing. This contradiction is inseparable from I-witnessing. Is this I-witness not the figure that is complicit in the denial and negation of the untold atrocities that always go un-witnessed? Let us not again be tempted to invoke an easy example to illustrate the aporia of the I-witness. One may, of course, be tempted to think of the ongoing U.S.-led Iraq war, whose countless dead-dying Iraqi victims—who must always remain uncountable without being reduced to a statistic—are rarely ever mentioned and *acknowledged,* let alone witnessed and accounted for, by our politicians and so-called journalists even as they ritually repeat the "number" of the dead and maimed soldiers of their *own* nation at press conferences and on news bulletins. (This is, of course, granting that not every dead Iraqi was a "terrorist.") These dead do not really "exist," *even* for those who initially supported the U.S. plan to invade Iraq but now wear the soothing balm of bad conscience and demand the end of war. This is so because the dead are hardly ever "witnessed" or have the possibility of being I-witnesses themselves, capable of testifying to their own deaths, under a sign of presence, standing in front of a camera or some microphone, hollering and ballyhooing that they be accounted for and compensated if not mourned. That is, of course, if one speaks of witnessing in the conventional sense of seeing. I am not speaking of that manner of seeing here. My point is that even if one hears details about their deaths or sees pictures of their bodies, the dead always remain un-witnessed. Indeed, they must. Yet they cannot be left alone. If the dead can never be really witnessed, they nevertheless demand of us recompense. And, yet, what possible "compensation" can there ever be for them?

Yes, even such an example must never be invoked, because it will make possible the un-witnessing of so many other (past, present, and future) victims of war and war-related "incidents" because they would not receive at least the obscure(d) and vanishing, aerial and ground, visions of bomb explosions in Iraq that we are intermittently blessed with. How would one ever witness the un-witnessable? Can the same figure of the I-witness, who prefers the empirical, the particular, the evident, or the event, and who can hence always deny the non-presence of that which cannot be seen, ever be accountable and responsible for the un-witnessable? The un-witnessable are always non-existent and non-present (as far as the I-witnessed is concerned) because the I-witness always demands the truth of knowledge, knowledge of their existences and deaths that must be verified, tallied on a sheet of statistics. (Need I remind that even when such accounts are available—let us not name recent reports of those accounts here—they are dismissed out of hand by our heads of state as "not credible," never to be interrogated by our reputable mainstream journalists.) And it is this un-holy alliance between knowledge and truth embodied in the figure of the I-witness that democracy and its apparatus of law and justice—along with our academia—compete to preserve. Let us not press this point any more except to note that the figure of the I-witness, who cares about the particular, is a figure of secrecy that conceals more than it reveals. I would even go so far as to wager that the power of the I-witness depends not necessarily on its capacity to reveal but on its right to conceal. But the I-witness conceals—I insist on this point however unbelievable it may seem—not what it knows but what it does not know. This is the logic and structure of the I-witness. If there is any way to exit the structure (and we might even say the aporia) of the I-witness, it must begin with *thinking* a future in which one can never be an I-witness—the "I" of oneself or the "I" of any other single/collective self—to anything. Will there ever be a future in which we might be able to think of politics, ethics, responsibility, and democracy from a standpoint—if that can ever be a "standpoint" as such—where we, none of us, have no recourse to the possibility of such an I-witness, where we witness nothing, where we have no possibility of testifying to anything? That would be a future in which we may acknowledge the un-acknowledgeable.

February 2007.

THE POLITICS OF POSTSECULAR RELIGION

Interruption.—Here are hopes; but what will you hear and see of them if you have not experienced splendor, ardor, and dawns in your own souls? I can only remind you; more I cannot do. To move stones, to turn animals into men—is that what you want from me? Oh, if you are still stones and animals, then better look for your Orpheus.   —*Friedrich Nietzsche*, The Gay Science

I understand by "improved"—much the same as "tamed," "weakened," "discouraged," "refined," "pampered," "emasculated" (much the same, then, as damaged).   —*Friedrich Nietzsche*, On the Genealogy of Morals

I never associated the theme of deconstruction with . . . the themes of "diagnosis," of "after" or "post," of "death" (death of philosophy, death of metaphysics, and so on), of "completion" or of "surpassing," of the "end." One will find no trace of such a vocabulary in any of my texts.   —*Jacques Derrida*, Rogues: Two Essays on Reason

I can interrogate, contradict, attack, or simply deconstruct a logic of the text that came before me, and is before me, but I cannot and must not change it.   —*Jacques Derrida*, "Others Are Secret Because They Are Other"

I Thinking the Un-improvable, Thinking the Un-inheritable

Democracy, Name, and Un-inheritance

In a number of his later works Jacques Derrida claimed that "democracy is a promise." By definition, a promise is something that is deferred. That which is deferred is not present or available. Nor is it simply absent. (Indeed, the deferred is irreducible to the binary of presence/absence). Understood this way, to live in a democracy, to be a citizen, to believe in democratic principles—freedom of choice, freedom of the press, human rights, justice, law, among others—is to live in a state of deferral. To believe in the deferred promise is to believe in the future. That is to say, by definition, that which is deferred belongs to the future. Put simply, if democracy is a promise, and if a promise is deferred, then to live in a democracy is to live in the future. This book is an attempt to think seriously about whether we can or cannot inherit such deferred futures of our democracy.[1]

This way of thinking about the future can provide an unheard-of perspective not only on the notions of democracy and secularism but also the concepts of memory, history, heritage, and indeed time itself.[2] It does so in part because the question of how we inherit the deferred democratic future cannot be separated from the question of how we might un-inherit the democratic past/present. That is to say, for Derrida, the future does not mark the point where the past and the present "end." The future does not mark the "post" of the past/present. (This is why Derrida in one of the epigraphs refuses to associate deconstruction with the themes of "post," "after," "end," or "death.") The future is very much animated by the past-present. But, needless to say, this is not the same old view that the past, the present, and the future are inseparable because a seamless thread of continuing time binds them together. On the contrary, the future is deferred by the democratic promise of the past-present. To put it more simply, if our (post)colonial modernity—by this I mean colonial pasts and postcolonial presents in the most rudimentary senses of the terms—is supposedly governed by democratic norms such as human rights, freedom of the press, justice, law, and so on, and if the full (utopian) perfection and realization of those norms can be only promised and hence deferred to the future, then we can only think about whether we can continue to inherit such a future. We can and must only think whether we can continue to inherit such a future, not only because (as some might argue rightly) untold atrocities have been committed in the *name* of defending and sustaining the very name/identity of democracy—one can imagine countless examples here—but also because democracy remains, in each of its futures, deferred, as a promise. As Derrida says, "even when there is democracy, it never exists." [3] It never exists because democracy, as Derrida argues, always "remains to come." I will have much more to say about the importance of the notion of the "to come" of democracy later, but if we begin at least to recognize something of the insight in Derrida's claim, the question that emerges here is: how (and how long) can we continue to bank on inheriting democracy as a promise that will always remain deferred, remaining to come in the future? Can we continue to pursue something that always remains deferred? I take up these questions in chapters 4 and 7 of this book, however, the point that I want to stress here is that as far as the identity or the *name* of democracy goes, the question of inheriting is always a question of un-inheriting. To think about inheriting the deferred future of our democracy is always to think about un-inheriting it.

Hence the word *inheriting* should be written as *un-inheriting*. By un-inheriting I mean a pathway of reflecting upon the postcolonial conceptions of heritage, history, and identity that is not reducible to a ready-made binary of remembering/forgetting or embracing/ abandoning. Such a binary surely plays into hands that would—for all sorts of convenient political, nationalist, racist, militant, separatist, humanist, or modernist reasons—want either to remember or to forget the violent legacies of our modernity. Rather, as far as our pasts, heritages, histories, and identities are concerned, the kind of un-inheriting I have in mind is not reducible to receiving or abandoning, remembering or forgetting, embracing or rejecting. For me, un-inheriting is a pathway of thinking about the (aporetic) heritage of our democratic modernity and all its (deferred) promises of the future that we cannot receive or reject. It is this pathway of thinking about our modernity that I call "mourning secular futures."[4]

The question of un-inheriting has received little or no attention in the literature of disciplines that range from religion and postcolonial studies to history, political theory, philosophy, cultural studies, and anthropology; indeed, it is safe to say that the disciplines (which are specifically concerned with questions of the postmodern or the postcolonial) do not have a theory or a language of un-inheriting at all.[5] My contention is that the lack of a theory of un-inheriting largely owes to, and is compensated by, a particular tradition and style of comprehending and critiquing the "problem" of our postcolonial-secular-democratic modernity; this tradition has become as pervasive as it is, perhaps, in the wake of the Foucauldian (or Foucauldian-inspired) postcolonial practice of writing genealogical histories (chapter 2). As Foucault explained it, the art of writing genealogies is a mode of "problematization," which is essentially about understanding how an object of knowledge (madness or discipline or sex) has become a historical "problem." Thus, it assumes that to understand how an object of knowledge became a historical problem is to have performed a critical labor. Yet problematization tells us almost nothing about how we might *think* (about and with) the historicized problem. Foucault offers no answers here, simply because his genealogy has no (certainly no explicit) concern with thinking about the question of un-inheriting. It is perhaps because we have no such thinking about un-inheriting that dominant postcolonial and postmodern works (be they Foucauldian or not) take for granted that even though democratic modernity— marked by norms such as freedom, justice, civic responsibility, individuality, human rights, and tolerance—has become a *problem,* it can and must be reconstructed, refashioned, and improved. There is an almost tautological argument here: democracy must be reconstructed because its very *name* cannot be easily abandoned. Hence reconstructing and improving democracy is possible and done *in the name of itself*. The argument boils down to a belief that there is always a core in the name—be it the name "justice" or "law" or "human rights"—that can be recovered, reconstructed, and changed. The core is the name itself. It is as if one could always reconstruct and return to the name, *in the name of the name,* if you will. In that sense the name is never expendable or exhaustible. It is always full of unrealized potential and hence always available for improvement and perfection. Once reconstructed and improved, from time to time and generation to generation, the name can be re-inherited.

This, largely, is how postcolonial critics approach the heritage of democratic modernity. Take, for example, Paul Gilroy, who argues in his book *Postcolonial Melancholia* for an "unorthodox defense of the twentieth-century utopia of [multicultural] tolerance, peace, and mutual regard," against the post-9/11 context that demands homogeneity and unity as a virtue of strength.[6] Gilroy impugns the idea of the "death" of multiculturalism heralded on many fronts, by popular U.S. scholars such as Samuel Huntington and by the so-called global war on terror, which, as he claims, is beginning to spawn a new climate of racism and ethnic profiling in England. But, unlike the United States, where racial groups are segregated more than ever, in England a hopeful (and an improved) culture of "multicultural conviviality" *already* exists in its urban centers. In this conviviality— aided in part by "years of tokenism" on the part of sports, pop music, advertising, the House of Lords, and now reality TV—what matters, Gilroy asserts, is not racial or ethnic divisions but daily differences in "taste, lifestyle, leisure preferences, cleaning, gardening, and child care. . . . Alongside those habits, racial and ethnic differences appear mundane, even boring."[7] For Gilroy, the "motley" crowds that came together to mourn collectively the death of Princes Diana and protest against the U.S. invasion of Iraq serve as other powerful examples of such conviviality. It is this multiculturalism, Gilroy insists, that must be recovered, defended, and retained as an alternative to the decade-long anti-immigration racism and the emerging post-9/11 xenophobia made possible in England by a discourse of national security. I will have more to say about the problem of multiculturalism in chapters 2 and 7, but my purpose here is to sketch how Gilroy seeks to recover and re-inherit the heritage of democracy. Surely he understands the problem with the old notion of multiculturalism and its politics of tolerance and he consequently speaks of the need for a kind of "new" multiculturalism. This new multiculturalism, he says, will refuse "state centeredness" and embody "a vernacular style," creating "conceptions of humanity that allow for the presumption of equal value and go beyond the issue of tolerance into a more active engagement with the irreducible value of diversity within sameness" (*Postcolonial Melancholia*, 67). The story, in a nutshell, is this: the new multiculturalism is not the same as the old one; it will be new. It will retain values such as equality but will go beyond the mere notion of tolerance. The adjective *new*, in other words, is another name for the reconstructed and improved form of multiculturalism. Hence, in order to re-inherit the heritage of the democratic values that have become problematic over the years, one must reconstruct them. This is Gilroy's theory of re-inheriting democracy, and he is not alone in advancing it. Similarly, in his wide-ranging book *Democracy and Tradition,* acclaimed as one of the best works since the publication of John Rawls's *A Theory of Justice*, religious studies professor Jeffrey Stout offers an indefatigable defense of democracy as a tradition of moral-civic responsibility against what he perceives as an increasing onslaught on the secular by certain philosophers and theologians, such as Stanley Hauerwas and John Milbank.[8] As I will demonstrate in chapter 3, Stout too sees democracy as a tradition capable of being reconstructed and enriched from generation to generation. Different contexts, he posits, make possible the enrichment of democratic principles, and each generation must attend to the task, in the name of democracy, in the name of re-inheriting the name of democracy.[9]

This view of inheriting democracy may not be same as the much-maligned Habermasian notion of (longing for the fulfillment of) the unfinished project of the Enlightenment, but the idea that the heritage of democracy can be remade from time to time has a deeper tradition itself. The view is rooted in the pragmatist tradition of the Deweyan variety.[10] Fundamentally, John Dewey held that the task of democratic citizenship is to remake democratic principles in each of its times, always returning to the very "idea" of democracy. The governing presumption in Dewey is that the heritage can (and must) be remade, *in the name of the name itself.* More generally, the same presumption about heritage and history can be found among postmodern critics of other disciplines. Consider, for instance, literary theorist Maurice Blanchot's argument about the notion of *philia*. As I elaborate in chapter 7, *philia* is the Greek term for what we know as "friendship," and the heritage of what it means is entrenched in a long history that made distinctions between not only brothers and nonbrothers but also between friends and enemies, from the classical Greek era to modernist (Nazi) times. The phallogocentric and genocidal heritage of friendship, as Derrida reminds us, is inseparable from the heritage of democracy. Democracy, like friendship, is rooted in a heritage of separating brothers from nonbrothers, friends from enemies. But Blanchot, among others, argues that, notwithstanding its *problematic* past, the Greek tradition of friendship can be transformed and "enriched." As he writes, "*philia,* which for the Greeks and even Romans, remained the model of what is excellent in human relations (with the enigmatic character it receives from opposite imperatives, at once pure reciprocity and unrequited generosity), can be received as a heritage always capable of being enriched." [11] The key point here is worth repeating: the problematic heritage of Greek *philia*/democracy can "always" be received and enriched. The overarching belief that connects these different thinkers, then, is that the name—be it the name of tolerance, democracy, or friendship—can always be received and retained while changing, modifying, and enriching its particular (no longer desirable) characteristics. To improve or enrich the tradition of democracy or friendship, one must retain its name. One cannot possibly speak of improving or enriching the name, however, without (retaining) the name. That is to say, the name must remain, but with *difference.* That which is improved or enriched may be different, but it must bear the "same" name. The name cannot differ without (retaining) itself. This quality, as Derrida noted, is the self-sovereignty of the name (*ipseity*). [12] In a word, then, one improves democracy *in the name of the name.*

I will have more to say about the aporia of the name/identity soon and about the concept of "difference" later (in chapter 3). For now my point is that there is something deeply questionable about the above logic of inheritance presented here. [13] Beginning to think about how we might un-inherit this way of inheriting the heritage/name itself has enormous political implications. The question I want to pose is this: can we continue to inherit the heritage of democracy and retain its name in the future simply by enriching it? Does the future lie just *after* the reconstruction of the heritage of democracy that we have received? Is this way of thinking about our political futures a legacy that we can continue to (re)inherit? When I question the above logic of inheritance, I am not intimating that we abdicate democratic norms in place of a *better* way of being. That would be too simple-minded a proposition. Indeed, I think we can neither defend—if such a thing is possible at all—nor abandon democracy. *This is the aporia of our postcolonial modernity.* My concern is with how we might *think* about this aporia itself, about which many contemporary works on democratic theory have precious little to say, and how such thinking may produce for us an unheard-of future.

My view of the aporia of modernity is radically different from the ways in which some postmodern critics understand the problem and crisis of the democratic modernity. One thinks of the intimidating example of Slavoj Žižek. A distinguished contemporary political critic of international standing, Žižek can be, without a doubt, described as wholly antidemocratic. In stark contrast to Stout and Gilroy, Žižek finds almost nothing redeeming about, or recoverable from, democracy. In his view democracy is a problem that we cannot and must not (re)inherit, particularly because of its present-day unholy consanguinity with capitalism. We can only renounce democracy-capitalism. One may, of course, argue that the politics of our democratic present have reached a dead end, yet we cannot, discard democracy as simply and easily as Žižek proposes. Žižek's alternative suggestion—if it can constitute an "alternative" at all—is to (re)inherit the "subversive core" of Christianity, which will be embodied within a new Pauline community, liberated and free from all fundamentalist accretions and corruptions. In fact, for him, the crisis of modernity calls for not only the death of democracy but also the death of Christianity itself, which, he argues, is Saint Paul's basic message. With the death of democracy and Christianity emerges a new and different Christian "community." However different it may be, this newly resurrected Christian-Pauline community will still bear the same (old) name: the (Christian) community. For Žižek, as for others, the name does not present a permanent problem because it can be renewed and therefore can become something "new." [14] The new redeems the old, if you will, but the new still retains the (old) name ("community"). As I point out in chapters 2 and 3, there is of course a whole host of problems with the very notion of community that Žižek uses to describe the new

Pauline Christianity. Is community not an intimate ally of the idea of democracy itself, the very identity that Žižek wants to abandon? Now Žižek could defend himself only by saying that what he wants to retain is a community without community, a Christianity without Christianity—that is to say, to have the name without the name! This is an im-possibility, and I shall demonstrate in this book why I think so.[15] Surely critics such as Žižek know at least something of the problem with wanting to have the name without the substance that makes it up—for example, elsewhere Žižek has rightly parodied the paradoxical practices of our permissive liberal society of control, of Coke *without* caffeine, beer *without* alcohol, cream *without* fat, sex *without* sex (which is virtual sex), and war *without* war (the Colin Powell doctrine). Yet, even at the end of his searing critique of liberal-capitalistic democracy, Žižek remains unable to suggest anything other than the name *without* the name, e.g., a Pauline Christianity, and this is in part because he has not thought adequately about the aporia of the name. If it is an overhauled democracy that Stout and Gilroy seek, Žižek envisions an overhauled Christianity. Even though Gilroy, Stout, Blanchot, and Žižek are animated by starkly different political orientations and seek to receive different ideological-political heritages, the logic of how they want to inherit them is the same.

If the contemporary postmodern or postcolonial theory of inheriting boils down to the preceding logic, I think it bespeaks an inability to think seriously about the question of the "post" in relation to the future of the political. But there have been, of course, attempts at thinking about the question of the post. In a recent book, *After Christianity*, the Italian philosopher-parliamentarian Gianni Vattimo ventures to meditate on the question of the post in terms of the future identity of Christianity.[16] For Vattimo, any consideration of the possibility of a post-Christianity in the West must take into account the process of secularization. Secularization, he asserts, is "the fulfillment of the central Christian message and prepares us for a new mode of Christianity." In so claiming, Vattimo is not thinking of the ways in which our democratic sovereignty is haunted by the spectral legacy of the secretive Abrahamic religions, an argument that Derrida makes (chapter 2, this volume). Rather, he is merely thinking about how we might recover Christianity after Christianity's own death, announced by postmodernist thought. "The postmodern pluralism," he writes, "has enabled (for me, though I mean it in a more general sense) the recovery of the Christian faith" (*After Christianity*, 5). Vattimo has in mind particularly Nietzsche's proclamation about the death of God as well as Heidegger's notion of the end of metaphysics. Vattimo claims that the death of a (moral) God does not equal the end of Christianity, but, rather, it creates room for the emergence of "new gods." Because Nietzsche could not and did not deny the existence of God, and because philosophy has now recognized that it cannot with certainty make claims about the "ultimate foundation," we no longer have a need for philosophical atheism. Hence, contrary to what most would say, Vattimo argues, "the end of metaphysics and the death of moral God have liquidated the philosophical basis of atheism" (17). This liquidation makes "it possible to take the Bible seriously in so far as it is the principal book that has marked deeply the 'paradigm' of Western culture" (7). For Vattimo, taking the Bible seriously does not involve returning to the Church or some fundamentalist Christian ideology. To the contrary, this new Christianity must "embrace the destiny of modernity" without becoming another sect (97–98). It must because the old Christianity can no longer have any say in the "intercultural conflicts," certainly with the collapse of the universal certainty of the western concept of reason (96). To embrace modernity, Christianity can no longer aspire to become a "strong identity," but it must deepen "its own physiognomy as source and condition for the possibility of secularity" (98). The general story here is that the death of (old) Christianity gives birth to a new Christianity; the very process of postmodern pluralism that kills Christianity creates a *new* Christian identity. I need not proceed with unpacking this argument: however complicatedly and differently it may be framed, the argument ends up echoing the familiar logic of inheritance—that is, as if one could easily pass through the (passage of the) death of the name to recover the name. The name can always be recovered, recycled, and reused after its death. Put differently, the general logic of inheritance is this: the heralded death of the name (which is democracy for Gilroy and Stout) can be thwarted, or the name (which would be Christianity for Žižek and Vattimo) can be resurrected after its own death.

I do not want to suggest that these thinkers are necessarily wrong in trying to improve and reshape certain features and principles of democracy or the Christian tradition. In fact, I do share especially Gilroy's and Stout's commitment to an (antiracist) culture of democratic tolerance and justice. I question, however, the conceptual rigor in their argument because it is based on a logic that returns to the name of the name. I am glad to yield to these critics, granted that their task of thinking the new or the post or the after cannot avoid the problem of the name. What I am suggesting, then, is that they have not rigorously thought through the relation between the name and its supposed postidentity or postincarnation.[17] It seems to me that if we begin to doubt this logic of inheritance, terms such as the *postsecular* also become deeply problematic. Can we possibly speak of a "post-secular" secularism in the sense that Vattimo speaks of an after- or a post-Christianity?[18] Note that I am not merely suggesting that these terms are unclear and hence need to be defined with greater clarity and precision. Rather, for the time being, I want to take it for granted that there cannot be such a thing as the postsecular because the secular cannot be reconstructed. In so doing I want to pose a different set of questions: what option(s) might be available if we began to think that there is no possibility of having secularism after secularism, democracy after democracy, Christianity after Christianity? What if we never have the possibility of reconstructing and improving the name? How would we even begin to think about the im-possibility of such an inheritance?

Deconstructive Thinking and the Un-improvable

This is where, I think, Derrida's notion of deconstruction and its relation to un-inheriting the aporia of the name can become important in ways not recognized earlier. Thinking about the very democratic possibility of the name as an aporia (a non-passage or an im-possibility itself) can give us a wholly different perspective than that which we can no longer reconstruct or improve. Contrary to what some may insinuate, such thinking is not an abstract mode of intel-lectualizing that one can oppose to a realistic, pragmatist view of the world. Such thinking can bear profound political implications, and the pragmatism of Richard Rorty's or Will Kymlicka's breed can learn much from it. (In fact, as I will show in chapters 5 and 7, the pragma-tist viewpoints of politics themselves are not as pragmatic as some fantasize, because they remain anchored in a deferred and abstract notion of justice and fairness.) To think the un-improvable name and the im-possibility of its inheritance, one must begin by understanding why that which is deconstructed can never be reconstructed. Note what Derrida says in one of the epigrams: "I can interrogate, contradict, attack, or simply deconstruct a logic of the text that came before me, and is before me, but I cannot and must not change it." [19] This is one of the clearest statements about deconstruction, and I show in chapter 7 the importance of such a deconstructive project in my reading of Derrida's opus, *Politics of Friendship*. What should be noted here is the profundity of this statement: that ("a logic of the text") which is deconstructed cannot be changed. My intimation is: what if we were to think of the name—the name of a book called the Bible or the name of a religion called Buddhism or Christianity or the name of a country called Sri Lanka or the name of a "religious-ethnic" group called the Sinhalese or the Tamil—as a text itself? [20] What if such a text is one that we can deconstruct because it has a history, a history within which so many have attempted to comment upon it—through wars, through genocides, through separatist struggles—so as to change and reconstruct it from generation to generation? What if we view any ethical-political name/identity (i.e., Sinhalese or Buddhist) as such a text, one that can be deconstructed but cannot be changed and improved? How would we begin to think about, meditate on, and respond to such a deconstructable yet unchangeable name/identity? Can we ever really begin to *respond* to the deconstructed name/identity that we embody and live with but cannot change? At the risk of restating the obvious, let me emphasize that I am not arguing that a person cannot change herself in terms of modifying her habits, her manners, her style, her tastes, her relations with others, and whatnot. Yet the heritage of the name/identity—into which we are installed and inducted (in which, as Althusser might say, we are "always-already") and which can be deconstructed—cannot be changed and improved. Note what Nietzsche says in the epigraph about the im-possibility of improvement: "I understand by 'improved'—much the same as 'tamed,' 'weakened,' 'discouraged,' 'refined,' 'pampered,' 'emasculated' (much the same, then, as *damaged*")." [21] For Derrida, in some sense deconstruction undermines, and perhaps damages, the logic of a text/name/identity, but it does not and cannot reconstruct it. At the same time, deconstruction is not about the end or death of the text; nor is it concerned with completing or surpassing or passing through the text. (This is the fundamental difference between Derrida's deconstruction and that of his predecessors, including the two

eminent German Martins, Luther and Heidegger.)²² I can imagine
at this point the reader is scratching her head in bewilderment: what
on earth does this deconstruction, which deconstructs but *does not
change name/identity*, have to do with "politics"? Yes, deconstruction
will have nothing to do with politics in the sense that it deconstructs
the very idea of what we know and cherish as politics. Viewed this
way—Derrida mentioned it innumerable times—deconstruction can
never be political. On the contrary, deconstruction poses questions
about the political that are irreducible to what we know as politics
now (be it the kind associated with a regime or a political party or
some other government or nongovernmental "political" organization). For me, as for Derrida, such a sense of politics is insufficient
for thinking about the aporia of the name. No politics, no democracy,
no regime, no political organization—"radical," "fugitive," or otherwise—can adequately respond to the aporia of the name.²³ (That is,
even if we follow early Marx's [1844] definition that "to be radical is
to grasp things by the root; but for man, the root is man himself,"
then democracy cannot be radical as such. If for democracy the root
is democracy itself, then once `democracy becomes radical and grasps
itself by the root, uprooting itself, will it still remain democratic?)²⁴
No democratic politics can ever solve the aporetic contradiction that
inheres in the name and the violent duality (e.g., Sinhalese/Tamil,
black/white, Muslim/Jew, friend/enemy) that it creates and sustains.
Indeed, the very notion of democracy is sustained by the name and its
opposite, identity and difference, and hence is fundamentally incapable of thinking of its (democracy's) own aporia. This incapability itself
is the aporia of democratic and postcolonial modernity; that is to say,
democracy cannot be improved to eradicate the problem of identity/
difference, minority/majority that sustains its very being. If by democracy and justice one means laws, then laws can be deconstructed:
old laws can be changed and new ones can be instituted to modify
and ameliorate the relations between the name and its opposites—
between, say, the Sinhalese and the Tamils—to create a *better* climate
of respect and mutual regard for one another. But such a climate will
never question the very political and genocidal distinction between
names such as Sinhalese/Tamils defined in terms of numerical categories like majority and minority. This is so because democracy/
justice, which authorizes and sustains such distinctions, can (no longer) be deconstructed (chapters 4 and 6). Democracy/justice cannot

be deconstructed, in part because it is a deferred promise, but also because any deconstruction of it in terms of improving laws cannot eradicate the aporia of the name/identity. Democracy/justice cannot ever eradicate the name/identity because it relies precisely on the logic of numbering, which counts and distinguishes identity from difference, self from other, Sinhalese from Tamil. No culture of tolerance can ever really solve the problem of number(ing). The question here is, can democracy ever function without numbers or what I call (ac)countability (see chapter 3)? Put alternatively, can there ever be a democracy *without* democracy? For Derrida there cannot be democracy without democracy, just as there cannot be the name without the name or religion without religion.[25] As he argues forcefully in the *Politics of Friendship*, the future of democracy does not lie at the end of the mere preposition: *without* (the preposition by which, as Žižek rightly notes, the politics of capitalistic consumption are animated). Thus, when Derrida argues that justice/democracy cannot be deconstructed (anymore), he means to attune us to the im-possibility of inheriting the name without the name, religion without religion. Need I repeat myself here? Once the name is deconstructed, it can never be reconstructed. The task here is to think about this aporia, that is, to think about how we may live with (and perhaps begin to respond to and un-inherit) the name that has been (already) deconstructed. That is precisely what I attempt to do in this book.

Postcolonial Modernity: Tragic or Aporetic?

Before I spell out more clearly the significance of viewing the heritage of postcolonial modernity in terms of aporia, it would be helpful to situate and distinguish this project in relation to Talal Asad's work on the problem of secularism. Arguably Asad is one of the most formidable thinkers today to contemplate the problem of secularism in singularly original ways, as in his work *Formations of the Secular*.[26] My purpose here is not to summarize this very complex work but only to emphasize an aspect of it that differentiates it from many works that critique secularism and democratic sovereignty (e.g., Žižek's). That is, even though Asad's thinking is obviously influenced by Foucault's genealogy and its mode of problematization, in *Formations* he is not offering *just* one more critique of secularism or the nation-state.

Certainly, he examines critically varying facets of the history of secularism in relation to such themes as pain, cruelty, human rights, law, and torture, demonstrating skillfully the ways in which the secular cannot simply be opposed to the irrational or the sacred. But, apart from this, there seems to be a potentially more interesting question that seems to haunt Asad's thinking. I say potentially, because the question is nowhere clear, let alone explicitly stated. Let me demonstrate what I have in mind by examining Asad's moving and witty "Responses" to a host of interlocutors of his works in a recent volume titled *Powers of the Secular*.[27] Lest I, like so many of Asad's interlocutors, misread his work, I want to focus on his responses to two interlocutors so as to tease out precisely the critical parts of his arguments. One of his responses is to the noted sociologist Jose Casanova, whose thesis on secularism Asad criticizes in *Formations*.[28] Casanova complains that Asad has misread his thesis, which states that the secular spheres (say, for instance, the modern state, the capitalist market economy, and the sciences) are different not only from each other but from the religious spheres as well. This thesis, Casanova believes, is "still the defensible core of the theory of secularization."[29] Asad, of course, disagrees. For Asad, the problem is that the thesis simply "equates secularism with modernity, as many sociologists have defined it."[30] In other words, Casanova takes secularization to be self-evident. As a result, Asad argues, Casanova's theory fails "to identify the different kinds of secular life and the political reasoning on which they are based" ("Responses," 208). Asad argues, for example, that the United States, whose population is largely religious, supposedly cultivates a neutral stance toward religion, but historically Christian movements in the country have lobbied and fought for causes such as abolition of slavery, prohibition, abortion (pro and con), and Israel's regional security. Moreover, U.S. federal courts often make decisions concerning questions of appropriate lifestyles under the Freedom of Religion Act, thereby making it possible for the state to "continually define what is true religion." Asad goes on to point out that although France's population is largely nonreligious, all church property belongs to the state and "priests, ministers, and rabbis are state employees." In this sense, Asad claims, "a state that maintains the basic conditions for the practice of religion in society is itself religious." Certainly, the United States and France are very different in their juridical and constitutional structures, and they respond "very differently to religious institutions and norms." Even so, Asad holds that "in neither case are state and religion completely separate." Hence, for Asad the problem with Casanova's thesis is that it hinders any inquiry into these sorts of historical twists and turns and "avoids examining the complicated prejudgments on which relations between religion and state appear to rest in constitutional law" (208).

Asad is thus interested in attuning us to these kinds of historical complexities. But he is not a historian in the familiar sense of the word. Asad is a genealogist in the most expanded Foucauldian sense of the word, through and through.[31] He argues he does "*not* describe historical development . . . in terms of a linear consequence of ideas, as Casanova and other sociologists often do ('Protestant Reformation' as a cause and 'secular modernity' as an effect), because genealogical investigation presupposes a more complicated web of connections and recursivities than a notion of a causal chain does" (210). What he wants to demonstrate is not merely that religion and the secular merely intersect, but also that

> (a) both are historically constituted, (b) this happens through accidental processes bringing together a variety of concepts, practices, and sensibilities, and (c) in modern society the law is crucially involved in defining and defending the distinctiveness of social spaces—especially the legitimate space for religion. In *Formations of the Secular*, I . . . [argued that] in modern society the law finds itself continually having to redefine the space that religion may properly occupy because the reproduction of secular life ceaselessly disturbs the clarity of its boundaries. I observed that "'the unceasing pursuit of the new in productive effort, aesthetic experience, and claims to knowledge, as well as unending struggle to extend individual self-creation undermines the stability of established boundaries.'" The point that interests me, therefore, is not that we need to be careful in drawing analytical distinctions. . . . My concern is with the *process* by which boundaries are established and by which they come to be defined as modern. (209)

This, then, is what Asad does so well, and this is what, he charges, historians and sociologists such as Casanova fail to do. Concurring as I do with almost everything that Asad says—I count myself among those who have learned much from his work—the question I want to pose is this: is it simply enough to demonstrate how the laws continually redefine the boundary between religion and state? More precisely, what sort of "thinking" is the genealogical inquiry supposed to produce? How are we to think about the problem of "law," justice, and democracy at the end of the genealogical investigation? This is what remains unclear at best in Asad's work. Here I am not posing a pragmatist question, that is, I am not asking if Asad's work has any "political" value. If anything, Asad *problematizes*—in the Foucauldian sense of the word—what is usually taken to be the domain of "politics," marked by the secular state and its laws, separated from the supposed private sphere. I ask again: how might we think (about) the problematized secularism/laws? Asad offers no answers to these questions.

David Scott, another of Asad's interlocutors in *Powers of the Secular*, reads a "tragic" sense into Asad's thinking about modernity. Scott claims that we can find a tragic sensibility in his work because Asad casts doubt on "the possibility or desirability of self-mastery" in our modernity, "drawing us away from the glad hubris that the world (including our own worldly selves) is there for the molding or the shaping and toward a more somber appreciation of the debt we owe to the past . . . and the extent to which are shaped by its contingent, passional, and sometimes catastrophic necessities" ("Tragic Sensibility," 153.) This is a very liberal characterization of Asad's work, and Asad himself modestly disavows any such sense of the tragic in his thinking about modernity ("Responses," 235). Scott claims that Asad's is a tragic view of modernity in part because in *Formations* Asad takes issue with a dominant reading of Sophocles' *Oedipus Tyrannus* and questions whether the notion of agency can be understood in terms of responsibility, answerability, and punishment. Contrary to scholars such as Bernard Williams, Asad argues in a chapter titled "Agency and Pain" that the tragic story of Oedipus cannot be understood as a narrative about responsibility: Oedipus did not suffer because he had to answer or respond to anybody but because he was "virtuous" (*Formations*, 96). Asad says that his interest in the Oedipus story had nothing to do with wanting to conceptualize modernity in terms of tragedy, however.

> My purpose in discussing the tragedy of Oedipus was . . . to explore some aspects of agency and pain in a secular context. It was not intended as a disquisition on tragedy as such. I was concerned neither with the thesis that human beings are in fundamental

disharmony (as Bernard Williams held in the book I cited) nor with the paradigmatic sequence of tragedy: confusion, violence, horror, and meaningless suffering resolved eventually into guilt, moral lucidity, the recognition of personal responsibility, and the calm recovery of meaning. . . . I simply wanted to say that if one reads *Oedipus* purposefully, one might see more clearly that moral agency doesn't necessitate the ideas of intentionality (in contrast to consciousness), responsibility (answerability to authority), and "just punishment." So I am reluctant to use that piece—or anything else that I have written—to claim a privilege for the tragic sensibility. . . . I think that a malign fate rules us collectively, often turning our best intentions against us. I am not sure that that amounts to a tragic vision. ("Responses," 233)

If it is not a tragic vision of modernity, is it more accurate to say that Asad's is a form of aporetic thinking? To be sure, aporia is not tragedy: thinking about the aporia of democracy is not thinking about how we do not have self-mastery or developing a somber appreciation for a modern world shaped by "catastrophic necessities," as Scott claims.[32] Asad mentions the word *aporia* at least once—so far as I can locate. In explaining why he considers religion itself a liberal product, he argues:

As a value-space, liberalism today provides its advocates with a common political and moral language (whose ambiguities and aporias allow it to evolve) in which to identify problems and with which to dispute. Such ideas as individual sovereignty, freedom, limitation of state power, toleration, *and secularism* are central to that debate. . . . In referring to religion as liberal, I refer to its adjustment to these (often incompatible) ideas. ("Responses," 210)

This is where Asad stops; nowhere does he ever think the notion of aporia. Here I am not criticizing Asad but only want to note the point where his genealogy of secularism leaves off. Certainly, I note the importance of understanding the "ambiguities" of the moral-political language of our secularism, but thinking about the aporia of secularism is a wholly separate labor. Asad does not proceed beyond examining the ambiguities, in part because the dominant method of his inquiry is not "deconstruction," at least not in the way that Derrida understands it. What Asad carries out is genealogical critique. (*And critique—be it Foucauldian or Marxist or postcolonial—is not deconstruction.*)[33] Even though Asad differs from most critics of our secularism, he does not have a theory of un-inheritance; he cannot tell us how we might begin to think about, much less mourn, the obvious *problems* of the heritage of the state/laws that redefine the boundary between religion and the secular. My point here is that the problem with Asad is *not* because he does not practice Derrida's deconstruction. Rather, even though he poses questions about memory and history—"what kinds of authorized memory and presentiment go into these contrasting definitions of religion in 'secular' societies?" he asks—nowhere does he spell out the implications for *thinking* (about) such questions in relation to the problem of un-inheritance ("Responses," 209). If, at the end of his genealogical critique, the history within which the laws are changed to define and redefine the distinction between religion and the secular appears as a problem, might we begin to think about mourning/un-inheriting that history instead of just seeing it in terms of its ambiguities? Is it just sufficient to go on problematizing such history? Or, simply put, can we continue to inherit the history of these ambiguities, in the name of secularism? This particular question is important, given that Asad does not seem to think that we can just receive the heritage of secularism, nor does he think we can simply abandon its legacy. Asad, whose genealogy attempts to pursue the secular through its "shadows," can never recommend easily forsaking the legacy of democratic modernity (*Formations*, 16).[34] If heritage is like a shadow, surely it is not easy to abandon or cast off. (Nietzsche, too, noted the difficulty of casting off the shadow when he said that even the shadow of God, whose death he announced, must be vanquished [chapter 2].) Yet Asad does not demonstrate any interest in posing these sorts of questions about the heritage of secularism. This is not just Asad's shortcoming. It is a general shortcoming anchored in the tradition of genealogical inquiry itself, and a pathway of un-inheriting is not available to it.

Unlike genealogical efforts, deconstruction does not just problematize but *thinks* about un-inheriting and mourning the irresolvable contradictions of modernity—that is, the deconstructed (name, identity, history, and laws) or the undeconstructable (justice, law, and political sovereignty). My argument here is that once our secularism, its apparatus of justice and law—again I am speaking of "law" and not of "laws"—is viewed as an aporia, as an irresolvable contradiction, then the *im-possibility* of thinking about un-inheriting the heritage of our democratic identity may have a future.[35] Note that I say "im-possibility," because, just as un-inheritance is irreducible to inheriting or abandoning, to remembering or forgetting, im-possibility is irreducible to any notion of possibility or impossibility. It is such a concept of un-inheritance that we could imagine should we begin to understand our modernity as marked and stalled by aporias.

Aporia, the Question of Death, and the Un-inheritable

No other thinker of late but Jacques Derrida has written tirelessly about the aporias that animate the legacies and inheritances of our democratic-secular beings and belongings. However, this aspect of Derrida's thinking is hardly appreciated, much less conceptualized, in terms of thinking about the questions of heritage and un-inheritance in relation to the futures of the political.[36] Derrida has commented on the notion of the aporia in numerous writings, but the most sustained disquisition on it is in his aptly titled *Aporias*.[37]

In *Aporias* Derrida begins with a question about how we might think about such concepts as "limits," "borders," and "beyond" by way of discussing the phrase *limits of life*. He claims that an irresolvable contradiction inheres in the phrase. Derrida asks if there is such a thing as "limits of life." He then goes on to ponder the question in relation to Diderot, who, in an essay purportedly on the life of the Stoic philosopher Seneca, claimed that the "limits of truth" must not be crossed lest it create a "'general defect.'" But, Derrida asks, does not the very word *limits* suggest that one can cross the limits, because it has the sense of being "limited, *finite*, and confined within its borders" (*Aporias*, 1)? The question that emerges is can that which is finite ever be confined within borders or limits? Derrida argues that "as soon as truth [or life] is a limit or has limits, its own, and assuming that it knows some limits, as the expression goes, truth [or life] would be a certain relation to what terminates or determines it" (2). Perhaps it is precisely because life/truth is finite that it must be contained and safeguarded within limits.

Hence a powerful irony: that which confines and safeguards life also terminates (or threatens to terminate) it. In other words, the limits of life presuppose and predetermine its end or death. But what is this end/death? Does one get to end/death by crossing the limits of life? Does life in its end, in its death, have borders? If so, can death then be contained within borders? The larger question that concerns Derrida here is whether we can ever really think of death as the end of life. That is to say, if one were to speak of the limits of life, one would already know about its end as a *possibility*. But can we really speak of the end/death of life as a possibility? This is why Derrida poses the seemingly senseless question: "My death—is it possible?" He goes on to think about the question with a brief reading of a text titled "On the Shortness of Life," by Seneca.[38] Derrida argues that Seneca's text is an exhortation, "addressed . . . to any one who finds himself at a major turning point in life, a day of some fearsome birthday," reminding them of "the absolute imminence, the imminence of death at every instant" (4). Seneca complains that we live as if we are immortals and waste time not contemplating our own mortality. We have, Seneca writes, "all the fears of mortals and all the desires of immortals" (quoted in *Aporias,* 5). For Seneca, to postpone, delay, and defer thinking about death until we are old is to negate our mortality. For Derrida, Seneca's treatise on death is about "a *rhetoric of borders*, a lesson in wisdom concerning the lines that delimit the right of absolute property, the right of property to your own life, the proper of our existence, in sum, a treatise about the tracing of traits as the borderly edges of what in sum *belongs to us*, belonging as much to us as we properly belong to it" (3). Thus, according to Seneca, the borders of life should be guarded jealously, more than a border of a country or a territory. And by extension one must learn to testify to the border of life because the "end" of it arrives too "early," too "prematurely," too "immaturely" (4; Derrida's words). As Seneca says, "come now, recall your life . . . look back in memory and consider. . . how little of yourself is left to you: you perceive that you are dying before your season" (quoted in *Aporias,* 4).

Derrida goes on to ask this question: if life is constituted by a border, then would death be that which crosses this border or would death be the ultimate border or something else? He asks, "What, then, is to cross the ultimate border? What is to pass the term of one's life? Is it possible? Who has ever done it and who can testify to it?" (8). In other words, can one really testify to one's own death, attest to it, provide

evidence for it? Here Derrida is raising a critical question about the
problem of "crossing" borders, borders of life and borders of identity.
To testify to death, death must be possible. This is why Derrida asks
the absurd question: is "my" death possible? But the question throws
into doubt the entire history of how the subject of death has been understood since the times of the Greeks, down to "our" times. Derrida
does not provide a detailed history here but makes brief references
to a few choice Greek and Latin words, as found in the writings of
Sophocles, Seneca, and Cicero, only to note how death has been seen
in terms of crossing a border, reaching an end (*finis*), moving beyond
(*peran*) life, or crossing the term (*terma*) of life. By extension, Derrida is interested in understanding how crossing the border of life
(or crossing any other political, juridical, or national border) is not as
easy as it sounds and indeed becomes a "problem." Crossing becomes
a problem, according to Derrida, because it involves trespassing upon
an "indivisible line."

> The crossing of borders always announces according to the move-
> ment of a step [*pas*]—and of the step that crosses a line. An in-
> divisible line. And one always assumes an institution of such
> an indivisibility. Customs, police, visa or passport, passenger
> identification—all of that is established upon this institution of the
> indivisible, the institution therefore of the step that is related to it,
> whether the step crosses it or not. Consequently, where the figure
> of the step is refused to intuition, where the identity or the indivisi-
> bility of a line (*finis* or *peras*) is compromised, the identity to oneself
> and therefore the possible identification of an intangible edge—the
> crossing of the line—becomes a *problem*. There is a *problem* as soon
> as the edge-line is threatened. And it is threatened from its first
> tracing. The tracing can only institute the line by dividing it intrin-
> sically into two sides. There is a problem as soon as this intrinsic
> division divides the relation to itself of the border and therefore the
> being-oneself of anything. (11)

Thus the crossing of the line always creates a threat, a threat to the
identity of the edge-line, be it the line of a territory, country, or some
juridical institution that assumes a certain "indivisibility" of itself,
from the very "tracing" of the line. The crossing of the line then

makes any form of "being-oneself" difficult, if not impossible, to maintain. Viewed this way, the crossing of any limits—the limits of life, or the limits of a nation, or the limits of a visa—has remarkable implications for thinking about the problem of name/identity. Name/identity itself remains within limits and borders, with the imminence of being threatened by its other, the "foreigner," the immigrant, the stranger, the unknown other, which is the figure of death itself. Hence, just as life is safeguarded within its borders, against death, so identity remains safeguarded (jealously) within limits, against the foreigner. No matter how hard one may try to qualify it, one cannot ever speak of name/identity without implying its borders and the figure of the stranger that it tries to keep away.

So far, the important point that should be taken from this argument, in the way I read Derrida's text, is this: that the very borders that safeguard life/identity threaten it; if this is so, the perennial binary between life and death (and, by extension, identity and difference, self and other) cannot be sustained. In other words, death can never be viewed as the end of life. (And, as we will see, this is perhaps why Heidegger tried unsuccessfully to blur the life/death distinction by saying that "[Being-toward-]death is a way to be that Dasein takes over as soon as it is." (But, ironically, Heidegger quotes Seneca—"As soon as a human being is born, he is old enough to die right away"—without considering carefully that Seneca's thinking operates in terms of a dichotomous view of life and death.)[39] The critical question here is this: if as soon as the borders of life/identity come into existence, they presuppose their instability, if not death, how are we to think about this problem? Can we even think of it *as* a problem? Can we think about and solve this problem? Derrida's answer here is that so long as one thinks of it as a problem, one can never *think* about it. The very word *problem* (which comes from the Greek *problema*) means "protection" or a "projection." It also means a "task to accomplish," a "barrier," or a "guard-barrier . . . behind which one guards oneself (*Aporias,* 11–12). Put differently, so long as one approaches the question of any border as a "problem" needing protection or guarding, one is engaging in a task that undermines and threatens that which is being guarded. One can never protect the borders of life/identity without ushering in their own deconstruction if not destruction.

By extension, this conception of borders, of course, will fall on the deaf ears of western nation-states, of their customs and border patrol, which increasingly define their *democratic* sovereignty in terms of defending borders and delimiting ("legal" and "illegal") immigration for reasons of "security," particularly in post-9/11 contexts. But, as Etienne Balibar has ably demonstrated, borders are the most non-democratic institutions of democracy, because borders assume that "they must be able to remain stable while all other democratic institutions are transformed":

> [Borders] must give the state the possibility of controlling the movements and activities of citizens without themselves being subject to any control. They are, in sum, the point where, even in the most democratic of states, the status of a citizen returns to the condition of a "subject," where political participation gives way to the rule of police. They are the *absolutely nondemocratic,* or "discretionary," *condition of democratic institutions.* And it is as such that they are, most often, accepted, sanctified, and interiorized.[40]

While Balibar's point about democratizing the borders is important, we must also recognize that no such democratizing will ever really eradicate the threat that democracy faces from itself. This is so because the borders of democracy, like the borders of life/identity, threaten to terminate the very identity of democracy. The irony, of course, is that democracy, like life/identity, cannot exist without borders!

Hence, what the very concept of the border of life produces is an irreducible and irresolvable contradiction: life-death. Life-death (written this way) is not a binary that can be reduced to life or death. This contradiction is not limited to life-death; it has far-reaching, powerful implications for beginning to think about un-inheriting the pervasive binary of identity/difference, self/other, democracy/foreigner, citizen/alien. Now what is important to stress here is that, if the irreducibility of life-death cannot be thought of as a problem that cannot ever be solved, it must be thought of as an aporia. Aporia is not a problem: aporia is not a barrier or a shield, behind which one can protect oneself; aporia has nothing to do with protection; that which becomes aporetic cannot be protected and guarded; it must only be thought as an im-possibility. As Derrida writes,

> There, in sum, in this place of aporia, *there is no longer any problem.* Not that, alas or fortunately, the solutions have been given, but

because one could no longer even find a problem that would constitute itself and that one would keep in front of oneself, as a presentable object or project, as a protective representative or a prosthetic
substitute, as some kind of border still to cross or behind which to
protect oneself. (12)

Thus, in a place of aporia, there can be no barrier that pro-
tects itself or separates itself from something else. In aporia there is
no self that is presentable "in front of oneself." There is no identity to
protect by protecting a border between oneself and another. A place of
aporia is a "non-passage," with no easy passage through. There is no
passage through the contradiction of life-death, leading us to separate
life from death. With aporia what we receive and inherit, then, is an
im-possibility. Derrida's labor is to think the im-possibility of inheriting this contradiction and to spell out the implications for understanding it as an aporia.

Derrida takes the word from Aristotle (*Physics* 4.217b). As Derrida
has demonstrated elsewhere, Aristotle uses the word to explain the
notion of time, which he understood in terms of points ("nows") on
a line that supposedly continues. The problem for Aristotle was to
understand whether the now of yesterday (or the now of some other
time) is the same as the now of today. To this extent, the now defines
the limits of time, not as part of time but as accidental to time. Aristotle found this to be an irresolvable problem and declared that time
both "is and is not." [41] By seeing the contradiction of time this way, Aristotle said that he had reached an "aporia," a place where "I am stuck,
I cannot get out, I am helpless" (quoted in *Aporias,* 13). The foremost
figures of modernity such as Kant and Hegel, Derrida argues, inherited the same concept of time, without ever sufficiently thinking of
its aporia (14). (Even Heidegger, to whom we will return later, tried
to break with such a "vulgar" concept of time, but in vain, because,
in Derrida's view, there can never be a concept of time that is not vulgar). Obviously, Derrida does not think that we can keep re-inheriting
this aporetic concept of time, and he un-inherits the heritage of time
by inventing the word *hauntology* (see especially chapter 4).

What is noteworthy here is Derrida's suggestion that thinking of
aporia, of being caught in a place where we have no easy passage, of
this place of im-possibility, may produce something unheard of. Put
differently, if life/identity cannot be protected or safeguarded because

the logic of its own borders, within which it wants to remain separate and separatist, predetermines its deconstruction, then we can only think about un-inheriting this sense of life/identity. Life/identity can only be thought of as an aporia, as an im-possible inheritance. If identity is an im-possibility, what can one inherit instead or in its place? Again, note that there can be no replacement of, "supplement" to, identity because, as Derrida remarks in the previous quotation, the aporetic life/identity cannot be given a "prosthetic substitute." Identity cannot be replaced or improved.[42] What is even more alarming and monstrous is that the aporia of identity cannot even be deconstructed: that which is aporetic has already been deconstructed; the deconstructed aporia cannot be reconstructed, given a facelift.

Derrida contends that contemplating this im-possibility can help us imagine, *not another (different) identity* but "a wholly non-oppositional other," that is irreducible to any name, or any self, or any identity (18). It surely will not be an identity that will retain its name with some "difference." (It will not be defined in terms of the political-moral-epistemological opposition between the Sinhalese and the Tamil, the Muslim and the Jewish.) The wholly, nonoppositional other is what he refers to as the *"arrivant"*:

> What we call the *arrivant* . . . is whatever, whoever, in arriving does not cross a threshold separating two identifiable places, the proper and the foreign, the proper of the one and the proper of the other, as one would say that the citizen of a given identifiable country crosses the border of another country as a traveler, an émigré or a political exile, a refugee or someone who has been deported, an immigrant worker, a student or a researcher, a diplomat or a tourist. They are all, of course, *arrivants*, but in a country that is already defined, and in which inhabitants know or think that they are at home (. . . this is what, according to Kant, should govern public rights, concerning both universal hospitality or visiting rights.) No, I am talking about the absolute *arrivant* who is not even a guest. He surprises the host—who is not a host or an inviting power— enough to call into question, to the point of *annihilating or rendering indeterminate, all the distinctive signs of a prior identity*, beginning with the very border that delineated a legitimate home and assured lineage, names and language, nations, families, and genealogies. The absolute *arrivant* does not yet have a name or an identity. It

is not an invader or an occupier, nor is it a colonizer, even if it can also become one. This is why I call it simply the *arrivant*, and not someone or something that arrives, a subject, a person, and individual, or a living thing, even less one of the immigrants that I just mentioned. It is not even a foreigner identified as a member of a foreign, determined community. Since the *arrivant* does not have an identity yet, its place of arrival is also de-identified: one does not yet know or one no longer knows which is the country, the place, the nation, the family, the language, and the home in general that welcomes the absolute *arrivant*. The absolute *arrivant* as such is, however, not an intruder, an invader, or a colonizer because invasion presupposes some self-identity for the aggressor or for the victim. Nor is the *arrivant* a legislator or the discoverer of a promised land.... It even exceeds the order of any *determinable* promise. Now the border that is ultimately most difficult to delineate, because it is always already crossed, lies in the fact that the absolute *arrivant* makes possible everything to which I have just said it cannot be reduced, starting with the humanity of man, which some would be inclined to recognize in all that erases, in the *arrivant*, the characteristic of (cultural, social, or national) belonging and even metaphysical determination (ego, person, subject, consciousness, etc.) Yet this border will always keep one from discriminating among the figures of the *arrivant*, the dead, and the *revenant* (the ghost, he, she, or that which returns). (33–35; emphasis added)

We cannot even imagine the *arrivant* that annihilates "all distinctive signs of a prior identity" unless we begin to see identity as being caught in such an irreducible contradiction. One way to imagine such an *arrivant* is to begin to understand life-death as an aporia. In so doing, we may begin to respond to the aporia of the name and uninherit its heritage.

One cannot understand the aporia of life-death so long as one sees life and death as dichotomous. This is what Derrida undermines by posing the question: is my death possible? For example, if I see life as that which is opposed to death, I am claiming to know not only life but also death. But is this knowledge really possible? Does one really understand or know death? Can one say that she knows death? Or, as Derrida puts it elsewhere, can one ever say, "I am dead"?[43] Given that testimony requires one's presence, can one ever testify to one's death?

Has one ever been present in, part of, one's death? (This is why even Maurice Blanchot speaks only of the "instant of my death," the "imminence of death," that is, death before death ever takes place. Or, as Blanchot says, "I die before being born.")[44]

The critical point to register here is that Derrida's questions make difficult not just claims to knowledge and experience of death but also thinking of death and mortality as a basis for any form of ethical or moral existence. When, for example, Emmanuel Levinas conceives of the ethical life in terms of the relation between oneself and another based on the other's mortality—he says, "it is for the death of the other that I am responsible, to the point of including myself in death. . . . I am responsible for the other in so far as he is mortal"— Levinas is making an im-possible claim to knowledge about death as a condition for an ethical life of responsibility. There can never be such a "mineness of death or being-toward-death"(Aporias, 39). I cannot possibly relate to the other merely by recognizing the fact that the other, like me, dies. I can have no possible knowledge of my or the other's death. It is because of the im-possibility of such knowledge that Derrida takes issue with certain anthropological-historical-sociological accounts and analyses of death. "The historian knows, thinks he knows, or grants to himself the unquestioned knowledge of what death is, of what being-dead means" (25). But historians and anthropologists rarely ask questions about death itself: "what is death in general or what is the experience of death itself. . . . From the outset, these questions are assumed to be answered by the anthropologico-historical knowledge" (25). Surely one can produce varying and rich accounts and knowledges of mortuary rights, burial rituals, and rites of mourning as they exist in different societies, but such accounts cannot pretend to say anything about death (42–44, 57–59). Thus no one can ever write a "history" or genealogy of death (not even master Foucault, I might add). Hence, as I explain later, the limitation of historicization in thinking about the question of the political.

How, then, might we begin to think about death as an aporia? Here Derrida turns to Heidegger, who haunted him for so many decades. As he does time and again in various places, in Aporias Derrida undertakes a devastatingly deconstructive and a characteristically dense reading of Heidegger's idea of being-toward-death. I will have more to say about this Heideggerian concept in relation to a question about politics in chapter 4, but we must note Derrida's pointed criticism of it, briefly, so as to appreciate the idea of aporia. Heidegger is one of those rare figures who refused to understand death in terms of the disciplines of biology, theology, or psychology because they "presuppose a meaning of death, a pre-understanding of what death is, or what the word 'death' means" (27; Derrida's words). For this reason Heidegger claims that his was an existential analysis of death. As it is well known, in Heidegger's view, being-toward-death is the most proper possibility of Da-sein. (In so doing, Heidegger claims wrongly, according to Derrida, that animals do not die.) Heidegger, of course, distinguishes the death of Da-sein from its end: Da-sein does not have to mature to die. This is why he says, quoting Seneca, as soon as one being is born, he is "old enough to die right away." Heidegger tries to avoid the problem of the separation between life and death. To make a long story short, Derrida does not think that Heidegger is able to avoid the perennial problem of death because he does not and cannot think of death in terms of its aporia.

If we think of aporia as the "impossible," Heidegger does speak of death as "the possibility of the absolute impossibility of Dasein" (quoted in *Aporias,* 69). In that sense, Derrida notes, there may be several aporias "internal to the Heideggerian discourse," but Heidegger cannot think the aporias because he ends up understanding life and death in terms of the binary of *here/there.* Heidegger prefers *here* (of life) to *there* (of death). Heidegger thinks about death from this side of Da-sein and not from the other side. To put it in simple terms, Heidegger asks questions about death within existential limits, trying to avoid anthropological, biological, and historical accounts of death. But Heidegger's desire to discuss death from "here" and not from "over there," from "the side of Dasein" and not from the other side, its afterlife, itself rests on a problem of "decision" (Derrida's words).[45] Put differently, Heidegger's decision—he just decides to do so—to ask questions about death from this side of Da-sein cannot possibly avoid the problem of the other side. When Heidegger privileges "this side" (*here*), which for him should not be crossed in the existential interpretation of death, he creates the possibility of crossing over to "the other side" (*there*) (51–56). Thus Heidegger ends up producing the very methodological problem of the anthropology of death that is rooted in a "Judeo-Christian theology" (55). With Heidegger we are back, Derrida contends, to the problem of *crossing the border.* Heidegger thought that he had broken with the previous western tradition by thinking of the death (and, by extension, of time) in terms of "not-yet." As Heidegger claims, "the not-yet . . . belongs to Da-sein"; "Da-sein . . . is *always already its not-yet*" (*Being and Time*, 226, 227).

Surely Heidegger's not-yet is an attempt to think about the supposed connection between life and death. Yet Heidegger's not-yet, Derrida argues, does not produce anything new. "In the 'not-yet' that bends us toward death," Derrida writes, "the expecting and waiting is absolutely incalculable; it is without measure, and out of proportion with the time of what is left for us to live" (69). Put differently, Heidegger thinks that the notion of not-yet solves the problem of delaying death or anticipating death against which Heidegger warned. Instead, for Heidegger, not-yet is a way of saying that life has always been short, no matter how long one has lived it. However, according to Derrida, Heidegger contradicts himself: if death is the most proper possibility of Da-sein, then death is the most "proper property" of Da-sein. But, as Derrida argues, "since [death] is also as far away as possible, far from any actual reality, it is the possibility of an impossible, of a non-real as impossible" (70). Thus, even though Heidegger thinks of death as "the possibility of the absolute impossibility," he can hardly think the notion of im-possibility. For Heidegger, to speak of death as the possibility of the impossibility is to speak of death as being faraway. This is not just Heidegger's problem: it is a problem that plagues the entire western heritage of understanding death, including the Judeo-Christian-Islamic experiences of death. As Derrida states,

> despite all the distance taken from anthropo-theology, indeed from Christian onto-theology, the analysis of death in *Being and Time* nonetheless repeats all the essential motifs of such onto-theology. . . . I'll just say, without being able to go into it in any depth, that neither the language nor the process of this analysis of death is possible without the Christian experience, indeed, the Judeo-Christiano-Islamic experience of death. (80)

Here, then, is a terrifying and monstrous proposition for thinking of the im-possibility of inheriting not just the legacies of the concepts of life and death but also the legacies of ethical-political names such as Christianity, Islam, and Judaism within which such concepts remain anchored. Thus, the text *Aporias* is not merely a critical treatise on the problem of death. It is a powerful exercise in coming to terms with, and indeed living with, the aporia of name/identity that is im-possible for us simply to inherit. It must be clear by now that one can only live with an aporia so as to think of un-inheriting it because that which is aporetic is already deconstructed, beyond reconstruction and salvaging. The name/identity, by its own logic of remaining within limits, threatens and undermines itself: name/identity has no place, no limits, no borders, no safe zones within which it can conceal itself. Whenever a border of identity is created, that border inaugurates its own dissolution. The very logic of identity is its own deconstruction. How does one live with an identity that one can never improve or reconstruct? How does one respond to one's political-moral-epistemological identity, one's name, whatever it may be—*Sinhalese, Tamil, Christian, Muslim*? Is it even possible to respond to the name that we can only un-inherit?

Our democracy, our modernity, our secularism, our secular ways of being and belonging, have not even come close to thinking of the im-possibility of un-inheriting the name. Our democratic modernity cannot ever do such a thing because it is in the business of improving and perpetuating the name. It wants to have the name without the name. It knows something of the "problem" of the name. It treats it as a problem. It believes that the problem can be corrected by improving it. Hence the pervasive emphasis on the importance of creating climates of multiculturalism, tolerance, and mutual regard these days. But the name is not a problem. The name is not a "shield" behind which it can recuperate and regenerate itself. Name is aporia. How does one respond to the name?

If democracy has not succeeded in doing so, have there been other traditions of responding to the name differently? Of course, as Derrida has shown, such traditions as "negative theology" have attempted to do just that. Negative theology has sought to speak of the name (of unknown God) in terms of apophasis: that is, to say the name (of God) without saying it. This tradition has a distinctive history that goes as far back as Angelus Silesius and perhaps even farther back. But, contrary to what its contemporary proponents believe, negative theology, Derrida contends, is a language with a distinctive tradition and heritage.[46] Negative theology cannot ever respond to the aporia of the name in any new way, no matter how hard it tries to say it without saying it. One cannot ever say the name without saying it and still try to lose it. On the contrary, like democracy, negative theology *saves the name*. Derrida argues in *On the Name*: "As if it was necessary both to save the name and save everything except the name, *save the name* [*sauf le nom*], as if it was necessary to lose the name in order to save what bears the name, or that toward which one goes through the name. But to lose the name is not to attack it, to destroy it, or wound it. On the contrary, to lose the name is quite simply to respect it: as name." [47]

Is it, then, even possible to respond to the name that is an aporia? Indeed, if there is such a thing as a responsible way of responding to the name, it cannot and must not ever save the name. Can one ever be responsible to the name, to oneself, to one's identity that one can only un-inherit? I will have more to say about the very problem of the notion of responsibility in chapter 3, but my wager here is that perhaps *to be truly responsible to the name is to be irresponsible to it*. To be irresponsible to the name is to develop an "unfaithful fidelity" to it. [48] If, as we will see in chapter 3, responsibility involves responding and answering to a secret other that we do not really know or understand (which can be the state, justice, or law), one cannot ever really respond to the name so as to un-inherit it. The double contradiction that lies in responsibility is that "one always has, one always must have, the right not to respond, and this liberty belongs to responsibility itself." [49] Hence, if there is any "true" responsibility—I doubt that there can ever be such a thing—it has to be conceived through the irresponsibility of un-inheriting the name, mourning the name, the very legacy of the name that we cannot ever really (re)inherit. I contend that no prevailing notion of responsibility, duty, or obligation associated with any form of democracy (or, for that matter, any concept of morality, ethics, or goodness associated with a given ethical or religious tradition or heritage) will ever help us to respond to the aporia of the name.

Thus, un-inheriting the name, thinking and mourning the very im-possibility of it, derives not from a pregiven sources of politics or ethics but from the aporia itself. The aporia of the name beckons, if you will, its own un-heritance because aporia is not dead; it has no association with anything that is post, after, or beyond. Nor is aporia simply alive. It is that which has survived. It is the "trace." It is the figure of the ghostly specter. (We will see some "examples" of the spectral figures that haunt our futures, the figures that cannot and must never be exemplified.) Aporia of the name is a ghost that haunts anybody and everybody who embody the name. One never has the luxury—she may think she does—of not being haunted by the specter of aporia so long as one bears the name. The specter of the name will haunt us and will survive us, haunting those who bear the name in the future. Even when "we" have un-inherited the name, in the future, in a future of the political that will be irreducible to democracy, we will still be haunted by the survived specter because un-inheriting, as I have already noted, is neither remembering nor forgetting, embracing nor abandoning. We will always live haunted by the surviving specter of the name, its legacies of ethnic cleansings, segregations, genocides, pogroms, and other separatist horrors, lest we forget them and think that that we may reappropriate the name one day. Such a future will be a future of what Derrida calls survival. We will all be survivors in the future to the extent that the specter of the name will survive all of us and live on. The future of survival, which is "living on," which means neither living nor dying, will make it impossible for us simply to forget or remember "history."[50] If we cannot simply forget or remember history, it will never be reducible to either absence or presence, past or present.[51] (This is what Derrida calls "the non-contemporaneity with itself of the living present," that is, a present that is not contemporaneous with itself; see chapters 4 and 6.) More simply put, in such futures of the surviving specter of the heritage of the name, we will not be able to pick and choose which aspects, features, and events of history we will want to forget (e.g., slavery or segregation) and remember (e.g., the 9/11 attacks). Such futures may appear as monsters because they threaten the very thing we the modern (and modernizing) citizens seek to embrace without embracing: the name. The question I can only pose here (and will elaborate upon later) is this: if such futures will be marked by the *arrivant*, which Derrida sometimes calls the "irreducible singularity," that is not subject to being numbered and counted, will our democracy, founded on counting its citizens, belong in the futures?

My larger point here is that thinking about the aporia of the name is a way of mourning the deferred democratic futures because democracy is the place where the name—not just the name *democracy* but the very possibility of the "name" itself, of being counted as Sinhalese, Muslim, Hindu, white, or as majority or minority in a given

democratic country—remains a promise, full of unrealized, unfulfilled potential. To mourn, then, the name of democracy, its political
sovereignty, its apparatus of law and justice, its politics of (ac)count-
ability, is to mourn the name itself. This is what is direly lacking in
our postcolonial, postmodern thought, and it is precisely what I attempt to do in this book.

I am so irreligious that atheism seems a religion to me.
　　　　—*Gayatri Chakravorty Spivak, "Use and Abuse of Human Rights"*

These deniers and outsiders of today, these absolutists in a single respect—in their claim to intellectual hygiene—these hard, severe, abstemious, heroic spirits, who constitute the pride of our [modern] age, all these pale atheists, anti-Christians, immoralists, nihilists, these spiritual sceptics, ephectics [who withhold their judgments on any issue], hectic ones . . .; these last idealists of knowledge, these men in whom intellectual conscience is alone embodied and dwells today—they believe themselves to be free from the very ascetic ideal, these free, very free spirits: yet if I may reveal to them what they themselves cannot see—for they are too close to themselves. . . . These men are far from free *spirits; for they still believe in* truth! *. . . It is in their belief in truth that they are more inflexible and absolute than anyone else.*　　　　—Friedrich Nietzsche, On the Genealogy of Morals

2　　Aporias of Secularism

Death of God and Secularist Complacency

Nietzsche tells us in his *The Gay Science* that one day, early in the bright morning, a madman arrived in a market with a lantern and jumped into the people's midst and pierced them with his eyes. "'Whither is God?' he cried; 'I will tell you, *we have killed him*—you and I. . . . God is dead. God remains dead. And we have killed him." Following this pronouncement, the madman poses a series of rhetorical questions about the event—from how it became possible for God to be killed to what might be invented to replace Him. He then yells at the silent, bewildered crowd:

I have come too early. . . . My time is not yet. This tremendous event is still on its way, still wandering; it has not yet *reached* the ears of men. Lightning and thunder require time; the light of the stars requires time. Deeds, though done, still require time to be seen and heard. This deed is still more distant from them than the most distant stars—*and yet they have done it themselves.*[1]

These are arguably some of the most evocative, elusive, and—if one can say this about a master of suspicion—corrosive words that *seemingly* represent one of Nietzsche's devastating attacks on the edifice of (Christian) religion, morality, and civilization sustained by European modernity.[2] Now, if these Nietzschean words constitute as self-evident a critique of religion, as they may appear to do at first sight, then it seems difficult, if not impossible, to pass through Nietzsche to arrive at the task of desecularizing secularism. In other words, Nietzsche's critique, it seems, endorses readily the secularist, Enlightenment claims about the dedivinized public spaces of rational argument that liberal thinkers ranging from Kant to Rorty and Rawls (in their own varying ways) have considered so essential to our modernity and its attendant virtues of tolerance, pluralism, and democracy.[3]

Nietzsche, of course, remained far less sanguine about the possibility that we would come to know, much less fathom, the gravity of the death of God so soon (even though we ourselves have done it). He suspected that it would take "thousands of years" before we would come to know it since the "shadow" of God would continue to appear in different guises. Viewing from a comparativist angle, Nietzsche claimed that "after the Buddha was dead, his shadow was still shown for centuries in a cave—a tremendous, gruesome shadow. God is Dead; but given the way of men, there may still be caves for thousands of years in which his shadow will be shown.—And—we—we still have to vanquish his shadow, too" (*Gay Science*, sec. 108). However, Nietzsche suspected that the shadow of this recent "greatest event," that is, the idea that "the belief in the Christian god has become unbelievable," was already beginning to hover over Europe, and with the dawn of the "breakdown, destruction, ruin, and cataclysm" of this belief, a new horizon "appears free to us again, if it should not be bright. . . . The sea, *our* sea, lies open again; perhaps there has never yet been such an open sea" (*Gay Science*, sec. 343).

The idea of the shadow of God constitutes, as I read it, an insurrectionary move on Nietzsche's part. On the one hand, it cautions against a lapse into complacency about the secularism of our political modernity. On the other, it forestalls the most obvious empirico-epistemological question: If God is dead, how and why does religion (Christianity) still operate as a visible discourse/practice in many parts of the world? Now some defenders of secularism would rush to warn us that this question is no longer worth asking today. They argue that, compared to the ways in which it was once visible a century or so ago, Christianity has lost its grip of power, prestige, and influence on the "first world." This is precisely the kind of argument that British sociologist Steven Bruce advances in his latest book, aptly titled *God Is Dead*.[4] Curiously lacking any reference to Nietzsche, yet illustrated by a front-page picture of a church that was converted—if this is the right word—to Mike's Carpet Stores: Discount Warehouse in West Yorkshire, England, *God Is Dead* is a post-Weberian confirmation, if not a celebration, of secularism's disenchantment with and indeed its gradual triumph over religion in the West. In this story of triumph, secularism comes to stand as a synonym for the decline in religion. By reference to a sociological archive of statistical data—from decrease in church membership and Sunday school attendance to what he calls the "Easternization of the West"—Bruce would have us believe "that the declining social significance of [Christian] religion causes a decline in the number of religious people and the extent to which they are religious" (3). (Bruce seems not to have read any postcolonial literature and seems unaware that the phrase "Easternization of the West" is itself founded upon a notion of colonial racism.) Differentiating his version from conventional notions, Bruce contends that secularism is caused not so much by science as by a certain kind of "indifference." As he elucidates, "Most people did not give up being committed Christians because they became convinced that religion was *false*. It simply ceased to be of any great importance to them; they became indifferent" (235). Bruce's is not an isolated argument. Charles Taylor, who might resist being labeled a secularist, seems to buy readily into Bruce's statistical claim, if not the secularist complacency embedded in it, when he cites the latter's previous work:

> The immeasurable, external results of [a postwar slide into a "fractured culture"] are as we might expect: first a rise in those who state themselves to be atheists, agnostics, or to have no religion, in many countries. . . . But beyond this the gamut of intermediate positions greatly widens: many people drop out of active practice, while still declaring themselves as belonging to some confession or believing in God. On another dimension, the gamut of beliefs in something beyond widens, with fewer declaring belief in a personal God while more hold to something like an impersonal force;

in other words, a wider range of people express religious beliefs that move outside Christian orthodoxy.[5]

For Bruce, then, and perhaps for Taylor, the former church cum discount carpet warehouse is an indubitable signifier of that indifference. Steeped in an academic tradition of objectivity in which sociologists "describe and explain" but do not "regret or rejoice," Bruce seems, at best, content with the emergence of this indifference to religion. Nietzsche, of course, would have railed against this self-satisfaction as premature and indeed unworthy of our political modernity because it might hinder the possibility of self-fashioning or fashioning "ourselves" that he considered crucial to freedom. Nietzsche questions this sort of complacency in *The Gay Science:* "I do not see how we could remain content with such buildings [abandoned churches] even if they were stripped of their churchly purposes. The language spoken by these buildings is far too rhetorical and unfree, reminding us that they are houses of God and ostentatious monuments of some supramundane intercourse; we who are godless could not think *our thoughts* in such surroundings." We could not remain content, Nietzsche argues, until our "godless" selves would become permanent parts of such buildings stripped of churchly purposes. We could not remain content, he avers in the most ironic sense, until we could "see *ourselves* translated into stone and plants [of such buildings]." We could not remain content until we could "take walks *in ourselves* when we stroll around these buildings and [their] gardens" (*Gay Science,* sec. 280). This Nietzschean refusal to remain content until we "could see ourselves translated into stone and plants" and until we would "take walks *in ourselves*" points to the kind of critical suspicion that we ought to cultivate concerning the available demarcation between religion and secularism or between what Nietzsche called "church and [public] life.

The Enemy/Adversary Within

Even though Nietzsche claims (in *Twilight of the Idols*) that "church is *inimical to life*,"[6] his almost comical vision of inserting our godless selves into the very being of the church does not permit the comfortable political distance that modern secularists labor to maintain from religion. In other words, here Nietzsche wants to dislodge us from the self-secure zones of political comfort and complacency about a transparent understanding of the parameters of our secular world and religion, church, and public life. If we take, in the most metaphorical sense, "church" for the Christian "religion" that Nietzsche considers his archenemy (most clearly in *The Anti-Christ*), the idea of translating "ourselves" into stones of the church alludes to the possibility of imagining a new kind of political relation between such seemingly opposed political categories as friend and enemy and, by extension, self and other, public and private. It is perhaps through reimagining this relation between enemy and friend that the emergence of the Nietzschean "overman" becomes possible, that is, the type of being/belonging antithetical to "'modern' men, to 'good' men, to Christians and other nihilists" (*Ecce Homo* 3.1; cited in *Twilight*, 105).

This is Nietzsche at his affirmative best. Antithetical though it is to modernity and Christianity, the identity of the overman—this is crucial to note—is not one that wallows in the simple negation of such concepts as goodness, belief, and truth. Rather, the identity of the overman is one of affirmation, affirmation of a kind of being that is "beyond good and evil." The overman, in other words, embodies the possibility of godless selves, those "who do not readily deny" but seek "honor in being *affirmative*" (*Twilight*, 25). Understood in broad terms, this Nietzschean affirmation of the kind of being and becoming that is opposed to "good men" and "modern men" cannot simply be cultivated by the comfort of distance and dissonance between enemy and friend, religion and secularism, now available to our political disposal. The practice can come from the formation of the "postsecular" politics of forging a new relation between religion and secularism, that is—if I may push the idea a bit further—by conceiving of a politics that would oblige us to honor the nonsecular "enemy within" the domain of secular politics.[7]

It is through a radical forging of the relation between friend and enemy, between "godless" selves and "godly" men, that the practice of taking "walks in ourselves" can, *perhaps*, see the light of day. In the sort of relation I have in mind, the enemy may cease to be the enemy. Now "enemy," as Foucault has reminded us, is not a helpful political category. An enemy is born out of polemics, not out of "politics." The difference between polemics and politics is that the former "establishes the other as an enemy, an upholder of opposed interests against which one must fight until the moment this enemy is defeated and either surrenders or disappears."[8] Here it is instructive to heed Foucault's argument, even though we may not follow him all the way. For Foucault, polemics is "nothing more than theater." The "reactivations" that polemics generate are similar to the histrionics characteristic of theater. In polemics/theater, he claims, "one gesticulates: anathemas, excommunications, condemnations, battles, victories, and defeats are no more than ways of speaking, after all" (*Polemics*, 112–13). Foucault goes on to ask, "Has anyone seen a new idea come out of a polemic? And how could it be otherwise, given that here the interlocutors are incited not to advance, not to take more and more risks in what they say, but to fall back continually on the rights that they claim, on their legitimacy, which they must defend, and on the affirmation of their innocence" (112–13). What is being urged by Foucault here is the possibility of a politics in which the enemy must cease to be the enemy as such. In such a politics the enemy is not to be either annihilated or tolerated. Now it is important to stress that such a politics does not necessarily abandon incitement or provocation. (Otherwise this would allow nothing but a liberal revamped notion of "dialogue.") Indeed, the enemy becomes—again to borrow a phrase from Foucault—a certain kind of adversary worth the political investment of a "permanent provocation." However, it is a politics of provocation, in which competing interlocutors—moralists and secularists, "fundamentalists" and atheists, nationalists and centrists—do not merely dismiss each other because of their a priori ethical convictions. Now Foucault may not be able to envision the possibility of eradicating the very category of enemy in the way Derrida (with Nietzsche) attempts to do (chapter 7). Nonetheless, it is helpful to begin to think of a politics in which adversaries take "risks in what they say" in a public sphere, with no recourse to *merely* defending the "rights" of what is being said. But, of course, we cannot possibly imagine such public spaces so long as we continue to invest in the politics of the defense of history that our secularized democratic present offers us.

My point here is that the secularist defense of history is akin to a defense of rights. As we will soon see, secularists have a certain sense of history, and, so long as they appeal to the virtue of that history, they can never take the kind of political risks crucial to fashioning new vistas of politics. They can only defend the rights of their historicist claims—however varying these claims may be—about secularism against their political enemies and critics. They can only fall back on the affirmation of their innocence because the epistemological grounds on which they engage their opponents are already familiar and hence safe. But, as I will show in this chapter, resorting to historicist claims and arguments can produce only a dead end of political despair. What I want to suggest is that thinking about the dead end of political despair will involve giving up certain cherished claims to the kind of history in which secularism remains anchored. This is what I call desecularizing secularism, and essentially it is a task of dehistoricizing history (chapter 6). As we will see in the following chapters, this will have profound implications vis-à-vis thinking about the future of our democracy in a way that is irreducible to law and rights. This is because the secularist (democratic) defense of history is a tacit defense of law. Can democracy (and secularism) exist without easy recourse to history and law? Seeing the problem of democracy from this angle will show us that today we have reached an impasse where we cannot continue to believe that the health of the democratic futures rests on improving our notions of law and justice, trying to convince ourselves that justice and law can be more fair and just. (John Rawls's notion of "justice as fairness" is only a modest example of this belief in the possibility of improving our democracy.)[9] Desecularizing secularism cannot even be attempted as long as the sort of complacency mentioned above dominates contemporary thinking on secularism.

Aporias of Secularism

The politics of complacency about secularism/secularization that Steven Bruce's *God Is Dead* offers us does not even question the self-evident nature of the boundary between religion and secularism, much less imagine new domains of politics. This much should be obvious by now. But there remains a more serious problem that is not so readily apparent in *God Is Dead*. The text's complacency about our secular present—understood in terms of that progressive "indifference" to religion—amounts to rehashing the dated dictum of "the-West-is-secular" that rolls off the tongues of many liberals and secularists these days. In this regard Bruce's *God Is Dead* is implicated in a broader problematic of the enduring western production

and canonization of the nexus of power/knowledge about the demarcations between identity and difference. Here I imagine some (anti-
essentialists) already registering complaints to the effect that not all
liberals claim that the West is secular or that liberalism cannot be
equated with secularism. As should be evident later, these sorts of
complaints remain misdirected in light of the complex deployment of
the-West-is-secular discourse. The dictum is no longer one that liberals alone employ; it is one that even critics of secularism or "born-
again Christians" use—albeit with a slightly different spin on it—in
the name of democracy today, and it is undergirded by a certain logic
of the supposedly liberal, secular notion of tolerance.[10] To put it quite
bluntly, this problematic, it seems to me, threatens to put out of business those liberal secularists whose political careers have been staked
on an exclusivist claim to the domain of secularism and tolerance.
This is perhaps what Talal Asad has in mind when he notes that "liberals are generally dismayed at the resurgence of the right, but the
notion of primordial intolerance will not explain it."[11] Put differently,
if the-West-is-secular discourse ceases to be the ideological commod-
ity of the secularists and atheists, we will have to confront the present
urgency of desecularizing secularism.

Something of the urgency may be recognized in light of a brief
speech that President George W. Bush gave during his nationally
televised visit to the Islamic Center of Washington, DC, six days after 9/11. Bush's seven-minute speech was supposed to allay the fears
of American Muslims, who had been threatened, attacked, shot at,
and killed by some white Americans in different parts of the country. Among some two hundred reported cases of the attacked and
murdered were non-Muslim South Asians who were "mistaken" for
Muslims of Arabic descent. Bush's attempt to allay the Muslims' fears
was simultaneously an attempt to allay the suspicions of his "fellow [non-Muslim-white-Christian] Americans" about *the* identity of
Islam and Muslims. To do so, in the speech Bush drew a distinction
between the suspected Muslim "evildoers" who masterminded the
9/11 attacks and ordinary Muslims, that is, a distinction between true
Muslims and terrorists who call themselves Muslims. "These acts of
violence against innocents," the president claimed, "violate the fundamental tenets of the Islamic faith. And it's important for my fellow
Americans to understand that." Perhaps the most profound moment
of his visit to the mosque was when the president, flanked by a few

American Muslim men and women, held up a copy of the Koran and asserted: "The face of terror is not the true faith of Islam. That's not what Islam is all about. Islam is peace. These terrorists don't represent peace. They represent evil and war." [12]

This moment of Bush's holding up the Koran and proclaiming that "Islam is peace" constitutes, for me, simultaneously a moment of the triumph of tolerance and a moment of the aporia of secularism and liberalism. It is a moment of the triumph of tolerance because it is the secular West's commitment to the practice of the "tolerance" of Others—a principle bound up with the "nonfanaticism" of the West—which presumably made it possible for George W. Bush, a self-proclaimed admirer of Jesus as the "best philosopher," to visit a Muslim house of worship and cite a passage from the Koran. As I watched Bush make these remarks on television, I wondered if one could, in some weird way, think of it as bearing some semblance to the ethnographic practice of "participant observation" that has defined and sustained the unstable proximity between the West, anthropology, and its constructed native others. Unlike a typical anthropologist, However, Bush did more than simply participate/observe; he *intervened*. He did so, not as an insider, but as a *tolerant* outsider, to insist that "Islam is peace." One cannot imagine anti-essentialist postcolonial critics and anthropologists ever advocating this kind of moral (indeed state) intervention in questions of what and who constitute the parameters of (an)other's "true" religious identity. Such intervention, they might claim (and perhaps rightly so), essentializes another's tradition, robbing it of its own voices. Today better informed postcolonial anti-essentialists might easily ridicule and discount Bush's intervention at the Islamic Center as a machination of a pretentious, not to mention right-wing, politician hardly familiar enough with the Koran or the nuances of the Arabic language to claim the English translation of a verse he cited "is not as eloquent as the original Arabic." However, my intention here is not to pursue such an anti-essentialist criticism which will accomplish nothing but a mere dismissal of that "intervention." It seems to me that we can no longer cultivate that sort of knee-jerk dismissal, for the sake of deepening our critique of colonial imperialism and essentialism and celebrating the agency of colonized native religions and cultures, without offering an alternative practice of politics. Such a summary dismissal would be unable to understand how the kind of tolerance that marked the Bush visit to the Islamic

Center produces a profound ethical problem that signals the aporia, if not the failure, of liberalism.

If a certain (post-Tocquevillean?) tradition of democratic tolerance enabled Bush to inform/remind non-Muslim Americans of Islam as a religion of peace, that tolerance became possible at a costly price. On the one hand, if that tolerance sought to extend to Muslims the generosity of the president's pleading for "fellow citizens to understand" and recognize what constitutes Muslim identity, it did so by making Muslims pay the price of being represented as misunderstood yet visible Arab American Others. The otherness of Muslims can only be comprehended by the abstract quality of "peace." On the other hand, if the possibility of this plea for non-Muslims' understanding and recognition of Muslims in America signals the triumph of tolerance, then the moment of that plea marks a moment of the aporia of secular liberalism that labors to foster, but *always* is threatened by, the divergent politics of cultural and religious pluralism. Put differently, the moment in which the plea was made was the moment in which pluralism threatened the "stable" relation that the secular state strives to maintain between the nation, citizenship, and freedom. If the discourse of freedom is crucial to the apparatus of the secular nation-state, to its guaranteeing and facilitating the "free exercise" of different religious and cultural choices among its citizens in a pluralistic society, the attacks by the "fellow citizens" on the "Muslims" in the immediate aftermath of 9/11 undoubtedly injured that freedom. Seen in this light, the relation between freedom and pluralism becomes unstable, indeed unsustainable, because it is not so much that freedom does not makes pluralism possible as that pluralism threatens the very survival of freedom. What can stabilize that unstable relation is tolerance—that is, "fellow citizens" extending tolerance toward (cultural-religious) others. Tolerance, however, cannot guarantee the lasting stability of that relation since pluralism, appearing as it does in diverse and shifting forms, will stand as a threat to freedom.

Freedom, then, will always have to live with the threat of pluralism, so to speak, always anticipating the injury that it may cause to freedom, since to eliminate that threat, to say no to pluralism, is to risk freedom's own demise. After all, freedom will cease to be freedom if it cannot sustain the moral space in which the "free exercise" of plural ethical and political choices of being is possible, either by the "majority" or the "minority" of a given democratic nation-state.

Understood this way, then, the Rawlsian idea of giving priority to liberty/freedom over all other values and goods simply becomes untenable, because freedom becomes secondary to, and often needs to be rescued by, tolerance.[13] My argument here then is this: If tolerance can never really eliminate the threat of pluralism to freedom, and if it can never really prevent "fellow citizens" from *misunderstanding* the differences of certain other citizens, the only effective strategy a state/ nation can take to reduce that threat is to periodically remind citizens of the virtue of the practice of tolerance, of its significance to secular freedom, which allows the democratic state to distinguish itself from other nonsecular (often nonwestern) nations supposedly lacking in that western virtue.

This reminding has a certain similarity to the-West-is-secular discourse, repeated in so many redundant ways by secularists such as John Rawls on the one hand and Steven Bruce on the other. So when George W. Bush rushed to assert that "Islam is peace," he did not just ask his fellow citizens to "understand" and tolerate Muslim others because of their alleged affinity to their Christian tradition of "peace"; he *also* extolled the West's tradition of secularism and tolerance momentarily forgotten by the fellow citizens. Thus what is demanded of fellow citizens in the plea is not necessarily respect for or understanding of Muslim others; what is demanded is certainly not the exploration of the spaces of differing Islamic practices in which "Islam" as such becomes irreducible to the homogeneous notion of "Islam-is-peace," practices that can thwart the rush to define what is and is not Islam and render problematic the very ideas of *understanding* and *respecting* the otherness of Islam/Muslims that supposedly stands in opposition to "fellow citizens." Rather, what is demanded here is respect for the West's own secular tradition of tolerance and its importance to freedom. So, for me, this plea marks a moment of the aporia of secularism not merely because it is made by a born-again Christian conservative, threatening (as he arguably does) to deprive secularists and liberals of their long-possessed privilege to make claims about secularism and tolerance; the plea marks a moment of the aporia of secularism because the politics of solution that it offers to the problem of pluralism and its perceived threat to freedom is based on the shaky principle of tolerance whose collapse can be (*temporarily*) averted by the-West-is-secular discourse. Obviously, then, the plea for tolerance can guarantee no lasting solution; it has to be made and remade as our sociopolitical circumstances may shift and fellow citizens forget the virtue of tolerance.

Here we return to the Nietzschean suspicion of secularism with which we started. If the discourses of "the-West-is-secular" and "Islam-is-peace" are two sides of the same coin, and if they constitute the most effective politics of responding to the problem of cultural and religious differences and safeguarding freedom, Nietzsche's refusal to remain content with secularism (that is, if we understand his comic refusal to be contented with the former "houses of God," stripped of their churchly purposes, as an expression of his dissatisfaction with secularism and modernity) poses a new demand for imagining alternative politics of reckoning with the cultural and religious differences of others in a new postsecular world.

In view of this discussion, we can suspect now that the route of seeking to understand minority "Others" usually takes us back to the temporary refuge of tolerance. The problem with the idea of understanding a minority religion is obviously that it revolves around the messy business of sorting through empiricist-historicist questions of which embodied concepts, ideas, practices, and debates constitute the proper identity of that religion. If the task of understanding such minority religions can produce any tolerance, that tolerance cannot be anything but an act of personal or collective generosity that someone or some group might extend toward others different from them. Tolerance can be only so because it is not clear why seeking to understand—in terms of reading and thinking about—the differences of another's religion or cultural tradition would be followed by one's tolerance, if not respect, toward it. One could be easily insulted, if not threatened, by another's perceived religious and cultural differences. This was clearly evident when, in the months following 9/11, U.S. televangelists (like John Hagee in Texas) in their sermons quoted passages from the Bible and compared them to those passages from the Koran to contend that, contrary to some popular claims, Christianity and Islam are not (and would never be) "sister faiths" because Islam is not a religion of peace. Seeing this as a selective reading-understanding of Islam by a misguided fundamentalist Christian will not suffice.

Now the demand for an alternative politics—if there can ever be such a thing—that sets aside the virtue of tolerance does not abandon secularism or democracy. Rather, thinking about the limits of tolerance is a new demand for secularism. That demand is for secularism to "desecularize" itself. Desecularizing does not mean we have more or less of secularism. It means that if tolerance, marked by discourses like the-West-is-secular and Islam-is-peace, constitutes the kind of politics through which secularism has sought to sustain its claims to the distinction between religion and the secular space, it needs to question those politics, because the terms of how and by whom that distinction is maintained have altered. My proposal here is that secularism can do this by setting itself a new task, which involves interrogating secularism's reliance on history.

Here I must insist on a fundamentally important point. Desecularizing secularism or dehistoricizing history is not about "reconstruction." There is an interesting relation between reconstruction and critique. If the defense of history, as I will show soon, is about affirming its innocence, reconstruction is concerned with reshaping history—perhaps by separating the good version from the bad one. In the way I conceptualize it, dehistoricizing or desecularizing begins with the doubt that that mere criticism of our pasts—in terms of whatever their problems may be—cannot reconstruct them (and render them available for our present). In other words, I begin with the doubt that what is deconstructable is not necessarily reconstructable. (Note our discussion in chapter 1.) The innocent question that one may ask is: What are we to affirm in the absence of the deconstructed? My answer is that so long as our contemporary politics is governed by the ways in which defenders and critics of secularism and democracy appeal to history, we cannot think of any new politics we might affirm. Hence, in what follows, I discuss the ways in which the questions of history, past, and legacy are understood by both defenders and critics of secularism. The defenders of secularism—as we see in the narrative I provide below about the American secularists and their arguments against the In-God-We-Trust motto on U.S. currency—appeal to history as a way of appealing to law/justice. For them, there is an intimate relation between history and justice. But the *critics* of secularism (if I may use that term broadly) claim that reconstructing, rescuing, and fighting for the "legacy" of nonsecular traditions like Buddhism and Christianity can offer a new politics. What I want to show is that both these positions are animated by the belief that answers to the problems of our political present are available within our present, within shouting distance of our modernity, within our reach, just beneath our feet. That is, they are available at the end of a defense of the history of secularism or a critique of that history, by way of a defense of a nonsecular history in our present itself. In other words, both seemingly opposing positions operate within the grips of history. I want to show that neither of these positions have anything new to offer, precisely because they do not have a concept of mourning and un-inheriting the aporia of our democratic modernity.

History at the Limits of History/Law

To do this, I now turn to a debate involving those who might be called atheists, fundamentalists, and the state in contemporary America. The debate is about the question of whether the In-God-We-Trust motto on U.S. currency violates the separation of church and state on the one hand and civil rights on the other. Obviously, the debate echoes general questions about the role of religion within American public life that (re)gained visibility within the public domain in the summer of 2003, particularly in the wake of a high-profile controversy involving a 5,280-pound granite monument displaying the Ten Commandments that Alabama's chief justice Roy Moore installed in the rotunda of the Alabama Supreme Court. Moore defied a court order to have it removed from the courthouse. Later, in August and November of 2003, respectively, against a modest opposition from some evangelical power brokers, Moore's own associates not only removed the monument from the rotunda (it was wheeled away on live television to a storage room in the courthouse) but also expelled Judge Moore himself from office. This was preceded by several other less familiar controversies about what seem, at least from the perspectives of self-described secularists or atheists, like attempts by radical Christians to insert religion into various levels of the secular space. For secularists, such attempts come in terms of Christian demands to adopt classroom prayer and the phrase "under God" in the pledge of allegiance in public schools and inscribe symbols of God within other public buildings. Generally the secularists see such demands as undermining the constitutional separation of church and state while the advocates (the so-called fundamentalists) view the opposition to them as efforts to deny the nation its religious "history" and heritage. (Indeed, Judge Moore flouted the court order to remove the monument, claiming that the law of the land was based on the law of God.)

These sorts of disputes are usually settled through the courts, often initiated with lawsuits filed by the American Civil Liberties Union (ACLU) on behalf of the plaintiffs. The secularists see favorable rulings as affirmations of the principle of the separation of church and state required by the First Amendment of the Constitution, which they claim is rooted in a secular "history." The courts' interventions in upholding the Constitution, deciding whether or not a given religious symbol or practice within the secular space violates the separation of church and state, are themselves an interpretation and affirmation of "history," that is, adjudicating if a given public act or practice (concerning religion) of the present violates the "original" principle or precedent of the past. In this sense, for the nonviolation of the original principle to exist, there must be a correspondence between the past and the present. For the secularists these juridical affirmations of history, sustaining that relation between the past and the present that safeguards the distinction between church and state, are a self-evident form of "justice." This idea of justice is clearly embedded in the conventional understanding that "law" (the courts' interpretation or affirmation of the Constitution/the First Amendment) delivers justice. In this view, justice is to be found in history, in a historic principle, which, in this case, is the principle of the separation of church and state, enshrined in the First Amendment. What I am after in the rest of this chapter is to understand if secularism can continue to think of history and justice in this way. Put differently, my interest in seeking to desecularize secularism, to understand if secularism can always have recourse to justice via history, is to explore how we might find justice elsewhere, outside of history, that is to say, justice from the present, and, if you will, from the "future of the present."

The debate about the In-God-We-Trust motto on U.S. currency constitutes an ideal site for this task. It is not a debate in the sense of a legal dispute between some branch of the federal government and the secularist citizens that remains pending to be settled through the intervention of a court ruling, at least not for the time being. Indeed, the absence of a call for an immediate legal intervention to settle the questions about the supposed (un)constitutionality of the motto on the currency points to the difficulty of resorting to history/historicist claims to defend and sustain secularist demands today. As the American atheists, arguably the most staunch defenders of secularism, explain:

> Across the country, there is a movement afoot. It isn't using picket signs, or a flood of letters to congress, or even a lawsuit—that's already been tried. Instead, some atheists and separationists are taking pen in hand and crossing out the motto "In God We Trust" from the national currency. Others are using rubber stamps, or inserting their own messages like "In Reason We Trust," or "Keep Church and State Separate." . . . Simply put, atheists do not like the "In God We Trust" slogan staring at us every time we pull out our wallets or purses. It has to go. But how?[14]

What is worth noting in this statement is not the obvious concession to the inefficacy, if not the failure, of the strategies that usually animate political protests—picketing, law suits, marching, etcetera—because they have "already been tried." But such strategies remain ineffective because they cannot combat the power of the *normalized* and, by extension, *legalized* history of the motto on the national currency. There is, in other words, an implicit admission in the above statement that the motto has become part of history, not just the history of the national currency, but the history of the United States. Put differently, the motto has become "history" itself. Unlike the adoption of class prayer in a public school or the installation of a religious symbol in a federal building, against which the strategies of picketing and lawsuits might spur quick legal action, protests against the motto do not seem to do so. This is perhaps because the "unconstitutionality" of the motto remains invisible to us today, hidden by history/time. It remains hidden by time itself because, as one might say, it has been there for some time. It has become not only normalized but also legalized by time, because one can locate the time(s) when its appearance on the currency was(were) made possible by (post-First Amendment) bills/laws. Then, perhaps, the atheists' admission is that the normalized and legalized status, and indeed the identity, of the motto on the currency makes it difficult for the secularists to appeal to law to recognize its unconstitutionality. What is interesting about this appeal is that it is really a demand for law to sever law's own relation to itself since the very being of the motto on the currency now remains "legal" today. The difficulty of challenging the legality/law is clear in the following statement:

One of the first legal actions to challenge religious sloganeering of this type was made in 1978 by American Atheists founder Madalyn Murray O'Hair. In the case of MADALYN MURRAY O'HAIR et al. v. W. MICHAEL BLUMENTHAL SECRETARY OF THE TREASURY et al. (462 F. Supp. 19—W.D. Tex 1978), the court opined: "Its use is of a patriotic or ceremonial character and bears no true resemblance to a governmental sponsorship of religious exercise." The U.S. Court of Appeals for the Ninth Circuit reached a similar conclusion in the 1970 case ARONOW v. UNITED STATES. Subsequent cases also fell short, even though they argued that the motto clearly encouraged religion and made a statement about god and theology. On September 14, 1988, then-President of American Atheists Jon Murray addressed the Subcommittee on Consumer Affairs and Coinage concerning proposals to redesign the nation's currency. At that time, Murray expressed concern about including "In God We Trust" on the national currency, suggesting instead a return to the secular "E Pluribus Unum" ("One from many") that was used earlier in the nation's history. ("In God We Trust")

If secularists seem to find it difficult to turn to law in the conventional way to prove the unconstitutionality of "religious graffiti" on the currency, then they must find an option beyond law. The readily available alternative, of course, is history/time itself. But this alternative does not provide easy solutions. In turning to history, the difficult question that the secularists face is whether or not they can establish a certain temporal distance between history and the motto—that is, if they can demonstrate that the distance between the (original time of the) First Amendment and the time of the appearance of the motto on the currency is constitutionally unbridgeable. In seeking to do so, they must find a way to deny any relation between the two. Now for the secularists to negate this relation is to negate the (existing) relation between the motto and the post–First Amendment law that "legalized" it. That is to say, they must show that the law that made possible the appearance of the motto on the currency is unjust because it violates the "original" time (or "original intent") of the Constitution/ First Amendment.[15] This, perhaps, is the only way for them to restore the original law of the Constitution/First Amendment.

To accomplish this, atheists must, then, narrate the history of the original law of the separation of church and state. This is precisely what the atheists do when they ask, "Where did 'In God We Trust' originate?" Contrary to what they claim is the common public belief that the motto has been on the currency since revolutionary times, atheists set out to delineate the history of how the motto came to be adopted as the national symbol and why it today conveys a distinctly religious message. The first national motto was E Pluribus Unum. Thomas Jefferson recommended it, and it was later endorsed by Benjamin Franklin; it became part of the Great Seal of the United States. All this happened just five years prior to the constitutional convention of 1787. The atheists contend that "it wasn't until a century later, though, that 'In God We Trust' was seriously proposed as a motto." Quoting Madalyn O'Hair, the author of "Freedom Under Siege," they claim that the argument for the case was made in 1861 by one Reverend M. R. Watkinson. Watkinson proposed to the secretary of the treasury that the motto be put on the coins because America is a "Judeo-Christian nation" and should recognize "there is but one God." Supposedly swayed by the arguments of the religious community that buttressed Watkins's claim, and conscious of the importance of the votes of that community, Congress passed the Coinage Act of April 22, 1864. The act authorized the inscription of the In-God-We-Trust phrase on the coins. The motto first appeared on the two-cent coin in 1864, on the one-cent coin in 1901, and it has appeared on dimes since 1916. Eventually it was imprinted on gold coins, silver dollars, and half-dollar coins.

According to the atheists, the real "religionizing" of the national currency took place in 1955, under the leadership of President Dwight Eisenhower, who signed public law 140, which required the imprinting of the motto on all currency, completely replacing the phrase E Pluribus Unum. Here the atheists remind us of the cold war background against which this religionizing of the currency took place.

All of this occurred at the height of the cold war tension when the political division between the Soviet Union and the western bloc was simplistically portrayed as a confrontation between the Judeo-Christian civilization and the "godless" menace of communism. Indeed the new national motto was only part of a broader effort effectively to religionize civic ritual and symbols. On June 14, 1954, Congress unanimously ordered the inclusion of the words "Under God" into the Pledge of Allegiance. By this time, other laws mandating public religiosity had also been enacted, including a statute for all federal justices and judges to swear an oath concluding with "So help me God."

For the secularists to tell the "history" of how In God We Trust became part of the national currency is to tell the history of how a nation conceived in the ideals of secular governance, with no privileging of one particular religion, was religionized. As the secularists claim, the public has taken this for granted to such an extent that the religionized identity of the currency is now assumed to be part of the identity of the nation. In other words, for many in the United States, the religionized identity of the currency is a self-evident testimony to the religious identity of the nation. The secularists remain understandably frustrated by the public's unawareness of an irony here.

> Ironically, religious groups and courts often use the same evidence to argue vastly different conclusions. Money and the "In God We Trust" motto is a case in point. While researching this story we discovered that the religious motto was often cited by religious groups as "proof" of the melding of government and faith, or in support of the notion that America is founded upon Christian religious principles. Other evidence included the opening of congressional sessions with prayer, the display of a Ten Commandments bas relief at the U.S. Supreme Court building, or the fact that the President of the United States takes the oath of office while swearing on a bible. The same sort of evidence, though, often appears in court rulings which decide establishment clause cases. Justices will cite the "In God We Trust" motto, for example, as evidence of a "civic religion," or maintain that it has a secular intent. ("In God We Trust")

This obvious frustration at the normalization of the relation between the religionized identity of the currency and the nation is not lessened, but only made more visible by the atheists' movement to deface the motto on the currency. This defacement of the currency seems to be the only option available for the secularists to remind the larger public of the irony of the religionized identity of the nation. But this option remains frustrating, not simply because "defacement" is necessarily a negation of an object but also because, as anthropologist Michael Taussig puts it, "[defacement] also animates the thing defaced, and the mystery revealed may become more mysterious." [16] If we follow Taussig's argument, we could argue that secularists remain frustrated because defacement does not adequately reveal the irony of the religious identity of the currency/nation, since this identity now has become a "public secret" and, by extension, has become the "truth." Seen from this perspective, the public already knows the irony (and does not need being reminded of it), because knowing it is crucial to maintaining it as a public secret.[17] Even though this way of understanding may be structurally useful, I wish to see it in a different (and less structured) way. I see defacement as a frustrating labor for atheists because it involves the double task of questioning not only the religionized identity of the currency/nation but also the law (title 18, section 33) that prohibits any defacement of the currency. The questioning of one law is prohibited by another law. The atheists' frustration clearly borders on a profound sense of despair, almost tantamount to a total resignation to the law (indeed the "reality") of the religionized identity of the currency/nation. As the atheists write:

> One thing remains certain. Despite the convincing evidence that "In God We Trust" has a strong origin in religious sensibilities, it is doubtful that courts today would care to revisit O'HAIR v. BLUMENTHAL, or any other case which proposes to take up this controversial issue. Scratching out "In God We Trust," or stamping separationist slogans on the currency displays the frustration that many Atheists have in dealing with a legal system which rarely holds to a stern and strict interpretation of the establishment clause. The wall of separation goes only so far. You can bet your money on it. ("In God We Trust")

If we see this atheist/secularist despair as an implicit surrender to the post–First Amendment law(s), to the "self-evidentness" of the religionized identity of an "originally" secular nation, then we must think of a way that can reach beyond law. To think beyond law, of course, is to think "beyond" history. As we have seen already, the secularists' insistence on the unconstitutionality of the In-God-We-Trust motto rests, to a large extent, on historicist claims, on returning to the history of the constitution/First Amendment. This, of course, is their version of the history, and some might challenge it. I am not interested in whether or not the atheists have gotten their history right.

Rather, my point here is that if what becomes possible at the end of the history they provide is merely this despair, then we must think beyond history.

But what is important to note is that this despair alone cannot make that move possible because the demand of the despair—if one can call it that—yearns for the *restoration* of the constitutional separation of church and state. The demand of this despair remains anchored in history, in a history of the past. Thinking beyond this history, then, means giving up the commitment to what is being demanded in the despair—that is, "history" itself. Giving up this commitment to history may be unthinkable for the secularists because it also involves recognizing the irrelevance of the very constitutional principle of the separation of church and state to the *contingent* demands of the present. After all, the laws that have made possible the imprinting of the motto on the currency were not accidental; they were historical products, products of debates in which specific individuals made particular claims for it, and the debates mark particular "changes"—if you will—in the history of the Constitution. If one sees these laws as examples of how history changes, there is ample evidence to dismiss the secularists' desires to restore the "original" Constitution. The secularists, then, will have to consider the unthinkable option of giving up their claims to history and imagine a different way of un-inheriting the problems of our modernity.

What I want to argue here is that if the above discussion has shown so far something of the problem of secularism and its reliance on history, then a mere critique of secularism is not going to help us understand how we can think anew about the aporia of our democratic existence. If the above debate is about the problem of history and heritage (that is, the problem of how we think about the legacy of secularism and democracy that we can neither abandon nor reject), then we may see this aporia in relation to the questions of the heritage of religion in a postcolonial democracy like Sri Lanka. I think doing so may shed new light on how we may "un-inherit" the very problem of heritage itself. Put more simply, by thinking about the above problem in relation to a postcolonial society like Sri Lanka, we cannot only (and merely) gain a cross-cultural perspective on the question of democracy and secular values but also think broadly about the place of received discursive traditions of religion within the framework of

democratic politics of our modernity. Or, to put it in more empirical terms, when a supposedly misguided fundamentalist like Judge
Moore claims that U.S. laws remain inspired by the Christian tradition and installs a granite monument displaying the Ten Commandments in a courthouse, or when secular feminists in India campaign
to ban public celebrations that have anything to do with the tradition of sati, or when the French government proscribes the wearing
of "conspicuous religious symbols" in public schools, they all speak
to problems of heritage and legacy. Seeing this problem of heritage
from such a cross-cultural perspective is also important in thinking
about the problem of "modernity at large"—to use Appadurai's felici-
tous phrase—that animates the politics of all postcolonial nationalisms and all secular questions of belonging.[18] And, more important,
if these questions of heritage today demand (and can perhaps never
be fully resolved by) the intervention of law/justice, then this cross-
cultural angle may help us think of another demand for a nonjuridical intervention and im-possibility. Needless to say, this way of ap-
proaching the theme of democracy and heritage can put an end to
the anthropological work of merely representing (to the West) what
is going on in other nonwestern cultures, dominated by area studies,
with its continuing penchant for "knowledge" about other cultures,
and begin to speak to the politics of places that are irreducible to a
(nonwestern) "case" or an example.

A Postcolonial Demand for Displacement:
History and Humanism

Indeed, the instance I am thinking of has as much to do with
the very problem of treating places like Sri Lanka as an object of anthropological knowledge as it has to do with engaging the questions
of history, heritage, and democracy in relation to such places. It is a
dispute between two Sri Lankan intellectuals about the question of
religion, heritage, and otherness that arose after the publication of
the novel Anil's Ghost (2000), by Michael Ondaatje.[19] As we will see,
this dispute has far-reaching implications, making it more than a Sri
Lankan case, and demands thinking of the question of democracy beyond the terms of area studies. Obviously, this is not because Ondaatje

is an internationally renowned author, whose earlier work *The English Patient* (1992) won the Booker Prize and was later adapted into an Academy award–winning Hollywood feature (under the same title) in 1996. Rather, the dispute that *Anil's Ghost* sparked asks profoundly disturbing questions about heritage and modernity that any discussion of secularism and justice cannot afford to ignore.

The dispute is remarkable because it reflects the ethical-political concerns of two important Sri Lankan intellectuals, Radhika Coomaraswamy and Qadri Ismail, who are both fundamentally committed to thinking about the questions of history, violence, and peace from nondominant, nonmajority angles of vision. A lawyer by profession, Coomaraswamy directs the International Center for Ethnic Studies in Colombo, one of the few nongovernmental organizations that seek to engage the questions of history, violence, and peace irreducible to the nationalist dictates of the government or the LTTE (Liberation Tigers of Tamil Elam) fighting for a separate state in Sri Lanka. Ismail, a postcolonial literary critic, trained and employed in North America, seeks to *abide by* the question of peace in Sri Lanka from a self-professed "leftist" perspective. Constituting different modes of becoming Tamil and Muslim respectively, Coomaraswamy and Ismail are interested in contesting the very parameters of the majority/minority distinction within which Sri Lankan (and all postcolonial) identities are authorized and sustained for the oppressive nationalist projects of the state or of the fascist and totalitarian regime of the LTTE. (Ismail contends that an organization like the LTTE cannot be described merely as an "illiberal" bunch of hooligans, as some liberal critics like Jayadeva Uyangoda describe it, because of its violations of "'even elementary norms of democracy, human rights, and pluralism.'" Indeed, the LTTE has to be seen as nothing but a "fascist or totalitarian" group of separatists.)[20] Nonetheless, Coomaraswamy and Ismail approach the questions of history and heritage from different standpoints. Ondaatje's *Anil's Ghost,* if anything, occasioned a brief yet critical forum where their different perspectives came to be foregrounded in a way that is critical to our discussion here.

In 2000 Ismail published a damning indictment of *Anil's Ghost* in an important, nonacademic venue in Sri Lanka, *Pravada.*[21] In contrast to *The English Patient* (which was a "phenomenal effort" that

speaks intelligently to subjects of war, racism, nationalism, and colonialism in places like India, England, and Canada), Ismail argues that
Anil's Ghost produces a "flippant gesture" toward a postcolonial society like that of Sri Lanka. The novel begins with the story of a forensic
anthropologist named Anil Tissera, a woman born in Sri Lanka but
trained in the United Kingdom and United States who visits the island in the midst of a political "crisis" in 1992. The purpose of her
visit, sponsored by a UN human rights group, is to team up with a
Sri Lankan archaeologist named Sarath Diyasena to reconstruct the
identity of a supposedly murdered person whose skeleton was found
in an ancient burial ground. As Ondaatje himself describes in the
author's note, the novel is "set" against the backdrop of the mid-1980s
and the early 1990s, a context of a "crisis that involved three essential
groups: the government [of Premadasa], the anti-government insurgents in the south, and separatist [LTTE] guerillas in the North. Both
the insurgents and the separatists had declared war on the government. Eventually, in response, legal and illegal government squads
were known to have been sent out to hunt down the separatists and
the insurgents." For Ismail, the word *set* in this description is merely
an indication of the problem that plagues the novel. (Indeed, it is a
problem that plagues most of the anthropological literature that produces disciplinary knowledges about Sri Lanka.) The novel is set *in*
Sri Lanka, but it is not *of* it. As Ismail complains, "The casual reader
might assume that the novel is *about* this political time and historical
moment. But Ondaatje, an extremely subtle craftsman, insists otherwise. The novel is merely 'set' in Sri Lanka. The country and its politics may turn out, ultimately, to be incidental to the plot." In Ismail's
view, Ondaatje pretends to do the impossible, that is, not to take sides
with any of the groups mentioned but to speak *of* Sri Lanka from a
distance, as most anthropologists do, to produce an objective knowledge about it. This is impossible, says Ismail, because whether or not
we (authors) intend, "texts always do [take positions]." Surely, then,
Ondaatje's text must find itself on some side. And that side, Ismail
avers, is the side of the Sinhalese Buddhist nationalism of the "majority." Indeed, much of the narrative is told from the familiar angle of
the history of Sinhalese Buddhism. In this respect, *Anil's Ghost* in-
criminates itself in championing "the relentless yet subtle" versions
of Sinhala Buddhist dominance and racism. Ondaatje does this by

"scrupulously" avoiding "a direct encounter with Sri Lankan politics."
This can be found in the way in which Ondaatje describes the war in
Sri Lanka. Ismail quotes Ondaatje:

> There had been continual emergency *from 1983, onwards,* racial at-
> tacks and political killings. The terrorism of the separatist guerilla
> groups, who were fighting for a homeland in the north. The insur-
> rection of the insurgents in the south, against the government, the
> counterterrorism, of the special forces against both of them. . . . It
> was a Hundred Years' War with modern weaponry, and backers on
> the sidelines in safe countries, a war sponsored by gun-and-drug
> runners. It became evident that political enemies were secretly
> joined in financial arms deals. *"The reason for war was war."* (Anil's
> Ghost, 42–43; Ismail's emphasis)

There are many problems in this description for Ismail to quarrel
with, not the least of which the claim *"The reason for war is war."* It reduces all the complexity of the war to *nothing but* war. Nowhere are we
told why the Tamils are fighting for a separate state. The politics of the
LTTE are reduced to "gun-and-drug runners." In other words, Ismail
writes, "The reason for war is not political—even though there have
been 'racial attacks and political killings'; the reason for war is war."
The reduction of this war to war enables Ondaatje to deny "the existence of what we have become used to calling an ethnic or national
conflict." Even though the year 1983 is mentioned, its significance
is never noted. (As we know now, 1983 is synonymous with the pogrom in which Sinhalese Buddhist nationalists murdered thousands
of Tamil civilians; it took place on the heels of the LTTE demand for
a separate state for Tamils in the north. Chapter 6 will have more on
this.) Ondaatje wants to see the war in generalized, humanist terms,
however. And this is why he suggests at one point that "the problem
here is not the Tamil problem, it's the human problem" (142). Seen
this way, the Tamils (and the LTTE, however bloody and indeed fascist their politics have been since they have been fighting for a separate state) have no grievances. The suffering endured by the Tamils
as the "minority" merely reflects the general story of human violence
and aggression that we encounter everywhere. And this human vio-
lence/aggression is synonymous with the present state of Sri Lanka.

As Ismail says, "there is nothing redeemable in the Sri Lankan present. . . . The state is horrible." "Since there is nothing but war in the Sri Lankan present, he [Ondaatje] "turns to the past, to Sri Lankan history."

Ismail's critique helps us see a crafty double move that Ondaatje makes here: to depict the war in generalized, *humanist* fashion is to deny the politics of the war. And, by extension, if this general violence pervades the present state of Sri Lanka, then what is redeemable may be found in the past. Thus, Ondaatje assumes, as so many nationalists themselves do, that there was a Sri Lankan past untainted by violence. As Ondaatje writes, "This is was once a civilized country. We had halls for the sick for centuries before Christ. . . . By the twelfth century, physicians were being dispersed all over the country to be responsible for far flung villages. . . . There were villages for the blind" (192). This nostalgic invocation of a peaceful past suggests not only that the violent problem of Sri Lanka is incurable, but that the source of the problem is modernity or politics itself. That is, Sri Lanka has failed to meet the demand of modernity defined by the problem of ethnic and religious diversity. And, therefore, Sri Lanka will remain (at least for the foreseeable future) in a state of war and chaos, unable to fully reach the goals of modernity. (Though Ismail does not put it this way, the understanding of politics and modernity that governs *Anil's Ghost* is worse than the familiar story that the only cure for the violence—and now terrorism—in the world is the full realization of the grand designs of modernity and democracy. But some societies can never live up to the demand of modernity and are doomed to remain in a permanent state of war.)[22] And this is why Ondaatje prefers to see Sri Lanka in "Asian" terms. Sri Lanka is part of the geography of Asia, which is "older" than "old" Europe (79). Once Asia/Sri Lanka is seen in geographic terms, it needs not be seen in "political" terms. And that is how Ondaatje's novel turns to the past of Sri Lanka. The bygone civilized past is to be admired; the present, reduced to war and chaos, is to be feared and kept at a distance. Thus, westerners may observe, visit, and even write about the present and the past; but they cannot be part of them. The point here is that, in the space of Sri Lanka that Ondaatje constructs, one cannot think the question of the political. One can only do humanitarian work! This is why, Ismail says, *Anil's Ghost* has almost an uncanny admiration for doctors, who are "a long way from governments and media and financial ambition" and who have no "cause or political agenda" (*Anil's Ghost,* 231), but attend to the victims of war, without taking sides. As Ismail has argued elsewhere, better informed and supposedly more theoretically sophisticated anthropologists writing about Sri Lanka treat the question of its politics no better than a novelist like Michael Ondaatje does today. The point here is that one cannot think the question of the political by merely admitting and discussing events of violence.[23]

Thus, Ondaatje's turn to the past is animated by a profound sense of humanism. But this humanist interest in the past is not as innocent as it may appear. Indeed, the turn to the civilized past is not merely an effort to find a redeeming essence that existed once upon a time in Sri Lanka. What undergirds this interest is an effort to sugarcoat contemporary violence and atrocities in Sri Lanka, making the country part of a unique history of Asia, which *was,* at one time, superior to the west. And it is this past that westerners may glimpse (and even admire), embodied in its *ruined* forms (found in ancient geographical areas, museums, texts, or discursive narratives). This view of the past/history is central to the novel. For example, take a key part of the plot in which Anil and her companion, Sarath, after failing to identify the skeleton, come to seek the help of a blind man named Palipahana. Palipahana, "the country's greatest epigraphist," was Sarath's (and his brother's) teacher. Palipahana lives a relatively ascetic life, in a hut, somewhere near Anuradhapura, an ancient ruined capital of Lanka, "a traditional home for monks" (88). (A section of the book is titled "The Grove of Ascetics.") Palipahana's conversation with Anil is replete with references to Buddhism and Buddhist history. Palipahana tells Anil stories about the past (of her forgotten Sri Lankan Buddhist heritage?). Palipahana relates stories from Sinhala texts of Buddhist history like the Chulavamsa. These are not the militant stories of how the Buddha conquered island of Lanka. (The fifth-century historical text Mahavamsa opens with this mythic narrative of the founding of the island in which the Buddha tames semidivine, malevolent beings, or *yakku,* in order to prepare the island for the future flourishing of his *dhamma* in Sri Lanka.) Rather, the sanitized stories Palipahana tells Anil are about the simple lives of ascetics who "were not really poor, but they lived sparsely" (86).

As Ismail claims, "these are the only ancient Lankan stories, or history, that appear in *Anil's Ghost.* Sri Lankan history, to this text, is

Sinhala Buddhist history. A more humane history than we are used to hearing, yes; but not a multi-ethnic history." For Ismail, this humanism is a feigned attempt to negate not only the presence of violence in the past but also the presence of non-Sinhala others who lived in that past. If what we see in the novel is a "nostalgia for lost sovereignty," it is only made more visible by the glaring fact that "all of the male actants in the novel have names that resonate with Buddhist iconography." To this extent, "*Anil's Ghost* is clearly on the side of the enemy." The enemy, for Ismail, is the Sinhala Buddhist nationalism that is responsible for racism and even genocide against the Tamils, who in turn gave birth to an equally genocidal Tamil nationalism embodied by the LTTE. In other words, the story that Sinhalese nationalism tells is precisely the story that *Anil's Ghost* also tells. In that sense, *Anil's Ghost* is nothing but a partner in Sinhala Buddhist domination.

There are many aspects of Ismail's no-holds-barred criticism that I would endorse. But my interest here is not in determining the accuracy of Ondaatje's depiction of the Sri Lankan past or of Ismail's representation of *Anil's Ghost*. My concern here is with the question about history and heritage vis-à-vis the present that Ismail raises. What Ismail's criticism demands, of course, is not a merely nuanced and critical history whose particular details account for the place of minorities in the Sri Lankan past, though such a history in itself would not be entirely unhelpful. What Ismail only implies in this critique, but states more explicitly elsewhere, is a doubt that any history, however critically revamped it may be, is going to weed out the problem of the Buddhist heritage and its relation to the present in Sri Lanka. A better, more accurate history of the past, Ismail seems to think, is not going to redeem the problems of our present, but rather would reproduce a false humanism. Ismail is following others who have already pointed out that the problem is with history itself. To do away with the problem of history, Ismail argues, we have to displace and deauthorize (the discipline of) history. As he writes, "if history, the discipline, is allowed to continue to have an authoritative claim upon the past, it will inevitably make a claim upon the present, which is why it needs to be deauthorized. For history, "even in the hands of its trendiest current practitioners . . . is predicated upon the possibility of an accurate recreation, representation, or narrativization of an object called the past" (*Abiding by Sri Lanka*, 164–65). Rather, "if history can be understood as narrative, as writing, as text . . . and not as the real telling itself, then the past cannot have a determining claim upon the present" (xxxix). Once this history/past is deauthorized, deprived of a "determining" claim to the present, the *postempiricist leftist*, who, like Ismail himself, desires "peace in Sri Lanka need not look to history . . . [or a] historian but to politics, ethics, and even literature" (xxxix). Thus, the argument is that there cannot ever be any relation between history and politics, that is, a relation between thinking about history and thinking about the question of the political.

I am attracted to the idea of displacement. Indeed, I find Ismail's insinuation that we must refuse to think, as Nietzsche would have said, that history has a purpose for life, quite helpful to thinking about the present. Yet I doubt that the idea of displacement or deauthorization (which Ismail contrasts to "dehistoricization") is entirely theoretically sound in the way he deploys it. That is to say, I do not agree that Ismail can deauthorize history and, by extension, "dismantle the category of 'Europe,'" merely through a critique (30). He fails to realize that even critique depends upon a certain kind of historicization or what Foucault called problematization. I will point out in the next chapter why a historicization of certain "problems" such as the category of "Europe" or history itself is not going to be politically worthwhile today. That is, I do not believe, as Ismail does, that our political futures lie merely at the end of a critique. Ismail believes too much in critique. This is why he says that if the "post" in postcoloniality is about "the project of getting beyond the thematic (and problematic) of Eurocentrism, it must entail the critique of the Enlightenment, the epistemological ground of Eurocentrism. . . . [It must be] the project that takes as its task finishing the critique of Eurocentrism—concept by concept, thought by thought (32–33). Of course, there is still much Eurocentric racism and hubris that remain to be criticized, and critique may still have a "purpose" in that sense. Yet we must not fool ourselves that such a critique can put a dent in the heritage of the Enlightenment, its haunting legacy of concepts like "justice," "democracy," and "law," which is often associated with the concept of "politics" or even "peace" today. Can a critique displace this heritage? In other words, postcolonial critics like Ismail cannot explain why, as Derrida contends, justice/law cannot be deconstructed in the way "laws" can be deconstructed (*Force of Law*). Postcolonial critics cannot explain this, because, as I have already noted, they lack an adequate conceptualization of the aporia of our secularism and political sovereignty.[24] (This is in part because the aporia of our modernity is no longer a "problem," that is, it is already deconstructed or can no longer be deconstructed.) For this reason I have profound doubts about any project that begins with the assurance that a critique can navigate toward an emancipatory future. What we need to interrogate is the very relation between problematization/historicization and critique itself, and doing so will demand, as I will explain in the next chapter, bidding farewell to a conceptualization of the present that Foucault has told us to appreciate, a conceptualization that is central to so many postcolonial works.

By way of getting to why I think that thinking of the question of the future should be irreducible to any kind of historicization or critique, let me engage the rejoinder that Radhika Coomaraswamy wrote to Qadri's assessment of *Anil's Ghost*. As I've already mentioned, this brief response echoes a broad set of concerns that animate the very problem of democracy and history. Coomaraswamy grants that some of Ismail's criticism of how *Anil's Ghost*'s history leaves out the presence of Tamils (and "other minorities") in the story/history of Sri Lanka that Ondaatje constructs is important. She shares his concern that Ondaatje's omission of the "ethnic conflict" can play into the hands of the Sinhala Buddhist chauvinism that denies the ethnic conflict and reduces the LTTE to a bunch of thugs or terrorists. That said, Coomaraswamy argues that the presence of Buddhism and history in the novel cannot be dismissed as easily as Ismail does so. Coomaraswamy writes: "The Buddhist presence in the book is a benign one. *Anil's Ghost* celebrates the non-dominant forms of Buddhism reflected in the heterodox traditions of Buddhism. Ondaatje highlights a monastic Buddhism as well as a Buddhist aesthetics. Ondaatje's Buddhism is not the political Buddhism of burning flags and stamping on minorities. He yearns for a Buddhist humanism that in some ways challenges very dominant forms represented in Ismail's critique."[25] Coomaraswamy complains that the problem with Ismail's critique is that it conflates "Buddhism humanism" with "Buddhism chauvinism." For her, Buddhism humanism, however sanitized or romanticized a version of it Ondaatje provides, can work to counter the hegemony of Buddhist nationalism. It does so because humanism, for her, is the "doctrine that privileges the concepts of human rights and human dignity as being more important than ideological doctrine[s] and structures." One could, of course, counter that "humanism" is not as a politically neutral and benign a category as Coomaraswamy would have us think. One need not look to Heidegger or Derrida but only glance at the history of colonialism to grasp the problem with it.[26]

But doing so would not deter Coomaraswamy from insisting on the value of Buddhist humanism. The kind of humanism she considers politically important is found within the history and tradition of Buddhism itself. For her, this Buddhist humanism cannot be ignored merely for the sake of criticizing a general notion of humanism. The horror of Buddhist nationalism has to be fought back with Buddhism. That is to say, it has to be attacked, not only from the outside but also from inside the tradition. After all, there are important insiders or allies who celebrate "an alternative Buddhism . . . by attacking the hatred and corruption from within the tradition." Here she identifies such well-known Buddhist intellectuals as Gananath Obeyesekere, H. L. Seneviratne, and Senake Bandaranayake, all of whom are branded by the Sinhalese right as "traitors" to the Buddhist heritage because they contest the supposed homogeneous identity of Buddhism and history in the island. Coomaraswamy fears that Ismail's broad-brush portrayal of all Buddhist history as participating in the oppression of non-Buddhist others could alienate those "brave" Buddhist allies who speak from the humanist tradition of Buddhism. "In today's context, they are brave people, and to alienate them with a sleight of hand is a great disservice to the struggle against racism." Thus, in a move that seemingly throws into question the crux of Ismail's critique of *Anil's Ghost,* Coomaraswamy identifies Ondaatje himself (who was born in Sri Lanka but perhaps is not a Buddhist) as "a powerful ally . . . an effective voice against brutality and terror, which takes place in Sri Lanka or the world." In other words, Coomaraswamy thinks that history or tradition has still got some work to do, and that one has to speak to the present from such a history to construct alternative visions of the future.

How would Ismail (and we) respond to this? Can Ismail debunk this argument about history and humanism in a new way that takes into account the "heterodox tradition of Buddhism"? Can Ismail respond in a way that does not "alienate" those who champion Buddhist humanism, and still insist on a notion of the present that is disconnected from the past? Can Ismail, or any postcolonial critic for that matter, respond to this demand to take history into account without reproducing the problem of humanism? In other words, can one, as Derrida might say, have *history without history, religion without religion,* or *community without community*? Is the past (history) too contaminated with the blood of its violence to be recovered in the form of a forgotten humanism buried within it? It must be clear by now that a critic like Ismail—who wants to think of the question of otherness and difference in relation to the present, irreducible to any pregiven sense of community, religion, or subjectivity, and who wants to imagine (in Adorno's terms) a space that would make possible "distinction without domination"—cannot possibly embrace any kind of humanism (*Abiding by Sri Lanka,* xlii). Such humanism, Buddhist or not, Ismail would protest, still fosters hierarchy or domination in terms of how self relates to the other. That is to say, if self relates to the other through some already available ground of being like humanism, self/ identity already comes first. (Even Heidegger's everydayness notion of Da-sein despises such a prioritizing of self.) Ismail thus insists that any kind of humanism "cannot be an option for postcoloniality." (In this regard, Ismail takes to task critics like Lila Abu-Lughod who advocate even a "tactical humanism" [251].)[27]

Concerned as he is with making history irrelevant to the present, Ismail says that an alternative to the problem of humanism and history has something to do with how we imagine a new kind of "proximity" between self and other in the present. Such proximity, he assumes, does not reproduce the problem of history. This is because such proximity—and here Ismail quotes Levinas—does not lead to the "'absorption or disappearance of alterity.'" Rather, it is "'the fraternal way of proximity to the other,' with the other being understood as a 'neighbor': literally, someone who is not distant or radically different but who is proximate or close by, who lives next door" (237). Such a conception of proximity does not "confirm 'oneself in one's own identity' or stay exclusivist, but [must] be prepared to put 'that identity itself in question.'" This, for Ismail, can open up a new way of conceptualizing the very question of peace that is "ultimately committed neither to identity . . . or to difference" (ibid.).

One cannot but rush to embrace the desire to think about difference and peace in this way. But does Ismail's (Levinasian) notion of "proximity" vis-à-vis "neighbor" really present a new option for us? Is this "neighbor," this fraternal figure, the figure of the *human,* the figure of the familiar, any different from the Christian "neighbor," who is commanded to love the person next door as *his* counterpart? Or, more specifically, are we not already living upon the (ruined) foundations of the politics of such fraternal-neighborly proximity? (Ruined perhaps because, before Freud, Nietzsche had already mutated, if not demolished, this idea of the "neighbor?") Ismail might not have read about Nietzsche's memorable injunction (in *Thus Spoke Zarathustra*): "flee from the neighbor." As we know, Nietzsche issues this injunction in a discussion of how "you flee to your neighbor from yourself and would like to make a virtue out of that."[28] Nietzsche suspects— he says, "I see through your [supposed] 'selflessness'" that lies in this "virtue." Nietzsche's contempt for fleeing to the neighbor, or rushing to love one's neighbor, is not merely a desire to live in solitude and love ourselves. Rather, it is a call to do something im-possible. As he says, "[My brothers], do I recommend love of the neighbor to you? Sooner I should recommend flight from the neighbor and love of the farthest!" (61). (Elsewhere he writes, "Our Love of our neighbor—is it not a lust for new *possessions*" [*Gay Science*, sec. 14].) For Nietzsche, the figure of the neighbor stands for that which we already know: the familiar figure, whose identity we can *appropriate* and possess. (Possession or appropriation, for him, is another name for "knowledge" and "truth.") To love this near and familiar one is the easiest (perhaps the most dangerous) thing to do. It is dangerous, because the neighbor stands for the familiar "identity," always subject to appropriation ("possession"). Nietzsche contrasts "neighbor" to "friend" (*Thus Spoke Zarathustra*, 61). "I teach you not the neighbor, but the friend." The friend, unlike the neighbor, is not somebody who is next to you, with easy "proximity" to *him*, but one who is "the farthest." "It is those farthest away who must pay for your love of your neighbor; and even if five of you are together, there is always a sixth who must die." These "farthest" friends are those that we do not know or recognize yet; they are our friends. The ones that we do not know yet are "ghosts." The demand here is to love the *ghosts/friends*, have friendships with those that we do not know or see. "*Higher than love of your neighbor is love of the farthest and the future; higher yet than love of human beings I esteem love of things and ghosts.*" Such "friendship" with the farthest is beyond "appropriation" (61; emphasis added). That which one cannot appropriate or possess is friendship, and that is its "right [just] name" (*Gay Science*, sec. 14). To love phantom friends, to love the farthest that one cannot possess, then, is to think about the unknown future itself, a future that might enable "a becoming of purpose out of accident [and chance]" (*Thus Spoke Zarathustra*, 62).

I will have much more to say about chance and the future later. But my point here must be obvious. Ismail wants to think of politics irreducible to history. But he invokes the idea of the neighbor, which is deeply historical. In so doing, Ismail brings us back to the very problem of humanism itself. This happens not because the idea of the neighbor—this point is crucial to note—is inherently Christian, but because it embodies a "history," a history that, as Derrida has shown, produces—from Aristotle to Augustine and Carl Schmitt—the distinction between "friend" and "enemy," a distinction of domination that has been central to the very sustenance of the idea of democracy (more on this in chapter 7). In other words, I do not think that today, perhaps still belonging to the posterity of Nietzsche, we can bring back this figure of the "neighbor" (or even the Nietzschean idea of the undoubtedly fraternal "friend") and continue to insist on a new conception of the present that is disconnected from the past. The ghost of Nietzsche, as we will see later in detail, stands where we come to the dead-end of the past, in which the shattered pieces of the image of the neighbor do not remain to be assembled and packaged for our present. Yet, at the same time, even Nietzsche's legacy of the "friend," which brings back the "brother," is not available to us today. (This is why we will have to read Nietzsche with Derrida.) [29] What I will argue in this study is that, to think of the problem of history, we will have to think of what I call anti-genealogical futures. In such futures we have to "lose" (in Nietzsche's view) or "un-inherit" (in my view) not only the kind of history/heritage (of the neighbor) that Nietzsche mutated but also the very name *Nietzsche* itself—which stands for a certain critique of community, history, and modernity. Nietzsche, who brings back the (Greek) brother/brotherhood, still retains a notion of history without history, community without community. *Losing* this name *Nietzsche* is Nietzsche's own "bid" in *Zarathustra*. To do so, we will need a new conceptualization of how to think about un-inheriting the problems of pasts and presents in our (still democratic, secular?) futures.

Hence a sophisticated postcolonial critic such as Ismail—with whom I share a profound disconcertion with the conventional ways of thinking the question of postcolonial difference within the confines of history and heritage and an uncompromising opposition to letting (the discipline of) history make claims about the present—can offer nothing but the guarantee of a false humanism, one perhaps no better than Coomaraswamy's. By now it should be obvious that this problem of humanism is intimately tied to the problem of history itself. Mere opposition to humanism then is not going to eradicate this problem of history and vice versa. In other words, one cannot have history without humanism. To illustrate this point, let me examine how a prominent critic of popular culture and capitalism, Slavoj Žižek, approaches the problem of history, heritage, and humanism. Žižek is an ideal figure in this regard, not only because he echoes the problem of history that has preoccupied us so far but also because he critiques humanism as a way of thinking of a "new beginning." In this respect Žižek is the opposite of Coomaraswamy. Žižek wants to have a certain history without its humanism. Can this antihumanist critic accomplish this task?

Humanism's "New Beginning"

This is precisely the kind of concern that Žižek brings to bear in his book, *The Fragile Absolute: Or, Why Is the Christian Legacy Worth Fighting For?*[30] One should not be fooled by the subtitle and assume that the book offers a fine-grained, detailed analysis of a *history* of Christianity that one should fight for. Žižek, of course, is not a historian of that sort. Indeed the first part of the book has almost nothing to do with Christianity. It deals with a psychoanalytic critique of a certain notion of a capitalistic present that guides our contemporary existence, from the consumption of caffeine-free Diet Coke to powerful democracies waging war in the name of (capitalist) humanity. For Žižek, the age of capitalist consumption that we live in is one of "obscurantism," in which we consume "nothing" for something. For example, he says,

> We drink Coke—or any drink—for two reasons: for its thirst-quenching or nutritional value, and for its taste. In the case of caffeine-free diet Coke, nutritional value is suspended and the caffeine, as the key ingredient of its taste, is also taken away—all that remains is a pure semblance, an artificial promise of a substance which never materialized. Is it not true that in this sense, in the

case of caffeine-free diet Coke, we almost literally "drink nothing in the guises of something"? (*Fragile*, 23)

This consumption of nothing for something is a miniature form of the epistemic violence of capitalism, whose power today is more "anonymous" yet "systematic" than ever. This capitalism, among other things, renders "*the cause of desire directly into our object of desire*" (21). (If I were being unfair to Žižek, I would say that the irony here is that, for him, the products of the capitalistic market work as self-evident, ready-made examples to explain the "anonymous" power of capitalism itself!)

One of Žižek's main contentions is that there is a direct relation between capitalism and secularization. "Capitalism entails the radical secularization of social life—it mercilessly tears apart any aura of authentic mobility, sacredness, honor, and so on." To buttress this claim, Žižek quotes Marx's famous words in *The Communist Manifesto:*

It has drowned the most heavenly ecstasies of religious fervour, of chivalrous enthusiasm, of philistine sentimentalism, in the icy water of egotistical calculation. It has resolved personal worth into exchange value, and in the face of numberless indefeasible charted freedoms, has set up that single, unconscionable freedom—Free Trade. In one word, for exploitation, veiled by religious and political illusions, it has substituted naked, shameless, direct, brutal exploitation. (*Manifesto*, 82; quoted in *Fragile*, 14)

The evil of capitalism, today, in its more subtle, fetishized, anonymous forms of doing nothing for something, anchors the entire project of "globalization." Sometimes referred to as the "Third Way," to Žižek it has become "*global capitalism with a human face,* that is, an attempt to minimize the human costs of the global capitalist machinery, whose functioning is left undisturbed" (63). In other words, in an ironic twist of fate, the anonymous, ghostly capitalism that Marx spoke of has appeared to us today with a "human face." But the human face of capitalism/secularization is no less evasive and delusional than its former, faceless, counterpart. This humanized face of capitalism may be seen in the western democracies' attempts at humanizing their militarism. Such humanization was evident in the way the neoliberal philosophers sold the NATO intervention in the former Republic of Yugoslavia. The mouthpieces for this intervention justified it in both religious and humanist terms. The intervention was not an attempt to contravene international law; indeed, it was a *defense* of human rights and international law. Some even claimed that the military defense was demanded by a "higher law" itself. Žižek quotes one such neoliberal apologist: "Human rights, human freedoms, and human dignity have their deepest roots somewhere outside the perceptible world . . . while the state is a human creation, human beings are the creation of God." (Žižek might say that this statement has a remarkable resemblance to the way in which the Bush administration sold the war in Iraq, in terms of a global attempt to spread freedom and democracy as a gift from the "Almighty" to every human being in the world.) The specific question that concerns Žižek here is, how does one criticize this militarism, its false humanism and religious fundamentalism, without falling prey to the pacifist-liberal position that insists that "'more bombs and killings never bring peace'"? (56–57)? The problem with this sort of military humanism is not its self-evident militarism but its humanism itself. This false military humanism cannot be combated with pacifist humanism.

> The problem is, rather, that this purely humanitarian-ethical legitimization [of war] . . . thoroughly *depoliticizes* the military intervention, changing it into an intervention in humanitarian catastrophe, grounded in purely moral reasons, not an intervention in a well-defined political struggle. In other words, *the problem with "militaristic humanism/pacifism" lies not in "militaristic" but in "humanism/pacifism"*: in the way the militaristic intervention (in the social struggle) is presented as help to the victims of (ethnic, etc.) hatred and violence, justified directly in depoliticized universal human rights. Consequently, what we need is not a "true" (demilitarized), humanism/pacifism, but a "militaristic" social intervention divested of its depoliticized humanist/pacifist veneer. (ibid.)

This statement should supposedly cast aside any doubt that Žižek is fundamentally an antihumanist or even anti–human rights. (At least so it seems so far. We will see if Žižek can stand his ground as he proceeds.) The alternative to this humanism of our military capitalism is to forge a social intervention through manufacturing an alliance between Christianity and Marxism. But the legacies of both Christianity and Marxism have to be rethought or reconfigured. Marxism has to deprive itself of "the utopian-ideological notion of communism as its inherent standard" and return to its critique of political economy to "break out of the capitalist horizon *without* falling into the trap of returning to the eminently *premodern* notion of a balanced (self-)restrained society" (19–20). Marxism should not be left to be defined by the "old liberal slander . . . [that] 'communist-parties-are-secularized-religious-sects,'" just as Christianity should not defined purely as the "process of the final deliverance of the faithful" (2). This alliance has a double task: it should fight not only capitalism but also the so-called "return of the religious dimension in all its disguised forms: from Christian and other fundamentalisms, through the multitude of New Age spiritualisms, up to the emerging religious sensitivity within deconstructionism itself (so-called 'post-secular' thought)" (1).

It is against the background of a critique of the secularized, humanized present of our capitalism that Žižek seeks to think of "the authentic Christian legacy," which he says is "too precious to be left up to fundamentalist freaks" (2). My interest here is in Žižek's concern with the very notion of legacy/heritage itself. Obviously, there are many questions we can raise about some of his formulations so far. For example, who would contend that "deconstruction" is interested in producing (non-Christian) "religious sensitivity" or multiculturalist diversity? Is this not the same (naive and careless) charge that Christian fundamentalists (and uninformed "journalists" and political commentators who have not read a word by Derrida or any other serious thinker) throw at deconstruction and even secularization? If so, can Žižek avoid echoing the very problem of fundamentalism that he seeks to contest and produce a new conception of (authentically Christian) heritage/history? Obviously Žižek promises to accomplish just that. So what precisely does Žižek mean by the authentic legacy/heritage (of Christianity)? How and why is this legacy *available* for separating it from a different legacy of Christianity that fundamentalists supposedly represent? Can this new legacy be the alternative to the problem of humanism that even capitalism itself (and its big brother, law) claims to embody? I ask these questions from a theoretical, not empirical, standpoint.

Needless to say, it is easy to agree with some aspects of Žižek's critique of capitalism, even though it hardly contains anything new we do not already know about its powers and horrors. Be that as it may, my point here is that there are serious problems with Žižek's exercise of laboring to think of some (Christian) heritage as an alternative to capitalist humanism. Indeed, in my view, they threaten to put him right back into the arms of the humanism and nationalism rampant in the West today. One of the problems has partly to do with how Žižek equates the legacy of Christianity with what he calls its "core." Žižek's contention is that there is a "subversive core" of Christianity to be found in the legacy of Saint Paul (119). This core is its "fragile absolute," and it has to be "fought for and regained again and again" (118). This talk of a core might immediately persuade some critics to dismiss Žižek as someone who is out of touch with the literature that has interrogated the colonial fantasizing and imaging of the very notion of core or essence, which has been central to the logic of colonialism. Žižek cannot and should not be dismissed so easily, because underlying his seeming innocent desire to rethink Christianity's core, to demand that Christians be "true Christians," is a sinister labor that perpetuates the troubling distinction between the "West" and the "East." For example, tucked away in a long footnote to a discussion concerning the question of finding an alternative to the "Western" desire for consuming nothing in the "Eastern" ("Oriental") idea of the "Void" or "Emptiness" is a reference to Buddhism (128). For Žižek, following Lacan, there is a

> global difference between "Eastern" and "Western" elementary symbolic matrixes. In the "Eastern" perspective at its most radical, the ultimate "reality" is that of Emptiness, of the "positive Void," and all finite/determinate reality is inherently "illusory," the only authentic way to the ethico-epistemological Truth is to renounce desire . . . to enter the impassive bliss of nirvana. (166n57)

What a remarkable set of claims! Surely, this celebrated cultural critic has contented himself with learning Buddhism from the old texts of Lacan and has not done his research. Weber, Hegel, Heidegger, and even Nietzsche might have been able to get away with this sort of ham-handed extension of the relation between Emptiness and Nirvana across the board. (Never mind the assumption that the West's penchant for consuming nothing for something is the same as Buddhist Emptiness.) What is astonishing is not this ghastly empirical

blunder; rather, it is the warped equation of "the 'Eastern' perspective" with Buddhism/Emptiness! Apart from the obvious epistemological violence committed, what Žižek is really concealing—and he
knows this better than anyone, because his hero Lacan's idea of the
Real is not about the obvious but about the "concealed"—is that the
East is the East. One can easily know the East by merely identifying and making a claim to an aspect of it: "Buddhism/Emptiness."
Once this knowledge of the East is established, no careful effort is
needed to explore other possible aspects of the East. There's no need
to bother glancing at, much less engaging, a decade of postcolonial
criticisms of precisely this sort of problem simply because what Lacan said about Buddhism sometime ago still holds true.[31] Note that
the problem here is not simply that Žižek does not bother to mention
other traditions of the East, but that he can speak of the East in these
generalized terms precisely because he thinks of Asia geographically
and not conceptually and politically. The East is a place, separated
(by a geographical distance) and different from the West. The place
is understood not in terms of its politics but in terms of its location,
defined by a specific tradition. If Žižek were to talk about the East in
terms of its politics, he could not possibly speak of the "Eastern perspective." Žižek would have to assume that, in contrast to the *notion*
of Nirvana or emptiness being buried in some text or somewhere,
the questions of politics—the *questions* of democracy, justice, law, and
government, secularism, minority rights, etc. that concern the lives
of those who live in Sri Lanka or India or elsewhere—change and
hence are irreducible to "the Eastern perspective." But for Žižek the
East is in the East. (Putting quotation marks around the word *Eastern*
is not going to redeem this assumption.) The presumption is clearer
when, at one point, Žižek parenthetically mocks an unnamed "highly
paid [supposedly a nonwhite, eastern] professor of cultural studies in
Western academia who thinks that his incessant self-condemnatory
critique of the Eurocentrist, etc., bias of Western academia somehow
exempts him from being implicated in it" (45–46). I can only imagine the troubling implication here: do not bother to criticize Eurocentrism and its racism unless one is really elsewhere, away from Europe, with no ties to it, monetary or otherwise. I would not want to
guess who Žižek has in mind here but should remind the reader that,
in his occasionally candid but largely misguided review of Gayatri
Chakravorty Spivak's *A Critique of Postcolonial Reason,* Terry Eagleton

leveled a similar racist charge at Spivak.[32] This racism is evident in how people in Euro-America constantly hound Spivak with questions about why she (like Homi Bhabha and others) is enchanted by (western) deconstruction and does not "write about my Indian hybrid soul" or "let the native speak."[33] Here Žižek could learn much from a critic like Ismail about *speaking to* the politics of anthropologized domains such as Sri Lanka not in cartographic but in textual terms. As Ismail writes, "The place [of Sri Lanka] is understood in this study in textual, not cartographic, terms. That is to say, Sri Lanka is not just a place on a map, a self-contained, discrete entity in which events (by and large) do not exceed its borders. Sri Lanka is a problem, an intellectual and political problem, ultimately for the theory of democracy, not of violence [and religion, if I may add]."[34]

The central problem in Žižek's argument is not the mere reduction of the East to Buddhism (which is precisely the kind of nationalism Qadri accuses Michael Ondaatje of promoting in *Anil's Ghost*). Rather, Žižek's very desire to speak of the core/legacy of Christianity becomes possible by virtue of his *ability* to identify the core/legacy of Buddhism/the East. By extension, then, the core of Christianity becomes the (forgotten?) core of the West. This western core is different from that of the East. Žižek drives home this point when he contrasts abruptly the subversive legacy of Christianity to the supposedly passive message of the Bhagavad Gita (129). If the contrast between Buddhism and Christianity sounds unconvincing, just bring in Hinduism, signified by the Gita! Again he does not entertain for a minute that this sort of contrasting has a distinct colonial history. The contrast is dubious not simply because it is colonial but because it assumes that the Gita is merely available for critique, right through so many historical interventions within it.[35] What is deeply troubling about this characterization of the eastern perspective/Buddhism/ Gita is that it comes from a man who presents himself as an enlightened critic of racism (5). One can easily ask whether, in an empirical sense, anything Žižek says can be trusted, since he is capable of constructing such a fallacious view of the East. *But that is not my question.* My point here is not that Žižek simply essentializes Buddhism or Christianity, a charge he expects. Rather, to refer to a core of Christianity, he must produce a cultural-religious difference. The pointed question I want to ask is this: how does Žižek presume that the difference be negotiated or dealt with? After all, as a self-proclaimed antiracist who would have nothing do with the Nazi past that sought to "cultivate full identification with one's ethnic community," Žižek must tell us how the supposed subversive core of Christianity would help Christians think about the question of difference within empty, secularized capitalism (129).

Does this mean that Žižek is finally coming around to abandoning the notion of "community" the Nazis bought into? We must not be beguiled here into believing that this shrewd thinker can so easily bid farewell to the idea of community. What Žižek wants to have is community without community, one that is a bit better than the Nazi version! That is to say, he wants to have Christianity without Christianity. For Žižek, this new community/Christianity is not a humanized one. Such humanism is fundamentally antithetical to the "true" Christian way of life. This is why, by extension, Žižek sees human rights themselves as diametrically opposed to the Decalogue.

As the experience of our post-political, liberal-permissive society amply demonstrates, human Rights are ultimately, at their core, simply *Rights to violate the Ten Commandments.* "The right to privacy"—the right to *adultery*, in secret, where no one sees me or has the right to probe into my life. "The right to pursue happiness and possess private property"—the right to *steal* (to exploit others). "Freedom of the press and of the expression of opinion"—the right to *lie*. "The right of free citizens to possess weapons"—the right to *kill*. And, ultimately, "freedom of religious belief"—the right to worship false gods. Of course, human Rights do not directly condone the violation of the Ten Commandments—the point is simply that they keep open a marginal "gray zone" which should remain out of the reach of (religious or secular) power: in the shady zone, I can violate these commandments, and if power probes into it, catching me with my pants down, and trying to prevent my violations, I can cry: "Assault on my basic human rights!" The point is this that is structurally impossible, for Power, to draw a clear line of separation and prevent only the "misuse" of a right, while not encroaching upon the proper use, that is, the use that does *not* violate the Commandments. (110–11)

Again, we may dismiss this seemingly fatuous statement as a less than serious attempt at thinking the problem of human rights or an unskilled and unflattering imitation of Nietzsche. (Why on earth otherwise would this intelligent man say "'freedom of religious belief'— the right to worship false gods"?) For example, note what Nietzsche said about human rights and humanity in a context in which he (and his "children of the future") refused to endorse the liberal claims of his day or be "condemned as eyewitnesses" to German "nationalism and racial hatred . . . that now leads the nations of Europe to delimit and barricade themselves against each other." Nietzsche writes:

> We "conserve" nothing; neither do we want to return to any past periods; we are not by any means "liberal"; we do not work for "progress"; we do not need to plug up ears against the sirens who in the market place sing of the future: their song about "equal rights," "a free society," "no more masters and no servants," has no allure for us. We simply do not consider it desirable that a realm of justice and concord should be established. (*Gay Science*, sec. 377)

At first the statement seems scandalous. But Nietzsche's opposition to liberalism and equal rights and justice indicates how he, who spoke of a "new justice," contends that the "realities" of "modern men" should not define the futures (339–40). Nietzsche's seemingly callous disregard for "equal rights" and "free society" points to a fundamental problem with the notion of equality he raised elsewhere. "'I don't like him.'—Why?—'I am not equal to him.' Has any human being ever answered that way?"[36] Obviously Žižek's questioning of human rights hardly measures up to Nietzsche's suspicion of rights.

Still, I want to grant Žižek the benefit of the doubt. I want to think of his statement as an attempt to be (however ineffectually) provocative, to coerce us to meditate on the problem of humanism and the question of otherness. In other words, Žižek is saying that the human rights of secular-juridical politics do not enable us to think of new relations between self and other. This is precisely what he seems to be saying when he claims that the same opposition between human rights and the Decalogue also exists between the Decalogue and the supposedly Christian injunction to "love thy neighbor." For him, this idea of loving the neighbor is founded upon a humanist notion that advances otherness. That is, it "calls for an activity *beyond* the confines of Law, enjoining us always to do more and more, to 'love' our neighbor—not merely in his imaginary dimension (as our *semblant*, mirror-image . . .), but as the Other in the very abyss of its Real, the other as a properly *inhuman* partner, irrational, radically evil, capricious, revolting, disgusting . . . in short, beyond the Good" (III–I2). For him, in other words, the "injunction prohibits nothing" (III). It still operates within the law of humanism. (For Žižek, Tim Robbins's film *Dead Man Walking* serves as the paradigmatic illustration of his point.) To that extent, "one can see how human rights and 'love for thy neighbor' *qua* Real are the two aspects of the same gesture of going beyond the Decalogue" (II2). To paraphrase Žižek, perhaps somewhat liberally, contemporary Christianity itself operates within the grip of the law of humanism and human rights (and not within the Decalogue), and hence it cannot really think about otherness without reducing it to some radical or "traumatic" evil explained "as the result of social, ideological, psychological, etc. conditioning." The problem with the fetishization of the radical evil (of the neighbor to be loved) is that it turns the neighbor into "the absolute Otherness (say, of the Holocaust) which is thus rendered untouchable, impossible to be accounted for in terms of a power struggle" (II2).

Some of this would not sound so bad, had Žižek not already produced (and fetishized) the otherness between the East and the West, between Buddhism and Christianity, in the way I have presented. After all, pointing to "the global difference between 'Eastern' and 'Western' elementary symbolic matrixes" is hardly a political engagement with otherness. No amount of Lacanian qualification is going to redeem his fetishization and deportation of Buddhism/the East/ the "Oriental" from the West. Can the trendy critique of liberal human rights/humanism—and explaining how the oppression of the "totalitarian populist democracy" works today by comparing it to the oppression of taking Viagra, a practice sustained by the very law of modern human rights—possibly exonerate Žižek? The hubris is that a critique of western democracy/capitalism somehow stands for antiracism, allowing one to politically engage the otherness and difference.[37] Can Žižek address the question of difference, however, and still save face? As a presumed antiracist, he must. So how, precisely, does he suggest new "Christians" think about otherness in a nonsecular, nonpolitically correct sense without succumbing to the temptation of the "religious sensitivity" of the modern day deconstruction? For Žižek, one must begin with what he calls the "unplugging" of the Christian notion of love/*agape*, "which has nothing whatsoever to do with the common 'humanist' idea that one should forget about 'artificial' symbolic predicates and perceive one's neighbors in their unique humanity, that is, see the 'real human person'" (ibid., 126). And that antihumanism is to be found in Saint Paul. Žižek cites Corinthians 5:16–17: "from now on, we regard no one from a human point of view; even though we once knew Christ from a human point of view, we know him no longer in that way. So if anyone is in Christ, there is a new creation: everything old has passed away; see, everything has become new!" (127).

This beginning anew, for Žižek, means rethinking all our relations to ourselves. The idea of the new here means "a symbolic death" of the old: "erasing the traces of one's past ('everything old has passed away')." Lest one misunderstand him, Žižek is quick to note that this erasing of the past traces does not mean the mere disappearance of all differences. It means rethinking the very idea of the familiar/beloved. Since there can be no (sudden) erasing of all differences, Žižek suggests that Saint Paul's message enables us not to love the neighbor, nor even to love the enemy, but to hate the beloved, which one does "out of love, and in love." Thus, this love, its "Christian unplugging is *not* an inner contemplative stance, but the active *work* of love which necessarily leads to the creation of an *alternative* community." This unplugging/uncoupling suspends everything, *"not just the implicit laws but, rather, their implicit spectral obscene supplement"* (129–30, 145). He opposes this love not only to the Gita's message of "indifference" to the world but also to (contemporary or inauthentic?) Christianity, which "supports participation in the social game (obey the laws of the country, even if your ultimate fidelity is to God), and thus generates the ideal subjects of existing social order" (129). In a remarkable sentence he explains the relation between the "proper" unplugging of love and the alternative community:

As every true Christian knows, love is the *work* of love—the hard and arduous work of repeated "uncoupling" in which, again and again, we have to disengage ourselves from the inertia that constrains us to identify with the popular order we were born into. Through the Christian work of compassionate love, we discern in what was hitherto a disturbing foreign body, tolerated and even modestly supported by us so that we are not so bothered by it, a subject, with its crushed dreams and desires—it is *this* Christian heritage of uncoupling that is threatened by today's "fundamentalisms," especially when they proclaim themselves Christian. Does not fascism ultimately involve the return to the pagan mores which, rejecting the love of one's enemy, cultivate full identification with one's own ethnic community? (128–29)

What a revealing, yet concealing, set of claims! Is there anything groundbreaking in the proposition that claims to inaugurate a new beginning as an alternative to secularism and liberal humanism? Or, to put it simply, is this call for Christians to be "true" Christians not a call that we have already heard from Enlightenment philosophers like Voltaire?[38] To look at it from a different angle, is this any different from Buddhist intellectual humanists asking Buddhist fundamentalists and nationalists to be true Buddhists by practicing "true" Buddhist compassion for Tamils in Sri Lanka? Is Žižek, then, not back to the problem of humanism and history that he wants to set aside? Is this Žižekian thinking of the question of otherness within the domain of (Christian) history not the fundamental logic of humanism?

My contention here is that any thinking of otherness reducible to history cannot escape the trap of humanism. Žižek would surely contest this charge. He would say that his notion of a *new beginning* (even though it comes from Saint Paul) has no relation to humanism; he is really speaking of a new Christian beginning, and not the old politics of multiculturalism and humanism.[39] How so? By enjoining Christians to do what the Nazis did not and could not do? By doing the active work of more than loving the "enemy"? By founding an "alternative community" (130)? Žižek would say that this interpretation is wholly unfair, because he is talking about not just loving the enemy, but also *hating the beloved,* which is the cardinal message of Saint Paul. But can one really hate the beloved and uncouple oneself from one's legacy while still invoking and attaching oneself to the *name* that connects to a legacy, (authentic) Christianity or (alternative) community? Does not the name, as we have already discussed, by its logic, return to itself? Can the adjectives *alternative* or *new* really change the name? Is *community* not the place where the very distinction between friend and enemy remains safeguarded, where the very possibility of ethnicity qua identity exists? Is not community the most fraternal idea of brotherhood, secured by the logic of number and law, monopolized and supervised by the state? Can the adjective *alternative* really *uncouple* the idea of community from its colonial-democratic-juridical heritage? How would Žižek answer these questions?

Thus my point here is that though Žižek claims that Saint Paul's message about hating the beloved is about inverting the injunction to "love thine enemy," it cannot really invert or bypass the legacy of that injunction because so long as one still talks about the "authentic" name, one is back to the history/legacy of Christianity. Within such a legacy only a humanist politics—i.e., "love thy neighbor" or "love thine enemy"—is possible. Hence my uncompromising insistence that Žižek's thinking about uncoupling sits squarely within the problem of humanism/history. That is to say, if I may repeat this point in a different way, Žižek cannot avoid the problem of "love thine enemy" and still talk about an alternative community of uncoupling. One cannot have one without the other, despite one's best intentions, despite one's appeal to the words "new" and "alternative." The new does not get rid of the old, because it still bears the old names: authentic Christianity or community. Let me put it this way: when Žižek calls for an alternative community, he returns to the problem of not only the history of Christianity but also the history of democracy itself. This is in part because, as Žižek might know, the category of *enemy*—which has such a close connection to the Nazi regime, particularly as it came to be worked out in the hands of the Nazi jurist Carl Schmitt—is a key ally to the very idea of democracy. (Moreover, his suggestion that such a community is the result of "repeated uncoupling," which requires fighting for it again and again, is very much the logic that is enshrined in the principles of democracy and human rights.) To be absolutely clear, my position (and my opposition to Žižek) here is not an empirical one. I am not opposed to Žižek *simply because* the concept of community he is proposing is "Christian." Such an opposition would ring hollow (at least for me) because the sort of future of the political I am imagining in this work has no already installed identity there to which the new (Pauline) Christian community can be opposed; that is to say, my opposition to Žižek is not self-evident. Rather, I am opposed to it on the very ground on which it becomes possible for Žižek to propose this new Christianity. What I mean by this is that for Žižek to propose this new Christianity (by way of fighting for its true legacy, again and again) is to oppose not only what he considers the fundamentalism that is corrupting Christianity but also the eastern or the "Oriental" perspective(s). The Oriental perspective for him stands for an other, and it cannot be simply tolerated (as multiculturalist humanism does) but must be *politicized* and engaged, even if it means opposing and doing violence to it. This is why he often attempts (however unskillfully) to compare/contrast a text such as the Bhagavad Gita to Christianity. In fact, he is almost obsessed with opposing the Gita. For example, take his comments on it in *The Puppet and the Dwarf.* In the most selective reading of it, Žižek goes so far as to argue that "the doctrine of noninvolvement, of disinterested action . . . [in the Gita] provided the justification for the burning of Jews in gas chambers." He claims that this is why "the *Bhagavad-Gita* was Heinrich Himmler's favourite book. . . . This means that Buddhist (or Hindu for that matter) all encompassing Compassion has to be opposed to the Christian intolerant, violent love." [40]

Now one may, perhaps rightly, retort that this is not a critical engagement with the political history of the text, but merely an attempt at redeeming the legacy of the West's genocide against the Jews: the problem with Nazism was not the Nazis themselves, but their supposed source of inspiration, the Gita! So ultimately the problem of anti-Semitism rests with the East. What Žižek fails to see is that, by thinking that the message of the Gita is available for adoption or critique in relation to a political project today, he is committing the same historicist horror enacted by the Nazis. Nevertheless, my point is a rather different one. If we grant him at least part of what he is claiming here, we can pose a question that might chip away at his entire argument. That is, when Žižek claims to oppose the Gita because of its "history" in being deployed for violent and fascist purposes, he supposes the text and its overarching Hindu message has exhausted itself, undermined itself, and hence cannot be appropriated today. If this is the case, then we might ask Žižek, can we not say the same thing about Christianity (and the Bible)? Has not Christianity outlived its usefulness because of its own fascist heritage? Žižek may answer that it is precisely because he recognizes Christianity has such a history that he is interested in fighting for the "true" legacy, the authentic heritage that has always been there, but has never materialized, so to speak, which is to be found in the new Pauline "alternative community." Here, then, is a dazzling sleight of hand. Yes, a new community, but one that is still "Christian," which is possible by invoking the very name Saint Paul. Thus I venture to say that what Žižek wants to have is a community without community, a Christianity without Christianity—i.e., to have the name without certain parts that have constituted it.[41] This can hardly be the uncoupling and unplugging that Žižek envisions. In the end, then, what Žižek desires is not very different from the logic of the permissive capitalist society he criticizes, and I would go so far as to argue that the desire for Christianity without Christianity is the same desire that goes into the logic of (Diet) Coke without caffeine—that is, to desire the property, the "proper" of the property, without the malignant substance that makes it up. Ultimately, and perhaps unwittingly, Žižek becomes a partner in the very logic of capitalism and democracy he opposes. Part of the problem here is that critics like Žižek think of concepts such as religion and community not as aporias, but as problems. Once concepts like Christianity, Buddhism, Hinduism, or identity are conceived as problems, one cannot go very far with them, except to labor to change and improve them. This, I contend, is exactly what Žižek ends up doing. Thus he rushes headlong into the recycling machinery of our capitalistic society, animated today by the greatest virtue of anti-essentialism, which, in its most simplistic (Euro-American) form, translates into the liberal self-help mantra "we are not all racists."[42] This self-righteous disavowal of (the undesirable parts of) one's heritage; this bloated celebration of one's difference and distance from (the bloody parts of) the name that has shaped one, this haughty claim to an improved identity, and, in a word, this narcissistic desire to have identity without identity—does this not conceal the most callous and dangerous *indifference* operating as an alibi for, if not a direct partner in, engendering and fostering incalculable and often unseen racisms, atrocities, and genocides in our permissive capitalistic, humanitarian society?

What this shows us, then, is that Žižek is situated in a long line of thinking that supposes that the solution to the problem of secularism can be found in history. In his case, he thinks his critique of capitalism and humanism can produce a new option. As we have seen in this chapter, neither the defenders of secularism nor its critics can offer alternatives to the aporia of secularism without finding themselves at the limits of history and humanism. Part of the problem is that such critics and defenders lack an adequate conceptualization of un-inheriting and mourning the aporia of secularism. Such a conceptualization of un-inheritance can come from a new understanding of our present itself. My argument here is, in order to produce such an understanding of the present, we will have to imagine a way of un-inheriting a concept of history that owes very much to the legacy of Foucault and even Nietzsche. So long as we continue to bank on the Foucauldian legacy of history, we cannot examine how we might think of new political futures and how perhaps to begin to "walk in ourselves," as Nietzsche put it. Ironically, such anti-genealogical futures, which neither abandon nor embrace our pasts and legacies, would not be Nietzschean either. In the next chapter I demonstrate how we can pose anew the problem of our Foucauldian present of history by way of interrogating two fundamental categories of our democracy, community and responsibility.

Giving an account of oneself comes at a price not only because the "I" that I present cannot present many of the conditions of its own formation but because the "I" that yields to narration cannot comprise many dimensions of itself.
—Judith Butler, Giving an Account of Oneself

Acts can have an ethical significance without necessarily having to be interpreted in terms of "answerability."   —Talal Asad, Formations of the Secular

One is never equal to a responsibility that is assigned to us even before we have accepted it. We have to recognize this without developing a culture of the bad conscience. But a culture of the bad conscience is always better than a culture of the good conscience.
—Jacques Derrida, "Others Are Secret Because They Are Other"

3   Postcolonial Community or Democratic Responsibility?

A Problem of Inheritance

Responsibility and Memory

To account for oneself is to count oneself. One cannot really account for oneself, give an account of oneself, be accountable, responsible, answerable without (always running the risk of) counting oneself, distinguishing oneself, differentiating oneself, among others or as opposed to others (and their cultures, races, religion, ethnic groups, or castes). That which one can account for can be counted. Hence accountability, in my view, is better written as (ac)countability. Thus, if (ac)countability is about counting oneself, then it is about fashioning a memory of oneself. One cannot count oneself without remembering oneself. In that sense, (ac)countability is tied to memory. Memory animates identity, the questions of a person's *being*. If (ac)countability is tied to memory, then any call—by one's religion, community, democratic citizenship, or conscience—to accountability/responsibility is a call to account for oneself *as oneself*. In (ac)countability or responsibility toward the other, the memory of oneself precedes the other. Thus I would argue that any sense of hospitality, care, or responsiveness toward the other begins with the distinction/difference between oneself and (an)other. (Ac)countability is founded upon the difference between self and other. The critical question here is this: if the future of "democracy" is a future of a radical otherness irreducible to the self/other difference or incalculable by the state or community, can we continue to invest in and inherit this notion of (ac)countabilitiy/responsibility as an ethical-political virtue? This question is paramount today since democracy is entirely dependent upon the notion of accountability. Thus to inherit democracy is to inherit this problem. If democracy/(ac)countability were to be part of the future of an irreducible otherness, can one liberate the notion of accountability from the problem of memory and countability? Can one have democracy without this notion of responsibility?

The sense of (ac)countability that I have in mind is not exactly the juridical sense that Nietzsche assigned to the notion of responsibility. Yet it does have some important parallels with the sense of memory that Nietzsche attached to it. In *Twilight of the Idols* Nietzsche argued that the modern idea of the "free," willing, "responsible" individual was "fabricated essentially for the purpose of punishment." "Wherever responsibilities are sought," he argued, "it is usually the instinct for *wanting to punish and judge* that is doing the searching." [1] For Nietzsche, in such a sense of responsibility, "becoming [as opposed to being] is stripped of its innocence" (31). Nietzsche's juridical sense of responsibility has an important lesson to teach us about the problem of memory (and history). In *On the Genealogy of Morals* Nietzsche elaborates on the relation between memory and responsibility. Memory, which he regards as antithetical to "forgetting," makes us *"calculable, regular, necessary."* [2] Thus he describes the history of responsibility as in part a history of calculability. Nietzsche sees in the origin of the practice of calculability the birth of the modern "sovereign individual," the "liberated man," the "free man." On the one hand, this liberated man is "an equal among equals"; on the other hand, the free man is the "individual who resembles no one but himself" (40–41). The free man embodies a distinctive characteristic: "The 'free' man— the owner of an enduring, indestructible will—possesses also in this property his *measure of value:* looking out at others from his own vantage-point, he bestows respect or contempt" (41).

Such a free man, who makes "promises like a sovereign" and vows to keep them against "fate" itself, begins to develop knowledge and mastery over himself (41). "The proud knowledge of this extraordinary privilege of *responsibility,* the consciousness of this rare freedom, this power over oneself and over fate has sunk down deep into his innermost depths and has become . . . a dominant instinct. . . . This sovereign man calls it his *conscience*" (41–42). Nietzsche goes on to make his case for how this concept of conscience has gone through "a series of transformations" and how notions of guilt and debt became complicit in producing what we know today as bad conscience. With bad conscience, man enters a contractual, legal relationship with community, and this relationship is like the one that exists between a debtor and a creditor, founded upon "buying, selling, exchange, wheeling and dealing" (45). The relationship between man and community is one that is sustained by pledges and promises.

> The community stands in the same important fundamental relationship to its members as the creditor does to his debtors. One lives in a community, one enjoys the advantages of a community (oh what advantages! we sometimes underestimate them today), one lives protected, looked after, in peace and trust, without care for certain forms of harm and hostility to which the man *outside*, the "outlaw" is exposed . . . since man has pledged and committed himself to the community as regards this harm and hostility. (52)

If man breaks these pledges, "the community, the deceived creditor, will see that it receives payment, and in so far it can, one may count on that" (52). The important point here is this: it is in this contractual relationship that "man first *measured himself* against another" (51). Such a relationship, a feature of every civilization, is sustained by the belief that "'everything has its price; *everything* can be paid off'" (52). This marks "the earliest and most naïve canon of moral *justice*, the beginning of all 'neighborliness,' all 'fairness,' all 'good will,' all 'objectivity'" (52).

One may quarrel with aspects of Nietzsche's argument. For example, one may argue that Nietzsche's view of responsibility in terms of a "free individual['s]" making promises fails to account for how community itself makes promises to the individual and hence how promise making as a modern norm is a mutual activity and animates the very existence of democracy today. As we will see in chapter 4, Derrida's argument that "democracy is a promise" seeks to account something that Nietzsche perhaps did not notice in the relation among promises, citizens, and democracy.[3] Nonetheless, what Nietzsche wants to show is that responsibility and its relation to community, defined by such cherished values as neighborliness, good will, and fairness, are not self-evident virtues of our democratic modernity. In particular, Nietzsche's mocking of the "free" individual is remarkable because it points to the problematic relation between identity and memory. The free individual is hardly "free." His freedom exists insofar as he counts (and accounts for) his actions; he measures and calculates them. As he does so, he remembers them. The memory of his actions enables him to "dispose of the future" (41). Thus, the (Nietzschean) man who calculates, measures, and remembers his promises and pledges is one who cannot imagine new futures. Note that what is being emphasized by Nietzsche here—remembering one's actions, promises, and pledges one makes to community—is more than an expression of one's commitment to fulfilling them. To remember them is to create a memory of who one fundamentally *is*. This memory is about identity and how it is different from the identities of others. For Nietzsche, the possibility of this memory is always ridden with the possibility of violence. "Things never proceeded without blood, torture, and victims, when man thought it necessary to forge a memory for himself" (42). The question that interests Nietzsche here is how one does away with this problem of memory and identity, and he recommends "active forgetting" of history as an option (see chapter 6).

Thus, responsibility, calculability, community, and memory cannot be easily separated, at least as far as Nietzsche is concerned. And, by extension, this sense of responsibility is inseparable from modern democracy. Indeed, one can easily argue that the contumacious logic of counting/accounting for oneself—forging a memory of oneself—lies at the heart of democracy and its intimate ally and alibi, *community*, the place where democracy's work of counting citizens and neighbors, holding them responsible, is carried out with (or without) their knowledge. Foucault has taught us the story of the power/knowledge vis-à-vis community/state, and we will return to the problem of community.[4] But granting, for the time being, that any modernist sense of responsibility cannot avoid the problem of community/democracy/countability, how can we continue to inherit it? Can notions of responsibility and community continue to define our future democratic aspirations and hopes? Put more broadly, if modern democracy today depends so much on the idea of responsibility, insofar as it is tied to the statistical principle of numbering/counting individuals, can democracy then exist without the notion of responsibility? And, more to the point, if responsibility/community/democracy is about the problem of (the) memory (of identity), and if this problem appears more and more acute in the wake of so many different kinds of murderous nationalisms throughout the world today, can democracy (and we the democratic citizens) continue to live with the problem?

One of my fundamental arguments is that we do not yet have an adequate way of thinking about this problem of responsibility/ community/democracy. This is so not because we still believe in the Habermasian story about the unfulfilled goals of the Enlightenment, modernity, and democracy. On the contrary, I think we have grasped the problem with this story quite well and, by extension, have understood something of the problem with democracy itself. Let me put it this way: Nietzsche bemoaned in *On the Genealogy of Morals* that his generation of modernists, those "seekers after knowledge," "English psychologists," "utilitarians," or "atheists," never permitted themselves to consider that "truth . . . should be a problem" (128). Nietzsche's unforgettable maxim was *"A new problem exists:* that of the *value* of truth.—The will to truth requires critique—let us define our own task in this way—the value of truth must for once, by way of experiment, be *called into question"* (128). I think it safe to say that today *we,* the postmodernists, the poststructuralists, and the postcolonialists, have come to realize that we can never take truth for granted and that the enlightenment values of modernity and democracy are not self-fulfilling prophecies. In that sense, we have become skilled executors of Nietzsche's prophetic injunction, and thanks are due, in large measure, to Michel Foucault. Arguably, more than any other thinker of late, Foucault has taught us how to criticize and *problematize* the givenness of particular concepts through the art of writing genealogies. I will have more to say below about the relation between Foucault's notions of problematization and genealogy and their relation to responsibility. But it is precisely because we have become skillful in the art of problematizing our democracy and seeing it as a "problem" that we today remain hamstrung and thus unable to imagine new domains of the political. No doubt this will be a controversial argument. Let me clarify my point. I am not suggesting we abandon the kind of critique of modernity that Nietzsche-inspired Foucault has taught us. I am suggesting we recognize that such critique/problematization itself will not enable us to think about the question of the political.

This is because critique/problematization, as I will show, does not and cannot stand for the political. Since critique/problematization depends very much on history, and any thinking of the political cannot take place without producing the problematic of humanism, which I have already demonstrated in the previous chapter, we need a different pathway of thinking of the futures of the political. One such pathway will offer in this book is active forgetting of history as a way of imagining anti-genealogical futures.

If Nietzsche contends that memory (of history and heritage) is accompanied by blood and torture, and if identity depends upon such memory in accounting for itself, a strategy of anti-genealogy will be critical to thinking about whether it is possible at all for identity to avoid the problem of memory/(ac)countability. In the above epigraph, largely following Foucault, Butler seems to suggest that it is possible for "I" (identity) to account for itself without being bound to the memory/history of itself. She suggests that, in accounting for itself, the "I" that narrates itself goes through a certain metamorphosis "not only because it cannot present many of the conditions of its own formation . . . but because it cannot comprise many dimensions of itself."[5] While I am sympathetic toward Butler's effort to think about the problem of identity in this way, I will disagree with her because she still relies on the Foucauldian notion of "critique." More generally, in contrast to Butler, I think, as Derrida asserts, "one is never equal to a responsibility."[6] This does not mean that one can never measure up to responsibility simply because responsibility is too stupefying a task. On the contrary, responsibility has a double contradiction built into it. Discussing the relation between secrecy and responsibility, Derrida argues in *The Gift of Death* that "one is never responsible enough, because one is finite, but also because responsibility requires two contradictory moments. It requires one to respond as oneself and as irreplaceable singularity, to answer for what one does, says, gives. But it also requires that, being good and through goodness, one forgets or effaces the origin of what one gives."[7] We will have occasion to return to this text in some detail. Suffice it to say that this contradiction inherent in responsibility, this aporia, this double demand of responsibility, is not something one can problematize and criticize so as to solve it or improve it. To think about this contradiction is to recognize the "im-possibility" of responsibility. And thinking at the limits of this im-possibility—or, to be parasitical on Spivak, "being responsible to the thinking of responsibility"—might enable us to imagine a future of the political irreducible to (ac)countability, memory, and the self/other distinction.[8]

Historicization and Responsibility, Community and Difference

My contention is that the Foucauldian idea of problematization/critique cannot even begin to help us think at the limits of this im-possibility. It seems to me that many scholars often assume, inspired directly or indirectly by the Foucauldian art of writing genealogies, that such problematization/critique/historicization itself would yield a certain sense of politics and indeed responsibility. For example, in an important book on the history of the invention of the category of world religions, Tomoko Masuzawa begins with the following complaint: "in the social sciences and humanities alike, 'religion' as a category has been left largely unhistoricized, essentialized, and tacitly presumed immune or inherently resistant to critical analysis."[9] Urged on by her sense of "inquisitive[ness] about the marvelously loquacious discourse on religions," Masuzawa goes on to subject the category of religion "as a whole to a different kind of scrutiny, a sustained and somewhat sinuous historical analysis" (2, 13).[10] And, after an exhausting delineation of the pluralization of world religions, which is a discourse of "othering" others, Masuzawa concludes the book with the following argument:

> If we are to be serious in our critical intention, the exorcism of an undead Christian absolutism would not suffice. Instead criticism calls for something far more laborious, tedious, and difficult: a rigorous historical investigation that does not superstitiously yield to the comforting belief in the liberating power of "historical consciousness." We must attend to the black folds, billowing, and the livid lining of the fabric of history we unfurl, the story we tell ourselves from time to time to put ourselves to sleep. This is one of the reasons historiography must include the historical analysis of our discourse itself. (328)

My interest here is not in challenging the assertion that religion has not been sufficiently historicized or subjected to sufficient scrutiny.

In fact, the claim has some substance to it, and I can appreciate part of the history Masuzawa provides (though it is the sort of history that we have come to expect from such a project). But rooted within some of the assertions is the wager that this criticism, by way of "historical investigation," would yield a certain *politics*.[11] Masuzawa does not address explicitly the question of the relation between criticism and the political. In fact, if pressed, she would probably tell us that it was not her purpose to address the question of the political because she assumes that this task of criticism/historicization can pass for the political.[12] Even though she does not regard her proposal for historicizing as carrying a sense of the political, she surely assumes that it is the *labor of responsibility* that awaits those of us thinking about the questions of religion, culture, and otherness. After all, can one write about "the discourse of religion as a discourse of othering" without some ethos of politics, ethics, and responsibility toward the "Other"? Thus, responsibility to historicize, it is presumed, counts for some sense of the political. One can address the question of the political without ever addressing it because historicizing itself constitutes a responsibility.

I want to raise a doubt about the assumed relation between historicization/criticism and responsibility/the political. I do so not necessarily to criticize Masuzawa, but only to understand if this presumed relation could hold. This is important because such an assumption is central to an already vast and still growing body of postcolonial literature, to which undoubtedly Masuzawa's work belongs. My worry is that this supposed relation between critique and historicization, at best, cannot tell us what this labor ought to yield. And, at worst, it runs the risk of producing the problems of memory, countability, identity against which Nietzsche warned. After all, the postcolonial genre of Masuzawa's work wants to show how the very practice of "counting" was instrumental in inventing the very myth of "world religions" (13). What is clear in Masuzawa's work is the hope that the *knowledge of the history* of this counting might redeem and liberate us, compelling us not to commit the same historical errors. But is this sufficient? Did not Nietzsche already raise profound misgivings about this concept of knowledge? Can we bank on the belief that knowledge of history— however "sinuous" it may be—would lead to this liberation? Masuzawa does not make it clear how we may think against, if not thwart and un-inherit, the problem of "counting" via the knowledge and indeed memory of the history she provides. It seems to me that in part the difficulty lies with a Foucauldian approach to writing genealogies and problematization.[13] I would argue that if we are to shed any new perspective on the problems of memory, (ac)countability, identity, and community, then we have to give up assuming that historicization and problematization would constitute the political. Let me be precise here. If this sort of historicization demands nothing but responsibility toward the othered other, it cannot really do anything but think about otherness on an already available ground of *difference* between oneself and another. In this way of thinking, one *as oneself* can only work to improve one's relations with the other *as the other*. This is partly the modern logic of responsibility, and I want to show how we might un-inherit and begin to think about the democratic futures of an irreducible otherness.

To do so, let me now turn to Donald Lopez's *Prisoners of Shangri-La: Tibetan Buddhism and the West*.[14] This postcolonial text is very much anchored in the tradition of the Foucauldian- and Saidian-influenced project of postcolonial historicization/criticism. Even though it does not announce itself as such, I would contend that this brilliant work can be read as a text on postcolonial responsibility. In fact, by extension the entire postcolonial field, I would argue, is animated by this question of responsibility.[15] Hence, at least in the way I read it, *Prisoners of Shangri-La* is not a narrow account about Tibetan Buddhism and the problems of its seeming encounters with the West. It echoes that general postcolonial problematic of responsibility. We can discern something of the concern with this problematic in how Lopez came to conceive the book project. It came about as a result of his discontent with the western romanticization and idealization of Tibet, its culture, and its religion, Buddhism. This romanticization, Lopez informs us, emerges out of a historical "play of opposites," in which differing western narratives depicted and produced Tibet either as a land of unsullied and peaceful (Buddhist) culture or as a place of demonic idolatry where a corrupt version of authentic Buddhism has mutated into "Lamaism" (4). The question of "history" is central to Lopez's discontent with this play of opposites. These narratives "deny Tibet its history . . . a real world of which it has always been a part" and deny "the Tibetans their agency in the creation of a contested quotidian reality" (11). This denial of history has been instrumental to the production of Tibet as an object of (western) knowledge about

which anybody can make general claims. In these representations
Tibet becomes a timeless place of universal values and qualities (like
"peace"). This Tibet exists "everywhere and hence nowhere," making
"it no longer necessary for us to go to Tibet when Tibet can come to
us" (10–13).

At the outset of the book, Lopez gives the impression that the interrogation of these romantic stereotypes may have a bearing on the
question of politics itself. This is somewhat clear when he says that the
play of opposites is dangerous because it hurts the cause of Tibetan
independence from the Chinese, who invaded and occupied Tibet in
1950. Indeed, for Lopez the play of opposites "strengthens the Chinese occupation" not only because such stereotypes produce "Tibet as
a [timeless] vacuum," making it possible for various "influences from
the outside" such as the Chinese to lay claims of ownership to it, but
also because they construct it as a place whose universalized essence
remains nowhere and everywhere. The critical question Lopez poses
is partly this: if Tibet is nowhere and everywhere and its essence is
universally appropriable, how can the argument for the independence
of Tibet as a real place be sustained? His point is that much of the
rallying support for the cause of Tibetan independence is based on
idealized images of Tibet and distinguishes Tibet from other places
with similar political predicaments. As he passionately writes, "What
sets the plight of Tibet apart from that of Palestine, Rwanda, Burma,
Northern Ireland, East Timor, or Bosnia is the picture of Tibetans as
a happy, peaceful people devoted to the practice of Buddhism, whose
remote and ecologically enlightened land, ruled by a god-king [the
Dalai Lama] was invaded by the forces of evil" (11). That myth is crucial to garnering western support for Tibetan independence because
"without it the Chinese occupation and colonization of Tibet seems
just one of many human rights violations that demand our attention" (ibid.).

Here, I think, is one of the most moving and powerful instances
in which Lopez opens up a space for thinking the question of the political. The question he does not pose but that emerges here is how
might we think about responsibility to Tibet—responsibility for sup-
porting its cause of independence without recourse to manufactured
idealizations and juridical notions of human rights. Unfortunately,
Lopez cannot and does not pursue this question, simply because he
does not have a concept of the political. He assumes (somewhat like

Masuzawa) that the labor of historicization that he undertakes passes for a certain kind of responsibility and politics. Indeed, the very space of the political that Lopez fortuitously opens up is immediately foreclosed when he (like a good Foucauldian genealogist) goes onto say that the book is not an attempt to "apportion blame and praise." "Neither is its purpose to distinguish good Tibetology from bad, to separate fact from fiction, or the scholarly from the popular, but to show their confluence. The question considered is not how knowledge is tainted but how knowledge takes form" (13). Even so, Lopez hopes, as he puts it modestly, "hidden in its pages, however, some may find a file with which to begin the slow work of sawing through the bars" of the prison of Shangri-La, the imaginary domain of Tibet in which we are all captives (13).

To point out the obvious, I am not asking Lopez to take sides, to know whom to blame, to abandon his seeming neutrality, or to show his cards, if you will. That is not the question of the political I am posing to this text. Such a question implies that the political already and always remains under a sign of presence. My suggestion is that Lopez (as some have suggested) may sound like a neutralist precisely because he thinks his labor of historical investigation can accomplish a politics of responsibility toward thinking anew about the Tibetan cause.[16] Lopez's historical investigation, as will be evident soon, ends up reinforcing some of the very problems that he wants so admirably to jettison. My quarrel here is not with the specific details of the history that he provides. In fact, one cannot help but appreciate many of the beautifully crafted chapters about divergent themes of interest. In my view, *Prisoners of Shangri-La* is a text worth reading carefully to learn much about the fanciful and downright racist views through which the supposed humanity of the Tibetan other has been produced as an object of knowledge. Each chapter is a masterly attempt at demonstrating how such objects of knowledge came to be authorized in terms of reducing Tibetan Buddhism to an adulterated form of "lamaism," reducing the Tibetan Book of the Dead (a mortuary text that has do with the complex Buddhist doctrine of rebirth) to a text that anybody could translate, comment upon, and psychologize about while comparing Buddhism to science, reducing *Om Mani Padme Hum* (a Tibetan mantra that has its "use" in invoking the name of Bodhisatva Avalokitesvara) to so many literal translations to find its original "meaning" (sometimes rendering it to mean "nipple is in the mouth"; 129), and reducing Tibetan art to products of some outside influence or to an imagination of some demonic decadence.

In each and every instance of the frenzied knowledge production about Tibet for many generations, Tibet is denied its history. Tibetans are rarely consulted and Tibetan sources are completely ignored. The objects of knowledge do not remain static; they take on lives of their own. (Here Lopez draws on the early Foucauldian notion of discourse to show how, once uttered, a statement "appears with a status, and enters various networks and various fields of use.")[17] In many instances, contrary to what Lopez hopes at the beginning of the book, fact becomes discernible from fiction in the way he organizes and presents the material. Lopez's contention is that Tibet is hardly recognizable in these fictitious representations. The implicit question here is in how one recognizes Tibet, its history, its agency, among these representations.[18] Lopez attempts to make such a recognition when he writes, at the end of a fascinating chapter on lamaism: "Tibetans are said to believe that if the la, the soul, leaves the body, the person becomes unbalanced or insane. With the formation of lama from la, the original meaning of la left lama, causing a loss of equilibrium that resulted finally in 'Lamaism.' My purpose here has been to attempt a belated ritual of 'calling the la' back to its lost abode" (45). The humorous question that begs to be posed to this humorous sentence, in an otherwise sober—even somber—work, is this: Is Lopez attempting to put the toothpaste back in the tube, so to speak? Surely Lopez sees the difficulty of this attempt, and it is reflected in the title of the book, *Prisoners of Shangri-La*. The fact that today much of the humbug of these views has been appropriated not only by westerners but also by Tibetans themselves exacerbates the difficulty! The questions of responsibility, memory, and community seem to haunt Lopez. How to recognize and liberate Tibet, its history, its agency, and its *own* community from the prison of the orientalist views of Tibet? (Including himself in this prison is an indication of the extent of the difficulty of breaking free from the prison.) It is this labor that he undertakes in his final and undeniably controversial chapter, "The Prison."

Thinking about this prison and those imprisoned within it is driven by a critique of the most influential name in the West associated with Tibet and (Tibetan) Buddhism, the Dalai Lama. To critique

the Dalai Lama is to understand Tibetan Buddhism in relation to
the problem of community and modernity. After all, the Dalai Lama
has been "the leading proponent of Buddhist modernism" since the
beginning of the Tibetan diaspora in 1959 (185). Thus any question
about Tibet and its history cannot ignore the Dalai Lama because he
is the sole representative of Tibetan Buddhism. "For many Tibetans
and non-Tibetans, where the Dalai Lama is, there is Tibet; the soul of
Tibet need not stand on the soil of Tibet" (184). As we know, following the Chinese takeover of Tibet, the Dalai Lama and fellow refugees
took up residence in India, while other Tibetans fled to different western countries, and with this "the nation has followed the exile into
diaspora" (184). It is in the diaspora that the Dalai Lama and other Tibetans have appropriated the "'lie' about Tibet" (184). For Lopez, this
appropriation is visible in the Dalai Lama's efforts to modernize (and
sanitize) Tibetan Buddhism, particularly in his interpretations of it to
western audiences. He has done so in several distinctive ways. He has
simplified complex Buddhist doctrines and reduced them to "peace,"
while portraying Tibet itself as a "zone of peace." He has sought to
sanitize Buddhism by prohibiting the worship of certain Tibetan deities, such as Shugden, for their terrifying and "demonic" features. He
has undermined the significance of certain key cosmological ideas
prevalent in the Buddhist tradition. These efforts appease not only
the modern senses and sensibilities of the westerners that patronize
Tibetan monks but also the fears and assumptions of the Chinese
government, which views the Tibetan demand for independence as
a threat. In these modernizing efforts the Dalai Lama not only reinforces the early orientalist views of Tibetan culture and identity, he
also jeopardizes the very cause that Tibetans are fighting for. After
all, why would Tibet, as a nonviolent zone of peace, "free of the weapons that harm humans and the environment, where the practice of
compassion is preserved for the good of humanity and all sentient
beings," need to be *governed* by Tibetans? (205). Wouldn't such a Tibet still remain a prison, needing the imperial protection of and safeguarding by the Chinese or the West? Wouldn't this portrayal of Tibet
itself make it possible for the Chinese to oppose the Tibetan cause?
The demand that Lopez puts forward (for Tibetans) is to think about
the cause of independence *within history*. To that extent, he is calling
for a Tibetan responsibility. To release themselves from the prison,
the Tibetans must release themselves back into the history that has

been denied them by westerners and members of *their own* community. To exist outside history is to propagate the lie about Tibet.

Now can one here accuse Lopez of essentializing the very idea of history and identity? Lopez would surely demur at such an accusation. He would likely say that the notion of history he has in mind is not an essentialized one, but one in which conflict, power, and movement are at work. If anybody, it is the Dalai Lama who essentializes Buddhism, refusing to recognize diversity and difference within that history. But one could argue that Lopez has in mind a very particular kind of "Tibetan" history. However different and divergent Tibetan identity may be within this history, it is one that is constituted by Tibetans' *own* "agency." The question here is this: how precisely can this history—the Tibetan return to it, if such a thing is possible at all—liberate the prisoners of Shangri-La? This is where, I think, Lopez's argument tends to deconstruct itself, making it possible for us to pose a new set of questions seemingly anticipated by the text. (And that in itself makes the book worth careful study.) If Lopez's demand is for Tibetans to recognize their agency in history, and Tibetan differences within that history, then it is a demand to return to and retain a certain sense of community. Lopez assumes that Tibetans may be Tibetans in such a community, recognizing their specific differences without giving up or compromising their *own identity*. Thus community is the place in which one can have identity *without* identity, be Tibetan without being reduced to an essentialized, universalized idea like "peace." It is the place where differences (among Tibetans themselves) are recognized and honored. It is the place where Tibetans may exercise the agency of their responsibility to their *own* diverse traditions, histories, and pasts.

Is this as theoretically sound an argument about history, community, and identity as it may seem at first sight? Surely it is a nonessentialized community that Lopez is constructing, but it is still a community. Can the mere nonessentializing of community really escape the problems of memory and identity? If community is the place where one can never be adequately responsible, always facing the incessant demand to account for oneself as oneself, can belonging within it really provide a safe postcolonial politics that can counter the Chinese claims about Tibet? Is community not the place where identity is held in check, supervised, subjected to (punitive) gaze, and even *imprisoned*, if you will, by its politics of the calculation of normal (versus deviant) citizens? It is unclear precisely how belonging in a Tibetan community/history itself would enable Tibetans to reconstitute the politics of their demand for independence. It seems to me that Lopez cannot sufficiently think about the problem of identity and memory except to view it in relation to the possibility of its being different. That is to say, Lopez wants to retain Tibetan "agency" while recognizing that it is constituted by *internal differences*. This is not a view that Lopez alone holds. Some go so far as to suggest that the future of postcolonial studies should be defined in terms of recognizing such internal differences or "non-Western ways of life." Take, for example, Richard King—to cite randomly the name of a former Buddhalogist turned "postcolonial scholar"—who claims that, against the old-school practice of comparativism, the labor to "anthropologize" and locate particular "non-Western ways of life" or differences should concern how we think and write about postcolonial cultures. In summarizing the scope of his book *Orientalism and Religion*, King writes: "The broad methodological stance that I have been advocating throughout this book could be described as an attempt to 'anthropologize' . . . in particular to render contemporary Western constructions of reality 'exotic' by drawing attention to the cultural particularity of such knowledge systems and their historical involvement in the systematic and violent suppression of non-Western ways of life."[19] Note how the friendly yet safe exercise of anthropologizing the violent western constructions of the non-West and emphasizing instead nonwestern cultural particularities is masqueraded and marketed here as a radical (political-theoretical) breakthrough. That is to say, the mere demystification of the "mystic" other and the delineation of different "non-Western ways of life" suppressed by colonialism are assumed to constitute something of a postcolonial responsibility. Does this responsibility produce anything other than the most naive, if not the most dangerous, sort of multiculturalism that still safeguards the racist-imperialist distinction between the "West" and the "East"? After all, demystification does nothing to un-inherit the distinction between the West and the non-West, us and them. At best, all it does is say, Yes! look, we all have identities, eastern and western; but there is nothing exotic about them; they are simply nonessential, marked by internal differences.[20] But, at the end of the day, after all the "complex" work of demystification and anthropologizing, these identities will *remain,* defined and confined by the epistemological-cartographic differences and boundaries between the East and the West. (Of course, if the differences between the East and the West didn't remain, how would scholars continue to write and teach better and more complex versions of histories [that orientalism suppressed] about "Asian" cultures and religions while furthering their professional careers as area studies experts?)[21] Lopez's work traffics in a similar set of troubling assumptions about identity. After all the vast amount of historical research that has gone into *Prisoners of Shangri-La*, after giving Tibet back its own history/histories, it simply ends by emphasizing the importance of difference(s) within (Tibetan) identity. Identity is harmless so long as it is nonessentialized. Identity can remain with difference. This emphasis on difference, the nonessentialized nature of identity, is supposed to constitute a postcolonial and democratic responsibility not only for the Tibetans living in the diaspora but also for those of us writing about the postcolonial cultures of others. Recognizing this difference in identity, it is assumed, constitutes a responsibility, and it is this responsibility that must guide postcolonial forms of being and belonging.

My point is not that the conceptual problem that grips *Prisoners of Shangri-La* undermines many of its biting yet humanist criticisms of colonial legacies of knowledge production. Rather, the problem points to the inadequacy of such criticisms and problematizations to thinking about the question of the future of the political. Indeed, much of the postcolonial literature, defined by a desire to historicize (or, in King's terms, "anthropologize"), remains immobilized because it cannot adequately theorize, much less think about un-inheriting, the problem of identity, memory, and history. It is as if postcolonial literature—if you can call it literature—has truly lived up to Nietzsche's demand: it now sees identity as a problem. But it assumes that the problem can be managed, if not solved, by pointing to differences that shape identity; hence the pervasive and tireless emphasis on the importance of not essentializing identity these days. The mere recognition of identity as being nonessentialized constitutes a responsible virtue. This is why much of the postcolonial literature, in my view, rarely addresses the concept of the political or responsibility. It just assumes that the problem can be solved, or kept at bay, so long as it can speak of the nonhomogeneous, fluid nature of identity. Put broadly, one may retain (the traces of) one's identity as "Tibetan," "Sinhalese," "Tamil," or "white," but still remain different. Whether the logic of this argument comes from postcolonial critics like Lopez or from more prominent theorists like Jean-Luc Nancy, it means one thing: one may be the same yet different.[22] (Even Julia Kristeva goes no further when she says, "the foreigner lives within ourselves: he is the hidden face of our identity.")[23] However complexly understood, this notion of difference or foreignness within identity does not eliminate sameness; it just subdues it, devalues it, de-exoticizes it, desovereignizes it, or even corrupts it. In a nutshell, difference simply *problematizes* identity. Note how Qadri Ismail, who is deeply and justly troubled by the ways in which claims to identity suppress differences (in the context of Sri Lankan Tamil nationalism), contends that what needs to be emphasized "is not that one and one don't make two but that one may not always equal one."[24] Part of Ismail's point is that "it is not that all claims to identity are false but that every claim to identity—the production of sameness through the self-evident, 'disinterested' logic of arithmetic—suppresses differences" (85). He argues that the "postempiricist" critic concerned with the responsibility of devaluing the privilege of number/counting/history that makes possible identity/community "would insist, in Jean-Luc Nancy's formulation, that all Tamils, not to mention Sinhalese, Muslims, Burghers, and Malays are 'singular plural.' Or perhaps more clearly, she would hold that the subjectivity of these two constructs are not identical but rhyme, that they must be understood as a mixture of sameness *and* difference" (86). Thus identity is recognized as a problem, and the way to combat it is to point to the differences that "rhyme" it. They are a "mixture." My point here is that a far weaker conceptualization is at work in *Prisoners of Shangri-La* (and surely Ismail, as we have already seen, adopts a deep suspicion of historicization that Lopez and his postcolonial colleagues do not even recognize). If this is how we have attempted to live up to Nietzsche's injunction, perhaps we have not really heeded it at all. Nietzsche could have hardly been satisfied with this sense of "responsibility," because he demanded much more than an attempt to keep the problem of identity/memory at bay. Historicization, then, cannot offer anything but the mere emphasis on difference in identity, and ultimately those who are against historicization cannot avoid the problematic, either. If postcolonial responsibility does nothing but reproduce an old problem in a new guise, can we continue to inherit the very idea of responsibility?

Democracy, Name, and Responsibility

Granted that postcolonial responsibility is sustained by a belief that the problem of identity/community can be rendered less problematic, if not solved, through the aforementioned logic of difference, a similar sense of it governs some of the recent efforts to defend the importance of the "tradition" of democracy. Here I am thinking specifically of Jeffrey Stout's book *Democracy and Tradition*.[25] This ambitious and stout defense of democracy—if I may call it that—is a defense of the very *name* of democracy. That is to say, it is a defense of the very *identity* and "idea" of democracy. For Stout, such a defense has to be articulated in relation to a "tradition" of democracy. Put from a different angle, just as Lopez thinks that any view of Tibetan Buddhism (and the Tibetan cause of independence) does not exist in a vacuum and cannot be separated from history, so Stout thinks that democracy cannot be separated from its tradition/history. What does Stout really mean by democracy as a tradition? The answer he provides is this: "Democracy . . . *is* a tradition. It includes certain habits of reasoning, certain attitudes toward deference and authority in political discussion, and love for certain goods and virtues, as well as a *disposition to respond to certain types of actions, events, or persons with admiration, pity, or horror.* This tradition is anything but empty" (3; emphasis added). This "disposition to respond" (which is responsibility) is embedded within the substance of democratic tradition. "The point of view of a citizen is that of someone who accepts some measure of responsibility for the condition of society . . . for the political arrangements that it makes for itself" (5). Thus responsibility drives the tradition of democracy. In stressing this relation between democracy and tradition, Stout does not want to simply subscribe to a static notion of democratic tradition. He wants to show the opposite. The very "substance" of this tradition makes it possible for us to subject democratic ideals to "critical scrutiny" (5). This is because democratic ideals and commitments are "constantly in dispute, subject to revision, and not fully determinate" (5). Hence the tradition of democratic responsibility demands the terms and parameters of that responsibility itself be scrutinized and revised from time to time, generation to generation. Democracy is something that can be made and remade, and this is the fundamental virtue of understanding it as a tradition.

Democracy can be improved. Stout quotes John Dewey to point out the centrality of this argument to the book.

> The old saying that the cure for the ills of democracy is more de-mocracy is not apt if it means that the evils may be remedied by introducing more machinery of the same kind as that which already exists, or by refining and perfecting that machinery. But the phrase may also indicate the need for *returning to the idea itself,* of clarifying and deepening our apprehension of it, and of employing our sense of its meaning to criticize and remake its political manifestation. (6; emphasis added)

Here, then, is a qualification. What Stout is suggesting is not having more and more of democracy, but rather a "return to the idea itself." This return requires that one not just appreciate democracy, but "criticize and remake" it. Stout traces this sense of reshaping and improving democracy not only to Dewey but also to Emerson. Stout quotes Emerson at the outset of *Democracy and Tradition:* "you shall not look through my eyes . . . or take things from me . . . [but] filter them from your self" (xi). As the term *filter* connotes, Stout considers the tradition/heritage of democracy to be one that needs constant refining. And, essentially, this is what democratic responsibility is all about. Democratic responsibility is the ethical inheritance of a people. "The continuing social process of holding one another responsible is chiefly what I have in mind when I refer to the ethical life or the inheritance of a people" (6). Responsibility is ethics. To belong to a democratic community is to belong to a community of ethics in which members can "reason with one another about the ethical issues that divide them" (6). Even if one is already a member of another ethical-religious-theological community (i.e., that of Christianity or Islam), one cannot abandon democratic responsibility. "Democracy will suffer greatly, I fear, if orthodox Christians [and other religious followers] are unable to maintain their own convictions while also taking up their responsibilities as citizens" (116).

If one were to be unfair to Stout, one might easily suggest that this argument about democratic responsibility sounds tautological. What demands (democratic) responsibility is responsibility itself! For Stout, it is a bit more complex, because citizenship is another name for that responsibility. To be responsible is to be a citizen and vice versa. Yet what is unclear is why this responsibility must be seen in democratic terms. Why not see it in terms of the beliefs, sensibilities, and obligations found in a religious tradition or community? Stout would perhaps retort that a democratic tradition is not like a religious tradition or community. The former demands obligations, commitments, and loyalty to a narrow group of people, whereas the latter is interested in "shared commitments" with respect to a wider citizenry, with differing religious and ethical persuasions. As Stout contends,

> The kind of community that democrats should be promoting at the local, state, and national levels of politics is the kind that involves shared commitment to the Constitution and the culture of democracy. In America, this culture consists of a loose and ever-changing collection of social practices that include such activities as quilting, baseball, and jazz. But its central and definitive component is the discursive practice of holding one another responsible for the actions we commit, the commitments we undertake, and the sorts of people we become. (303–4)

Lest he be mistaken for another romantic liberal championing a new version of old secularism, Stout wants to make a distinction between new traditionalists and secularists, secularism and secularization. On the one hand, by depicting democracy as a tradition, Stout seeks to fend off the criticisms of new traditionalists (represented by John Milbank, Alasdair MacIntyre, and Stanley Hauerwas), who, somewhat like Žižek, charge that modernity, liberalism, and secularity are nothing but expressions of a capitalist market economy, devoid of ethical and moral contents. For Stout, at best these criticisms do not take into account the complex character of democracy (as a tradition of virtues) and at worst they undermine democracy itself. On the other hand, Stout wants to think of democracy as a tradition precisely because it is not simply a *secular* (empty) doctrine. "Modern democracy is not essentially an expression of secularism as some philosophers have claimed and many theologians have feared" (11). Here he wants to part company with philosophers such as John Rawls and Richard Rorty who claim that religious expression flies in the face of democratic reasoning. In Stout's view, this claim is not accurate because "the ethical discourse of most modern democracies is *secularized*" (93), and a secularized discourse does not mean the absence of ethics in democratic reasoning. This is why he argues that secularization is different from secularism. Secularized democracy does not controvert theological beliefs or banish them from the public sphere; however, it just does not take it for granted that such beliefs have "default authority" in a religiously pluralist society (99). Indeed, "this leaves open the possibility that citizens who hold one or another set of religious commitments could be rationally entitled to those commitments" (99). Hence to speak of democracy as a tradition of responsibility is to speak of a culture of ethics. Such a tradition, like any tradition, is not empty, and it needs to be refined from time to time. This culture of secularized responsibility should not frighten religious people; rather, it should compel them to embrace it.

This is how Stout partly constructs the relation between the tradition of democracy and the idea of responsibility. Now my purpose here is not to question whether democracy can yield the kind of responsibility that Stout supposes it does or whether such a notion of responsibility fosters the kind of civic community of shared commitments that he envisions. My interest here is to question whether this very labor of seeking to remake and improve the democratic tradition by way of "returning to the idea itself" is a worthy pursuit. Stout seems to be unaware that the Deweyean overture toward returning to the idea of democracy is not as groundbreaking as he believes. Let me put it simply: The idea of the (re)turn to democracy is already inscribed within democracy (and its name) itself. Any attempt to improve it, to remake it, can go nowhere but back to itself. In other words, one cannot really both remake and improve democracy and return to it at the same time. One cannot render it different. In many ways, Stout's thinking about democracy is entirely founded upon the logic of difference already discussed. He wants to retain democracy, its "name," with a difference. That is what he means when he says, "democracy is better constructed as the name appropriate to the currents in this particular time and place" (308). Meanings of the name differ at particular times and places, but the "name" remains! Can this logic really hold? Can (the name of) democracy really ever differ from itself? Does not that which differs from itself always return to and retain itself? For example, in a fascinating discussion of the Latin notions of *ipseity* ("the power that gives itself its own law") and *rota* (rotation), Derrida shows how democracy has a self-sovereign "law" that returns to itself. Derrida writes: "This [democratic] sovereignty is a circularity, indeed a sphericity. Sovereignty is round; it is a rounding off." [26] Democratic sovereignty can go nowhere but to itself; it returns to itself. This is its power, its own force, its *ipseity*. Like the Greek word *autos*, this *ipseity* of democracy is defined by the possibility of its "automatic turn, or rather return to self, toward the self, upon the self" (10). Derrida goes on to argue that it is difficult to think of democracy "without the rotary motion of some quasi-circular return or rotation toward the self, toward the origin itself, toward and upon the self of its origin" (10) The point here is that a democracy that turns and returns to its own power, "the *autos* of autonomy," its own self, is not something that one can change or improve, in the hope of inheriting a better, a different version of it. In other words, democracy is not something that can really differ from itself.

Hence difference does not really differ at all. At the same time, the logic of difference requires that it (democracy or identity or self) always have some relation to *itself* from which it differs. We cannot expect democracy to be different and not have "more democracy." By criticizing and remaking it, by making it different, one gets nothing but more (of the same) democracy. This, I think, is the fallacy in Dewey's pragmatism, and Stout cannot see it because he, like the postcolonial genealogists, believes that the task of democratic responsibility is to insist on difference while retaining sameness. Stout cannot entertain that there might be a problem with this way of thinking about the heritage of democracy because to him the heritage, the name itself, "the ethical inheritance of a people," renders the problem less problematic. That is to say, he thinks the problem can be continually problematized (and criticized) and made better. Stout acknowledges, perhaps undermining his own argument, "there is no guarantee that things will go well" in a democratic community (303), but the heritage, the name of it, the memory of it, makes it worth pursuing the unguaranteed! To believe in democratic responsibility, then, is to pursue something that is not guaranteed, by extension, something that is inaccessible and transcendent. (Soon we will see how this notion of responsibility indeed has a deeply problematic Christian-messianic sense attached to it.)

For Stout, this way of thinking about democracy, community, identity, and responsibility is almost unquestionable because of his inability to appreciate that the problem of democracy cannot be done away with simply by problematizing it. As I discuss in the next chapter, this problem becomes more acute when democracy, as Derrida says, works as a "promise," something fundamentally deferred.

Stout, of course, would simply dismiss thinkers like Derrida as "postmodernists" who pose a threat to democracy (303). Because he dismisses such thinkers so easily, he is able to completely disregard the relevance of postcolonial (particularly subaltern) criticisms of colonial modernity to any discussion of democracy. He does so partly because his account of democracy buys into the fallacious notion of "multiple modernities," which feeds the colonialist-racist-capitalist thinking that modernity of the West is different from the modernities of the third world, because the third world's transition to capitalism, as Chakrabarty argues, is assumed to always remain "incomplete and lacking." Thus when Stout suggests that America make a "persuasive argument on behalf of democracy" for the third world, he becomes, perhaps unwittingly, party to such thinking, uncritically promoting a democracy whose promise will always remain deferred and allowing so-called democratic governments to get away with so much.[27] My point here is that if democracy is something that cannot be improved and re-inherited, then it must be mourned. What is clearly lacking in Stout's view of democratic community and identity is any concern with the possibility of mourning, of thinking about how we might un-inherit this problem. Such a concern with mourning can never really emerge so long as we continue to believe that the problem of identity can be continuously criticized, (re)problematized, and improved. Mourning democracy, as will be evident in the succeeding chapters, does not mean rejecting it. But it does involve a more serious labor of *thinking* about the problem of memory that informs the legacy and heritage of democracy. Any possibility of such mourning is completely absent in works of Stout's kind because they simply advocate more and more democratic responsibility as the ready-made alternative.[28]

It must be evident that my point thus far has been that our modern sense of responsibility—be it the call of postcolonial genealogists to historicize community or of democratic theorists to return to democracy—cannot really think about the problem of memory, heritage, and identity.[29] The modern (post-Deweyian or postcolonial) sense of responsibility is an alibi that defers the problem of memory and identity by way of the logic of "difference." At the risk of repeating myself, I would say that ultimately such a notion of responsibility is responsible to itself because it fundamentally returns to itself. Hence democratic responsibility cannot be anything but (ac)countability. Can one, then, really think of responsibility differently, without producing this problematic of the return to (it)self? Can one have identity without the problem of memory? In her recent study of responsibility, Judith Butler attempts to do just that. Does she accomplish the task without reinscribing the problematics that govern this thinking about (ac)countability and responsibility?

Butler understands well the *problem* of responsibility. To be sure, unlike Stout, she is suspicious of the dangerous proximity between responsibility and the possibility of its return to (it)self (though she does not see it exactly as Derrida describes the relation between *ipseity* and rotation). For that reason, she begins her account of how one can give an account of oneself with a modest disagreement with Nietzsche. Although she values Nietzsche's account of responsibility, she claims that it misses other aspects of responsibility. In her view, Nietzsche's notion of responsibility is too juridical and punitive: for him, one gives an account of oneself because of the fear of punishment or guilt. This is only partly true, Butler argues, because fear, guilt, revenge, and aggression are not the only mediums through which one can give an account of oneself. (Here she confesses that she herself perhaps too hastily bought into such a sense of the punitive aspects of self-formation in her previous work, *The Psychic Power of Life*.) There are other forms of address, particularly those of "the interlocutory scene in which one is asked what one has done, or a situation in which one tries to make plain, to one who is waiting to know, what one has done, and for what reason" (*Giving an Account*, 13–14).

For her, giving an account of oneself is not just telling a narrative of oneself. There is something of the narrative form in such an account. But the two are different. In giving an account, the one who responds to another's query is not an already-formed, self-mastering subject. Rather, one gives up and abandons something of oneself in an interlocutory context. A certain moment of "unknowingness about oneself," an "opacity to the self" takes place when one enters into an interlocutory relation with another (20). She adds: "The very terms by which we give an account, by which we make intelligible to ourselves and to others, are not of our making. They are social in character, and they establish social norms, a domain of unfreedom and substitutability within which our 'singular' stories are told" (21). Thus the relations that occur between oneself and another when we make ourselves intelligible do not allow us to remain simply self-mastering, free, unsubstitutable subjects but rather produce a domain of "unfreedom" in which we become exposed and vulnerable to being substituted by others. In these relations, we risk forsaking self-knowledge and unrecognizability of ourselves.

One of Butler's fundamental concerns is to understand how it is possible to be responsible and accountable at all if one who is exposed to the vulnerability of the narration of oneself that is "always undergoing revision" (40). (Unfortunately, Butler's concept of self here sounds very much like Stout's idea of democracy, which is always undergoing revision.) How can the subject have any sense of ethics and responsibility if the subject itself is made unrecognizable and unknowable to itself by the changes it undergoes? Contrary to those who associate this kind of poststructuralist thought with nihilism, Butler contends that unrecognizability and unknowingness about oneself can produce ethics. She suspects that "an ability to affirm what is contingent and incoherent in oneself may allow one to affirm others who or may not mirror one's own constitution" (41). Thus to unrecognize oneself is to recognize and affirm others. To understand the possibility of such an affirmation, she turns to several major critics, including Levinas, Adorno, and Foucault.

The challenge for Butler here is to understand the difficulty of narrating how we are formed by the interlocutory contexts before our own self-constitution. And if doing so produces a limit to our agency and ability for self-narration, then responsibility has to be rethought at this limit. This limited agency does not indicate a lack in our capacity to aspire to a better sense of humanity, but it is "the sign of our humanity" (83). This limit indicates that an attempt to account for oneself cannot ever be undertaken without the other. How can it be? If we are formed only when we respond to others, we cannot think about nothing but responsibility to others. As she writes (perhaps without intending to echo Julia Kristeva), "I speak as an 'I,' but do not make the mistake of thinking that I know precisely all that I am doing when I speak in that way. I find that my very formation implicates the other in me, that my own foreignness to myself is, paradoxically, the source of my ethical connection with others" (84).[30] Needless to say, the interlocutory relation between oneself and another is not always a peaceful one. Sometimes it is fraught with the possibility of harm, danger, even trauma. How does one think about accountability here? How does the other manifest in oneself in situations of violence (e.g., the Nazi persecutions of the Jews), where one is the wounded, the tortured, and the victimized? How does one conceptualize responsibility from the standpoint of being wounded and persecuted? Here she finds Levinas's thinking about responsibility relevant. For Levinas, injury is almost the ideal conceptual site within which responsibility must be thought. As he said, shockingly, persecution leads to responsibility. Or, "wounds and outrages . . . [are] proper to responsibility itself." [31] This does not mean that the persecuted are responsible for the persecution committed upon them. It means that persecution is the site in which the formation of the ego (*moi*) takes place prior to one's own being. Since, for Levinas, self- or ego-formation takes place "outside of being," thinking about persecution enables him to understand the relation between self and other in a way that does not depend on the notion of will or freedom. Persecution exposes the face of the other, and this face, which is irreducible and irreplaceable, makes it impossible for one to renounce the other. As Butler writes, "whatever the Other has done, the Other still makes an ethical demand upon me, has a face to which I am obliged to respond—meaning that I am, as it were, precluded from revenge by virtue of a relation I never choose" (91). While Butler values Levinas's effort to think of the ways in which we become implicated in relations with others without free will and agency, she finds Levinas's essentialist and even racist claims—he claimed persecution is the core heritage of Judaism and that "masses of Asiatic . . . and underdeveloped people" have no culture of responsibility and that they threaten Jewish authenticity—not helpful, to say the least (94). In particular, she considers Levinas's attempt to link the Jewish sense of responsibility to a "preontological being" (his terms) highly problematic. She finds in Foucault ways of grapping with the problem that are more helpful.

I will discuss her engagement with Foucault shortly. What should be noted in Butler's reading of Levinas is that her effort to think about responsibility beyond the notion of bad conscience still operates within the binary of self/other. Whether she understands that relation in terms of the "other in me" or" "my own foreignness to myself" or my being shaped by another prior to my own being—all as a way of bypassing the problem of free will and agency—her thinking still remains anchored in that binary. *To anticipate my argument, let me say at this point that ultimately Butler cannot conceptualize an otherness that is irreducible to such a binary.* This is partly because she believes too much in a Foucauldian project of continuing to desubjugate the subject. That is to say, Butler ultimately believes too much in the notion of critique. For example, following an insightful engagement with Adorno, she writes: "Foucault, like Adorno, maintains that ethics can only be understood in terms of a *process of a critique,* where critique attends, among other things, to the regimes of intelligibility that order ontology and, specifically, the ontology of the subject" (109; emphasis added). Butler, of course, does not do the sort of history or historicization that Masuzawa or Lopez recommends. Nonetheless, she pins her hopes on the "virtue" of the Foucauldian critique.[32] (Foucault himself remarked, "there is something in critique that is akin to virtue.")[33] What precisely does the virtue of critique set out to do, if not accomplish?

As Foucault defined it, "critique is the movement by which the subject gives itself the right to question truth or its effects of power, and to question power on its discourses of truth. . . . In a word, the politics of truth" (32). Thus, critique in a nutshell is the "desubjugation of the subject" (32). It is precisely this sense of the desubjugation of the subject that is central to Butler's labor to rethink one's relation to another. Butler believes, like Foucault, that the relations between oneself and another can be re-formed by way of critique. As Butler explains, for Foucault, critique operates in relation to a given regime of truth, norms, and discourses that governs, orders, subjugates, and obliges oneself. To question that regime of truth is to question oneself, one's own identity, in relation to that regime. In this self-questioning one begins to ask what one may become given one's own ordered and subjugated being within such a regime. This becoming, for Foucault, is not merely to recognize one's own true self prior to subjugation but involves, as Butler claims, "putting oneself at risk, imperiling the very possibility of being recognized by others, since to question the norms of recognition that govern what I might be, to ask what they leave out, what they might be compelled to accommodate, is, in relation to the present regime, to risk unrecognizability as a subject" (*Giving an Account,* 23). Thus Foucauldian critique (as opposed to the Kantian notion of critique) desubjugates oneself by way of producing unrecognizability of oneself.[34] Butler grants that what Foucault does not show is how this self-criticism would foster what sorts of relations with others. Even so, Butler contends, such a critique can make possible the formation of new relations between oneself and another. After all, it is only within a given history of a regime of truth that one exists as oneself, to be recognized by others (115–16). To question that regime must, then, mean to question one's pregiven relation to others. It is through such a critique that one can begin to give an account of oneself.

I am not persuaded by this argument, but not because I think critique somehow fails to desubjugate the subject. I am prepared to accept what Foucault and Butler claim it does. Critique is what it is. It is a "movement" or a "process." It interrogates the process of the formations of the subject through genealogical investigation, which supposedly enables the subject to desubjugate itself. What Butler does not show is that this Foucauldian critique is tied to a key concept in Foucault's thinking: problematization. She sees critique's connection to genealogy. This is clear when she quotes the following sentence by Foucault: "Genealogy of the modern self . . . is one of the possible ways to get rid of a traditional philosophy of the subject" (113). But the notion of genealogy is inseparable from what Foucault called "problematization."[35] It is this genealogy that supposedly enables us to problematize identity/subject. Desubjugation is possible only through genealogical problematization. My misgiving here is precisely about this relation between critique and problematization. I doubt that critique can be the strategy on which we can continue to bank. It seems to me that the task of the desubjugation of the subject, made possible by genealogy/problematization/critique, is not sufficient to the task of mourning that concerns me here. Critique cannot help us to think about the problem of un-inheriting the legacy of our pasts so as to imagine new, anti-genealogical futures.

My wager is that what such futures need is not a continuing "process" of critiquing subjects and their subjectivities, but to mourn the already desubjugated and deconstructed identities of aporia that haunt us. Critique cannot offer such a theory of haunting and mourning. In other words, critique/problematization does not attend to the spectral pasts that haunt our present. A critique-inspired project of giving an account of oneself—even the sort of account one may give through the art of "confession" that concerned "final Foucault"—can find no way to account for such pasts and legacies. Democracy is one such legacy. The problem with this legacy is that it cannot be criticized and problematized any more. Critique surely cannot help us understand those "deferred" promises of democracy. In other words, what we need are not more and more strategies of problematizing our identities, as I discussed in chapter 1. We need a pathway of thinking about how we may live with those identities, the identities that are beyond problematization, that are no longer a "problem." To do so, we have to give up thinking that our identities (including the identity of democracy itself) remain to be criticized from time to time. To do this, we need an anti-genealogy, and neither Butler nor the postcolonial and democratic critics can help us here. Critique that relies so much on history has no concern with an antigenealogy. I will have more to say about haunting, specters, and anti-genealogy later in the book. In what follows, I want to show why critique/problematization cannot attend to our haunting pasts and why it has to be folded into the Derridean project of deconstruction and mourning, if you will. To do so, I need to show how Derridean deconstructive mourning differs radically from the liberal-pragmatist project of responsibility that scholars such as Stout and Richard Rorty advance.

Problematization, Deconstruction, and "Accounting" for Specters: Un-inheriting the Unproblematizable

In a series of fascinating lectures given at UC Berkeley in the fall of 1983 on the Greek and Roman notions and meanings of *Parhesia,* usually translated as "free speech," Foucault sought to define problematization in terms of a distinction between a "history of ideas" and "history of thought."[36] The history of ideas was concerned with an analysis of a specific concept or notion "from its birth, through its development, and in the setting of other ideas which constitute its context." The history of thought, on the other hand, is "the analysis of the way an unproblematic field of experience, or set of practices, which were accepted without question, which were familiar and 'silent,' becomes a problem, raises discussion and debate, incites new reactions, and induces a crisis in the previously silent behavior, habits, practices, and institutions" (74). More specifically, the history of thought is "the way people begin to take care of something, of the way they become anxious about this or that—for example, about madness, about crime, about sex, about themselves, or about truth" (74). It is this analysis of the history of thought that Foucault calls problematization. Problematization is about "how and why certain things (behavior, phenomena, processes) became a *problem*." Problematization, he says, does not deny the "reality" of that which is problematized," such as madness or crime. (It is not "historical idealism.") Nor does it lack a historical context. Nonetheless, a "given problematization is not an effect or a consequence of a historical context or situation, but is an answer given by definite individuals" (172). Foucault elaborates:

> The fact that an answer is neither a representation nor an effect of a situation does not mean that it answers to nothing, that it is a pure dream, or an anti-creation. A problematization is always a kind of creation; but creation in the sense that, given a certain situation, you cannot infer that this kind of problematization will follow. Given a certain problematization, you can only understand why this kind of answer appears as a reply to some concrete and specific aspect of the world. (172–73)

Seen this way, problematization is not so much a task that an author does as it is something that a given "people" do. And a given situation can never anticipate what sort of problematization will materialize. So problematization is hardly a seamless genealogy; it is contingent to the extent that its demands are made possible by a given situation.

If at the end of this distinction between history of ideas and history of thought we are left wondering how problematization may be brought to bear on the question of the political, or that of responsibility, Foucault might say that the problematization itself has a certain kind of politics and responsibility. But it is a politics that does not (and cannot) become available in advance of the situation and its problematization. Problematization is a series of answers provided to questions generated by a "problem." Politics—Foucault means, I think, the politics of the liberal/leftist, humanist/progressivist, or Marxist/activist traditions in which "we" remain invested—can never come prior to questions/answers. Any such politics of responsibility has to emerge and be worked out in relation to the domain of questions/answers that a problem demands. The relation between problematization and politics becomes clearer in an interview Foucault gave less than two months before his death, later published under the title "Polemics, Politics, and Problematization." Here he does so by renouncing the idea of "we" in terms of thinking about the domain of politics. In responding to Richard Rorty's claim (or charge?)[37] that Foucault never appeals to a "we" (and hence has no politics of responsibility or moral obligation) in his works, Foucault contends:

> I do not appeal to any "we"—to any of those "wes" whose consensus, whose values, whose traditions constitute the framework for a thought and define the conditions in which it can be validated. But the problem is, precisely, to decide if it is actually suitable to place oneself within a "we" in order to assert the principles one recognizes and the values one accepts; or if it is not, rather, necessary to make the future formation of a "we" possible by elaborating the question. Because it seems to me that "we" must not be previous to the question; it can only be the result—and the necessary temporary result—of the question as it is posed in the new terms in which one formulates it. For example, I'm not sure that at the time when I wrote the history of madness, there was a preexisting and receptive "we" to which I would only have had to refer in order to write my book, and of which this book would have been the spontaneous expression. Laing, Cooper, Basaglia, and I had no community, nor any relationship; but the problem posed itself to those who had read us, as it also posed itself to some of us, of seeing if it were possible to establish a "we" on the basis of the work that had been done, a "we" that would also be likely to form a community of action.[38]

Here Foucault throws down the gauntlet in the path of any facile attempt to mask the invocation of a "we" for a politics of responsibility and care. He is clearly suspicious of those who might think that merely identifying with a given political cause could constitute politics. Surely such easy identification can only pass for shedding the worn-out mantle of political neutrality. But shedding this neutrality alone does not qualify for or guarantee securing a sheltered domain of a "we" from which we can always define our political commitments and moral obligations. Thus, Foucault insists on saying,

> I have never tried to analyze anything whatsoever from the point of view of politics, but always to ask politics what it had to say about the problems with which it was confronted. I question it about the

positions it takes and the reasons it gives for this. I do not ask it to determine the theory of what I do. I am neither a partisan nor an adversary of Marxism; I question [Marxism] about what it has to say about the experiences that ask questions of it. (115)

It would be difficult (and surely mistaken) to accuse Foucault of practicing political neutrality and having no sense of responsibility. Yet this seeming distance from a sense of responsibility, this seemingly hands-off practice of *problematization* can be frustrating to self-labeled liberal critics like Richard Rorty. For them, Foucault is too much of "an ironist who is unwilling to be a liberal," too unwilling to demonstrate his political-ethical commitments ("Contingency," 61). Indeed, Rorty, who quotes the first few sentences of the above passage regarding Foucault's opposition to a "we," says that Foucault, like Nietzsche and Marx, recognizes that he cannot "propose any alternative to the society we have now" because "our imagination and our will are so limited by the socialization we have received" (64).

Given our discussion above of Foucault's stance on the question of politics, undoubtedly Rorty misconstrues Foucault here. Rorty does so, I think, because of the liberal tradition of responsibility from which he hails, a tradition in which politics can be delimited prior to the questions/answers demanded by a situation, a tradition to which scholars like Stout belong, with some caveats. This is partly because Rorty shares too freely in the (largely Habermasian) distinction between public and private conceptions of politics. For this reason, Rorty thinks that the hopes of "self-creating ironists like Nietzsche, Foucault, and Derrida," who are—in Bernard Yack's phrase—"longing for total revolution," cannot "ever be embodied in social institutions" (65).[39] They are simply not responsible enough. Rorty grants (contrary to Habermas, whom he criticizes for not being enough of an ironist) that Foucauldians have a role to play in "accommodating the ironist's *private* sense of identification to her liberal hopes." Yet, Rorty contends, "as *public* philosophers [Derrida is included among them] they are at best useless and at worst dangerous" (68). The indictment seems damning. But it is completely misguided and misplaced. In my view, Foucault, or Nietzsche for that matter, could hardly be characterized as sitting on the sidelines merely waiting for a total "revolution" to come. If Rorty is thinking of Nietzsche's notion of the "overman" or the "new man" or the "new philosopher" to come, the possibility of that figure, according to Nietzsche, would hardly materialize through a revolution.[40] Neither Nietzsche nor Foucault was ever so materialistic as to anchor the future of his hopes entirely in a revolution to come. Be that as it may, my quarrel here is not with whether Rorty has misunderstood Foucault based on the "passages" he cites. Rather, Rorty's disagreement with or worry about Foucault's refusal to become a liberal ironist—that is, to sign up for a "we" (which is a code word for responsibility)—cannot possibly yield a new purchase on politics. This is so not because Foucault thinks that such a politics of "we" is entirely impossible. He does not deny the possibility of such a politics when he says that he has never analyzed anything "from the viewpoint of politics." Indeed, an appeal to Marxism or liberalism, for example, can constitute such a politics. But what Foucault is saying is that when one approaches one's subject/object of discourse from the "viewpoint of politics," from the viewpoint of an already available "we," of a ready-made sense of responsibility, one is already located and secure in the comforts of the well-tested vocabularies of the liberal or Marxist tradition. When one appeals to a "we," one cannot imagine any new horizons or take "political risks" (as noted in chapter 2), but must continue to be bound by the terms of the political tradition that has made such an appeal possible.

Rorty claims (incorrectly) that Foucault seems to be suggesting what is required is "the constitution of a new we." Even though Rorty believes that "we have a moral obligation to feel a sense of solidarity with all other human beings" (192), he claims that this "we" vis-à-vis solidarity must be formulated differently. This is so partly because what Rorty is urging is not "something which stands beyond history and institutions" (189). He sums up: "The fundamental premise of this book is that a belief can still regulate action, can still be thought worth dying for, among people who are quite aware that this belief is caused by nothing deeper than contingent historical circumstance" (189). To be sure, then, Rorty is not trying to co-op us into merely identifying with "humanity as such" because he understands the possibility of the contingent formations of a "we"—that it cannot easily equate with a notion of "common humanity" (196–98). The sort of "we"/solidarity Rorty seeks is contingent and different. (Here he sounds very much like Stout.) Yet this solidarity must be understood in terms of a practice of distinguishing between the questions "Do

you believe and desire what we believe and desire?" and "Are you suffering?" Rorty concludes that "distinguishing these questions makes
it possible to distinguish public from private questions, questions
about pain from questions about the point of human life, the domain
of the liberal from the domain of the ironist. It thus makes it for a
single person to be both" (198).

Thus the task of this new we/"solidarity" entails a vague idea of
navigating between these two questions, between the private and
the public domains—not necessarily a total transition from one to
the other, but an embodiment of the stakes of both questions. Rorty
could have put it this way: one should be less worried about the question "Do you believe in . . . what we believe?" and be more concerned
with the question "Are you suffering?" Attending to the latter does
not mean giving up what *we* necessarily believe and desire. Rather, it
can help us reformulate our sense of "we." But Rorty could not put it
in such explicit language because it would appear to be self-contradic-
tory. That is, Rorty does not want to appeal to a notion of "common
humanity," yet he wants to find a sense of a "we" that cares about the
cruelty, pain, and suffering of others. On this account, Foucault could
easily respond that what Rorty is really offering is not a new sense of
we, "something smaller and more local than the human race" (191),
but a mix-and-match hybrid, romantic notion of humanity. Foucault
could also say, more profoundly, that one could not possibly attend to
the question "Are you suffering?" without an a priori question about
a "we" and all its moralist hubris. Rorty in turn could rebut that "*we*
have to start from where *we* are"—if this is a rebuttal at all (198).
Foucault might retort that this is precisely the point: one can appeal
to a "we," but always at the risk of reproducing the givenness of the
values, morals, and histories of the liberal tradition onto the object
one is analyzing ("Are you suffering?). As Heidegger might say, with
Rorty's notion of "we," we are simply "thrown" into a world that is already "there," a world that is not "objectively present" or self-evidently
"disclosing" but appears *seemingly self-evident* by our very being in the
world.[41] In turn Foucault would argue that his notion of problematization attends to the unmasking of this seemingly familiar givenness
of our world, and hence it does more than simply pose the question
"Are you suffering"?

Thus, if the Rortyan demand for us (and Foucault) to be both a responsible liberal and a responsible ironist rings hollow, what different

sort of question might we pose to Foucault to find politics beyond responsibility in his work, despite the latter's insistence that problematization does perform a certain kind of politics? It is a politics that does not owe its allegiance to a pregiven political party, moral tradition, or ethical foundation, however. This is where Derrida becomes relevant. The kind of question that Derrida might pose to Foucault is not the one that Rorty poses about responsibility. In other words, the question of responsibility, the question whether he can respond to the problem of human suffering, is the wrong one to pose to Foucault. It must be clear that for Foucault there is no direct relation between such a sense of responsibility and "politics." (Butler does not see it this way.) To this extent, then, I agree with Foucault about the limitation of the notion of responsibility to thinking about the question of the political. What sort of question would Derrida pose to Foucault, then? Derrida cannot ask Foucault to care about suffering and cruelty, not so much because he does not care about them but because for him suffering does not remain under a "sign of presence." (Looking for suffering under a sign is the easiest thing to do; that is what law or humanism/humanitarianism does.) Derrida cannot pose to Foucault a humanist question of the Rortian sort because the former cares too much about ghosts and specters, the invisible, or the visible-invisible. (As we will see in detail, for Derrida the ghost is the figure for "non-presence" or the "visible-invisible.) If one cares about ghosts, about ghostly pasts, about ghostly presents, and about ghostly futures, if one cares about sufferings and atrocities that one cannot see, under a sign, those that go unheeded by us, our nation-states, one cannot ask Foucault to care about suffering in the way Rorty does. At one point, Rorty—quite surprisingly for one who knows his Nietzsche, Heidegger, and Foucault—invokes the unsettling idea of *national fellowship* as opposed to "common humanity" as a way to care about human suffering: "Do we say that these people must be helped because they are our fellow human beings? We may, but it is much more persuasive, morally as well as politically, to describe them as fellow Americans" (191).[42] (One wonders if Rorty held the same communal view in the wake of 9/11 nationalism/racism in America.) By now it must be at least faintly clear that replacing the idea of common humanity with that of national fellowship does not produce a new conception of community.

What Derrida demands of Foucault is not a mere refashioning of this idea of community. Indeed, Derrida is interested in radically revaluating, if not un-inheriting, the idea of community. This is why Derrida says that problematization falls short of attending to ghosts. In *Specters of Marx* Derrida writes: "problematization itself is careful to disavow and thus to conjure away (we repeat, *problema* is a shield, an armor, a rampart, as much as it is a task for the inquiry to come). Critical problematization continues to do battle against ghosts. It fears them as it does itself." [43] Derrida makes this complaint in the context of discussing Marx's own fascination with, and (his later) effort to conjure away, "the ghost, the fetish, and religion as cloudy apparitions" as well as noting Europe's current efforts to conjure away the ghost of Marx as a philosopher (164; also see chapter 6). Yet I suspect that Derrida is thinking of Foucault here as well. Even if the living Derrida never really had Foucault in mind, I want to imagine the "living-dead" ghost of Derrida (as Derrida might have put it) calling on the ghost of Foucault (and all his genealogist adherents) to hear this complaint. One could argue that Foucault's problematization itself attends to the question of politics, in that problematization is not something that an author does, but rather something that a "people" do in terms of raising questions and fashioning answers to a given "problem." Hence the question of politics should not (and cannot) be superimposed on the "problem" from a transcendentalist outside. Indeed, one could argue that Foucault's problematization bears some resemblance to deconstruction, since Derrida insists that deconstruction itself is a certain kind of justice. It is concerned with "nothing else" but the "problem of justice," perhaps only obliquely and indirectly. For Derrida, the question of justice cannot be addressed "directly." [44] In a similar vein, one could say that deconstruction, like problematization, does its work on its own; namely, it deconstructs all by *itself*. This means that deconstruction has already been done. As we will see in this chapter, and in chapter 7 in more detail, this self-propelling work of deconstruction—to use an egregiously bad phrase!—is partly what concerns Derrida in *Politics of Friendship*. (It will be evident that, for Derrida, anti-genealogy becomes important precisely where such concepts as democracy and justice can no longer be deconstructed or improved.)

Yet, notwithstanding this seeming parallel between problematization and deconstruction, a Derridean would still insist that Foucault is too much of a "genealogist" to be truly attentive to the question of the political vis-à-vis ghosts. Derrida and Foucault part company at the point where the former (in his supposedly later "ethical turn")[45] is not interested in deconstruction as a programmatic, methodological, or political end.[46] Indeed, as Derrida himself argues, "I do not think that there is such a thing as a deconstructive politics."[47] On the contrary, Derrida is interested in deconstruction to the extent of locating the possibility of the im-possible, "the experience of the impossible." For Derrida such an experience of the im-possible is beyond deconstruction! Indeed, as Derrida writes in "Force of Law," "deconstructive questioning starts by

> destabilizing, complicating, or recalling the paradoxes of values like those of the proper and of property in all their registers, and thus of the *responsible* subject, of the subject of right, the subject of law, and the subject of morality, of the juridical or moral person, of intentionality. . . . Such a deconstructive questioning is through and through a questioning of law and justice, a questioning of the foundations of law, morality, and politics. This questioning of foundations is neither foundationalist nor antifoundationalist. Sometimes it even questions, or exceeds the very possibility, the ultimate necessity, of questioning itself. (235–36; emphasis added)

It is in this regard that Derrida would contend that deconstruction differs from a Foucauldian problematization. The work of deconstruction is concerned not only with questioning the subject of law and justice and so on but also the possibility and indeed the necessity of the *questioning itself.* It is at the point of the questioning of the questioning itself that the unquestionable, the undeconstructable, the impossible, might become possible. Here, I agree with Derrida that Foucault's problematization does not attend to ghosts insofar as it is not concerned with the unproblematizable. To attend to ghosts of our pasts, to think about un-inheriting those pasts that haunt us, problematization has to be concerned with the possibility of the unproblematizable. The unproblematizable does not become possible by abandoning problematization. It becomes possible through *exceeding* problematization itself. In light of this, I would argue that to interrogate our democratic present, to mourn the "democratic" identity that we can no longer deconstruct, a mere critique of our contemporary democratic-juridical sovereignty, of its values, its paradoxes, is not sufficient. To criticize our democracy is to criticize law. To criticize law is to ask law to be more just. As we shall soon see, doing so is not going to produce anything new. A criticism of law can yield nothing but law, just as a criticism of democracy can yield nothing but democracy. On the contrary, we have to reorient criticism with an eye toward imagining new domains of the political that are irreducible to mere deconstruction or problematization. If democracy and justice today remain no longer deconstructable, then, thinking about that which is beyond deconstruction may produce an entirely new domain of the political. This yet-unheard-of domain of the political is not a linearly realizable future in itself because the new political irreducible to number and calculation demands something other than deconstruction, a new sort of "thinking" it, its possibility, the possibility of its impossibility. Such thinking attends to the past as it does to the future. But it is thinking of the specter. "Thinking of the specter, contrary to what good sense leads us to believe, signals toward the future. It is a thinking of the past, a legacy that can come only from that which has not yet arrived—from the *arrivant* itself" (*Specters*, 196).

In chapter 4 I spell out what such a theory of mourning "looks" like. The preceding discussion should demonstrate that problematization may raise doubts about the problem of responsibility, but it cannot escape the problem of memory that Nietzsche warned us against. Nietzsche himself gave only a few clues to how the problem of memory might be rethought, except for recommending elsewhere the active forgetting of history itself. This is where Derrida's ideas of mourning and haunting come into play. So, to be clear, I am not recommending the total abdication of the practice of genealogical problematization and critique; I only want to suggest that it be guided by a way of haunting and specter thinking. We can no longer simply historicize and assume, as many postcolonial genealogists do—perhaps in a way that Foucault himself did not expect—that historicizing can pass for a politics of responsibility. Nor can we merely insist, as defenders of democracy do, on the ideas of responsibility and community. Neither approach, I have argued, can guide our thinking about the question of the future of the political. The future of the political cannot continue to be thought in light of these approaches because they will yield more and more democracy with "difference." Such a logic of difference is not something that we can aspire to inherit. To inherit it is to inherit that enormous problem of (ac)countability and memory without which modern democracy would cease to exist as we know it today. The appeal to this notion of difference "returns" to the problem of a self that is always different from another. (Even Foucault—despite Butler's effort to reread him—cannot tell us exactly how to grapple with the logic of difference.) Viewed in terms of that logic, the relations between oneself and another can only be improved. For a thinker like Derrida, such a distinction is not one that we can inherit in our political futures simply because we already have it. This is why Derrida often speaks of what is called irreducible otherness, irreducible to the logic of difference, to the logic of law and democratic counting. For Derrida, to begin to think about such otherness, one must abandon thinking that there is something still salient and outstanding to be found in the practice of democratic responsibility. He makes a persuasive case for this in *The Gift of Death*.[48] I want to read succinctly the major arguments of this text because it shows that responsibility is tied to a "secret other," which comes to be embodied by modern political sovereignty. Thinking at the aporetic limits of the secrecy of this responsibility should not compel us to yearn for more and more responsibility, but rather to reflect more deeply on the problem of sovereignty that can no longer be problematized.

Im-possibility of Responsibility and the "Secret Other"

In *The Gift of Death* Derrida begins with a deconstructive reading of *Heretical Essays on the History of Philosophy*, by the late Czech philosopher Jan Patocka. In many ways *The Gift of Death* is haunted by Patocka, who died in 1977 of a brain hemorrhage suffered at the hands of the police, who had interrogated him for eleven hours. The irony perhaps is that Patocka, the coauthor of Charta 77 of the human rights declaration of 1977, conceptualized ultimate responsibility as a gift of death itself.[49] For Patocka, the history of responsibility is the history of Europe. It begins with the tradition of Platonism, inherited and refined by Christianity. As Patocka sees it, Christianity both refines and represses the Greco-Roman heritage but still retains something of its "demonic mystery." (For him, the term *demonic* is synonymous with irresponsibility. Hence the religion of responsibility is different from the religion of demonic irresponsibility.) Christianity has not yet embodied authentic responsibility and has not lived up to its true identity because it has not entirely purged itself of the residues of the heritage of Greco-Roman demonic mystery. In Derrida's words, "Christianity has not yet come to Christianity."[50] For Christianity to come to itself is for it to separate between the demonic mystery and the Christian mystery of responsibility. This true responsibility of Christianity is the *mysterium tremendum*. It comes from "a supreme being" who is inaccessible to human gaze but "holds us in check" (31; Patocka's words). Embodiment of such responsibility constitutes the true heritage of Europe. Thus the question for Patocka is about history and memory. Europe's modernity has become blind to its own history. It suffers "from ignorance of its history, from a failure to assume its responsibility, that is, the memory of its history, *as* history of responsibility" (4, 50; Derrida's words).

What is particularly important to Derrida here is the distinction that Patocka makes between Christianity and Platonism in terms of the idea of the "gift." For Patocka, Christianity is different from Platonism because the former considers responsibility a gift. The complete transition from Platonism to Christianity would mark the "death" of the former. The transition gives a gift of death. To embody true responsibility that comes from the supreme being, which is *mysterium tremendum*, Christianity must receive the gift of the death of Platonism. As Derrida puts it, to apprehend this death is to apprehend the gift that is "received from the other, from the one who, in absolute transcendence, sees me without my seeing, holds me in his hands while remaining inaccessible" (40). There is something of a contradiction in Patocka's formulation. Responsibility comes from an inaccessible supreme being, but it must be marked by the death of Platonism.

Let me cut short the elegant deconstructive reading that Derrida does of *Heretical Essays*. In demonstrating Patocka's sense of responsibility, the point Derrida wants to make is not that the modern concept of responsibility is founded upon his onto-theological-historical assumptions. Rather, he wants to make a general point about the sense of secrecy that is inscribed within the notion of responsibility. Such a sense is, of course, contrary to the general assumption that responsibility is about openness, that is to say, about "acting and signing in *one's name*" (58). Yes, responsibility is (ac)countability, but it is not about just making oneself public and visible in terms of giving an account of oneself. In being (ac)countable and responsible, one does not reveal oneself to everybody and anybody. One reveals oneself to a secret other. Responsibility is about acting and signing in for the sake of a secret other. If responsibility is about responding, one responds not in the name of one's opening oneself up to another human being, making oneself vulnerable to not being recognized by that other. Responsibility reinforces the sense of the secrecy of one's self because one responds to the call of a secret other. So, for Derrida, the secrecy of this responsibility boils down to this: "I am responsible to any one (that is to say to any other) only by failing in my responsibility to all the others" (70).

This is what Derrida attempts to explain by undertaking an inimitable reading of the story of Kierkegaard's *Fear and Trembling*. The title of Kierkegaard's essay echoes Patocka's notion of the *mysterium tremendum*, itself an indirect allusion to Saint Paul. As Derrida notes, "one can understand why Kierkegaard chose, for his title, the words of a great Jewish convert, Paul, in order to meditate on the still Jewish experience of a secret, hidden, separate, absent, or mysterious God, the one who decides, without revealing his reasons, to demand of Abraham that most cruel, impossible, and untenable gesture: to offer his son Isaac as a sacrifice" (57–58). This God who orders Abraham to sacrifice his only son is a secretive, jealous God. He demands absolute duty. Absolute duty demands maintaining absolute secrecy. To maintain this secrecy, Abraham must forgo all his ethics, all his loyalty and fidelity to his loved ones. (This is essentially the message of Saint Paul, which a critic like Žižek thinks holds out new hopes for us.) Abraham cannot divulge to his family anything about his plan to sacrifice his beloved son. To do that would be to renege upon his absolute responsibility. Because of his responsibility to the jealous God, Abraham has no hesitation. He decides "in the instant," as Kierkegaard puts it (65). Absolute responsibility is about this capacity to decide without hesitation. In this regard, Abraham is quite unlike the Greek figure of Agamemnon. Abraham has no sense of tragedy or mourning because of his absolute responsibility to God, to whom he says, "Here I am" (62). This is not the Kantian sort of responsibility that "acts out of duty." "Kierkegaard sees acting 'out of duty,' in the universalizable sense of the law, as a dereliction of one's absolute duty" (63).[51] Absolute duty is a "gift of death" in the metaphorical-literal sense. The absolute duty toward God must be done without any sense of duty or debt. It functions as a sacrifice of all our obligations to others.

(To sacrifice Isaac to God is to sacrifice all of Abraham's obligations to his family.) In the name of absolute duty, all other duties are forgone. As Derrida writes memorably, "absolute duty absolves him of every debt and releases him from every duty. Absolute ab-solution" (73).

If it is not already clear, what is the moral of the story? Surely, as Derrida says, we are not children of Abraham. "We no longer know who is called Abraham, and he can no longer even tell us" (79). This is not because Abraham is a figure of a mythic past. Nor is it because we find the terror of the message of his story unthinkable in our modern times. (Kierkegaard himself says that he could never do what Abraham set out to do. This is despite God's sending an angel to hold back the arm of Abraham about to slay his son.) For Derrida, we cannot really know or inherit this story, because it is about a "secret." A (story about a) secret is not knowable or transmittable. Can we really know this story then? Does it amount to a story or history? As usual, for Derrida the answer is both "yes" and "no" (80). We share something with Abraham's story without really sharing it. "We share with Abraham what cannot be shared, a secret we know nothing about, neither him nor us. To share a secret is not to know or to reveal the secret, it is to share we know not what: nothing that can be determined. What is a secret that is a secret about nothing and a sharing that doesn't share anything?" (80). What is this secret? It is hidden in the absolute responsibility itself. Absolute responsibility is secretive because an other who is faceless and unknowable demands it. It is God, "as the wholly other [who] is to be found everywhere there is something of the wholly other" (78). This concept of God, Derrida argues, "disturbs" and deconstructs Kierkegaard's text (and, by extension, Patocka's) (80). As Derrida writes, "in one case, God is defined as infinitely other, as wholly other, every bit other. In the other case it is declared that every other one, each of the others, is God inasmuch as he or she is, *like* God, wholly other" (87). (Needless to say, this is not the sort of irreducible otherness that Derrida seeks to imagine.) That is, the God that demands absolute responsibility and secrecy becomes wholly other like every other. God has to become this other to demand secrecy from Abraham. Abraham can promise absolute responsibility only to such an other.

Abraham's decision [in the instant] is absolutely responsible because it answers for itself before the absolute other. Paradoxically it is also irresponsible because it is guided neither by reason nor by an ethics justifiable before men or before the law of some universal tribunal. Everything points to the fact that one is unable to be responsible at the same time before the other and before others, before the others of the other. If God is completely other, the figure or name of the wholly other, then every other (one) is every (bit) other. *Tout autre est toute autre* (77–78).

Here is the haunting contradiction that inheres in the idea of absolute responsibility. Absolute responsibility is absolute irresponsibility. It absolves one of all ethical commitments and obligations to everyone except to a secret other. This is why Derrida contends that the "knights of good conscience"—he might include Stout and Rorty among them—who accuse him and others of failing in their ethics and duties when they do not address the question of responsibility in their works. The point here is that the mere appeal to responsibility does not constitute ethics or politics in itself. Such an appeal cannot solve the contradiction in responsibility. This contradiction in absolute responsibility haunts the politics of the modern state. Even though we do not know Abraham or anything about his secret, the unthinkable terror of the sacrifice, the logic of his absolute responsibility, is "inscribed in the existence of today." In a profoundly candid and revelatory moment, Derrida contends that by embodying our modern citizenship itself, by speaking the languages that we do, by living where we do, by holding the jobs we hold, today we, like Abraham, are always failing in our responsibility to millions of others whom we do not know, those dying of starvation, suffering from hunger, malnutrition, international economic sanctions, and war. Their sufferings, agonies, pains, and horrors are hardly justifiable before any court, any law, or any tribunal. To live in a culture of capitalistic, responsible citizenship, for Derrida, is to "offer a gift of death, [and to] . . . betray [those suffering and dying others], and I don't need to raise my knife over my son on Mount Moriah for that" (68). To live in a democratic system, within the juridical confines of being and belonging, is to be responsible to a secret other that demands irresponsibility.

This secret other of our modernity is democracy itself, its political sovereignty, its "law," its justice. This democracy/law/justice is secretive not because it is simply invisible, but because it remains deferred and hence unavailable and inaccessible. Thus one cannot begin thinking simplistically that responsibility already remains within democracy. Like the jealous and secretive God, the law of democratic sovereignty and citizenship demands absolute responsibility. Responsibility of citizenship binds me to law as myself, different from all others to whom I can never really respond. One must answer to and give an account of oneself before law in one's own singularity, failing in the possible responsibilities toward all the others. Hence one can never be responsible enough. One cannot be really responsible enough because that to which responsibility seeks to respond is deferred, remaining to come! Like the wholly other, democracy/law/justice remains a deferred and inaccessible other to which we as citizens pledge absolute responsibility. Can one ever really be responsive enough to something that is deferred? How does one think about this aporia? No problematization or critique will solve this problem of democracy. It requires something other than responding (and responsibility) to law. It requires mourning. In the following chapter I want to demonstrate what such a politics of mourning would be, what sort of new way of thinking about modernity, democracy, and law might be possible through it, and how such thinking could be vital to imagining new domains of the political.

Necessity has no law.
> —*A Roman saying; cited in Agamben,* State of Exception

By virtue of being self-evident, these truths are pre-rational—they inform reason but are not its product—and since their self-evidence puts them beyond disclosure and argument, they are in a sense no less compelling than "despotic power" and no less absolute than the revealed truths of religion.
> —*Hannah Arendt,* On Revolution

Community as com-mon auto-immunity: *No community [including democracy itself]* <is possible> *that would not cultivate its own auto-immunity, a principle of sacrificial self-destruction ruining the principle of self-protection (that of maintaining its self-integrity intact).* —*Jacques Derrida, "Faith and Knowledge"*

4 Toward Mourning Political Sovereignty

A Politics "Between a No-Longer and a Not-Yet"?

The "No-Longer" Present and the Deferred "Promise"

Part of the phrase that forms the subtitle of this chapter— "Between a No-Longer and a Not-Yet"—comes from one of Hannah Arendt's classics, *On Revolution*. Commenting on how the American Revolution, influenced by particular kinds of legendary narratives, marked a break in historical time, Arendt writes: "The revolution—at least it must have appeared to these men—was precisely the legendary hiatus between end and beginning, between a no-longer and a not-yet."[1] She goes on to elaborate:

And these times of transition from bondage to freedom must have appealed to their imagination very strongly, because the legends [like the biblical story of the exodus of Israel's tribes from Egypt and Virgil's story of the wanderings of Aeneas after he had escaped burning Troy] unanimously tell us of great leaders who appear on the stage of history precisely in these gaps of historical time. Moreover, this hiatus obviously creeps into all time speculations which deviate from the currently accepted notion of time as a continuous flow; it was, therefore, an almost natural object of human imagination and speculation, in so far as these touched the problem of beginning at all; but what had been known to speculative thought and in legendary tales, it seemed, appeared for the first time as an actual reality. If one dated the revolution, it was as though one had done the impossible, namely, one had dated the hiatus in time in terms of chronology, that is, of historical time. (205)

Despite the unguarded romanticization of the American Revolution we find in this passage, the problem of time/history that Arendt seeks to tackle is enormously interesting. I will engage *On Revolution* later and argue that Arendt's conceptualization of historical time enables us to think about the relation between law and modern political sovereignty in a new (albeit limited) way as well as to think of a politics of mourning that sovereignty, which she does not offer. However, to understand something of the terminology that is critical to Arendt's perspective on time/history, we have to pass through the offices of her teacher and mentor Martin Heidegger.[2] After all, the expressions "not-yet" and "no-longer" (as well as the notion of "gaps in time") are not entirely Arendt's. The expressions, at least in the way Arendt uses them, were formulated by Heidegger in his *Being and Time*.[3] In *On Revolution* Arendt does not attribute or discuss them in relation to Heidegger, perhaps assuming her readers' familiarity with the latter's work. Yet Arendt's use of these terms implies the sense in which Heidegger defines them. In part 3, section 2, of *Being and Time*, Heidegger deploys these expressions to rethink the conventional relation between the past and the future, the beginning and the end. He does so in his discussion of Da-sein's "being-toward-death" as a possibility of recognizing its wholeness. For Heidegger, death does not mark an end, just as birth does not mean merely a beginning. In that sense, life and death do not constitute separate domains, the latter producing the end of the former. (But, as we have already seen, Derrida argues that Heidegger fails to sustain this argument.) It is only by being-toward-death that Da-sein can recognize itself, its whole, "authentic" being, without going "astray" (228, 132).[4]

Whatever the theoretical value of this controversial idea of the wholeness of being may be, despite its now well-known Christian metaphysical and humanist implications, Heidegger is not suggesting that one should die to become whole and authentic.[5] Indeed, Heidegger insists that "being-toward-death" does mean its "actualization"

(241). Nor does it mean "thinking about" death (which would be an impossibility for Derrida). That would simply amount to brooding over death and "calculating how to have it at our disposal," and that weakens the possibility of being-toward-death (241). For Heidegger, one cannot anticipate or expect death as something possible this way. "To expect something possible is always to understand and 'have' it with regard to whether and when and how it will really be objectively present" (242). This is why Heidegger says that in "in death, Da-sein is neither fulfilled nor does it simply disappear; it has not become finished or completely available as something at hand" (228). Rather, as soon as one is born, one is being-toward-death, and this is Da-sein's authentic being. "[Being-toward-] death is a way to be that Da-sein takes over as soon as it is. 'As soon as a human being is born, he is old enough to die right away'" (228). (Here, as Derrida reminds us, Heidegger is quoting Seneca about the "essential immaturity of the human being who is dying. . . . Dasein does not need to mature when death occurs.")[6] In that sense, he claims that being-toward-death is not a being toward an end. It is "a being *toward a possibility*," a possibility that has to be cultivated *as possibility*, and endured as *possibility* in our relation to it (241). Thus, being-toward-death is being toward that which is "not yet." The not-yet is not something that lies far away, outside of Da-sein. "The not-yet . . . belongs to Da-sein." "Da-sein . . . is *always already its not-yet*" (226, 227). Seen this way, the very minute one is born, one is "no-longer" just living, or merely objectively present; rather, one is being-toward-death. "In being-toward-death, Da-sein is related to *itself* as an imminent potentiality of being" (233–34). Thus, in being-toward-death, one is both no-longer and not-yet.

This way of thinking of life and death, it seems so far, has a very interesting relation to the possibility of the future. The future here is not something that lies *after* the present, after the end of a present way of life. But the future is "not-yet." This not-yet is very much a possibility, always within the domain of the "worldliness" of life. This is why Heidegger insists that his "analysis of death remains purely 'this-worldly' in that it interprets the phenomenon solely with respect to the question of how it *enters into* actual Da-sein as its possibility-of-being. We cannot even *ask* with any methodological assurance about what 'is after death'" (230). This perspective on death is extremely suggestive. As Magda King notes in her commentary on *Being and Time*, "what would seem to us the natural course to take, to start from the beginning, is tacitly passed over by Heidegger. The implication is that even the beginning, the birth, can be understood only by coming back to it from the end."[7] What Heidegger is suggesting is that if one wants to think about the present, one has to think about it from the future. This formulation runs counter to what Heidegger, in the section on temporality and history, calls the "vulgar" interpretation of time.[8] This is partly the view that time is "infinite," followed by a "successions of nows," with "no gaps" (388). Such a vulgar view of history assumes, among other things, that

> this or that already belongs to "history." Here "past" means on the one hand "no longer objectively present," or else "indeed still objectively present" [such as an object from a different time period], but without "effect" on the "present." However what is historical as what is past also has the opposite significance when we say that one cannot evade history. Here history means what is past. (346–47)

This past is often contrasted with the present, which is understood "in the sense of what is real 'now' and today" (437). As he says, "'the past' has remarkable ambiguity here. Here 'the past' belongs irrevocably to an earlier time; it belongs to former events and can be objectively present 'now'—for example, the remains of a Greek temple. A bit of the 'past' is still 'present' in it" (437). For Heidegger, this view of history becomes very problematic when we think of human beings vis-à-vis the past. That is, one can use the word *past* to describe and explain things and even events. But human beings who lived in the past cannot be seen simply as belonging to the "past" in the way "things" do. They have to be seen as *"having-been-there."* The "past" (of things) is different from the "having-being there" (of human beings; 348–49). For Heidegger, this way of thinking of history is important because he wants to insist on the betweenness of time. Being-toward-death is a way to do this. As he says, "death is, after all, only the 'end' of Da-sein, and formally speaking, it is just *one* of the ends that embraces the totality of Da-sein. But the other 'end' is the 'beginning,' 'birth.' Only the being 'between' birth and death presents the whole we are looking for" (342). Conceived in this manner, "birth is never something past in the sense of what is no longer objectively present," and death is not something that "will come" and hence is "not yet objectively present." Both of these "'ends' and their 'between' *are*" (343). Put more simply,

Heidegger wants to insist that the past and the future are not separate "ends," constituted by the "between" of our present, but are part of the very experience of being-toward-death.

Obviously, this meditation on Heidegger is not an attempt to understand his views of death but rather to grasp his concepts of "no-longer" and "not-yet." What is crucial about Heidegger's formulation of the two concepts is the doubt it casts on the idea of the present as a point instant. (In her use of the terms, Hannah Arendt is, I think, interested in pursuing this doubt.) What I want to argue is that if we follow Heidegger to the extent that I suggest we do, then we can begin to conceptualize our democratic present, the one that we are supposedly passing through, as something that is "no-longer." This is not to say that our democratic present does not "exist" or that it has become undemocratic or less democratic. Rather, I am supposing here that the modern conception of political sovereignty, guided by a concept of promise, constitutes the identity of our democratic present as an aporia. *Here I am following Derrida and parting company with Heidegger. Heidegger, as we have already seen, does not have a notion of aporia, certainly not in the way Derrida conceptualizes it. (And eventually Heidegger's conceptualization cannot overcome thinking about life and death in terms of the binary of here and there.)* If our democratic present is constituted by a promise, it marks, for Derrida, an irreducible contradiction (aporia). Hence to live in this democratic present of the promise is to live in an aporia. By extension, I am arguing that our democratic present of the promise is no longer available *for a certain kind of critique and reconstruction.* By this I do not mean that there are too many critiques of our democracy and we have, therefore, exhausted all criticisms. Rather, I mean that our democratic present, its politics that depend upon notions of law and justice, is fundamentally animated by a deferred promise. My argument is twofold. First, if our democratic present is defined by a deferred "promise," such a present is no longer available for criticism and improvement. (Note that Heidegger does not have such a notion of deferral. For him, both the present and the future, the not-yet and no-longer, *are* [already available].) Second, the deferred (no-longer) present has a distinct relation to the future. That is, the present that is deferred is one that is deferred to the future. Any question of the deferred present is tied to that of the future! Thus, thinking of the present will have to be fashioned through thinking of the deferred future. Seen this way—it is important to stress—there can be no mere overcoming of our present, transcending it, or moving *beyond* it. There can be no easy "after" the present.[9] Thus, in contrast to Hannah Arendt or Heidegger, I am not so much interested in a politics "between" a no-longer and not-yet as I am in a politics of the deferred present-future itself. The questions that arise here are enormously difficult: if the future is animated by a deferred promise of our democratic present (not to mention all its problems of violence and bloodshed), would the politics of the promise continue to be part of the future that we want to inherit? By extension, can we inherit a future that is not tied to our democratic present, which we cannot wholly embrace or abandon today? How are we to think about the aporia of this democratic present? That is to say, if our modern political sovereignty is marked by the irreducible contradiction of living simultaneously in a state of law and in a "state of exception" (which is the absence of law), how are we to think about this contradiction? Can we continue to criticize this contradiction and make it better? These are not easy questions, and to formulate answers to them, we need a conceptualization of "mourning" and un-inheriting the aporia of our modern political sovereignty. Theorists who offer varying critiques of the *problem* of political sovereignty and its relation to law—from Hannah Arendt to Giorgio Agamben—cannot help us in this regard. In this chapter I want to show how we might formulate something of a "politics" of mourning, and why such a "politics," irreducible to notions of law, rights, and responsibility, is critical to thinking about the irresolvable contradictions of our modernity.

Notwithstanding the above qualifications, my suggestion about the present's being *no longer* available for critique and improvement may raise some eyebrows. Some may claim that we still have much work to do for the present, for its political problems, for all its unactualized goals of justice and equality. I recognize the importance of the immediacy of the present's political challenges and predicaments, and I am by no means gainsaying them. What I am suggesting is that thinking of the present as something no-longer (hence something that cannot be merely *improved*) is itself a different way of coming back at, and attending to, the idea of the present differently. Such a perspective obviously runs counter to the Marxist, progressivist notion of time or the (more recent) view of the "incompleteness" of our modernity.[10] Yet we have no shortage of voices continuing to impress upon us the urgencies of our present. They tell us that the "now" is so important that it should define and concern all of our (academic and nonacademic) thinking. Indeed thinking itself, we are advised, has to be in, on, and about our present. Questions are raised about theory's relevance to the present's politics. Indeed, theory is demanded to be *responsible* enough to return to the problems of the present, beyond the confines of academia, "outside senior common rooms."[11]

"Rational Construction of Politics" and the Promise of the "Now"

A flavor of this kind of argument about the present can be found in an editorial symposium organized by the journal *Critical Inquiry* in 2003. The symposium was to address, among other things, whether theory today has "backed off from its earlier sociopolitical engagements and its sense of revolutionary possibility and has undergone a 'therapeutic turn' to concerns with ethics, aesthetics, and care of the self."[12] Here the question of politics is contrasted with the question of ethics (and aesthetics). Theory is suspected of being concerned with "ethics" and not with "politics." Politics is, by extension, thought to be synonymous with the present. Of the statements on the subject by several well-known thinkers, Dipesh Chakrabarty's comments, aptly entitled "Where Is the Now?" stand out. As Chakrabarty points out, most of the "commentators share a concern with being able to name, designate, and describe the time or period we are passing through."[13] Chakrabarty singles out a few commentators to show how they share this concern. Robert Pippin quotes Hegel (*Philosophy of Rights*): "Philosophy is its own time comprehended in thoughts."[14] Catharine Stimpson notes that theoreticians "must live in and work for our century."[15] Teresa de Lauretis writes that "to the extent that it [thinking] is invested in figuring out the now—that is to say, the enigma of the world, thinking of theory is political."[16] What Chakrabarty finds "troubling . . . is our readiness to assume that both the now and the political are easily divined" (460). As he writes, "when we begin defining the now in a very particular way as our first step of analysis, we have in a sense already committed ourselves to certain understandings of the political. These very understandings themselves, however, may need to be more interrogated than assumed" (459).[17]

We cannot, Chakrabarty argues, speak to a *now* as such because the "political formations" that constitute it are always shifting. That is to say, the politics of a given group of people—for example, the oppressed dalits challenging the social hierarchy in India or the aboriginals competing for recognition in Australia—"do not any longer look to theory classes of the university for political guidance" (460). They may employ our rhetorical styles "pragmatically," but they do not "conform to any theoretical version of a global subject; they are not the proletariat; nor Hardt and Negri's 'multitude'" (461).[18] They do not belong to a politics of the "right-wing" or the "left-wing" order. To be sure, they are moved by a sense of justice. Yet their sense of justice "is fragmented, contextual, and always shifting." Note this argument is not as familiar as it may sound. What Chakrabarty is suggesting is that when theory classes attempt to speak to the "now," they assume its audience has an interest in what they have to teach. That is, he says, the "implicit faith in a rational construction of politics. Being exposed to a rational elaboration of the state of the world, it was [always] assumed, would help people act rationally." As Chakrabarty puts it so poignantly, "This has been the Left's romance of truth" (461). He elaborates:

It seems to me that today's disjuncture between theory and the [present] world is not a mere repetition of the old problem of reality failing to measure up to our categories. It is not, therefore, a question of . . . [our theory] finding a politics that corresponds to [our] time. To be sure, future theory and criticism will have to come to terms with developments in science and technology and in particular with changes in technologies of transmission. But . . . theory will also have to joust with what today exceeds the grasp of "Western" political thought in the domain of the political. For it is only by acknowledging the murkiness of the political today that we will configure a now so plural as not to be exhausted by any single definition. (460–61)

I cannot emphasize enough the importance of this argument. Seen from a broader vantage point, what Chakrabarty is noting has a critical bearing on how we might think the question of the political vis-à-vis the present. That is, if we cannot have a "rational construction of politics," which is another name for our contemporary desire to speak to the urgency of the present, what Chakrabarty is suggesting here is in fact the other side of my argument about the no-longer present. I want to extend Chakrabarty's argument, however, and emphasize two points. We cannot have a rational construction of politics not just because the senses of justice in particular social contexts vary and shift but also because the very idea of justice itself belongs to the present that I have been calling the "no-longer present." Hence, when our theories (and we) attempt to speak to the now, in which there are such multiple, shifting senses of justices, we will only be trying to improve what is already available.

The belief in working to "improve" justice must assume justice is present and possible, but it is not quite perfect yet or it has not been perfect in every case—the belief that there are too many inequalities in the world and justice has not quite attended to them all. It is as if we could indeed make our justice system a little bit better, better than it already is, if we just refocus it. This is a belief in justice. But this belief in justice, the belief in the possibility of working to improve it by making it attend to the now, is not just a belief in justice. It is a belief in the "promise" of justice. If justice is not as good as it could be, or if it has not yet attended to all social and political inequalities in all places, justice has yet to deliver on its promise. Without this promise, justice would not be justice. Justice is founded upon this promise. This promise defines justice. Justice can only be a promise. Otherwise, justice cannot be justice. Hence any attempt at working to improve justice is a pursuit after its promise. It is a pursuit that believes in the promise that it will always solve our existing political problems. My point here is this: when Chakrabarty questions the possibility of " a rational construction of politics" or when Derrida insists on the "impossibility of Justice,"[19] they both are raising a suspicion about this promise of justice in different ways. But more important, they are also raising a doubt about the present where justice exists as a promise. The promise of justice inhabits the present. It may not deliver its justice to all in the immediate present. Yet justice is a promise. *This promise is a promise about the future.* If not today, the promise of justice may come through the next day, the day after tomorrow. So this promise then keeps justice (and the belief in it) intimately connected to both the present and the future. But this promise also has an intimate relation to the past. Justice delivered in the future will always be justice for the (past) present. But there is something very problematic about this belief in the promise of justice, because the belief in the promise partly expects the promise to be more promising. *Can a promise be more promising?* By extension, can justice be more just? Let me make myself clear here: if a promise, by definition, is something that is deferred, expecting it to be more promising is nothing other that allowing the promise to remain deferred even longer. Hence, by definition, a more promising promise is only a promise deferred: deferred longer, to the future. Perhaps that is why a promise cannot be more promising, since justice cannot be more just!

My point here is that, if justice is a promise, our political present is defined by that promise. (And this is partly what Derrida means when he says "democracy is a promise," as discussed in chapter 1.) If we begin to see it this way, then we will have to pause in our rush to speak to the present and the now as such. An attempt at speaking to the present is an attempt at demanding that the promise of the present be more promising. If we assume that a promise can only be a promise, and it cannot be more promising, then we will have to question the enormous significance we attach to the present. This is hardly a suggestion to abandon the present and engage in wishful thinking about the future. *However, seeing the democratic present as being deferred may help us realize that our attempts at any rational construction of politics are themselves grounded on a belief in the promise of deferred justice. Hence there can be no rational construction of politics.* The critical point I want to make here is this: if it is a belief in the idea of the promise, the rational construction of politics—without our knowing—is only a strategy of allowing the promise to remain deferred. This is where thinking about our present as no-longer might become important to a different way of conceiving of politics. My contention is that if we think of our present itself as a deferred promise, then understanding the present as no-longer does not mean simply the fact that we are just "beyond" or "after" it. Following Derrida, we cannot subscribe to such a notion of an after or beyond. To view our present as no-longer is merely to recognize that we exist in the wake of the deferred promise of the democratic present. Such a present is not something one can abandon for the sake of inheriting a better future.

The question that arises is what other conceptual strategies today

are left at our disposal if we can neither speak to this present nor abandon it. To answer this question, we have to look at ongoing critiques
of our modern democratic sovereignty. My argument is that a critique
of our political sovereignty and modernity alone is not going to produce many breakthroughs these days. This is so perhaps because any
critique of political sovereignty aims at improving it in relation to our
present. Such a critique still pursues the promise of democracy. If
our democratic sovereignty itself is a promise, such a promise cannot
be criticized. If critique is partly about reconstruction, then a critique
cannot ever reconstruct the promise(d). If one still insists on the idea
of critique, it has to be accompanied by a different way of thinking of
un-inheriting the very question of history, which I have been calling
mourning. To do so, I will discuss two concepts that are fundamental
to the formations of modern political sovereignty: necessity and the
absolute. What we will see is why this relation between necessity and
sovereignty, as it has been configured and constructed in different
contexts, demands more than an attempt at the mere reconstruction
or improvement of what we have today.

Necessity and the Absolute

Here I return to Hannah Arendt's *On Revolution. On Revolution* is, on the one hand, a moving story of the idea of revolution,
with a particular focus on the French and the American revolutions.
For Arendt, the French Revolution ended in a disaster because it was
"haunted by the desperate urgency of the 'social question'" (221).
Guided by the social question, like all revolutions, the French Revolution sustained the belief that violence would eliminate poverty. On
the contrary, the American Revolution, even though it had, to begin
with, such an interest in the social question, was "brought into existence by no 'historical necessity' and no organic development, but
by a deliberate act: The foundation of freedom" (216). Yet America
later forgot that "revolutionary spirit" defined by the political realm
(221).[20] *On Revolution* is a critical evaluation of the notion of political
sovereignty, particularly in terms of the relation between violence and
"necessity." Necessity, as we shall later see, is one of the foundational
principles upon which political sovereignty heavily depends in terms
of its power to decide on a "state of exemption."[21]

Arendt's Heideggerian phrase "between a no-longer-and a not-yet" with which I began this chapter is an effort to think not only about the problem of time but also the problem of law and its relation to modern political sovereignty. When she claims that the revolution marked a "legendary hiatus between end and beginning, between a no-longer and a not-yet," she is speaking of the ways in which revolutions—she has in mind the French Revolution in particular—sought to come to terms with the problem of authority (205). That is to say, the "men" of revolutions always wrestled with the question of how to authorize the very basis for the revolution. More specifically, the question they faced was where does the power to revolt come from. The question becomes doubly difficult because the idea of revolution, for Arendt, is founded upon a "hiatus" between beginning and end. With all modern revolutions, time begins anew. This time is more or less secular time (26).[22] Yet beginning anew is not without difficulty. The question Arendt poses here is this: how would this "hiatus," this new secular beginning that revolution inaugurates, "found a new authority"? (182). That difficulty is confounded by the law of the revolution itself: "'a revolutionary law is a law whose object is to maintain the revolution and to accelerate or regulate its course'" (183). The idea of revolution, its spirit of beginning anew, may have negated the idea of the "absolute," yet it still appealed to "law" as an "immortal legislator" (the term is Robespierre's; 184). This was clearly the case with the French Revolution. The new appeal to law was bound to create a "vicious cycle." As Arendt writes,

> the vicious cycle in legislating is present not in ordinary law making, but in laying down the fundamental law, the law of the land or the constitution which, from then on, is supposed to incarnate the "higher law," from which all laws ultimately derive their authority. And with this problem, which appeared as the urgent need for some absolute, the men of the American Revolution found themselves no less confronted than their colleagues in France. (184)

There were, of course, unmistakable differences between the French Revolution and its American counterpart. The men of the French Revolution, for their part, attributed "all power" to the people, defining power as a "natural force." This force/power was not political. Ultimately, the power of the people became synonymous with violence. "This force was experienced as superhuman in its strength, and it was seen as the result of the accumulated violence of a multitude outside all bonds and all political organization" (181). Surely the violence ended the old regime of the monarch, but that was not enough to sustain the revolution. The men of the American Revolution, however, understood power to reside within the domain of the political. "To them, power came into being when and where people would get together and bind themselves through promises, covenants, and mutual pledges" (181; note the word *promise* here). This political power was "real power"; it did not come from a king or monarch (181). Yet, Arendt concedes, the people assembling together and making mutual promises themselves were not enough to create a government that would be one "'of law and not of men'" (182). The mistake made in the French Revolution was the "deification of the people," and it favored obtaining law and power from the same source of authority: the people. The mistake relied on Rousseau's notion of general will. Indeed, the French revolution rested on the principle that "'law is the expression of the General Will'" (183).[23] For Arendt, who undoubtedly favors the "enlightened" secularism of the men of the American Revolution, the Rousseauean notion of "general will" embodied by the French revolution ironically contained an element of divinity! As she quips, "the will which needs only to will produces a law" (183). For Rousseau, the problem was to "find a form of government which puts the law above man" (Rousseau's words; quoted 183). [24] Yet Rousseau understood the difficulty of doing so when he claimed—perhaps comically—that to "establish the validity of man-made laws, *il faudrait des dieux,* 'one actually needs gods'" (184). This claim is not surprising; even Locke claimed "appeal to God in Heaven" was the only way to help men who came out of the "state of nature" to create a law guiding civil society (185). Similarly, just as James Madison spoke of "the worship of a Supreme Being," which he called "the Great Legislator of the Universe," so Jefferson spoke of "the laws of nature and nature's God" (185).

Arendt does recognize the paradox here. The "enlightened," deist men of the eighteenth century undoubtedly wanted to separate church from state, but they still appealed to a certain conception of religion. For Arendt the paradox was made possible by the very "crisis" that inhered in the revolutions, that is, the crisis of founding a new authority. Yet Arendt contends that though the men of revolutions looked to the past for guidance, they did not do so out of longing or nostalgia. She claims the men of the American Revolution came close to resolving the paradox. They had to resolve it because when they changed the line "magnus ordo saeclorum"—whose author is supposedly the first-century Roman poet Virgil—to "novus ordo saeclorum," they were setting out to create not "'Rome anew'" but a "'new Rome'" (212). For Arendt, the best example of the manner in which they sought to create a new authority can be found in the celebrated words (in the preamble to the Declaration of Independence) attributed to Thomas Jefferson: "We hold these truths to be self-evident." This new authority would seek to replace, but become more or less a substitute for, the "absolute" of the despotic power of both monarch and religion. Arendt offers an interesting reading of the Jeffersonian words:

> Jefferson's famous words . . . combine in a historically unique manner the basis of agreement between those who have embarked upon revolution, an agreement necessarily relative because related to those who enter it, with an absolute, namely with a truth that needs no agreement since, because of its self-evidence, it compels without argumentative demonstration or political persuasion. By virtue of being self-evident, these truths are pre-rational—they inform reason but are not its product—and since their self-evidence puts them beyond disclosure and argument, they are in a sense no less compelling than "despotic power" and no less absolute than the revealed truths of religion. (192)

My interest is not in evaluating whether the men of the American Revolution, who supposedly acted out of "political wisdom" rather than "religious convictions" (193), really solved the paradox. I suspect that some historians and constitutionalists would quarrel with some of Arendt's claims, as often the case with such historicist claims. Contributing to such a debate is irrelevant to me. Rather, I am interested in Arendt's claims about the relation between necessity, violence, and sovereignty.

Arendt is careful to note that the new absolute embodied in the Jeffersonian claim about the self-evidence of truths is not the same thing as the power (and the violence) of an "avenging God" or the "sovereign will" of a prince who declared divine sovereignty on earth (193–94). The new absolute had to be different from either one.

Indeed, Arendt claims that, although it might have contained certain elements reminiscent of the absolute in religion, the new absolute born of the American Revolution differed in one important respect because it did not dictate violence, that is, the kind of "violence necessary for all foundations and hence supposedly unavoidable in all revolutions" (213). In other words, there was no relation between the necessity of violence and the American Revolution. The American Revolution did not "break out" in the way the French Revolution did. Rather, it was "made" by men, made on a foundation of promises and pledges. "The principle which came to light during those fateful years when the foundations were laid—not by the strength of one architect but by the combined power of the many—was the interconnected principle of mutual promise and common deliberation" (213–14). Not only does Arendt consider mutual promise making to be central to the foundation of "good government," but the pursuit of such promises themselves to constitute the task of the government's citizens. For this reason she often raves about the "genius" of the men of the American Revolution.

I am neither as certain as Arendt of such a pursuit's merit, nor do I think, as she does, that the American idea of the absolute (at least the early version of it) could so easily escape the relation between violence and necessity merely by virtue of the "act of foundation" embodied in the forefathers' instituting and worshiping of the constitution as a kind of "religion" (125, 196, 198, 204). To be fair, I must note that Arendt is careful to suggest that America escaped the most terrifying form of the absolute (sovereignty) precisely because it was not conceived to be a "nation." As she notes, "America was spared the cheapest and the most dangerous disguise of the absolute ever assumed in the political realm, the disguise of the nation" (195). This, of course, is not a hard argument to accept, given that the very idea of the nation, as we know it today, was unimaginable to the men of the American Revolution. Be that as it may, what is important and interesting to me is not this particular argument. Rather, it is the configuration of the relation between violence and necessity that Arendt provides in her narrative about the emergence of a "new absolute" in the American Revolution.

Arendt's general argument is that violence and war, in whatever the form they may take, "conquest, expansion, defense of vested interests," have an intimate relation to the principle of necessity. All wars "are recognized as necessities, that is, as legitimate motives to invoke a decision by arms" (13). Ironically, there is an interesting relation between necessity and the idea of the justification (of war). (As we will see in the course of this chapter, this was given a new direction by the late Nazi jurist Carl Schmitt in his contribution to the formulation of the modern notion of political sovereignty). To allude to this relation between necessity and justification, Arendt quotes the Roman historian Livy, who claimed that "war that is necessary is just" (13). In her view, the relation between violence and necessity has not been studied critically. Arendt rightly mocks political theory that has taken this relation between war, necessity, and justification to be self-evident, always leaving the phenomenon of violence to its "technicians." (How true is this even today?) And that is why "a theory of war or theory of revolution, therefore, can only deal with the justification of violence because this justification constitutes its political limitation" (19). What Arendt wants to show is that the relation between violence and politics cannot merely be reduced to a theory of justification. For this reason, she says that, despite having a recorded history, more often than not violence is assumed to be outside the domain of "politics." By extension, for Arendt, to confront the relation between violence and politics is to confront the relation between sovereignty and necessity. Put in simpler terms, the story of the centrality of violence and its necessity in maintaining "politics"—with which we popularly associate abstract notions of citizenship, law, order, responsibility, justice, democracy today—is the story of the centrality of the doctrine of necessity in maintaining political sovereignty. What Arendt writes about this doctrine of necessity has some bearing on the politics of the contemporary waging of war.

> [The] well-known realities of power politics were not only actually the causes of the outbreak of most wars in history, they were also recognized as "necessities," that is as legitimate motives to invoke a decision by arms. The notion that aggression is a crime and that wars can be justified only if they ward off aggression or prevent it acquired its practical, even theoretical significance only after the First World War had demonstrated the horribly destructive potential of warfare under conditions of modern technology. (13)

For Arendt such a notion of "politics"—animated by violence and necessity—is diametrically opposed to "freedom."[25] This is why she declares, for example, that necessity, based on the notion of "the needs of the people," made possible the doom of the French Revolution. "Thus the role of the revolution was no longer to liberate men from the oppression of the fellow men, let alone to found freedom, but to liberate the life process of society from the fetters of scarcity so that it would swell into a stream of abundance. Not freedom but abundance became now the aim of the revolution" (64). Here Arendt is critical of both Hegel and Marx. We see in both the surrendering of freedom to necessity. "Marx . . . knew this very well, and it was the most potent reason why he was eager to believe with Hegel in the dialectical process in which freedom would rise directly out of necessity" (63). She notes something of the problem of reducing freedom to necessity in *The Human Condition*. "Necessity and life are so intimately related and connected that life itself is threatened where necessity is altogether eliminated. For the elimination of necessity, far from resulting automatically from the establishment of freedom, only blurs the distinguishing line between freedom and necessity."[26] Surely, there are problems with her occasional view of freedom as an "objective state of human existence" and its implications for a notion of "pure politics" (71).[27] Yet what she writes about the relation between freedom and necessity is not undermined by such a view. For Arendt, freedom cannot be reduced to necessity. Freedom is about the political; at least this was her position in *On Revolution* (published almost five years after *The Human Condition*). Freedom is not about the order of society but about the form of government. (As she sees it, this was the central concern in the American Revolution.) Reducing freedom to necessity cannot ever make freedom possible.

Privileging necessity over freedom is nothing but a belief in the (secularized) notions of compassion and, indeed, pity. It is the belief in the "magic of compassion"—that, in Robespierre's words, "torments of misery must engender goodness" (*On Revolution*, 81). (These words should not sound so strange, particularly in the wake of Hurricane Katrina. The hurricane that displaced hundreds of thousands of poor blacks and some whites made possible the celebration of the "goodness" and "compassion" of an American public contributing to the humanitarian relief effort.) As Arendt shows, Rousseau, who privileged the idea of general will over selfishness, introduced this notion of compassion into political theory rather than discovering it. According to Rousseau, the general will requires the relinquishment of selfishness. To relinquish selfishness, one has to battle against oneself, because the idea of the general will, the multitude, indeed the people, takes precedence over (the interests of) one's own self. Overcoming selfishness is achieved by overcoming "the innate repugnance of man to see his fellow creatures suffer" (Rousseau's words; quoted 81).[28] Indeed, the very idea of "the people" (le peuple), which meant not just the people "who did not participate in government . . . but the low people," is synonymous with the principle of compassion. As Arendt shows, "the very definition of the word was born out of compassion" (75). Nietzsche would have concurred with Arendt's judgment on compassion; as he registers it, the western notion of morality is partly founded on that notion. He regarded the "morality of compassion . . . [as] the symptom of the sinister development of our European culture."[29] For him, compassion is not only a disguised form of will to power. It is also an attempt to harbor a *"pathos of distance,"* the difference between oneself and the weak (Genealogy, 12). As Arendt goes on to elaborate, reminiscent of Nietzsche, that compassion has a certain affinity to pity. "Compassion . . . was discovered and understood as an emotion or a sentiment, and the sentiment which corresponds to the passion of compassion is, of course, pity" (On Revolution, 88). Pity's alternative is solidarity (I wonder if Richard Rorty has heard about this). Solidarity is the supposed bond that one establishes with a "community" of the oppressed. But there is a certain danger to pity. Pity cannot exist without the "presence of suffering." To that extent, pity indeed glorifies suffering. Pity becomes a "virtue" in itself (90–92). The task of pity-virtue becomes one of exposing the "hypocrisy" of society and "tearing the façade of corruption down and of exposing behind it the unspoiled, honest face of the *peuple*" (106). Arendt's point is that exposing hypocrisy itself becomes a virtue, leaving aside the question of freedom. (Again, how true is this of our contemporary liberalism, which thrives on, among other things, the virtue of exposing hypocrisies and lies as a practice of radical politics? One of the dominant international anti-Bush slogans in 2003–2004 was "Bush lies." Surely such a conception of politics continues to believe in the relation between empirical knowledge and truth, to believe that knowledge produces truth *and* freedom. It is precisely this sort of sanctimonious empiricism that must be opposed. For the sake of the empiricists in our disciplines, let me cite an unsophisticated undergraduate example: when slavery existed and prospered, people knew about it and might have even thought of it as a kind of hypocrisy. But what eradicated slavery was not that knowledge—the *truth* about slavery. Perhaps it was "necessity" [in the spectral form of a "law"] that eventually made it *illegal,* but this necessity/law, as we know today, hardly created freedom.) This, for Arendt, was exactly the case with the French Revolution, where the new, bloody politics relied so much on a conception of natural rights. These rights, which were "prepolitical rights," entitled human beings to the "necessities of life." The old regime was charged with depriving men of these rights and not "the rights of freedom and citizenship" (109).

Understood this way, defending and safeguarding this necessity require nothing but necessity itself. Hence the violence of the revolution is founded upon the idea of necessity. The idea of necessity authorizes safeguarding those prepolitical, natural rights. This is the problem of the irony of necessity, so to speak. And, if anything, Arendt's *On Revolution* is exceptionally good at pointing to this *problem.* What she reveals, then, is that, beyond its popular connotations, the concept of necessity bears profound politico-epistemological implications. I think that Nietzsche himself alluded to something of its political significance when he remarked that "necessity is not a fact but an interpretation."[30] Let us listen to Nietzsche at length to understand something of the problem of the general concept of necessity:

> From the fact something ensues regularly and ensues calculably, it does not follow that it ensues *necessarily.* That a quantum of force determines and conducts itself in every particular case in one way and manner does not make it into an "unfree will." "Mechanical necessity" is not a fact: it is we who interpret it into events. We have interpreted the formulatable character of events as the consequences of a necessity that rules over events. But from the fact that I do a certain thing, it by no means follows that I am compelled to do it. Compulsion in things certainly cannot be demonstrated: the rule proves only that one and the same event is not another event as well. Only because we have introduced subjects, "doers," into things does it appear that all events are the consequences of compulsion exerted upon subjects—exerted by whom? again by a "doer." Cause and effect—a dangerous concept so long as one thinks of something that causes and something upon which an

effect is produced. . . . Necessity is not a fact but an interpretation. ("Will to Power," 297)

What Arendt shows is the way in which such a concept of necessity, refined in the context of the French Revolution, came to be tied to "violence" in general. This violence of necessity, this necessary violence, is intimately tied to the very idea of modern political sovereignty. Modern political sovereignty itself is a certain "absolute," though it supposedly differs from the absolute of the prince or the monarch. Arendt does not have very much to say about modern political sovereignty in *On Revolution*. Yet her discussion offers clues to the story of the emergence of this problem of sovereignty, and the concept of necessity is one integral part of it.

Critiques of the Promise: Modern Sovereignty and The State of Exception

Today a few critics have only begun to allude to the important relation between modern political sovereignty and the idea of necessity. For example, when Derrida writes, in *Specters of Marx*, "this 'it is necessary' is necessary, and that is the law," he means to point out that what lies behind the seemingly innocent appeal to necessity (in our ordinary parlance and in power politics as well) is indeed an appeal to "law."[31] Put more simply, when someone or some politician says, "the war is necessary" or even "it is necessary," necessity acquires a status of law in itself. Necessity has a certain sense of law attached to it. Where necessity is invoked and present, law as such may not be needed. Necessity itself becomes (a substitute for) law. This does not mean that necessity and law are the same. Yet the appeal to necessity can make law irrelevant. As Agamben has demonstrated, this is what the Roman saying "necessity has no law" implies.[32] Seen from this standpoint, it is not helpful to worry if violence can be justified or whether there is a "contradiction" in a just war theory of violence.[33] Any argument against violence and war based on such a worry plays right into the hands of the technicians of war. It is not an argument that can really be won. In other words, that which is necessary does not have to be justified! (Hence the fallacy of the notion of "justification" of violence.) This relation between necessity, law, and violence is central to the modern conception of political sovereignty.

The modern conception of political sovereignty, it is widely assumed, can be attributed to Carl Schmitt, as he articulates it in *Political Theology* (1922).[34] Schmitt is considered to be largely responsible for the formulation of the relation between sovereignty and the state of exception. As critics like Balibar have demonstrated, Schmitt defined sovereignty in terms of the power to "decide on the state of exception."[35] For Schmitt, "the sovereign is he who decides on the state of exception" (5). In defining sovereignty this way, Schmitt, Balibar says, tries to make it difficult for us to think of a "'sovereignty without a subject'" (136). The decision of the sovereign concerns the *necessity* of maintaining and preserving the order and safety of the people. The state of exception is a function of the sovereign subject, because the constitution (which upholds law) delays it. In a state of exception, "the state remains, whereas law recedes" (*Political Theology,* 1) This is the basic problem of sovereignty. The democratic state without law cannot remain democratic. In other words, in a state of exception, the "state" runs the risk of being an anarchy. Yet, according to Schmitt, there is "order" even in the state of exception. The order may not be juridical, but neither is it anarchical (13).

This is not the only problem with Schmitt's notion of sovereignty. The other problem has to do with the question of the subject: who decides on the state of exception—the state or the people? Something of this problem was detected by Nietzsche in the allegory "I, the state, am the people."[36] As Balibar goes on to show, Schmitt, who does not trust Machiavelli, wants to avoid conflating the state with the prince; even so, Schmitt wants to insist "on the impossibility of detaching the state from a personal unity capable of making a decision, and to whom decisions can be imputed" (137). This is why he even speaks of a "'guardian of the constitution'" to whom the power of decision making is relegated (137). Here Schmitt turns to such figures as Jean Bodin and Thomas Hobbes for a new construction of the figure of the sovereign.[37] Bodin, whose notion of the prince was different from that of Machiavelli, still spoke of the prince's right to suspend law "if the need be" (21). Schmitt claims that Bodin "incorporated the decision into the concept of sovereignty" (*Political Theology,* 8). This is a distortion of what Bodin actually says. Unlike Schmitt, Bodin considers "the state of exception as an exception, whose status and treatment depend on the constituted norm" (*We, the People*, 142).

This, then, is a brief and partial story of the modern concept of sovereignty and how it came to be associated with the state of exception. As Agamben will remind us, there is more to the (hi)story or the genealogy of this relation between sovereignty and law. For example, Agamben argues that in fact this modern notion of sovereignty/state of exception, though widely attributed to Carl Schmitt, can be traced back to the French Revolution, particularly with the establishment of the Constituent Assembly's decree of July 8, 1791 (11). Agamben does not stop there. He goes on to show how the problem of "law" versus sovereignty can be found even in Roman times. What we know by the technical term *law* today was recognized by the Romans as decrees. For example, the syntagma *force of law*—which is precisely what is at stake in a state of exception, to the extent that what remains is not law but the "force of law" (hence it has to be written "force-of-law")—is found in the Roman notion of the sovereign. Agamben writes, "Thus, when the roman sovereign begins to acquire the power to issue acts that tend increasingly to have the value of laws, Roman doctrine says that these doctrines have the "force of law" (38). What we see here is the "confusion between acts of the executive power and acts of the legislative power." The same confusion, Agamben claims, was manifest in the Nazis' repeated claim, "'the words of the Fuhrer have the force of law'" (38).

I am not entirely comfortable with this kind of history tracing, in which concepts like law or the state of exception can somehow be traced back to a distant past. This past is almost always a past that is part of the West. I know that some may view this criticism as an updated version of the familiar denunciation of Eurocentrism. But my question here is a broader one: what are we to do with a history of a kind in which undoubtedly our modern democratic sovereignty, whether it be traced to ancient Roman times or the French Revolution or the works of Carl Schmitt, remains a problem? To be fair, what Agamben and Balibar offer is a *problematization* of the modern notion of democratic sovereignty. As is evident from chapter 3, this problematization alone is not sufficient. Of course, Agamben and Balibar know this well. That is perhaps why at the end of the story they see the emergence of a crisis and/or an aporia marking our modernity. In so doing they seem to recognize that what is needed is not a mere criticism of sovereignty, law, necessity, and the state of exception, but something else. What Agamben writes in this regard merits quoting in full.

> Of course, the task at hand is not to bring the state of exception back within its spatially and temporally defined boundaries in order to then affirm the primacy of a norm [like law] and of rights that are themselves ultimately grounded in it. From the real state of exception in which we live, it is not possible to return to the state of law [*stato di diritto*], for at issue are the very concepts of "state" and "law." But if it is possible to attempt to halt the machine, to show its central fiction, this is because between violence and law, between life and norm, there is no substantial articulation. Alongside the movement that seeks to keep them in relation at all costs, there is a countermovement that, working in an inverse direction in law and in life, always seeks to loosen what has been artificially and violently linked. That is to say, in the field of tension of our culture, two opposite forces act, one that institutes and makes, and one that deactivates and deposes. The state of exception is both the point of their maximum tension and—as it coincides with the rule—that which threatens today to render them indiscernible. To live in a state of exception means to experience both of these possibilities and yet, by always separating the two forces, ceaselessly to try to interrupt the working of the machine that is leading the West toward global civil war. (87)

To live in a democratic sovereignty, then, is to live in (the ever immanent possibility of) a state of exception. Any hope, any resolution, if you will, cannot be found apart from or beyond the state of exception. We live in it. There is no living beyond it. No easy transcendence! Living in it, we cannot merely aspire to reverse it, stop it, hoping to live permanently in a state of law, because to live in a state of law itself is to live in a state of exception. If there is any countermovement, a counterforce, if you will, it lies in the very nexus between law and the state of exception. To live in a state of exception is to see and "experience" how "artificially and violently" the distinction between life and law has been fashioned in our political sovereignty as a fiction or as *artifactuality*.[38] There can be no separation of life from law, just as there can be no separation of anomie from law. If I may add to this, the state of exception is part of the promise of our democracy. Democracy cannot exist without this promise. The problem of the promise is that it is deferred. No amount of criticism of the promise can get rid the problem. In other words, there can be no criticism of the promise. We live in the promise. But to live in the promise is to live in the deferral of the promise. One cannot criticize that which is deferred. In a sense, to live in the promise, to live in a state of exception, is to live in the no-longer present. What is deferred is no-longer present. It is both present/absent. Living in it, we can neither easily abandon the promise nor improve it by critiquing it. I suspect, as detailed in the previous chapter, that Stout, Lopez, and others, in their different takes on community and democracy, still believe in this promise. I also suspect that even Hannah Arendt, who evinced skepticism about the relation between law and violence, still sees some value in pursuing something of what this promise may contain.

As Agamben goes on to show, a Durkheimian might think that mourning the state of exception as a kind of anomie—Durkheim introduced the word *anomie* into the social sciences to explain one cause of suicide—would help us come to grips with the problem. That is, it would help us think of the state of exception as a certain kind of social instability. Yet this thinking is an attempt to do away with the anomie, hoping that some kind of normalcy can be restored. But today, given the artifactual link between law and anomie, there can be no mourning *away* the problem—no easy doing away with it. But might it be possible to think of another mourning? How would such mourning think of the question of un-inheriting the relation between law, sovereignty, and anomie without trying to do away with it?

Here Arendt, Agamben, or Balibar, I contend, is not going to be of much help. Even though a critic like Agamben himself speaks of the importance of *interrupting* the machine of law and sovereignty, he offers no other conceptual strategy to go about doing so.[39] This is perhaps no intellectual fault of these thinkers. Perhaps our modern democratic sovereignty, law, and the state of exception are so complicatedly tangled that finding an easy strategy of interrupting the machine is difficult, if not nearly impossible, today. The question I want to pose and wrestle with in this chapter—and in the entire study— then, is this: how might we un-inherit this relation between law and life, anomie and sovereignty, past and present? My suspicion is that what is needed is less a way of "interrupting" than a way of inhabiting the relation between law, sovereignty, and violence.[40] In the remainder of this chapter I want to explore how that way of inhabiting the law and violence of our modernity might gain us a different purchase on it, one that does not seek merely to overcome it or interrupt it. I think this way of thinking about our modernity might enable us to recognize that inhabiting our modernity cannot transcend it, negate it, or deny it, but can only think the question of un-inheriting it, un-inheriting that which is so artifactually constructed. After all, if we see our modern sovereignty as a deferred promise, and if we cannot criticize this promise—at least not theoretically—then we can see why we cannot easily interrupt it. Can one interrupt that which is deferred? On the contrary, we may inhabit a promise. At least I suspect so. Inhabiting this promise demands living in a state of its deferral. It seems to me that such a conception of inhabiting might help us think about mourning the problem of democratic sovereignty and its promise in a radically new way.

Inhabiting the Modern:
Toward the Mourning's Political

As a modest measure of exploring this possibility, I want to turn to *Habitations of Modernity,* by Dipesh Chakrabarty, one of the most profitable thinkers of our time.[41] Even though the term *habitation* is part of its title, the book's concern with the questions of mourning and un-inheriting may not be entirely apparent. Yet I think that we can tease out some aspects of it that speak to important ways of mourning the impasse between law and modernity. What is distinctive about this work—*even though it does not say so anywhere*—is that it is not just one more critique of modernity. Chakrabarty does engage critics and defenders of modernity, from India and elsewhere. Yet he does not classify the ethical-political concerns and interests of such thinkers in terms of the tired western/nonwestern distinction. Rather, as we shall soon see, he considers them an important part of the discussion of the globalized question of democracy and modernity. Indeed, interested as he is in the question of "how . . . we think about the global legacy of European Enlightenment in lands far away from Europe in geography or history" (xxi), Chakrabarty wants to think of modernity beyond the axis of such habitual (and indeed racist) demarcations. (One of the most grotesque examples of this distinction is found in a statement made by a character in Salman Rushdie's novel *The Satanic Verses:* "Battle lines are being drawn in India, secular versus religious, the light versus the dark. Better you choose which side you are on" [80].)[42] This is partly why Chakrabarty contends, contra those who speak of alternative or plural modernities or those find no value in the term *modernity*,[43] that *modernity* "is a word that we cannot do without in the everyday context of discussions of democracy and development" (xx). For Chakrabarty, the challenge here is how to think about the inability to do without modernity and "resist the . . . violence that accompanies imperial or triumphalist moments of our modernity" simultaneously (xxi). Thus, as I read him, there can be no superimposed critique of modernity, standing back, away from it, at a distance, from a geographical or conceptual standpoint. It is only through *inhabiting* modernity that we may begin to "envision . . . ways of being modern that will speak to that which is shared across the world as well as to that which belongs to human cultural diversity" (xxi).

The challenge of this habitation becomes more pronounced because what it involves is not just a mere *coping with* the violent predicaments of modernity, envisioning new ways of being modern, but also a thinking about the past and its relation to the present in a new way. For Chakrabarty, this demands, as he argued elsewhere, seeing the past as being both "dead and alive."[44] Here Chakrabarty is building on the Kierkegaardian question "why bother to remember a past that cannot be made into a present?"[45] Note that this not the same as Eric Hobsbawm's exhausted claim that "if there is no suitable past, it can always be invented."[46] Rather, what Chakrabarty wants to do is to understand how all our pasts, "humans from any other period and region . . . are always in some sense our contemporaries" (*Provincializing*, 109). What is new about this approach to thinking about the past is that it is not another sophisticated injunction in the fashion of Fredric Jameson's call to "always historicize."[47] Indeed, Chakrabarty distrusts the political value of the very distinction between "good history" and "bad history." For example, historians like Hobsbawm never tire of reminding us that "bad history is not harmless history. It is dangerous."[48] Hobsbawm does not realize, Chakrabarty argues, that "good" history was often used by colonialism to subjugate people in places such as India (97, 275). And today, more often than not, even good histories that many anthropologists write about the natives produce nothing but the old liberal logic of "respect" for the others, that is, "'Yes, I respect your beliefs, but they are not mine'" (*Habitations*, 43).

Chakrabarty is hardly uninterested in the task of historicizing. Indeed, he considers a certain kind of historicizing, that which produces "subversive" histories, significant to the subaltern project of which he is a founding member. Yet, *pace* Jameson and Hobsbawm, Chakrabarty wonders how at times "refusing to historicize . . . [may produce] a life possibility for the present." Such a refusal, he muses, may help us view "any particular 'now' one may inhabit" as being disjointed (*Provincializing*, 108). This way of viewing history can enable us to shed new light on the relation between the past and the present, the modern and the nonmodern, that conventional historicizing cannot. That is, if the present itself is non-contemporaneous with or disjointed from itself, then we can begin to imagine the relation between the past and the present, the modern and the nonmodern, beyond the mere notion of continuity or discontinuity.

Here, I think, is a provocative proposition to take the past seriously without necessarily being bound to or dictated by all its concerns. This conception of the past and the present governs *Habitations of Modernity*. The obvious (Derridean) question that emerges here (and Chakrabarty does not put it this way) is this: how does one inhabit the present of modernity if it is already disjointed from itself? I will have more to say about Derrida's take on the political significance of seeing time/history as "disjointed." But in *Habitations* Chakrabarty points to some interesting ways in which we might conceptualize the notion of the disjointedness of the past/present into something of a politics of mourning, a "politics" that would be irreducible to conceptions of law, responsibility, or humanism.

Habitations, as noted earlier, is not another sophisticated contribution to the existing archive of critiques of modernity. Take, for instance, the chapter titled "Modernity and the Past." It is more or less a self-reflective evaluation of the contemporary criticism of modernity by way of engaging the controversial writings of Ashis Nandy.[49] Nandy appears to some as defending "a certain kind of atavistic nativism" precisely because of his critique of modernity. This was clear in the wake of a vituperative debate between Nandy and Indian secularists

about a Rajastani woman named Roop Kanvar who committed suicide and became a sati in 1997. Part of the debate was about the ("ir-
resoluble") question of the woman's agency. Nandy charged (Indian)
feminists and others, who sought to impose a ban on the public celebration of anything that had to do with the practice of sati, with seeking to impose an anglophile version of secularism on India. In turn,
secularists and feminists indicted Nandy (who is not a Hindu but a
Christian) of practicing a certain neo-Gandhianism and anticolonial
nativism, undermining western rationalism and thereby condoning
practices like sati. Chakrabarty finds no merit in the polemics of the
debate. Nandy, Chakrabarty argues, is wrong to dismiss his accus-
ers as "uprooted" Indian anglophiles (*Habitations*, 42). After all, "being westernized is one way of being Indian" (42). At the same time,
the secularists' accusation against Nandy is, at best, unfair. Indeed,
Nandy has written in no uncertain terms against the oppression of
the practice of sati. After all, Nandy is a self-described practitioner of
"critical traditionalism," which is "neither about a completely willful
rejection of the past nor about viewing history as a process of dialectical overcoming of the past [and its horrors]" (41). Hence Chakrabarty
insists that "one would be mistaken to see Nandy as anything but a
modern intellectual" (42). To listen to Nandy is to listen to an intellectual critic of modernity who "takes his bearings in the world from
concerns that are unmistakably modern" (42). Yet Chakrabarty finds
it difficult to reconcile Nandy's critical traditionalism with his call for
respecting the tradition of sati. Surely this is not a negation of the horrors of sati. In fact, Nandy recognizes this when he remarks that sati
represents a "dark" side of Indian culture. At best, Nandy's respect for
the tradition of sati is a way of thinking critically about the numerous
discourses within the Indian tradition—represented by various texts,
festivals, and figures like Mahabharata, Durga Puja, Kabir, Rabin-
dranath Tagore, and others—that discuss, honor, and even invoke the
name of sati. Needless to say, the (colonial) law that banned sati for
all sorts of juridical, humanist, and moral reasons can hardly attend
to these instances in which the knowledge about the (myth) of the
tradition still exists in modern society. Sati, of course, is more than a
myth existing in modern religious celebrations of goddesses that per-
sonified it. Despite the (still existing) ban on it, there are widows who
commit suicide to become satis.

That is why Chakrabarty wonders how Nandy's plea for respecting tradition could produce the kind of just society about which Nandy has written eloquently and powerfully. Can this respect for the tradition of sati ever attend to its "monstrosity" in a way that neither modern colonial law nor contemporary parliamentary bills banning its celebrations can? We know now, as Chakrabarty reminds us, that the anonymous yet universal "law" that observes and punishes can never confront human suffering and cruelty *"face to face"* (103–5). What Chakrabarty is intimating is that if modernity (and its laws) cannot think against the monstrosity of sati, neither can further historicizing of its pasts. This, I think, is a powerful incitement to think with. If we today exist at the aporetic nexus of having (exhausted) the options of appealing to the humanist notion of respect for the past (of sati) or to modern law that seeks to censor it, then we are in need of a different way of thinking about it. Thinking against the cruelty and violence of sati has to be accompanied by a different way of "thinking" about the past and the present, the modern and the nonmodern. This cannot come from one more critique of democratic modernity that outlaws (and disrespects) certain features of tradition like sati.

The kind of thinking that Chakrabarty has in mind, a thinking or theory that "takes a leap in the dark," is animated by what he calls (in a somewhat Heideggerian terms) "fear and anxiety." [50] As he says, "fear and anxiety have to be the other effects with which the modern intellectual—modernity here implying a capacity to create the future as an object of deliberate action—relates to the past" (46). This mood of fear and anxiety is about not knowing "with any degree of certainty that a sati will never happen again or that an ugly communal riot will never break out" (46). What I would add to this is that that mood of fear and anxiety is exactly what is missing in our democratic modernity and its apparatuses of law and responsibility. Law and democracy are founded upon a politics of assurance (of freedom from fear and anxiety themselves)! That is, democratic politics (and the campaigns of the politicians running for state offices these days) centers on the "promises" to eliminate fears and anxieties that supposedly threaten democracy itself, be they poverty and high taxes or big government and terrorism. In such a politics of assurance, fear and anxiety exist only with the promised possibility of their eventual elimination in the future. But can fear and anxiety become part of democracy? Can democracy live with this mood of existence? As Derrida once remarked, to do anything political, one should never seek assurances. One should always "be afraid and anxious." [51]

Yet, for fear and anxiety to define politics in a way that politics can never seek to banish them, they have to be understood in relation to the notion of being haunted. That is, we can only understand the importance of fear and anxiety to our democracy if we see the past as something that can haunt us. That is why, Chakrabarty reminds us— with a brief reference to Derrida's *Specters of Marx,* a text about which I will have much to say—"the pasts have the power to haunt us." To understand how the pasts can haunt us, for Chakrabarty, the past has to be seen as something that can "survive." That which survives, of course, can never be the same, which is why Derrida reinvented the figure of the ghost that has no form, the ghost that is visible/invisible (chapter 6). But Chakrabarty's notion of survival, I think, offers something radically new to think about the past so as to imagine new futures. We can draw out such a notion of survival in his discussion of the contemporary political significance of *khadi,* the Indian (male) politician's white uniform. (I say draw out, because the way I think about the notion of survival vis-à-vis un-inheriting is not how Chakrabarty sees it.) Chakrabarty explains the distinctiveness of this uniform:

> There is a strong Gandhian semiotic that still circulates in the Indian public life and marks the public man—the politician—out from others. The most general uniform for the respectable public servant in India is the safari suit; for the politician, however, it has been, from the time before independence, white *khadi,* the coarse, homespun cotton that Gandhi popularized in the 1920s. Its symbolism, as intended in the official/nationalist rhetoric, is clear. The white of *khadi* symbolizes the Hindu idea of purity (lack of blemish, pollution), its coarseness an identification with both simplicity and poverty; together they stand for the politician's capacity to renounce his own material well-being, to make sacrifices (*tyag*) in the public/national interest. *Khadi* indicates the person's capacity to serve the country. (52)

This is one important "meaning" of *khadi.* But the question that Chakrabarty raises is how *khadi* "persists" in public life today, when its (Gandhian) meaning has disappeared. That is to say, *khadi*, at least in the dominant public reading of it, stands not for purity and renunciation but for the "corruption" and "thievery" that exists in Indian (and world) politics today. The *khadi*-clad politician is not going to fool anyone into accepting "the Gandhian convictions of the wearer" (64). In that sense, one important meaning of *khadi* has faded from view, overshadowed by another. But how do we explain the persistence of *khadi*? Surely, one could say that it is simply a pretense of piety. Yet, as Chakrabarty illustrates

> it does not explain why *khadi,* or at least the color white, remains the most visible aspect of a male Indian politician's attire. The question is, Why does such a transparently hypocritical gesture persist even today? Why do politicians do that which fools nobody? In other words, if I assume that the hypocrisy of *khadi* is visible to everybody, then its (effective) purpose cannot be to deceive people into thinking well of the wearer. What has been read as a transparent gesture of hypocrisy must, then, because of its persistence, be amenable to another reading. (53–54)

Here, Chakrabarty, like Arendt, does not think that identifying forms of hypocrisy and bigotry alone can help solve the problem of our modernity. Therefore, is it possible to read this seeming hypocrisy as a way of communicating something entirely different, something the politicians themselves do not intend? In other words, can the persistence of *khadi* be seen as providing us with "alternative constructions of the values of public life" (54), those that exist in constitutive tension with the logic of capital that governs our modernist ways of being? Put more broadly, the persistence of *khadi* provides an important site to think about how we cannot aspire to easily inhabit the contemporary modernity of capital or return to the modern past of Gandhian politics.

A word about Gandhi's modern. As I read Chakrabarty, Gandhi was, of course, not just the most visible Indian example of nonviolence, as conventional (textbook) perspectives would have us think, nor was he just a shrewd politician, as some see him. Gandhi constructed a new sense of the modern by collapsing the difference between the private and the public. If the European, Christian notion of the modern depended upon the assumption that our private lives

are ultimately narratable and knowable, Gandhi defied such narration. "Gandhi . . . shunned the idea of privacy—sleeping naked and
completely asexually with others was one of his experiments in this
regard" (61). Gandhi invited a certain gaze upon himself and said to
others, "'Watch me closely'" (61). This is not to say that some aspects
of his private life were not knowable, but "whatever the private man
was, it was not for narration to others" (61–62). Gandhi's statement,
"things which are known only to oneself, and to one's maker . . . are
clearly incommunicable," distinguishes his modern distinctly from
European political theory's concept of citizenship (62). Indeed, the
Gandhian collapsing of the private/public distinction poses an important challenge to our increasingly secretive democracies. "The idea
of a completely narratable public life and a completely nonnarrat-
able private one corresponds to the idea of a completely transparent
government—'Examine my motives carefully,' as Gandhi said. The
modern state, however, cannot ever fulfill this requirement—*national
security, political intelligence,* etc., are its watchwords" (62). The point
here is that *khadi,* in its initial meaning of purity and renunciation,
emerged out of such a Gandhian politics of defying the private/public
difference in an anticolonial context. Today, *khadi,* persisting as the
politician's national dress, without either the colonial context or its
meanings, haunts those who inhabit the modernity of secretive democracies and the logic of its capital. In other words,

> the qualities that Gandhi demanded of the public man . . . do not
> sit easily with the logic of capital accumulation. The condition of
> Gandhi's success was colonial rule. . . . With the dawn of indepen-
> dence, Indian capitalism and democracy have developed their dis-
> tinctive characteristics, different from both the tenets of Gandhian
> politics and those of European classical writings on either of these
> phenomena. (63)

Yet, of course, *khadi* "survives"!

In my view, *kadhi's* survival, disjointed from its Gandhian time and
its politics, can only be as a ghost. It does not have its former form. It
is present, but not quite present. This surviving ghost of *khadi* cannot
fully belong within the politics of modern capital. It can only exist
in constitutive tension with capital. It haunts capitalistic modernity
and all of us who inhabit it. In other words, as we live within our

modernity, we exist within the possibility of being both haunted and not haunted by this ghost. That is, this (now almost unrecognizable/misrecognizable?) ghost of *khadi* that haunts our public space may cease to haunt us. It may disappear, without indicating when and how and in what form it may return. Are we ready for the possibility of *khadi*'s disappearance, which, "were that to happen, would signify the demise of a deeper structure of desire that would signal India's complete integration into the circuits of global capital" (64)? He may sound somewhat nostalgic here, but, in my reading of Chakrabarty, to inhabit this context of *khadi*'s survival as well as its (possible) disappearance is to inhabit a context of "fear and anxiety." Global capital, by its very logic, its desire to produce bourgeois citizenship, to eliminate all (always visible) hypocrisies, anxieties, and fears from a sanitized public space, of course finds the ghost of *khadi* menacing.

My point here is that, viewed from this angle, *Habitations* constitutes a powerful attempt at mourning our modernity and its logic of capital in relation to the past. It does not (and cannot) advocate to merely critique and eliminate this logic. We are all products of it. Inhabiting this logic, we also inhabit the possibility of fear and anxiety being eliminated from our politics. As should be clear by now, fear and anxiety run counter to the promise of our democracy. The promise is deferred and no-longer. Such a deferred promise cannot exist in proximity to the fear and anxiety the ghost produces within us. But can these two opposites coexist? If we cannot criticize the promise of democracy, would fear and anxiety help us relate to the promise differently? Neither Arendt nor Agamben nor Balibar tells us how to think about un-inheriting the possibility (and indeed the danger) of a future without fear and anxiety. Chakrabarty, as I have attempted to read him so far, at least attunes us to some of these sorts of questions.[52]

If *khadi*'s persistence haunts our modernity, reminding us of a past Gandhian politics of being modern, then its past is one to which we can never return, not simply because it is the past, but because the heterogeneity of our now violently racialized and religionized identities cannot be accommodated within its admittedly narrow Hindu yet secularized (and Christianized) purview. At the same time, of course, this heterogeneity does not remain settled neatly and peacefully within capitalistic modernity. If it did, we would be living in a violence-free society! Hence persisting *khadi* haunts us to think about the possibility of forms of *becoming* not beyond but within our modernity of law, citizenship, and number, through all of which the modern state constructs our "human" subjectivity. Chakrabarty is partly after thinking about this very difficult possibility.

For Chakrabarty, thinking of such alternative ways of becoming does not mean abandoning the category of the human, however problematic it may be. As he says, "far too hastily, it has often seemed to me, we now equate being human with being political" (xxiv). What this means is that our continuing to add to the available knowledges of the juridical constructions of our being, to continue to tell, in early Foucauldian vogue, the story of how law saturates our very human being, is not sufficient. Chakrabarty, of course, knows all too well that there can be no easy separation of law and the "human." (Here I cannot do justice to all the rich ways in which he illustrates the relation between modern citizenship, law, capital, and subjectivity [65–97].) In this respect, Chakrabarty would agree with critics who fault thinkers like Arendt for seeking to produce a concept of "pure politics" or advance a pure notion of "the human condition."[53] Yet, for Chakrabarty, such criticisms of "pure politics" have to be accompanied by thinking about how "being human" is a way in which we may come "face-to-face" with forms of cruelty, suffering, and oppression. Thus, being human—as opposed to the humanism of bourgeois citizenship—is not a way of shunning violence and relegating it to some corner of our existence, concealing and denying its presence. For example, more often than not, violence, be it communal rioting or the oppression of widows in India, is characterized as "inhuman" (142). Even so, the "inhumanity of . . . violence is, after all human. The inhuman is in humans, and in that sense, is better written as *in-human*" (142). Yet state and law teach us to see such violence as "inhuman" as opposed to the "human." Thus, when we hear "harrowing descriptions of oppression," we not only may generate emotions of anger and outrage but also "want to intervene and do something" (102). We know how such social-political interventions and actions are implicated within the terminology of rights, law, justice, and state. That is to say, our efforts to "do something" politically or socially, all our "emancipatory visions," operate within the confines of law and state. For Chakrabarty, the dilemma is how one is to "square" this desire to intervene and seek justice "with [one's] knowledge of the violence on which the nation-state and its laws are founded, the violence of the same modernity that teaches us to think of law as the key instrument of social justice" (102). This view of violence is Derridean (31), but Chakrabarty's notion of the *"in-human,"* and its relation to violence, is singular. If state/law can see violence only in inhuman terms, it cannot ever truly "confront" it. It confronts it to oppose it, to stop it. Yet it cannot come *face-to-face* with it. The long arm of law can reach far, and it can touch, grab, seize, and punish criminal(ized) bodies, yet it cannot touch or confront pain and cruelty. "The very same [legal] entitlement that causes a woman [in Bengal] to ask for affection from her in-laws makes her vulnerable to their acts of cruelty" (112). The state may (rarely) punish the in-laws, but it cannot ever attend to the widow's cry for affection. The widow's "cry is not a cry for general affection, that is, affection from anybody and everybody." The state cannot attend to that cry because "the problem of the state is solved by a theory of general affection" (112) Now we know, by way of Nietzsche and Arendt, that this general affection of the state (which sometimes comes to us in the form of "compassion") is bound up with the very idea of *le peuple.* Justice today passes for this general affection. But can justice, affection of justice, heed the call of the other, to see the other who cannot be seen, to hear the voices of the "dead" who cannot speak?[54] This is, of course, assuming that we can at least begin with "an affirmation that every life," as Amitav Ghosh puts it, "leaves behind an echo that is audible to those who take the trouble to listen."[55] In that sense, one may ask, how different is the unheard voice of the Bengali widow from the unheard voices of the incalculable dead/dying in Iraq, Darfur, and elsewhere? Will they ever receive and know the affection of justice of the local and international states that are complicit in reducing them to mere ashes and dust, beyond recognition, obliterating all traces of their former and future im-possible lives? Will justice, if such a thing were ever to materialize, be even acceptable to these unrecognizable others? But the powerful irony here is that to hope for justice for them is to hope for the continuation of the *state of exception* that renders *necessary* the very machinery of war that generates the dead.

For Chakrabarty, to heed the call of the other, we have to think of a different way of constituting "proximity" to human beings. One way to do so would be to think of a sense of responsibility. Here, he quotes Levinas: "politics must be able in fact always to be checked and criticized starting from the ethical. . . . This would be a responsibility [for the other] which is inaccessible in its ethical advent, from which one

does not escape, and which, thus, is the principle of an absolute indi-
viduation" (*Habitations,* 112).[56] We know now (as seen in chapter 3) that
this (Levinasian) notion of responsibility is not an entirely safe venue
through which we can think of the question of otherness. Any appeal
to responsibility always returns to the problem of law. Responsibility is law's companion. Responsibility is indebted to law. Law always
demands (repaying) the debt of responsibility. I think Chakrabarty is
aware of this because he is not interested merely in this notion of
"responsibility for the other" as a way of confronting the other's pain
face-to-face. He knows the danger of it because the other for him is
not easily recognizable. Can one be responsible for the other whom
one does not yet know or recognize? This is perhaps why Chakrabarty
stresses (with reference to Heidegger) the importance of "the capacity to hear that which one does not already understand" (36). Hence,
even as he suggests the importance of constructing a certain "proximity" to the other, he stresses that all our pasts, "the humans from
any other period or region [those others we have never met or will
never meet] . . . are always in some sense our contemporaries." Here,
then, is a challenge.

My argument here has been that, to meet this challenge, we must
consider a pathway of mourning. Chakrabarty's *Habitations,* in the
way I have read it, constitutes an important attempt, even though it
does not see mourning in the way I do. In particular, his notion of
survival is important to any thinking on (mourning our) modernity.
But what I want to suggest is that if we are to hear the unrecognizable other, to think about how all our pasts are our contemporaries,
we need to think about how we may be haunted not only by our pasts
but also by our deferred futures. That is to say, to live in the deferred
promise of the present is always to remain haunted by the past and
think the future of the political irreducible to democracy, law, and
justice. What I want to suggest is that thinking of how we might be
haunted by dead-alive ghosts of our pasts may guide us toward living
in tension with law and responsibility. To live in tension with law and
responsibility is to live within the deferred promise of the futures.
To live within the promise, one has to be guided by a mood of fear
and anxiety made possible by the ghosts of our pasts. Such living
might mean un-inheriting the juridical idea of responsibility (for the
other) and opening up a future of a life of *being haunted* (by the other,
its legacies, pasts, and histories that are aporia, no longer problems,

already deconstructed, and hence un-improvable and un-inheritable).
(This is to assume that ghosts do not demand responsibility or justice
but only fear and anxiety.) How would being haunted free us from
our appeal to notions of debt, law, and guilt that animate responsibility? It seems to me that in "being haunted," we cannot appeal to any
conception of ethics or responsibility guided by a sense of "ought."
Derrida once noted, "I would never say 'ought'—without adding two
or three qualifications." [57] If this juridical (Kantian) notion of "ought"
and the sense of debt attached to it are entrenched in the idea of responsibility, then being haunted may produce something other than
a responsibility toward the other. In being haunted, one is not engaging in any act, that is, one is not doing or giving something to/for
the other. In an act of giving and doing, one's self always comes first,
seeking to solve the problems of other(s), thereby exorcising and casting away the troubling other. On the contrary, in being haunted, one
has no monopoly over the other that one cannot know or apprehend.
One is always haunted prior to the self's initiating any act of contact
with the other. Being haunted, one may not even (easily) "recognize"
the other. It will not be a familiar other. Understood that way, can
one (as Levinas wants to do) even "speak" of the other, attempt a face-
to-face encounter with her?[58] Thus being haunted by the other (e.g.,
khadi) might mean being haunted by the very legacies of our pasts,
our names, our identities, and our differences, which we cannot inherit or abandon. It is in being haunted that the im-possibility of un-
inheriting might have a future, a future of (at least imagining an) irreducible otherness that is not even thinkable now, in the time of the
"now," in the now that values the empirical and the pragmatic, the
present and the signified—that is to say, the now that cares so much
about justice.

In the three chapters that follow I attempt to show how we may
imagine ways of thinking such otherness, which cannot be solely defined by the existing parameters of law, rights, justice, and responsibility, that is, the very apparatus of our political sovereignty. I will have
much to say about ghosts and haunting, active forgetting of history,
and imagining anti-genealogical futures. These concepts will be crucial to questioning some of the cherished features of our democracy:
tolerance, law, minority rights, the idea of the human, friend, enemy,
and freedom. To begin this task, in the following chapter I discuss the
contemporary politics of secularism in relation to an unprecedented,

nationwide "religious" debate in postcolonial Sri Lanka. Here we shall see how questions of otherness emerge in ways with which the secularism of the postcolonial state cannot easily reckon as well as consider the importance of certain religious voices that seek to speak (however imperfectly and imprecisely) to the concerns of minority politics, multiculturalism, and postcolonial difference. Recognizing the limitations of the politics of the postcolonial state and even the nonstate (religious) voices that attempt to speak to questions of minority differences and rights can help us imagine, in chapter 6, a space of the political that I call active forgetting of history.

If the adherents of a religion enter the public sphere, can their entry leave the pre-existing discursive structure intact? The public sphere is not an empty space for carrying out debates. It is constituted by the sensibilities—memories, aspirations, fears and hopes—of speakers and listeners.

—Talal Asad, Formations of the Secular

Do I recommend love of the neighbor to you? Sooner I should recommend flight from the neighbor and love of the farthest . . . But you are afraid and run to your neighbor. —Friedrich Nietzsche, Thus Spoke Zarathustra

5   Im-passable Limits of Fugitive Politics

Identity for and Against Itself

My purpose in this chapter is twofold: to offer a proposal for thinking anew the relation between religion and public sphere and to suggest that in so doing we may begin to conceptualize the questions of otherness and difference in a way irreducible to history, state, and law. I say begin because the agonistic moment of a demand for identity to be for and against itself that I want to locate in this chapter still remains at the aporetic limits of the postcolonial politics that continues to sustain and enforce distinctions like minority and majority, Tamils and Sinhalese as numerically, morally, and politically significant differences. We know today the danger of the view that authorizes one group as "majority" as opposed to another as "minority." In this regard, critics like Qadri Ismail are quite correct to argue that, so long as postcolonial politics remains hemmed in by such distinctions, new political horizons cannot be imagined. Viewed from the vantage point of such distinctions, postcolonial conflicts and violence between minorities and majorities demand nothing but a politics of "management." Such a politics can hardly attend to the pressing question of "peace," that is, the question of how to imagine an Adornian politics of "distinction without domination."[1] But we have seen that even such a view of peace cannot produce a conceptualization of otherness without retaining the political-epistemological binary between identity and difference. Now political scientists like William Connolly suggest that one way to deauthorize such normalized distinctions between minority and majority is to imagine new political domains in terms of what he calls a "fugitive abundance of being." For Connolly, the space of such fugitive abundance

> judges the ethos it cultivates to exceed any fixed code of morality; and it cultivates critical responsiveness to difference in ways that disturb traditional virtues of community and the normal individual. It does not present *itself* as the single universal to which other ethical traditions must bow. Rather, it provides a prod and counterpoint to them, pressing them to rethink the ethics of engagement, and, crucially, to rework their relations to the diversity of ethical *sources* that mark a pluralistic culture.[2]

In my view, there is an interesting relation between what I call identity for and against itself and the figure of the fugitive. In this chapter I want to find out how we might begin to imagine a fugitive space that demands identity be both for and against itself and if such a space can entirely do away with the problem of history and humanism, that is to say, the problem of the political-epistemological distinction between majority and minority, identity and difference. I want to do so by examining an unprecedented public "religious" debate that emerged in late-1990 Sri Lanka about questions of otherness and minority rights vis-à-vis the secular state and its national identity. The debate has profound implications for thinking about the very aporia of democracy in all postcolonial societies. In this fierce nationwide rhetorical contest, which lasted for weeks over the issues of who could speak to the space of minorities within the secular nation in terms of its historical (and constitutional) link to Buddhism, something of the possibility of (at least a demand for) a fugitive identity came into view, at least momentarily. The virtue of thinking of the relevance of this debate to democracy is that it demonstrates not only the poverty of the existing theories about religion and public space but also the aporetic limits of the postcolonial politics within which we continue to conceptualize the question of otherness today.

My argument is that the figure of the fugitive is a figure of aporia. (Even though Connolly does not put it in these terms, he probably has something of this contradiction in mind.)[3] In other words, even as it produces a demand for identity to be fugitive–to flee from a certain "history" of its definition–the politics of the debate cannot escape the aporetic limits of history within which it conditions the possibility of the demand. The debate shows that its demand for identity to be both for and against itself still remains in proximity to a certain history, threatening to produce the problem of humanism previously detailed. To put it differently, the moment of identity for and against itself was a fugitive moment. The fugitive, of course, is, by definition, the figure that "flees." Somewhat like Nietzsche's imagined antineighborly figure who runs (or is called upon to run) the farthest, away from the neighbor, the fugitive I have in mind flees (or at least tries to flee) her/his debt and responsibility to history. Yet the aporia is this: the fugitive (identity) remains never entirely free from history, as a fugitive is never really free from its debt and responsibility to law. The fugitive cannot run very far from law and responsibility. The fugitive identity/being is always haunted/hounded by its debt to history, a history in which it is compelled to define itself in a particular way (as Sinhalese or Tamil, majority or minority). Even though the fugitive seeks to run from its debt of bondage, it cannot proceed far beyond the limits of law. Hence the fugitive moment, if one may call it that, is a moment of aporetic limits. My wager here is that thinking about the debate in terms of these limits may help us imagine, in the following chapter, different futures of the political irreducible to history itself.

Getting to the public debate I have in mind will require recasting some fundamental presumptions that govern modern democratic theory about religion and its relation to public space. To do so, we have to set aside not only the nationalist presumptions about the interrelation between religion and politics; we also have to de-anchor secularist, Enlightenment assumptions about the separation between religion and public sphere. This does not mean abandoning secularism. But secularism/secularist theory will have to figure out how it may attend to the shifting political conditions in which new forms of postcolonial nationalisms, organized by particular religious groups, come to dominate the public sphere. In other words, secularism will have to give up the assumption that its politics has a self-evident safeguard. Secularism cannot do as long as it hangs on to the view that the best form of democratic politics and pluralist belonging can thrive only in a "de-divinized" state, a view represented differently by critics rang-ing from Kant and Rousseau to Chantal Mouffe and Richard Rorty. The following is such a secularist, indeed Enlightenment, view on religion and democratic politics by Mouffe, a renowned contemporary political theorist:

> Modern democracy requires the affirmation of a certain number of "values" which, like equality and freedom, constitute its "politi-cal principles." It establishes a form of human existence which re-quires a distinction between the public and the private, the separa-tion of church and state, of civil and religious law. These are some of the basic achievements of the modern democratic revolution, and they are what make the existence of pluralism possible. One cannot therefore call these distinctions into question in the name of pluralism. Hence the problem posed by the integration of a re-ligion like Islam, which does not accept these distinctions. Recent events surrounding the Rushdie affair show that there is a problem here which will not be easily solved. We find ourselves faced with a real challenge: how are we to defend the greatest possible degree of pluralism while not yielding over what constitutes the essence of modern democracy?[4]

Now I do not want to malign this obviously problematic statement. I share with Mouffe the idea of the importance of democracy and plu-ralism relative to the context in which we are living today. But I do not share her assurance about the indisputable distinction between dem-ocratic politics and religion. In other words, I do not think that merely invoking the "value" of the distinction between religion and politics can easily sustain pluralism and democracy. My simple contention here is this: the appeal to a self-evident demarcation between religion and politics ignores the important ways in which the intervention of religious discourses within the public sphere may help us pose the question of democracy vis-à-vis minority differences in a new way. As Asad notes in the above epigraph, when religious adherents enter the public sphere, they enter a space of sensibilities, hopes, and fears. Thus, for Asad, the public space is not an empty one. Asad's point here is that the religious adherents who enter the public space "may *have* to disrupt existing assumptions to be heard."[5] While I agree with this, I would suggest that such intervention seeks to disrupt not just the politics of the public space and its listeners but also the politics of the speakers. The hopes, fears, anxieties that constitute the identities of the speakers themselves may undergo a disruption. So, far from being a liberal forum for agreeing to disagree, the kind of debate that I am interested in examining *attempts* to create a space of fugitive politics for thinking against the normalized sense of being. Ignoring such debates will be detrimental to the kind of pluralism that secular liberals like Mouffe desire to sustain in democracies. Even so, as we will see, the debate does not provide a model for the futures of democracy that we are seeking to imagine in this work. If anything, the debate exposes the political, historical, and juridical limits within which questions of identity and difference are conceptualized, helping us see how thinking at those limits can only force us to imagine new domains of actively forgetting history itself. Now I want to turn to the debate by way of musing over the broader questions of democracy, violence, minority rights, tolerance, and religion in contemporary Sri Lanka.

Nation-State and Religion, Tolerance and Neutrality

For most anthropologists and like-minded postcolonial scholars, Sri Lanka—to use Bernard Cohn's memorable term—constitutes an "anthropologyland."[6] That is, they view Sri Lanka as a readily available ethnographic, empirical example of a troubled country, located in a far-off corner of South Asia, a place on the map where violence between the majority and the minority has disrupted the normalcy of life. One cannot, of course, deny the fact that, over its postcolonial career, Sri Lanka has witnessed differing contexts of abductions, tortures, killings, and massacres on the part of many different people. But such practices of violation do not remain available for self-evident disciplinary identification and explanation, particularly in terms of a conflict or "violence" between the majority and the minority. Yet, more often than not, this kind of narrative constitutes the typical form of (western) disciplinary representations of the island nation and the problems of its democracy and minority politics. Take, for instance, the following statement from the introduction to anthropologist Michele Gamburd's book on Sri Lankan migrant workers and transnationalism:

Roughly the size of West Virginia, Sri Lanka, the island nation off the southern tip of India, is home to more than eighteen million people. . . . Rivalries between the Sinhala-speaking Buddhist majority and the Tamil-speaking Hindu and Muslim minorities have disrupted the course of post-colonial government, plunging the country into an armed conflict that has claimed tens of thousands of lives since 1983. In addition to the civil war in the North and East, two insurgencies in the South, the first in 1970–71 and the second in 1988–90, have further torn the fabric of national unity.[7]

What is problematic here is not just the attempt at making known (supposedly still unfamiliar) Sri Lanka in terms of the (familiar) geography of West Virginia. Rather, it is her explanation of violence in relation to the cultural-religious difference of the Sinhalese and the Tamils. Violence is the product of the conflict between the minority and the majority. Sinhala-Buddhists are the majority; Tamil-Hindus and Muslims, the minority. (What is even more dubious about Gamburd's explanation of the violence is that her ethnographic account stands almost totally detached from the politics of the country's prolonged war, in which ideas of minority and majority came to be fought out.) Put differently, a certain kind of transparent Sinhala-Buddhistness and Tamil-Hinduness, it is assumed, defines a priori the demarcation between majority and minority. The majority and the minority are opposed to each other in terms of language, religion, or ethnicity, and these things form the essence of difference between them. This essential difference between Sinhalas and Tamils, punctuated by two particular insurgencies, has "torn the fabric of national unity."

What emerges from this story is the significance of "unity" to the democratic, peaceful existence of a postcolonial nation. The achievement of this unity, however, remains virtually impossible, since the supposedly essential religious, ethnic, and linguistic differences between the majority and the minority always tend to stand in the way. Now what I want to suggest is that this is not simply a Gamburdian, Sri Lankanist anthropological problematic, but rather a Kantian, and more generally, western Enlightenment problematic. For instance, in one of his influential essays, "To Perpetual Peace," Kant saw such differences precisely as the cause of war both within and between nations. He claimed that "the desire of every nation (or its ruler) is to establish an enduring peace, hoping, if possible, to dominate the

entire world. But nature *wills* otherwise. She uses two means to prevent people from intermingling and to separate them, differences in
religion and *language,* which do indeed dispose men to mutual hatred and pretexts for war."[8] This judgment is based on Kant's understanding that "there is only a single *religion,* valid for all men in all
times. Those [faiths and books like the *Vedas, Koran,* and so on] can
thus be nothing more than accidental vehicles of religion and only
thereby be different in different times and places" (125). Seen from
this Gamburdian-Kantian viewpoint, the solution to this problem
would be for the *majority* to cultivate tolerance toward the *minority*
differences. This practice of tolerance, understood in terms of the recognition of existing differences, obviously privileges the idea of the
majority, and, by extension, the nation-state.

I want to complicate this story and, in so doing, recommend revis-
iting the notion of toleration. Critics like John Gray, Partha Chatterjee, and David Scott have already warned us, in distinct ways, of the
poverty of some aspects of this theory of toleration.[9] Tolerance itself
is not an entirely bad concept. Can we explore ways of constructing a
politics of tolerance that does not remain subject to the calculus of the
nation-state and its supposed majority/community? As we know, the
notion of tolerance inheres in a liberal conception of toleration that
Locke deemed essential to sustaining the unity of a civil society. The
problem with this Lockean concept of tolerance, however, is that it is
ironically predicated on a principle of exclusion, which becomes the
right of the magistrate/state: "No doctrines opposed or contrary to human society or to the good mores necessary for preserving civil society, are to be tolerated by the magistrate. But of these examples in any
church are rare: for no sect is wont to progress to such insanity that
it would teach doctrines for religion, which manifestly undermine
the foundations of society, and are indeed condemned by the judgement of all mankind."[10] In this view the magistrate and, by extension, the state become equated with the "judgement of all mankind."
Differences and disagreements (that is, in Locke's words, opinions of
whether polygamy, divorce, etc., are lawful or unlawful) can be en-
tertained and tolerated, so long as they do not result in "disturbance
of the state, or do not cause greater inconveniences than advantages
to the community."[11] The state is equivalent to the "community" insofar as the state safeguards the interests of the community. This
notion of community is clearly animated by a majoritarian principle

of exclusion, since the state determines, on behalf and for the sake of the community, who and what ought to be tolerated. So the state, then, stands for the "judgment of all mankind." It is easy to see that what Locke envisions is the cultivation of a state/community in which collective agreement and consensus make possible a world of peace free from "fraud and violence of one another" (135).

Here Locke, I think, comes close to Kant's notion of rational consensus. Kant, who believes that the "state of nature is one of war" and that "the state of peace must therefore be *established*," argues that "greater agreement regarding men's principles [should] lead to mutual understanding and peace" ("To Perpetual Peace," III, 125). This agreement, Kant goes on to show, must, if necessary, be constructed "with force." This is so because the goal of peace in civil society, as Kant foresees it, can be reached by

> only the will of the *all together* (the collective unity of combined wills). The solution to so difficult a task [achieving perpetual peace] requires that civil society become a whole. Implementing this state of right (in practice) can only begin with *force*, and this coercion will subsequently provide a basis for public right, because an additional unifying cause must be superimposed on the differences among each person's particular desires in order to transform them into a common will. (127–28)

One can, of course, think of others like Rousseau, who (though not necessarily considered a liberal) argued in the *Social Contract* in favor of this general will over that of the individual, claming that the general will produces "public utility" and, by extension, a civil society of peace.[12]

Thus the concepts of unity, public will, rational consensus, and community that the thinkers of liberalism and the Enlightenment thought so crucial to achieving civil society based on the "will of the *all together*" simply privilege the will of the sovereign (state) over that of the people. In so doing they preempt the space of disagreement. This is not because these thinkers assume that individual voices do not count. In fact, elsewhere Kant concurs with the proposition that "*whatever a people cannot decree for itself cannot be decreed for it by the legislator.*"[13] But there is a clever sleight of hand at work here. What Kant wants to do is to authorize the people to the extent of authorizing the legislator/ruler who can, in turn, dictate the terms of who and what can count as authoritative. (Kant sometimes uses words like *legislator, ruler, monarch,* and *government* interchangeably.) Kant, like Rousseau, thinks that the legislator/ruler knows best and cannot err because "in the idea of the original contract he actually has in hand an infallible standard [of right], one that is, indeed, *a priori.*" ("On the Proverb," 79). This is why he insists that "resistance to [the government] in word or deed should never be mustered" (83).

Kant goes so far as to suggest that even though people, who in every nation must practice "an *obedience* to coercive laws" (83), may possess the common will, they do not possess the right to protest against the ruler who represents the public will. As he puts it, "the people never have the right of coercion (neither in word nor in deed) over the nation's leader" (81). Even in saying this, Kant does not want to deny the "*equality* of subjects." The equality of subjects exists so long as subjects can coerce and protest against *each other.* However, the ruler is exempt from this coercion because "if he could be coerced, he would not be the nation's ruler" (73). Hence Kant's claim: "Only a ruler who is himself enlightened and has no dread of shadows, yet who likewise has a well-disciplined, numerous army to guarantee public peace, can say what no public may dare, namely: *Argue as much as you want and about what you want, but obey!*"[14] People can argue, if they do so within the confines of law, and the preferred outcome of public argument is not disagreement but agreement and unity ("On the Proverb," 77–78).

Secularism and the Authorization of Religion

In pointing to this obviously problematic liberal authorization of the nation-state as the final arbiter of the collective good, I want to stress that the public space of agreement and unity that this Kantian rhetoric labors to secure is one that is transparently "secular." The distinction is clear in the Kantian demarcation of the private sphere of church and the public sphere of the (rational) state. This is based on the idea that salvation is the business of the church and the public welfare the business of the state. Hence, as Locke puts it, church and state are separate just as heaven and earth are separate ("A Letter Concerning,"). It is in this secular space of the state that rational discussion and argument can take place without the intervention of the "dogmas of religion." This is why thinkers like Rousseau, for example, prefer "civil religion." For Rousseau, there can be "a purely civil profession of faith, the article of which it belongs to the sovereign to establish, not exactly as dogmas of religion, but as sentiments of sociability, without which it is impossible to be a good citizen or faithful subject" (*Social Contract*, 226). It is this civil religion embodying sentiments of sociability that should govern the lives of the citizens. This is so not because Rousseau wants to make some room available for "religion" within the secular sphere. Rather, Rousseau, in defining what counts as "civil religion," authorizes the sovereign to expel those who do not abide by civil laws from the state "not for being impious but for being unsociable, for being incapable of sincerely loving the laws and justice" (226).

What is significant to note here is that crucial to the imagination of this secular, civil sphere of law and justice is the *normalization* of an essential difference between religion and tolerance, which, by extension, is a distinction between intolerance and tolerance. For example, Rousseau contends that there can be no difference between "civil intolerance" and theological intolerance. They are, Rousseau tells us, "inseparable." Now this should not beguile us into thinking that Rousseau is claiming that practices of intolerance take place in both public and private spheres. On the contrary, from Rousseau's perspective, civil religion in a secular space can never create intolerance because it embodies "positive dogmas." Only a religion of "negative dogmas" can create intolerance because, as Rousseau says, all the negative dogmas amount to "just one" thing: "intolerance" (226). So part of my argument is that the modern, Enlightenment discourse of secularism (be it liberal or otherwise) has proven fundamental to the demarcation between what does and does not count as tolerance and intolerance. And this demarcation in turn has influenced the idea that the state, belonging to and representing the public sphere, is authorized to cultivate *neutrality* toward those beliefs, sentiments, and practices that it deems not secular. This is evident in Locke's statement that "every church is orthodox onto itself" ("A Letter Concerning," 34).

Neutrality, as we know, is not necessarily an apolitical attitude of indifference since to cultivate neutrality is itself to take a certain position. The issue for me is not, therefore, whether neutrality/tolerance is an impossible practice.[15] On the contrary, what I want to stress is that the Enlightenment doctrine of secularism that enabled the delimiting of a public sphere, in which tolerance and neutrality could be practiced, has been critical to a particular kind of authoritative definition of religion—that is, the demarcation of a line between what does and does not constitute the terms of *authentic religion*. So when Kant claims in *Perpetual Peace* that "differences . . . in religion dispose men to . . . war" and when Rousseau insists in the *Social Contract* that "there are no wars of religion" (220), they seek to produce a universal definition of authentic religion in a particular way.[16] (This does not imply that there are no substantive differences between Kant, Rousseau, and Locke; rather, the public sphere they seek to construct, however differently, is a secularized one in which an authoritative definition of religion becomes possible.)

Today neo-Kantian liberal critics like John Rawls, Chantal Mouffe, and Richard Rorty, who (perhaps unwittingly following Rawls) continue to instruct us in the virtues of secularism and tolerance, participate in such a universal definition of religion.[17] Rorty and Mouffe in particular seem to be unaware that the secularism, tolerance, and pluralism considered possible within a "de-divinized" state—to use Rorty's own word[18]—end up reproducing the very Enlightenment problematic of rational consensus and uniformity they strive to set aside. This is certainly the case with Mouffe, who, at times, emphasizes the affirmation of difference and "value-pluralism" as salient features of a democratic society but nonetheless falls prey to championing uncritically the separation of church and state and of civil and religious law. For example, she thinks, as we noted earlier, that such separations are "the basic achievements of the democratic revolution and they are what make the existence of pluralism possible. One cannot therefore call these distinctions into question in the name of pluralism." The logic of this argument is Rawlsian. For Rawls, the separation guarantees not only "the protection of secular culture" but that of "all religions" as well (166). This notion of secularism, because it seeks to secure for itself, a priori, a privileged purchase on what counts as religious or secular, clearly preempts the space of any competing criticism of it. It is this self-evident knowledge of the secular/religious boundary that authorizes the "secular" state to forestall or simply turn a deaf ear to "religious criticisms" as such. One thinks of famous statesmen like Thomas Jefferson, who argued that "the way to silence religious disputes is not to take notice of them."[19]

Pluralizing the Secular?

If we are to counter this privileged notion of secularism, we ought to abandon thinking of secularism as a site in which religion remains located in a traditional past from which a dedivinized modernity has liberated itself. If it is still possible, secularism, as Connolly argues, ought to be thought of more usefully as a particular kind of "political settlement rather than as an uncontestable dictate of public discourse itself." This is because the "the possibility of reworking that settlement under new conditions of being takes on new significance."[20] I think this is what Connolly means by pluralizing the secular. The task of pluralizing the secular, then, cannot be achieved by taking secularism (as Rorty does) to mean "anti-clericalism" in contrast to "atheism" (*Achieving Our Country*, 142n8). Nor can it be done by taking it to mean (as a post-Rawlsian like Gutmann does) the "nonreligious" distinct from the "public space." Gutmann contends that "the identification of secular with nonreligious also has the great advantage of not presupposing as a matter of definition that all secular reasons, by virtue of being secular, are more publicly acceptable, or accessible than all religious reasons."[21]

I am not persuaded by the logic of these arguments. I am not at all persuaded, in other words, that thinking of the secular as anticlericalism or as nonreligious can point us to a safe exit from the problem of definition. After all, to call something nonreligious is to rely on, if not to construct, a definition of what counts as religious. As I noted earlier, this problem of the universal definition of religion has been pivotal to the Enlightenment discourse of secularism. My worry about the disciplinary conception of religion that Gutmann appeals to is not so much that it reflects an Enlightenment understanding as that it is produced in advance of altering conjunctures of debates in which different and differing forms of definitions of religion emerge. Thus, Gutmann's version finds itself in competition with those shifting definitions instead of navigating through them to conceptualize their conditions of possibility as significant to the cultivation and affirmation of something other than an updated version of old secularism.

That is why I am also somewhat wary of recent efforts to make more room available for religion within democracies, which is the stated purpose of a recent collection, *Obligations of Citizenship and the Demands of Faith,* edited by Nancy Rosenblum; Amy Gutmann's essay is included in it.[22] The volume is admirable insofar as it seeks to scrutinize (but not abandon) the conventional distinction between church and state that critics such as Mouffe would rather leave unquestioned. But the volume's logic, "accommodation of religious faith in democracies," is guided by the problematic conception of religion discussed earlier. For instance, in her introduction to the volume, speaking of a "proliferation of faiths" in the West, Rosenblum writes: "In short, contemporary demands of faith deviate from the modest Christian duties Locke described: 'Charity, meekness, and toleration.' More and more they are removed from inward-looking matters of doctrine, worship, ritual, and authority. Ministries expand outward. Except for rare, genuinely closed and separatist groups, the idea that faith is relegated to the private lives of individuals . . . is plainly misleading" (12). On this view, a certain shift in religion from "inward" to "outward" is what demands of us the recognition that religion is no longer a matter of the private sphere and that it be allowed greater accommodation within democratic politics.

Insisting on such an idea of accommodation presupposes fitting religion into an already available mold of democracy, leaving it up to the state to determine whether it should take notice of, listen to, or discount what kinds of "religious" discourses, debates, and disputes, under what kinds of circumstances. It seems to me that this notion does not adequately address, much less solve, the Kantian and Jeffersonian problematic; it only perpetuates the disciplinary problem of seeking to canonize universal definitions of religion. I want to suggest that one way to exit from this problematic is to explore how particular debates *may* enable plural persons, discourses, and practices, standing within and speaking from their respective positions of secular/religious domains, to authorize themselves to come into central view and battle out questions of what constitutes religious identity, pluralism, and difference. This is not the same thing as saying, as Rorty argues, that the goal of democracy is to reach "a point where we treat *nothing* [even] as a quasi divinity, where we treat *everything*—our language, our conscience, our community—as a product of time and chance" (*Achieving Our Country*, 22). This is Rortian antifoundationalism, either at its best or its worst, and it cannot grapple adequately with the relation between the religious and the secular.

The point I want to underscore is not that distinctions like secular and religious and state and church be erased. Rather, the debates and disputes about what such distinctions should embody, how and in what kinds of ways they should to be drawn, take place in discursive spaces not determined by the available conceptions of the public and the private. Such debates can hold religious/secular distinctions in constitutive tension, never losing sight of their *political* formations, the "possibility" of their reformations, to the extent that the nation-state cannot afford to not take notice of certain claims because they represent "religion."

Religion, Public Debate, and the "Dustbin of History"

What I wish to do in the remainder of the chapter is to sketch briefly the conjuncture that produced such a tension between secular/ religious boundaries in relation to a particular dispute, that between monks and lay Buddhists in late-1990s Sri Lanka, and to demonstrate how the dispute may mark the aporetic limits of a certain postcolonial politics even as it labors to contest and "refashion" the minority/ majority distinction. The dispute that I have in mind, broadly put, centered around the emergence (and later dismantling) of a hegemonic discourse of *polgahima* (lit. "coconut breaking"). The discourse emerged in vituperative opposition to Mangala Samarweera, the minister of media in the People's Alliance (PA) government who said that that a controversial Sinhala nationalist document called the Interim Report should be put in the "dustbin of history." The report was released on September 17, 1997, by the Sinhala Commission.

The Sinhala Commission was set up about a year before by the National Joint Committee—representing about forty nonstate Sinhala commercial and Buddhist organizations—to inquire into and rectify the presumed injustices committed against the Sinhalas over the last two hundred years. It came into being in a context in which the People's Alliance government of Chandrika Bandaranaike (elected in 1994) had been undertaking new constitutional reforms in terms of what was called the devolution package. For almost two decades, punctuated by several unsuccessful cease-fire agreements, the LTTE (Liberation Tigers of Tamil Elam) has been fighting a war demanding a separate state (Elam) in the northern and eastern provinces, which they consider their "Traditional Homelands." Central to the devolution package was the issue of war. As the text of the draft constitutional provisions explained, "All Sri Lankans, irrespective of distinctions of race, religion, or social status have, for the last several years, suffered the debilitating effects of one fundamental problem. It is the ethnic crisis which has evolved into the war, which currently engulfs the North East. It has adversely affected every facet of Sri Lankan public life, seriously impairing every progressive move that we, as a nation, have striven to make" ("Draft Provisions of the Constitution"). The devolution package sought to redress Tamil grievances and devolve power, giving greater political autonomy to Tamil regions to end the war. The devolution of power, the government assured, would create a political space in which "all communities" could "express . . . [and] promote . . . their distinct identity," "enjoy their own culture," "profess and practice their own religion and nurture and promote their own language."

The Buddhist nationalists on the Sinhala Commission saw the constitutional reforms as an effort by a liberal, secular government to undermine the "unitary state" (mentioned in the 1972 constitution) and divide the country. (The draft provisions of the constitution proposed to define Sri Lanka as a "union of regions," abandoning the concept of the "unitary state.") The commission, consisting of a variety of elites from former supreme court judges to university professors, issued the Interim Report to call into question the terms of the constitutional reforms. The report sought to do so by refuting the LTTE's claims about how the Tamils have always suffered at the hands of the Sinhalese majority. It represented the Sinhalese as the victims of oppression produced by centuries of colonial rule and by the postcolonial politics of *accommodating* the (predominantly Tamil) "minority" at the expense of the "majority." Indeed, some of the Sinhala Commission's umbrella organizations, such as Veera Vidhana, overseen by successful middle- and upper-class business persons in Colombo, made no bones about their commitment to the promotion of Sinhalese commercial interests as a way of redressing the supposed threat of competing Tamil and Muslim businesses in the country.[23] Such commitments have been animated by narratives of how the Sinhala Self always did and will continue to come under attack by the non-Sinhala Others at various junctures in the history of the supposed "Sinhala" nation. We know that these narratives are not age-old timeless realities that constitute an essential Sinhalaness, as some nationalists would have us believe. Rather they are recent inventions, fashioned and refashioned, invested with and divested of varying meanings in differing colonial and postcolonial conjunctures.

The Interim Report sought to construct and normalize a set of such nationalist narratives. The issues of injustice toward the Sinhalas that it addressed were not injustices that happened in the past, but those that might in the future. The possibility of such injustices, the report claimed, loomed large in the face of the government's redrafting of the constitution to devolve power. Put in a nutshell, the report opposed the devolution package, claiming that it would "destroy the unitary character of Sri Lanka . . . preserved for over 2,500 years [and] . . . impoverish in particular the Sinhala people who are already in a disadvantaged section of the population despite their comprising three fourths of it" (2). More interesting, perhaps, was its claim that the package would have a devastating impact on Buddhism since "splitting the Sinhala majority areas" would divide the Buddhists, creating the "the real possibility of disputes arising between them" (28–29). Ironically, what gave the report the kind of national news exposure that it sought was less the pomp and fanfare that accompanied its release than the very disputes (it wanted to prevent from) emerging among Buddhists about its worth.

On September 25, 1997, Minister Magala Samaraweera, an ardent supporter of the devolution package, was quoted by newspapers as having said that the Interim Report should be put in the "dustbin of history" (*Island*, September 28, 1997). The minister charged that the report spelled disaster for all (non-nationalist) Sinhala Buddhists, since "its contents . . . will make people like Velupille Prabhakaran [the leader of the LTTE separatist war], arms dealers and Tamil racists happy. These people will now brand all Sinhalese alike [as chauvinists]." These remarks flashed across the front pages of Sinhala and English newspapers and were featured on the radio and television news for several weeks. The minister's dismissal of the report reflected the Chandrika Bandaranaike government's widely suspected distrust of the right-wing nationalist Buddhist monks and lay elite behind the Sinhala Commission as viable partners for a negotiated political solution to the war, which the government promised as part of its political campaign. The dismissal was also a clear departure from the religious policies of the late President Premadasa, who maintained close political ties with Buddhist monks. The Chandrika Bandaranaike government sometimes openly criticized Premadasa's highly publicized political alliances with pro-Sinhala monks and saw them as political henchmen. However, as we shall soon see, it built up its own loyal, pro-devolution monks who would eventually challenge the authority of the Sinhala Commission monks.

The Sinhala Commission monks saw themselves as the guardians of the nation. Nothing infuriated the Sinhala Commission and its monks more than Minister Samaraweera's calling into question the uniform majority-Sinhalaness they had labored to claim and normalize for Sri Lanka in the report. In particular, the commission's assumptions on the absence of disagreements among Buddhists suffered a painful blow. A reprisal seemed inevitable. The Sinhala Commission sent one of its most vocal monks, Maduluwawe Sobhita, to the fore of the debate to denounce and censure the minister's statement. A well-known Buddhist preacher and staunch defender of the Sinhala Buddhist "unitary state," Sobhita had campaigned tirelessly to derail the previous Jayewardene government's plans to give political autonomy to Tamil areas and end the war in the 1980s. On September 29, 1997, he held a press conference at the Abhayaramaya temple, which is overseen by one of his monk friends, Muruttewe Ananda, and has served as a center for many pro-Sinhala nationalist meetings in the past. The monk stated that that the minister's comments offended and disgraced the entire Sinhala race and all Buddhists. He demanded that the minister withdraw his statements about the report within seventy-two hours and make a public apology to the monks and the rest of the country. Sobhita also announced that ten thousand monks would soon gather at the Vihara Mahadevi Public Park in Colombo to protest and render visible the "entire" Sinhala community's opposition to the minister's comments about the report. Other esteemed monks, like Piyadassi of Vajiraramaya Temple, shared Sobhita's arrogance to speak for the "entire" Sinhala Buddhist community (Island, September 30, 1997). This arrogance was short-lived.

On October 1, 1997, about two thousand (not ten thousand) monks and some fifteen hundred lay people gathered at the public park to stage a satyagraha ("peaceful demonstration"), and I, having arrived in Sri Lanka a few days before, found myself amid the crowd. Sobhita and other monks, representing the National Sangha Council (a nationalist monastic organization founded in the late 1990s in alliance with the Sinhala Commission), sternly echoed the commission's previous denunciation of the minister's comments. The monks warned

that if the minister failed to withdraw them they would take the protest to his hometown, Matara, and would break one hundred thousand coconuts to coerce (balakaranava) him into doing so. This event
was followed with mudslinging by the Sinhala Commission protago-
nists against the character of the minister in numerous newspapers.
These warnings and threats did not produce the desired effect, the
minister's withdrawing his comments and apologizing to the monks.
Rather, they became instrumental in arousing a competing Sinhala
monastic and lay force seeking to contest the National Sangha Council's and the Sinhala Commission's representation of "Sinhala Buddhist identity." When several thousand monks and lay people of the
National Sangha Council and Sinhala Commission convened to protest, recite slokas ("imprecatory verses"), and break coconuts at the historic bo tree in Matara, countless voices were raised depicting this as
a practice that contravened Buddhism, thereby questioning the very
Buddhistness of the Sangha council's satyagraha. The act of breaking
coconuts, in particular, which was shown on television and in which
a handful of monks did take part, came under scrutiny.

What is crucial to note is that breaking coconuts is not an entirely
"un-Buddhist" practice. Indeed, lay Buddhists, too, break (husked) coconuts, hurling them onto a hard surface, sometimes in front of an
image of a Buddhist deity (deva), to mark auspicious occasions. Sometimes it is done to make or fulfill a vow (baraya) to a deity. In fact, the
practice takes place inside Buddhist temples where there are shrines
(devala) dedicated to particular Buddhist deities. But there are other
uses of this practice, as well: sometimes a coconut is broken at the
beginning of a long journey or pilgrimage; at other times it is done
at wedding ceremonies, near the feet of the wedded couple. These
uses suppose that breaking coconuts is a positive (Buddhist) act that
can safeguard one from the troubles, misfortunes, and dangers of the
"worldly" life. It should be noted, however, that though polgahima is
an acceptable lay Buddhist practice, Buddhist monks, so far as I am
aware, rarely take part in it, at least not in public; it is performed by
lay people or lay priests who officiate at shrines. Perhaps one reason
why monks do not take part in polgahima is that it is considered a
"worldly" ritual designed to produce material benefits, which monks
ideally must forsake.

Therefore, when the monks broke coconuts in this public space,
it came as a surprise to many. The forces of opposition—from

prominent university professors to monks, movie stars to journalists, newspaper editors to cartoonists—began to portray the monks' act as an "un-Buddhist" practice representing violence and separatism and sought to divest it of any previous Buddhist, positive connotations. They connected it with the Sinhala Commission monks' political position, that is, as they saw it, their defense of a racist document that fueled the war. They dubbed the monks "nutcrackers." One newspaper columnist reinterpreted the practice, stating that breaking coconuts is done maliciously, so that "the enemy concerned should literally go into pieces in the same manner the coconut goes into pieces when dashed on the stone." He also claimed that it violated the fundamental Buddhist doctrine of compassion (*Daily News*, October 10, 1997). Others questioned whether the monks involved in the act were really monks at all (*Daily News*, October 10, 1997). Mangala Samaraweera himself (backed by Buddhist monks and lay people who vociferously defended his right to disagree as a virtue of "Buddhist democracy") drew a direct relation between the "nutcrackers," violence, and terrorism. They claimed the nutcrackers were defending a document (the Interim Report) that impeded the country's effort to solve the separatist war and hence advocated violence. A slew of newspaper articles berating the Sangha Council monks portrayed them not only as nutcrackers but also as "blood-thirsty," "hate-mongering," "treacherous" separatists and racists (*jativadiyo*) who advocated war and hindered the peace process (*Divayina*, October 5, 1997; *Daily News*, October 6, 1997).[24]

Perhaps the fiercest opposition to the National Sangha Council and the Sinhala Commission became centrally visible when a group of monks called the All Lanka Bhikkhu Organization held its own massive counterrally, protesting their hubris in speaking for Buddhism and the Sinhalese. This organization, formed in the immediate wake of the nutcracker debate in 1997, sought to rally an anti-Sinhala nationalist monastic force to contest the claims of the Sinhala Commission and its monks. Needless to say, this organization, which fully endorsed the devolution package, was supportive of the Chandrika Bandaranaike government. (Some founding members of the organization, like the late Atureliye Indaratana, also worked as advisers to the government's Ministry of Buddhist Affairs. Other monks who were members of the All Lanka Bhikkhu Organization were well-known supporters of the state; they included Kamburugamuwe

Vajira, the head of the government's Buddhist and Pali University and a presidential appointee, and Watinapaha Somananda, an adviser to the president.) These monks picked the same place, Vihara Mahadevi Park, as their public venue for the showdown. An estimated five thousand monks were in attendance. Speaking in three languages, Sinhala, Tamil, and English—itself an attempt to mock the monolingualism that governs nationalist discourse—these monks castigated the Interim Report and its defenders, asserting that the latter did not "represent views of the majority of the people" (*Island*, October 7, 1997) and charging that it was unethical for Buddhist monks to speak of "one race" (*Daily News*, October 7, 1997).

One notable feature of the rally was the donation of two truckloads of coconuts and woven fronds to North East families who had been rendered homeless by the war. This act was surely an explicit attack on their opponents' breaking coconuts in Matara. The contrast drawn here was not simply one between breaking (*polgahima*) coconuts and donating (*polbedima*) them. It reflected a more general ethical-political distinction between Buddhism and violence and between separatism and peace, suggesting that Buddhist monks do not and must not stand for war and racism (*jativadiya*). In addition, All Lanka Bhikkhu assailed the Sangha Council with seven specific questions, demanding to know why they had not broken coconuts during the slaughter of monks and citizens and other atrocities in the eighties and nineties (this is a reference to a bloody battle between the Marxist youth movement People's Liberation Front [JVP] and the Premadasa government in the late 1980s; the government's paramilitary forces had crushed the JVP, killing thousands of its members). Thus, in the wake of these seemingly insurmountable questions about their Buddhist identity, the National Sangha Council and Sinhala Commission found themselves in the predicament of having to defend the Buddhistness of breaking coconuts instead of defending the Interim Report.

The debate raged on in the letters columns of the newspapers, with people taking varying stands on the issue. Then, on October 15, 1997, a massive truck bomb exploded in the parking lot of the five-star Galadari Hotel in Colombo, killing several dozen people and devastating the building and nearby hotels and businesses. The bombing did not end the debate, but it began to divert the nation's focus toward matters of national security. Some charged that the bombing was the work of the LTTE, which intended to disrupt a critical process of disagreement and dissent among Sinhala Buddhists. However, the LTTE must have found such disagreements detrimental to its own separatist, racist campaign, aimed at constructing a monolithic Sinhala Self to stand against the Tamil Other.

Surely, this debate generated questions about what counts as Sinhala-Buddhist identity and who can speak authoritatively about it. But, apart from the significant divergence of narratives, how might we think about this debate, as far as presenting a moment in which identity was demanded to be both *for* and *against* itself? What does it say about the formation of the relationship between the secular/religious, identity/difference boundaries? How can we navigate through such boundaries? Can they be conceived as making possible a critical space of pluralism and difference (one that neither the state nor other monolithic nonstate organizations—like the National Sangha Council or even the All Lanka Bhikkhu Organization—can dictate), despite the fact that such pluralism is ultimately inadequate? The questions are all interrelated, and I hope that the way I have read this debate has already shed light on them. But let me, by way of alluding to the limitations of the kind of politics the debate produced, make some remarks that address these questions.

The government of Chandrika Bandaranaike found All Lanka Bhikkhu Ogranization's opposition to the Sinhala Commission more than congenial to its political agenda, to say the least; this was evident in the way the state newspaper jockeyed to represent its satyagraha as a monumental "Buddhist" event, as opposed to the National Sangha Council's "unBuddhist" nutcracking (*Daily News,* October 8). In fact, there were widespread rumors that anti–Sangha Council posters carrying the question "Buddhagama or Yuddhagama?" (Religion of Buddhism or Religion of War?), which appeared throughout the city of Colombo, were the work of the government (*Divayina,* October 9). Indeed, in an interview at the outset of the debate responding to the monks' demands that he withdraw his statements, Minister Samaraweera himself declared that he belonged "not to the religion of war, but to the religion of Buddhism" (*Divayina,* October 5). Rival nonstate newspapers like the *Island* clearly favored the Sangha Council position and decried the state's support for the opposition. Calling the anti–Sangha Council allies "nutty anti-nut crackers," an editorial in the *Island* opined:

The sudden desire for the renaissance [of] pristine Buddhism in government propaganda organs, we hope, will continue long after the confrontation between Mr. Samaratunga and the Mahasangha [monks] is over. Since the PA government itself speaks of secularism, we recommend that they . . . stop using the members of clergy of all religions for political purposes . . . for the sake of principled politics. (October 9)

If these statements are any indication of the state's support for the anti–Sangha Council force, that "support" marks an attempt on the part of the state to "rework" the secular/religious relationship. What we see in this attempt is a "secular" postcolonial government finding a particular "religious" ally with whom to stand and defend its proposal to enable peace. Put in more general terms, this debate is an example of a state's being unable to take notice of "religious" disputes and differences (as Jefferson, Kant, or Rawls would have preferred) but finding itself *obliged* to listen to competing religious viewpoints and, indeed, take sides. The state's taking sides with the All Lanka Bhikkhu Organization in this matter reminds us that it did not, and could not, cultivate the kind of religious neutrality on which the liberal tradition places a high premium.

In making possible an attempt to rework the secular/religious boundary, the significance of the debate lies not simply in the state's "recognition" of a competing group as "religious" and siding with it. In my reading of it, the debate constitutes a particular "public" battle that one could not (as Amy Gutmann would have preferred) enter armed with a priori conceptions of what counts as religion and combat any opposing views. Rather, the questions that were asked about religion, and the answers that were provided, were produced by the circumstances of the debate. In other words, the state's recognition of the All Lanka Bhikkhu Organization as a specifically "Buddhist" force battling the nutcracking, "un-Buddhist" Sangha Council did not emerge in advance of, but was made possible by, the terms of the debate. However, if the state had insisted upon defending the conventional boundary between secular and religious, public and private (as Rorty would have recommended), it would have simply dismissed the critical opposition and difference of the All Lanka Bhikkhu Organization as a religious dispute that deserved no "political" investment.

(After all, the major architects of this debate were speaking not as secular figures but as contending Buddhist spokespersons, including the minister himself.) The kind of ethos of recognition cultivated by the state in this debate may be important to rethinking the relationship between religion and the public space. Renewed theories of the "accommodation of religion within democracies," grounded as they are in the assumptions about religion mentioned earlier, cannot critically attend to this task. However, the politics of recognition that the secular state can cultivate toward "religion" is not contingent upon already available parameters of democracy; rather, the situation is one in which democracy begins to meet the challenge of disputes about the very demarcation between the religious and the secular. Democracy can ill afford to leave these disputes to religious technicians.

Politics of Agonism and Limits of Fugitive Politics

Can we think of the dispute in Sri Lanka as constituting a moment of the political in which identity is obliged to be both for and against itself? Is the moment of agonism (or what some call agonistic democracy) that was made possible by the debate a moment of the political? According to Michel Foucault, a moment of agonism can be a moment of freedom. Writing about power, subject, and freedom in the early 1980s, Foucault argued, "Rather than speaking of an essential antagonism, it is better to speak of 'agonism'—of a relationship that is at the same time mutual incitement and struggle; less of face-to-face confrontation that paralyzes both sides than a permanent provocation."[25] As we know now, Foucault is alluding here to his reformulated "productive conception" of power/discourse, which does not simply dominate, constrain, and negate but produces, enables, and authorizes individuals to break away from, to undermine, particular modes of power-domination and to practice different forms of freedom ("Subject and Power," 342).

This is why Foucault thinks that we should not understand power and freedom as mutually opposed to each other and should not assume that power simply gets exercised where freedom does not exist. Power and freedom should be recognized rather as existing in "a much more complicated" relationship in which freedom may make possible the very exercise of power (342). By such a power relationship, then, Foucault means "individual or collective subjects who are faced with a field of possibilities in which several kinds of conduct, several ways reacting and modes of behavior are available (ibid)." Needless to say, such a relationship is hardly like slavery. There can be a power relationship not "when a man is in chains" but "only when he has some possible mobility, even a chance of escape" (ibid). Alternatively, he argues that

> to say that there cannot be a society without power relations is not to say either that those which are established are necessary, or that power in any event, constitutes an inescapable fatality at the heart of societies such that it cannot be undermined. Instead, I would say analysis, elaboration, and bringing into question of power relations and the "agonism" between power relations and the intransitivity of freedom is an increasingly political task—even, the political task that is inherent in all social existence. (343)

This conception of power/discourse is evident in the final Foucauldian attempts at understanding forms of fashioning the self in relation to oneself. For Foucault, such a fashioning enables "the ethic of care for the self," as outlined in the third volume of *The History of Sexuality*.

This caring for the self (far from the Cartesian notion of the self or, for that matter, John Stuart Mill's preoccupation with the freedom and liberty of the individual)[26] involves one's forming, changing, and modifying oneself to attain "a state of perfection, of happiness, of purity" and so forth.[27] This care does not privilege one's self over others, the self's domination over others.[28] Caring for the self is "the development of an art of existence that revolves around the question of the self, of its dependence and independence, of its universal form and of the connection it can and should establish with others, of the procedures by which it exerts its control over itself, and of the way in which it can establish a complete supremacy over itself."[29] (This "question of the self," as Butler might say, is for Foucault one "responsible" way to give an account of oneself.) So in this process, Foucault would say, the other is never lost sight of because the fashioning and refashioning of the self, giving a critical account of oneself, becomes possible in relation to the other. Or, as Martin Heidegger wrote, "'The others,' whom one designates as such in order to cover over one's own essential belonging to them, are those who *are there* initially and for the most part in everyday being-with-one-another." [30] Therefore, folding Heidegger into Foucault, as it were, one could argue that an ethic of care for the self has to be an ethic of care for the other.

The cultivation of such an ethic of care for the self/other, identity/difference *perhaps* became possible because of the demand of the debate. The Sinhala Commission and the National Sangha Council sought to authorize a certain kind of nationalist Buddhist Self/Identity (distinct from Tamil and Muslim Others), laboring to arrogate to itself a space in which it alone and no "others" could make claims about it. These claims, of course, operated in a conjuncture—a field of power, if you will—that enabled them to be undermined by the rival claims of the All Lanka Bhikkhu Organization. To make the rival claims and arguments it did, that organization did not arrive in the field of the debate as an unrecognizable difference/other insofar as it represented itself as Buddhist. However, the Buddhistness of this opposition appeared differently in that its *claims* about what counts as Buddhism clearly differed from those of the Sinhala Commission and the Sangha Council. The opposition demanded representing and caring for a particular kind of Buddhist self, perhaps "(an)other Buddhist self," if there can ever be such a way of being. This provocation of caring for a differently argued and differently authorized "(an)other Buddhist self" is the moment of identity's being both for and against itself. Surely, Foucault would argue that caring for this kind of (an)other Buddhist self may open up to non-Sinhala-Buddhist Muslim or Tamil "Others" new ways of cultivating new relationships, recognizing, as Heidegger says, that the "'other' being itself has the kind of being of Da-sein" (117). Such care for the self, then, is a way of "being a self and being with others" (37). This is, of course, granted that, as Nietzsche would have put it, the self, that is, any political-moral conception of a self, does not "negate and deny [itself] something" and does not "strive with open eyes for [its] own impoverishment." [31] Hence the demand of the debate for such a self was, by extension, to devalidate it, to deauthorize it, to tame it, and perhaps to weaken and even to neutralize it. However imperfect such a demand may appear to us, it is still important to thinking against our normalized present of pluralism, tolerance, and democracy.

Thus the conception of the political that emerged in the context of the debate is both important and limiting. To be sure, the debate does help us understand flaws in the theories of secularism. Secularism, accompanied by notions of pluralism, unity, neutrality, and peace, and formulated and reformulated by figures ranging from Kant and Rousseau to Rorty and Mouffe, does not help us understand, let alone appreciate, the important intervention of religion/religious figures in the debate. One crucial point I want to make is that, if we are armed with a strict understanding of the secular and the religious, we cannot understand the competing narratives that produced this debate. Secularism, however variously defined and redefined, offers precisely such a limited understanding of the religious and the secular. What we need, then, is not merely an updated version of secularism trumpeting the importance of cultivating more tolerance and pluralism to peaceful democratic existence. We need rather to realize that the demarcation between the religious and the secular is contingent and fleeting. Once we recognize this, we may begin to oppose (often deadly) nationalisms that insist on an unchanging relation between religion, nation, and identity and to affirm other non-nationalist, non-hegemonic practices of being and freedom. By demonstrating how the dispute in Sri Lanka produced a provocation for identity to be both for and against itself, I have wanted to affirm the possibility of such a non-nationalist conception of identity. Current theories of secularism can gain much by paying attention to such debates not for their empirical value but for their relevance to the question of democracy.

That said, however, the above debate does not fully resolve the problem of the secular state and its inability to attend to the question of otherness. Surely the debate marks a critical moment in which "religion" intervened within public space and spoke to the questions of otherness in a way that the liberal-secular state could not have even attempted. Yet, at the same time, the debate demonstrates that the questions of otherness it addressed remain within the confines of history. That is to say, even as the major non-nationalist religious figures sought to counteract the nationalist hegemony of religious zealots, they did so within the domain of history in which a conception of identity (in terms of what constitutes a pristine Buddhism of peace), however radical or fugitive it may be, still remains. The debate's demand for a fugitive identity that flees from a certain nationalist conception of itself still remains tied to history. If that is so, can this moment of identity for and against itself really be fugitive at all? Can a fugitive identity really flee history, its attachment to history, to its name (*Buddhism*), resisting the gravitational pull of its self-sovereignty? Or can a fugitive identity be really fugitive? Does the fugitive identity, which can never really flee very far, not constitute an aporia in itself? The fugitive identity is already deconstructed, if you will; it shows its own limit, its bondage to history, its inability to flee very far, being bounded and haunted by the history of its name (*Buddhism*), which is its own irreducible contradiction. The fugitive identity cannot be deconstructed any more; it cannot be more fugitive. Perhaps the debate's provocation for identity to be both for and against itself constitutes a demand for an "impossibility": to be a self and to be a different self at the same time. Can one be (a Buddhist or any other) self and still be a different self? Can one have one without the other, trying to neutralize one predicate by another? Can one still retain the name/identity (*Buddhist*) without all its history behind it? Can such a politics of identity define our new political futures? In that respect, then, did the debate really produce anything new?

We cannot and should not dismiss the importance of this debate simply because of its reliance upon a category of history. The debate has too many important "worldly" implications for democratic governance in a postcolonial country such as Sri Lanka, where the Sinhalese and LTTE nationalists relentlessly pursue their own fascist agendas by seeking to produce notions of hegemonic selves opposed to each other. The fact that the debate "deconstructed," at least momentarily, the meaning of coconut cracking and represented it as a symbol of violence says something of the possibility of a public debate's producing at least a demand for thinking publicly about the question of otherness. Thus, if anything, the debate's provocation to be an(other) Buddhist self shows not so much its own failure to produce an entirely satisfying alternative to the problem of postcolonial religious/ethnic difference as it shows the aporias of the political spaces within which postcolonial questions about difference are thought. But, given our discussion of the problem of history in these chapters, we cannot remain content with the agonistic moment of this debate. Let me hasten to repeat myself: the debate constitutes, in my view, an unprecedented attempt at rendering problematic the state-monopolized politics of secularism as the sole arbiter of justice and rights vis-à-vis minorities. To that extent, the debate proves wrong secularist thinkers like Mouffe and Rorty who never tire of arguing against religious involvement in public thinking about the questions of justice and otherness and its possible effect on state policies concerning minority rights. However, the agonistic moment that the debate generated might still leave the specter of Derrida, always in-visible in the background, looking askance, hardly content. Derrida might complain that it is all fine and good for Heidegger and Foucault to claim how the *others* come first and that the same care for the self ought to be cultivated for the other. "Yet," Derrida might ask us, "does this thinking not begin with a profoundly problematic presumption about the innate political-moral difference between self and other?" "Might there be another way of thinking about postcolonial difference, one that does not remain reducible to the logic of history, one that does not inscribe the logic of the binary itself?" "Would such a way of thinking about otherness produce an unheard-of concept of 'justice' itself?" These are precisely the kinds of questions I seek to grapple with in the next chapter. I will demonstrate that, to get at some of these questions, we have to conceive a pathway of actively forgetting history that sees time as being out of joint with itself. This is one important way of un-inheriting the distinction of majority/minority that remains so crucial to the idea of democracy.

Time is out of Joint.   —William Shakespeare, Hamlet

I can find nothing more remarkable in the present day humanity than its distinctive virtue and disease which goes by the name of "the historical sense."
          —Friedrich Nietzsche, The Gay Science

There could be no happiness, no serenity, no hope, no pride, no present, without forgetfulness.   —Friedrich Nietzsche, On the Genealogy of Morals

Humans from any other period or region . . . are always in some sense our contemporaries.   —Dipesh Chakrabarty, Provincializing Europe

What is a specter? What is its history and what is its time?
          —Jacques Derrida, Specters of Marx

6   Active Forgetting of History, the "Im-possibility" of Justice

Can we in the same sentence, in the same breath if you wish, think "nonjuridical" justice and its possibility? Is there such a thing as "nonjuridical" justice at all? Can the juridical really ever be nonjuridical? Or, more simply put, can justice be anything other than justice? Can justice ever be separated from the juridical, from the aporia of law? If this sounds like an im-possibility (as Derrida writes the term), I want to suggest that thinking (about) that im-possibility may help us gain a new purchase on not only the concept of justice but also the concept of history, because any thinking of the im-possibility of justice will have to do with thinking of (the im-possibility of) justice irreducible to history itself.

By now both the importance and the im-possibility of "thinking justice" (as Derrida calls it) that cannot be reduced to the confines of history must be obvious. Importance, because any conceptualization of justice, any thinking of ethics, any imagining of the future of the political that remains reducible to history always runs the risk of producing the aporia of humanism, law, and responsibility. In other words, the category of the human or humanism is not an apolitical concept, with no relation to law and its juridical apparatus. So any thinking of human or humanist relations within history cannot easily avoid the aporia of law. That is to say, so long as we think of the question of otherness reducible to history, we get nothing but the distinction between self and other. History/law/humanism cannot ever do away with that distinction. Any thinking of otherness within the parameters of history cannot do anything other than seek to *improve* the relations between self and other, Sinhala and Tamil, Hindu and Muslim, majority and minority. (That is why we must not be satisfied with Levinas's proposition, "relation to others—that is to say justice."[1] Even though Levinas argues that "justice consists in recognizing in the Other my master," he is still thinking about the other in *relation* to self.[2] So long as we think of justice in terms of such a binary, we can have only a politics of improving relations between other and self. Such a politics cannot and should not be an option for us today.) Even in the unprecedented public debate discussed in the previous chapter, we see how our postcolonial present still runs short of producing a politics that abandons the distinction between self and other, because its politics remain tied to history. If anything, such a debate clearly shows that the aporetic present we inhabit makes it almost im-possible to think about justice without recourse to history/law/humanism. The questions that interest me here are these: how might we think about this im-possibility of justice irreducible to law and history? Once it is irreducible to history/law, would justice ever look like justice? Would we still recognize it as justice? Would we still call it by the name *justice*?

My contention is that thinking of this im-possibility itself might produce an irreducible concept of the political. Now, in my view, today there is no more provocative thinker than Derrida with whom to think about this im-possibility (of justice). As we know now, for Derrida, *im-possibility* is a way to set aside the conventional distinction between the possible and the impossible and, by extension, the distinction between the present and the absent. As in the case of his conceptualization of *différance*, which cannot be reduced to the notion of presence or absence,[3] im-possibility cannot be reduced to possibility or impossibility. To Derrida, "always, im-possibility—the possible as impossible—is linked to an irreducible divisibility that affects the very essence of the possible."[4] To put it in somewhat plain terms, and always at the risk of doing some violence to Derrida, we might say that the possibility of any politics and any justice has to be thought in terms of the im-possible. This is why Derrida at times speaks of the "possible im-possible" (80). Put even more plainly, thinking of the im-possible has something to do with thinking of the future itself. Such an im-possible future cannot be separated from *perhaps* and *chance,* as we shall see in chapter 7. Yet thinking of the future by way of the "im-possible" is not to dream of utopia. Derrida writes:

> Utopia has critical powers that we should probably never give up on, especially when we make it a reason for resisting all alibis and all "realistic" or "pragmatic" cop-outs, but all the same I'm wary of the word. There are some contexts in which *utopia,* the word at any rate, can be too easily associated with dreams, or demobilization, or an impossible that is more of an urge to give up than an urge to action. The "impossible" I often speak of is not the utopian. Rather, it gives their very movement to desire, action, and decision: it is the very figure of the real: it has its hardness, closeness, and urgency.[5]

Here is a formidable challenge to take up, that is, to think of the im-possible in the sense of "hardness," "closeness," and "urgency." Yet the hardness and urgency of the im-possible cannot be viewed in terms of familiar notions like realistic or pragmatic, which often define our contemporary democratic senses of justice, fairness, and rights. Broadly put, we could say that for a pragmatist or realist, justice is possible precisely because it always remains under the sign of presence, that is, under the sign of law. In that sense, *justice can be done* either by contesting an old (oppressive law) or by inventing a new law. Here, justice exists in relation to law, its presence and its possibility. Be it the Rortyan or the Rawlsian kind, a pragmatic or realistic view equates justice/law with presence and possibility. Justice is possible because law is present, present in the sense that old laws can be improved or contested *in the name of justice.* It is the very presence of the idea/name of law/justice that makes the improvement or contestation of "laws" possible. Derrida, of course, does not dispute the importance of such a view of justice. Indeed, he says that "effective responsibility for an engagement ought to consist in doing everything to transform the existing state of law . . . and of inventing new laws, even if they always remain inadequate for what I call justice (which is not the same thing as law, even if it has to guide the history and progress of law" (124). This is why Derrida says that "laws" can (and must) be deconstructed. But he warns that we must not delude ourselves that deconstruction of laws can really eliminate the aporia of justice/law. Unlike laws, Derrida insists, justice/law cannot be deconstructed.

> On the one hand, you have the law which is deconstructible; that is, the set of legislations, the set of positive laws which are in constant transformation. They are deconstructible because we change them, we improve them, we want to improve them, we can improve them. For instance, the Declaration of the Rights of Man has been improved for the last two centuries, there have been a series of declarations which have added new rights for the workers, for women and so on and so forth. So we can improve the law, the legal system, and to improve means to deconstruct. *It is to criticize a previous state of the law and to change it into a better one.* That is why the law is deconstructible. On the other hand, *justice, in the name of which one deconstructs the law, is not deconstructible.* So you have two heterogeneous concepts, if you want, two heterogeneous ends, the law and justice.[6] (emphasis added)

Laws may be criticized, deconstructed, and improved. We can criticize and improve the legal system. We can do that "in the name of [justice]." But justice itself cannot be deconstructed. It cannot be criticized and improved. One may, of course criticize it, but one cannot improve it, except for improving a law in the name of justice. In other words, one cannot change justice into a "better" one in the same way one can change a law into a better one. (We know the various ways in which the adjective *better* is being politically prostituted these days. Much of the platform of the 2004 democratic presidential campaign rested on the slogan "we can do better.") This is the reason, as I have already noted earlier, that the notion of critique is insufficient to thinking the aporia of our political sovereignty, which is also the aporia of justice/law. The aporia of justice cannot be deconstructed. And it cannot be problematized (anymore). It has to be thought differently. It has to be thought as the "im-possible."

But how does one really think the "im-possible"? Here Derrida, unlike any other thinker, offers a truly original way of thinking the aporia of justice. For Derrida, the im-possible has to be viewed as that which is deferred (*différance*). It has to be thought in terms of the syntagma *to come*. Here we must not misunderstand Derrida. We must not assume that by this phrase "to come," Derrida is thinking of a "better" kind of justice that remains to come in the future. Nor should we rush to associate "to come" with some religious idea with strict messianic connotations. Rather, by "to come," Derrida is pointing to the very notion of the promise that is inscribed within the idea of justice. As I have already noted, a promise remains deferred, to be fulfilled, and hence to come. The undeconstructible justice has to be seen precisely in this sense of "to come." What is so important about seeing justice this way is that it undercuts the conventional distinction between presence and absence. Justice that remains deferred cannot be understood in terms of either presence or absence. To put it in rather crass terms, the virtue of seeing the aporia of justice this way is that we will not be deluded by a justice that always has the luxury of escaping us, escaping our grasp, our apprehension, our demands. Justice always escapes us because justice remains deferred. It can elude us, it remains deferred, precisely because it is a promise. This capacity of justice to escape us is its own "auto-immunity," its own way of safeguarding it from apprehension, from making it be present, from making it be present right here and now, all the time. Yet, for Derrida, justice is never really present.[7] That is why, as we shall see, Derrida argues that even when justice is present, it is never really *there*. Thus to speak of justice is to speak of an im-possibility. To want to have justice is to aspire to having something that is deferred. This justice that is deferred does not remain under a sign of presence. Yet it is not absent either. It remains deferred. In this sense, it can be understood only in terms of "to come." In "Force of Law," speaking of justice and its relation to law—by law, he means the general idea of law itself, rather than a particular set of laws—he explains how this idea of "to come" that escapes us is inscribed within justice/law itself.

> The foundation of law remains suspended in the void or over the abyss, suspended by a pure performative act, that would not have to answer to or before any one. The supposed subject of this pure performative would no longer be before the law, or rather he would be before a law still undetermined, before the law as before a law is still nonexisting, a law still ahead, still having to and yet to come. And being "before the law" that Kafka talks about resembles this situation, both originary and terrible, of the man who cannot

manage to see or above all to touch, to catch up with the law. . . .
One "touches" here without touching on this extraordinary paradox: the inaccessible transcendence of the law, before which and
prior to which "man" stands fast, only appears indefinitely transcendent and thus theological to the extent that, nearest to him, it
depends only on him, on the performative act by which he insti-
tutes it: the law is transcendent, violent and nonviolent, because it
depends only on who is before it (so prior to it), on who produces it,
founds it, authorizes it in an absolute performative whose presence
always escapes him. The law is transcendent and theological, and
so always to come, and always promised, because it is immanent,
finite, and thus already past. Every "subject" is caught up in this
aporetic structure in advance. Only the "to come" will produce the
intelligibility or interpretability of this law.[8]

Note here the importance of the "extraordinary paradox" of law: its
"inaccessible transcendence." The law escapes and transcends; its
presence is inaccessible. Yet one can almost touch without touching
the law that we can never "catch up with." The point here is that even
though law is transcendent and inaccessible, its presence escaping, it
is hardly nonexistent or absent. It is present, yet inaccessible. It is precisely because of its inaccessible presence/transcendence, which is its
"aporetic structure," that only the "to come" can make any intelligibility of it. Hence thinking of justice in terms of "to come" is not an attempt to let justice have its own way, so to speak, to let justice remain
simply deferred. Rather, it is an attempt to think against the power of
justice/law having the luxury of always remaining "to come."

My point here is that to live in a democratic system or government of justice/law is to live within a domain of an im-possibility. If
that im-possibility can be thought only in terms of "to come," then
we *may* think the im-possibility of justice *without* law. And doing
so is precisely what I set out to do in this chapter. I want to think
of an instance of "nonjuridical justice"—to call it so for the sake of
clarity—that can help us imagine new political futures. My argument
is that if we are to think about the futures of such nonjuridical justice,
which is irreducible not only to law but also to distinctions like that
between self and other, majority and minority, we must meditate on a
Nietzschean suggestion for the "active forgetfulness" of history. Such

an active forgetting of history has to be accompanied by a conceptualization of our present as being "out of joint" with itself. To succeed in this task, we need not only Nietzsche but also Derrida, whose reading (in *Specters of Marx*) of Hamlet's cry "Time is out of Joint" produces an unheard-of idea: the present that is non-contemporaneous with itself. This is a concept of the present that is haunted by the figure of the Ghost.[9] The haunting of the ghost, or *hauntology*—a term Derrida coined to oppose the word *ontology*—does not mean either presence or absence (10). The notion of a non-contemporaneous present, one haunted by ghosts, is fundamentally critical to thinking about nonjuridical futures. The idea of a non-contemporaneous present makes it difficult to either abandon the past or remain merely bound to it. Hence active forgetting of history is not a way of abandoning our pasts; we cannot easily abandon our pasts, because all our pasts, as Chakrabarty put it so memorably, are in some ways all our contemporaries (see chapter 4). Rather, the active forgetting of history is a way of thinking about (and mourning) the past's relation to the present and the future in such a way that the past (and history) cannot really determine the futures. Yet those futures are haunted by the ghosts of the pasts.

One of my contentions in this chapter is that this way of understanding history/time offers a conception of otherness that cannot be defined in terms of the available distinctions of self/other, majority/minority. Thus, through reading a particular "event" or "date" in the history of the bloody conflict between the LTTE and the Sri Lankan state, I want to imagine the im-possibility of a "political" space in relation to a certain active forgetting of history. To belong within *and* constitute this space, one cannot be just either *Sinhalese* or *Tamil*. The very moment of active forgetting of history is a moment of un-inheriting a certain pregiven way of "being" (Sinhalese or Tamil). The space of active forgetting I have in mind is not an obliteration of the past and its history; instead, it is a space haunted by the very past that one actively forgets. Imagining such spaces can have a powerful impact on how we think about the future of a democracy that cannot continue to depend on the juridical practice of counting individual singularities in terms of majority/minority, self/other, Sinhalese/Tamil oppositions. In other words, such spaces of active forgetting are critical to thinking about the very question of peace, which cannot be reduced to a politics of settlement of bloody conflicts between communities of moral-political distinctions by way of a peace treaty or a constitutional amendment or a "law."

History After "But So What?"

To think of a space of the active forgetfulness of history, I want to turn to the anthropologist David Scott's recent intervention in a postcolonial intellectual debate about the problems and dangers of appealing to history in modern Sri Lanka. Indeed, my initial attempt at thinking about the aporia of secularism, law, and history, which I discussed in chapter 2, was inspired by Scott's intervening to reshape the direction of the historicist debate about nationalism, the past, and identity in Sri Lanka. Since, as I see it, the problem of secularism's reliance on law and history can be rethought (if not abandoned) by relinquishing secularist claims to history, thinking with and through Scott's call for "dehistorizing history" is both necessary and critical. Even more important, meditating on the question of history in relation to the contemporary concerns of Sri Lanka can, I think, help us see how the ostensibly western debate about religion, history, law, justice, and democracy can find an unconventional partner in thinking the problem of democracy in a postcolonial society. This is important at a time when nonwestern societies are often financially and politically parleyed with and palavered by the powerful western nations into becoming partners not in thinking the question of democracy but in helping to combat the troubling menace of terrorism. The West is often thought to be democracy's (and its contemporary political theory's) center of gravity. That is why the "area" of South Asia in particular is often left to the caprices of scholars of religious studies, history, anthropology, and even postcolonial studies to be historicized and anthropologized as a place of myth, ritual, religion, and, more recently, nationalist politics, violence, and colonial legacy—without their ever bothering to *think* the question of the political.[10] The way I approach Scott's intervention in the debate about history and identity in Sri Lanka will, I hope, undercut, if not render irrelevant, this sort of area studies that remains cosseted within the garrisons of our liberal disciplines.

The debate that Scott details is between two prominent scholars of ancient and medieval Sri Lankan history, R. L. H. Gunawardana and K. N. O. Dharmadasa. Trained in England and Australia respectively, today both scholars hold academic positions at the prestigious Peradeniya University in Sri Lanka. The debate between them is well-known among intellectuals in Sri Lanka and Sri Lankanist scholars in the West. I think it safe to say that, although the works of the two historians are often cited in the bibliographies of numerous academic works, on the whole, Sri Lankanist scholars in the West remain deeply suspicious of, if not down right hostile to, the politics of Dharmadasa's historiography and regard him as a historian of a certain nationalist leaning who defends, more or less explicitly, the ideological norms of Sinhala Buddhist chauvinism. Gunawardana, however, is esteemed as a liberal historian with certain commitments to the politics of the left. Now it is hard to deny that Gunawardana's liberal historiography has an alluring political appeal to those of us writing about Sri Lankan identity politics in the shadow of the island's two-decade-long separatist war. The debate between the two historians, then, is not a narrow academic quarrel; it reflects broader questions of nationalism, history, and minority belonging. Despite Sri Lankanist scholars' familiarity with the debate, Scott's intervention into it, in an essay titled "Dehistoricizing History," remains unknown at best and unappreciated at worst, considering that it has appeared in two different venues since 1995.[11] Obviously my concern is not so much with the nationalist debate as it is with (a belated assessment of) the relevance of what Scott's intervention has to say to the problem of interrogating the question of history in relation to the notion of active forgetfulness. While I consider Scott's labor to dehistoricize history seminal, I think it is not entirely adequate and needs to be questioned in terms of the (post-)Nietzschean idea of active forgetfulness of history.

"But so what?" This is the central question that Scott puts to the historicist debate in Sri Lanka. The question was first directed at Gunawardana's lengthy historiographic essay "The People of the Lion." This essay, first published in the 1970s, is, as Scott says, interested in showing not so much the political danger of Sinhala nationalism as the unsoundness of the nationalist history of Sri Lanka and the indefensibility of its political claims. Gunawardana wagers that our contemporary understanding of the Sri Lankan past (history) has been saturated by Sinhalese nationalist ideology, which, among other things, makes claims to the priority of the Sinhala race (as a numerical and a moral "majority") in Sri Lanka. This ideology has become so normalized that most Sri Lankan writers assume that it has a "very old history." (Note how eerily similar this is to what the atheists say about the history of the In-God-We-Trust motto.) Gunawardana dismantles the edifice of this assumption piece by piece, carefully sifting through a massive pile of historical facts and myths, and demonstrates that the nationalist ideology has gotten its history wrong. At least Gunawardana contends so. At the end of his essay, Gunawardana becomes a "historians' historian" wanting to relieve "us of our anxiety about the past of 'Sinhala.' Not only is the past rationally reconstructible within the ordered prose of professional history, but the evidence assembled pointedly demonstrates that history is, as it were, on our [liberal-progressivist] side," Scott says (101). But no sooner was Gunawardana—supported by other leftist intellectuals in Sri Lanka—assured of the soundness of his own reconstructed history than Dharmadasa published a rebuttal challenging the veracity of the former's findings. "Suddenly a fresh set of daunting questions seem to present themselves, questions about adequate data, sound scholarship, sources of evidence, strategies of reading, etc." (102). Loyal historian that he is, Gunawardana could think of no other critical strategy than to craft his own historicist rejoinder, full of new facts, to counter Dharmadasa's rebuttal.

This is the point of the debate at which Scott intervenes. In the wake of the rebuttal-after-rebuttal stalemate of this historicist debate, Scott asks, "what if, at the end of . . . this masterful tour-de-force ["People of the Lion"], Gunawardana simply and deliberately asked: But so what? What does this history really prove? How does it help us decide the questions of political community in Sri Lanka today?" (94). Scott admits satirically that it will be difficult for a historian of Gunawardana's caliber to heed this ostensibly comical Nietzschean suggestion.

> How could he, we would have asked ourselves incredulously, how could this esteemed professor of ancient and medieval Sri Lankan history, an historian so well known for his commitment to the craft, to the technologies of its muse, to its forms of narrative, to its orders of evidence, how could he in so singular and intemperate a gesture, heap such thoughtless ridicule upon this distinguished practice of Truth? (94)

Simply put, Gunawardana (perhaps as secularists do) "believes too much in history." But if Gunawardana had risked fidelity to his profession and asked the question "But so what?" contends Scott, he "would have disconnected the story of the past from the politics of the present and thus made itself invulnerable to historicist criticism" (104–5). Such a question would have delivered a severe blow to nationalists, who would no longer be able to argue with that question by resorting to history. Instead, they would have to resort to the politics of the present in which that claim is located. To extend Scott's argument a bit, I would suggest that the strategy of making nationalists reckon with the politics of the present, in turn, would—as Foucault would have suggested—enable them to take more political risks, rendering unavailable the possibility of affirming the "innocence" of their history.[12]

Scott's question "But so what?" constitutes, for me, an unprecedented critical strategy to think about the problem of history vis-à-vis nationalism in Sri Lanka or anywhere else, for that matter. But, concerned as I am with the questions of secularism, history, and active forgetting, I suspect that Scott's strategy requires more elaboration if it is to gain clarity as a political plausibility (or should I say impossibility?). To be sure, Scott grants that it is "not the penultimate gesture in . . . a getting *beyond,* so much as the initial move of what needs to be an extended elaboration" (105). What I am attempting here is a step toward such an extended elaboration. Needless to say, my attempt is by no means exhaustive. My modest proposition is that the question "But so what?" may be viewed as a post-Nietzschean political im-possibility if we think of it in relation to Nietzsche's idea of "active forgetfulness," coupled with Derrida's meditation on Hamlet's "Time is out of Joint." If Scott's question aims at disconnecting the history of the past from the politics of the present, forgoing the past's relevance to the politics of the present, the question needs to be thought in relation to an im-possibility of actively forgetting history. My wager here is that, to think of the im-possibility of active forgetting, we need a conceptualization of not only the present as a moment of disjunction, a moment in which time is out of joint, disconnected from the past/history; we also need a concept of the present that is separated from and non-contemporaneous with itself. Such a view of the present might help us imagine the im-possibility of an other, or *arrivant,* who renders indeterminate all distinctive signs of a prior identity. The non-contemporaneous present might be the space in which we can imagine a sense of nonjuridical justice, irreducible to the democratic notions of law and justice. Ultimately, then, Scott's proposal is not adequate to such a task.

Active Forgetfulness and the Ghostly Present: Nietzsche and Derrida

The way of forgetting, as I conceive it, is not a passive form or a static being. It does the active work of ceasing to remember/re-member the past vis-à-vis the present. This notion of active forgetting harks back to Nietzsche, who introduces it in his classic essay, "On the Uses and Disadvantages of History for Life." There Nietzsche speaks of the "art and the power of forgetting" as a way of "delivery from the malady of history."[13] This is possible through the art of the unhistorical. For Nietzsche, the art of forgetting and the "unhistorical" are interrelated. He says that "the ability to forget, or expressed in more scholarly fashion, the capacity to feel *unhistorically* during its duration" is more or less the same (62). Concerned as he is with "history for the purposes of life," that is, history for the future, Nietzsche insists that "the historical sense no longer conserves life but mummifies it"(75). He detests what he calls "the historical sense without restraint." "When the historical sense reigns *without restraint,* and all its consequences are realized, it uproots the future"(95). On this view, to be unhistorical is by extension is to be concerned with the future.

Nietzsche does not want to abandon the historical altogether, but wants to have a balance between the historical and the unhistorical. This balance, by extension, is a balance between remembering and forgetting ("to forget at the right time so as to remember at the right time" [63]). Here Nietzsche, I suspect, would have, if one can believe it, agreed with Wittgenstein's argument that remembering, which is so privileged today, is "not the description of a present experience." "When I say: 'He was here half an hour ago, that is remembering it—this is not the description of a present experience." Remembering cannot be a present experience because, unlike the experience of "tingling," how would one know it? That is why Wittgenstein makes the seemingly self-evident point, which is hardly self-evident, that "man learns the concept of the past by remembering."[14] For Nietzsche, the balance between remembering and forgetting is *"necessary in equal measure for the health of an individual, of a people and of a culture"* (63). The lack of this balance results in the historical sense reigning supreme and taking over life and its future. "With an excess of history man ceases . . . to exist" (64). On this account, forgetting is a way of restoring life and the act of living to the present. "Forgetting is essential to any kind of action" (62). This act of living life in forgetting is an act located in the present. For Nietzsche, in this present of forgetting, "every moment really dies, sinks back into night and fog, and is extinguished for ever" (61). My point is that this present must have a particular relation to the future. If Nietzsche, as quoted above, contends that "history uproots the future," the present he speaks of must be related to the future. But Nietzsche's understanding of the future is very different from that of the "historical men." This difference is captured when he says,

> looking to the past impels . . . [historical men] towards the future and fires their courage to go on living and their hope that what they want will still happen, that happiness lies behind the hill they are advancing towards. These historical men believe that the meaning of existence will come more and more to light in the course of its *process,* and they glance behind them only so that, from the process so far, they can learn to understand the present and desire the future more vehemently. (65)

Seen in this anti-Hegelian way, the future is hardly the culmination of a "process." One cannot desire to arrive at the future by merely passing through the present. Better yet, one cannot hope to bypass the present, hoping for a better future. One cannot wait for the end of the present at which point one leaps on to the future. The future is not just beyond the present, not just "over the hill" one marches toward. One cannot inhabit the present and anticipate reaching the future this way. *It cannot be anticipated this way because the present is not only disconnected from the past and the future but also disconnected from itself.* It is disconnected from itself because in it "every moment really dies, sinks back into night and fog, extinguished for ever" (61). One cannot escape this ever-dying, ever-extinguishing moment of the present in the way that one who is drowning in a whirlpool may struggle to reach the surface for a gasp of air and eventually reach the shore of safety. To be in this Nietzschean present is to be fully caught up in its dying moment. In other words, if there is any future, one has to find that future in the present. Such a future, as Heidegger would have suggested (whether we agree with him not), is not that which will be. The future is the present that already *is* (extinguishing).[15]

Now my point here is that if the task of forgetting is possible at all, it is possible (for Nietzsche) only in the present, because one cannot practice forgetting for the sake of the future. At the same time, if forgetting is possible in the ever extinguishing moment of the present, it must be so for the sake of the present. As we shall see, this forgetting is possible (and im-possible) in the present precisely because the present is marked by its vanishing moments or the moments of its constantly being disconnected, disjointed from itself. But there is another point to be made about forgetting and its relation to living in the dying moment of the present. Nietzsche's idea of living with(in) forgetting is not at all akin to "living without memory." Active forgetting is not a form of amnesia or inertia. Nietzsche grants that people may live without memory and even be happy. Yet, he asserts, "it is altogether impossible to *live* at all without forgetting" (62). Note that what Nietzsche is doing is carefully separating the practice of living with(in) forgetting from that of living without memory. This distinction is clear when he contrasts forgetting to sleepiness of the historical. Sleepiness of the historical, he stresses, is dangerous. *"There is a degree of sleepiness, of rumination, of the historical sense, which is harmful and ultimately fatal to the living thing, whether this living thing be a man, or a people, or a culture"* (62). Forgetting, then, is hardly sleepiness. It is active. Nietzsche elaborates on the active sense of forgetting in the *Genealogy of Morals*, albeit with a certain psychological gloss on it.

Forgetfulness is no mere *vis inertiae*, as the superficial believe. It is rather an active—in the strictest sense, positive—inhibiting capacity, responsible for the fact that what we absorb through experience impinges as little on our consciousness during its digestion (what might be called its "psychic assimilation") as does the whole many-fold process of our physical nourishment, that of so-called "physical assimilation." The temporary shutting of the doors and windows of consciousness; the guaranteed freedom from disturbance by noise and struggle caused by our underworld of obedient organs as they co-operate with and compete against one another; a little silence, a little *tabula rasa* of consciousness, making room for the new, making room above all for the superior functions and functionaries—those of governing, anticipating, planning ahead (since our organism is structured as an oligarchy)—such is the use of what I have called active forgetfulness, an active forgetfulness whose function resembles that of a concierge preserving mental order, calm, and decorum. On this basis, one may appreciate immediately to what extent there could be no happiness, no serenity, no hope, no pride, no *present*, without forgetfulness.[16]

If there can be no happiness, no living, no present without this forgetfulness, then forgetting and the present are not two separate strategies of being. Just as forgetting becomes possible in the present, so the present becomes possible in forgetting. They constantly animate each other. The possibility of this mutual relation between forgetting and the present, between forgetting and living, can be grasped better if we view it in light of Derrida's recent effort to think of the question of justice vis-à-vis Hamlet's overture "Time is out of Joint." Doing so is crucial because forgetting, as I think with Nietzsche, is a way of coming to terms with the "disjointedness" of the present. The disjointedness of the present is precisely where Derrida contends that the question of justice remains to be asked. Hence, if forgetting for Nietzsche is about happiness, about living, and about the present, then for Derrida forgetting (as a synonym for the disjointedness of time) is about the im-possibility of justice. Put simply, Nietzsche's contention that there can be no happiness without forgetting is fundamentally about justice, and we need to pass through Derrida to grasp better the relation between forgetting, justice, and the present.

Derrida's meditation on Hamlet's outcry is positioned against Fukuyama's neo-evangelistic announcement of the "end of history." Fukuyama's announcement was generated by, among other things, the supposed collapse of Marxism as a political possibility, an announcement masqueraded as an "event." Derrida's meditation is pervaded by a particular interest in the figure of the specter or the ghost. For Derrida, to meditate on the figure of the ghost is to meditate on the disjointedness of time. He thinks about the relation between the figure of the ghost and the disjointedness of history vis-à-vis the celebrated death of Marxism. If Marxism is dead, he says, one can only speak of its "non-presence" (101). For Derrida, the figure of the ghost is synonymous with this non-presence. This means that, if we are to talk about Marxism, we can talk only about its specters, ghosts, and apparitions. Derrida begins with Marx's opening line in the *Communist Manifesto* that "a specter is haunting Europe." Marx, of course, because he greatly prefers the material, the real, does not like ghosts. Just as specters can never assume a content of being, Marxism can perhaps never really materialize. But Marx's ghosts haunt us. (And that is why Derrida, who is hardly a Marxist, is against the European alliances—as he calls them—to exorcise and chase away the ghost of Marx too quickly. As he puts it, Marx "belongs to a time of disjunction, to that 'time out of joint' in which is inaugurated, laboriously, painfully, tragically, a new thinking of borders, a new experience of the house, the home, and the economy. . . . He [like the "clandestine immigrant" of whom one must not make an "illegal alien"] is not part of the family, but one should not send him back, once again, him too, to the border" [174]). Thus, perhaps like the clandestine immigrant, if I may say so, "the ghost never dies, it remains always to come and to come-back" (99). But the ghost "will never be there. There is no *Dasein* [being] of the specter." The specter does have a "certain visibility," however. It is "the visibility of the invisible." "And visibility, by its essence, is not seen, which is why it remains . . . beyond the phenomenon, or beyond being" (100).

There is a particular relation between the ghost and the present. When Derrida says that the ghost "remains to come," he is not speaking of an "event" that will happen in the future. Far from it. There is no relation between the specter and the future (as that which will be) because the specter has no being that it can take into the future. The specter's invisible presence, the "visibility of the invisibility," is fleeting; it comes and goes, appears and disappears.[17] It can neither be anticipated nor apprehended. This "place of spectrality" is synonymous with the present that is out of joint with itself. It is the place where one may await "what one does not expect yet or any longer" (65), and it is perhaps the space in which we can, as discussed earlier, be shaped by fear and anxiety. This is Derrida's ghostly history. Inhabited by specters appearing and disappearing, flitting in and out of sight, the ghostly present is where one cannot await what one wants. One can not await what one expects in this present because the present does not march or progress forward. As Wendy Brown puts it, "In Derrida's reformulation, history emerges as that which shadows and constrains, incites and thwarts, rather than that which moves, directs, or unfolds. History as a ghostly phenomenon does not march forward—it does not even march. Rather, it comes and goes, appears and recedes, materializes and evaporates, makes, and gives up its claims. And it changes shape."[18]

If the present is the place of spectrality, the ghostly present, the fleeting present, it is in such a present that one must do the im-possible work of "thinking [nonjuridical] justice," without an "event," without history, right, and law (*Specters*, 65). Justice seems impossible without history. As we shall soon see, thinking about nonjuridical "justice" is not merely to have justice *without* history and law. Derrida would say that to have justice without law is im-possible because justice is so engrained in law. But to think about this im-possibility is to think about how we may un-inherit the aporia of justice in our futures, and such thinking may produce a new future. Derrida is proposing the seemingly im-possible because the present (as he conceptualizes it) where justice is to be thought is deprived of any recourse to history. What makes (thinking) justice possible in the present is the present's own disjuncture, and that present cannot have recourse to history. "The necessary disjointure, the de-totalizing condition of justice, is indeed here that of the present—and by the same token the very condition of the present, and of the very presence of the present" (28). It is here in this disjointed present that one can think the "undeconstructible justice," which, as we discussed, always remains to come, "beyond all living present." If this disjointed present has any contemporaneity, that contemporaneity ought to be considered ghostly. That is why he speaks of what he calls "the non-contemporaneity with itself of the living present" (xix). This is, the disjointed present; this is the time out of joint. The present is not and cannot be contemporaneous with itself because the very promise of justice and the possibility of its presence always remains deferred to a future that will never be present.

Derrida does not see any hope in understanding justice in the disjunction of the present in terms of the familiar terms of *doing* or *rendering* justice. Such a conception of justice smacks overmuch of a politics of "restitution," a politics in which one merely gives justice to the other (27). "Thinking justice," as he calls it, should move beyond this juridical, restitutional, reparational politics of justice. Restitutional justice always needs history, right, and law. Justice by means of restitutional politics becomes justice by means of "punishment, payment, expiation," a lesson we have learned well from Nietzsche. It is what Derrida calls justice with "vengeance." Such justice operates within the horizon of culpability, debt, right, and accountability (25), and Derrida wants to think of the im-possibility of separating justice from such juridical connotations. Indeed, when Derrida says that "law and right stem from vengeance," one can think of many instances in which justice is sought within juridical and nonjuridical domains— from federal courtrooms to organizations like South Africa's Truth and Reconciliation Commission.[19] Even nonjuridical, nonstate organizations are concerned with law and right, and this is precisely the case with the American Atheists organization. All these juridically minded organizations undoubtedly do some sort of "justice," and one cannot deny the importance of it. But Derrida's contention here is that justice conceived in terms of law or right is often a way of doing or giving justice to the other as the *other*, who is always present *under a sign* (we already noted some of the problems with this sort of thinking). This is why Derrida asks: "if right or law stems from vengeance, as Hamlet seems to complain that it does—before Nietzsche, before Heidegger, before Benjamin—can one not yearn for justice that one day, a day belonging no longer to history, a quasi-messianic day, would finally be removed from the fatality of vengeance?" (21). Might that be the day when justice will be concerned with those who are not merely "present," seen and heard, without written records of complaint, available at some official's finger tips, to be retrieved in a computer database or some dusty archive? Will justice attend to those who have no such records, whose presence was never known, whose complaints were never heard?

I want to underscore that Derrida's attempt at thinking justice beyond accountability, law, right, etcetera, in the disjunction of a present that no longer belongs to history produces a radical conceptualization of the other, an other "not yet *there*."[20] To do this, Derrida suggests that we give up thinking of justice in terms of giving or doing justice to the other. Thinking beyond this sort of distributive justice is an important way to divest justice of any association with law or right or accountability. One might, of course, ask, can one think of justice as a gift so as to separate it from any link to law or right, a gift that belongs not to the giver, not even to God, but only to the other? Derrida, who has written so much about the im-possibility of gift, would

respond with a counterquestion: even if one were to understand justice as a gift beyond accountability, calculation, and commerce, "the
gift to the other as gift of that which one does not have, and which
thus, paradoxically, can only *come back* and belong to the other, is
there not a risk of inscribing this whole moment of justice under the
sign of presence?" (27). Put another way, the idea of justice as a gift,
whether it is beyond law or commerce, or whether it ultimately comes
back and belongs to the other, presupposes the existence of justice
somewhere in the present, under "the sign of presence," pointing to
its being *there*. This way of thinking about justice presupposes not
only that justice exists out *there*, but that the other as the other (or as
the victim) also always exists visible out *there*, waiting to receive justice. Clearly, for Derrida neither justice nor the other's needing justice
exists under a sign of presence. One cannot merely see them *there*.
They are neither apprehensible nor identifiable. They do not wait under the sign of presence. They cannot because they have no apprehensible *dasein*. They cannot because the sign of presence cannot exit
in the disjointed present. If "disjuncture is the very possibility of the
other [*arrivant*]," and if the disjunctured present is the ghostly present, neither justice nor the other can possibly remain out *there*. So,
we may ask, how might we speak of justice and the other if we cannot
find and apprehend them under a sign of presence? Derrida's answer
would be: "Not yet *there*." For Derrida to speak of justice "not yet *there*"
is simultaneously to speak of the other as not yet *there* as well. Thus,
by extension, the question of justice becomes a question of the other.

> Of justice where it is not yet, not yet *there*, where it is no longer,
> let us understand where it is no longer *present*, and where it will
> never be, no more than the law, reducible to laws or rights. . . . No
> justice—let us not say no law and once again we are not speaking
> here of laws—seems possible or thinkable without the principle
> of some *responsibility*, beyond all living present, within that which
> disjoins the living present, before the ghosts of those who are not
> yet born, or those who are already dead, be they victims of wars,
> political or other kinds of violence, nationalist, racist, colonialist,
> sexist, or other kinds of exterminations, victims of the oppressions
> of capitalistic imperialism, or any of the forms of totalitarianism.
> Without this *non-contemporaneity with itself of the living present*,

without that which secretly unhinges it, without this responsibility, and without this respect for justice, concerning those who *are not there*, of those who are no longer or who are yet *present and living*, what sense would there be to ask the question "where?," "where tomorrow?, "whither?" (xix)

What is important to note here is that the phrases "not yet there," "not yet born," "no longer present," and "will never be" do not simply mean that justice and the ghostly others have no location. Rather, they are terms to speak of the *ghostly location*, if you will, of justice and the other, the place of spectrality. If the ghostly, disjunctured present is the very possibility of the other, it is also the im-possibility of justice beyond law. In other words, ordinary notions of justice that is possible here and now does not help us think about those others who are dead, who are no longer present, who are victims of imperialisms, totalitarianisms, or other racist colonialist exterminations. To think of them, we need a conception of justice that carries "beyond all living present."

It would be easy to do justice for the victims we can see in our present, but can justice attend to those we (and it) cannot see? And this is the reason Derrida suggests that the question of justice must "carry beyond the *present* life" (xx). But justice beyond the *present* life does not merely appeal to a "better" future. For Derrida, the appeal to such a future is neither acceptable nor possible. One cannot appeal to such a future because one cannot leave behind the already dead and the presently living; one cannot appeal to such a future because one cannot just leap onto the future from the disjointed present. Thus, he disagrees with neo-evangelist futurists who fantasize that "there is even a more final end of history to come," supposedly after the complete universalization of democracy and capitalism. Such futurists consider a future "necessary" for the supposed well-being of the world. This necessity—expressed in terms of how we "must/should" aspire to a better future—becomes just another "law" ("'*it is necessary*' *is necessary, and that is the law*" [73]). But inhabiting as we do the ghostly present, the disjointed present, we cannot appeal to such a future. The disjointed present has no contemporaneity with itself. It does not, because time is out of joint. This is why Derrida speaks of the "non-contemporaneity with itself of the living present." If any justice, any future, is to be located, it has to be located in the non-contemporaneity of the living present with itself. This is where the impossibility of justice irreducible to law may be thought.

Only thinking of the living present in terms of its non-contemporaneity with itself, can one think of the question of justice as an impossibility beyond all living present. As Derrida says,

> If it is possible, and if one must take it seriously, the possibility of the question of justice, which is perhaps no longer a question, and which we are calling here *justice*, must carry beyond *present* life, life as *my* life, or *our* life. *In general.* For it will be the same thing for the "my life" or "our life" tomorrow, that is for the life of others, as it was yesterday for the other others: *beyond therefore the living present in general.* To be just: beyond the living present in general—and beyond its simple negative reversal. (xx)

Note the importance of what Derrida is saying here. The non-contemporaneity with itself of the living present, then, makes it difficult to think justice within one temporal domain or in relation to one ethnic or religious community that we might call mine or ours. Indeed, conceiving justice this way makes it possible to transcend—so to speak—ethnically or religiously bounded notions of us and them, self and other, citizen and alien. It does so precisely because it has no contemporaneity with itself; it is off the hinges. Inhabiting this ghostly present, one cannot leave behind the past or its atrocities or injustices for the sake of a utopian future that will happen one day (but the promise of justice is predicated precisely on such a notion), nor can one simply remain attached to a supposedly stable past and resist the future. The past and the future have only the relevance they do in the ghostly present. The past and the future are ghosts. Ghosts do not belong to, remain attached to, time—that is, to specific temporal location (xx). As he writes,

> A spectral moment, a moment that no longer belongs to time, if one understands by this term the linking of modalized presents (past present, actual present: "now," future present). We are questioning in this instant, we are asking ourselves about this instant that is not docile to time, at least what we call time. Furtive and untimely, the apparition of the specter does not belong to that time,

it does not give time, not that one: "Enter the ghost, exit the ghost, re-enter the ghost" (Hamlet). (xx)

If Derrida speaks (as he does) of ghosts of the dead and ghosts of the yet to be born, he must mean that the past and the future can belong nowhere else but in the ghostly present. In this ghostly present they appear and disappear; they haunt us—all of us. They enter, exit, and reenter. They cannot be conjured, exorcised, and sent back to the proper place of their "presence." They do not belong to time; if they belong to time they cannot haunt. Yet haunting is not ahistorical. "Haunting is historical, to be sure, but it is not *dated*. It is never docilely given a date in the chain of presents, day after day, according to the instituted order of a calendar" (4). This is perhaps why Derrida characterizes the time of the ghostly present as "not a time whose joinings are negated, broken, mistreated, dysfunctional, disadjusted, according to a *dis*-of negative opposition and dialectical disjunction, but a time without *certain* joining, a determinable conjunction" (18). Clearly, Derrida does not want to disregard and negate the past and whatever its (famous or infamous) entailments, imagined or not, merely because they are the past. If one is to take the past seriously, one can do so only in the non-contemporaneous present. It is in such a present that the past's possible joining or relevance to the present (or the future) can be constructed. I think that is what Derrida means when he says: "To maintain together that which does not hold together, and the disparate itself . . . all of this can be thought . . . only in a dislocated time of the present, at the joining of a radically dis-jointed time, without a certain conjunction" (17). (This is what history, anthropology, and religious studies, despite whatever qualifications they may offer, do in their attempts to construct historical-ethnographic narratives and accounts of what happened, where, and when. Can these disciplines ever attend to a time without a determinable conjunction? Can they even imagine the chance of such "time"?)

The critical point I want to make here is this: insofar as the non-contemporaneous present is where one has to labor to "maintain together that which does not hold together," the im-possibility of forgoing (forgetting) that which does not hold together can become available. Put differently, we need Derrida's ghostly present to make better sense of Nietzsche's active forgetting. Nietzsche's idea of how forgetting becomes possible in the present, and the present in forgetting,

gains greater clarity when we see it in tandem with Derrida's conceptualization of the spectral present that is disjointed with itself. If Nietzsche's present is where every moment dies, sinks back into night
and fog, forever extinguishing, and Derrida's notion of the ghostly
present is haunted by the untraceable and unmappable appearance
and disappearance of ghostly moments, then forgetting in such a
present can become *a ghostly reality*. That is, granted the ghostly present is haunted by disjointed traces, traces that can be conjoined only
by a disciplinary tool such as history or anthropology, forgetting such
traces of history (a history of what happened prior to us in the past, or
who did what to us) becomes synonymous with the ghostly present.
Forgetting is about living on. That which is forgotten does not disappear but lives on or survives. (Living on is neither being nor nonbeing; ghosts live on just as languages or books without their authors
live on.) But how can this forgetting in the ghostly present produce
justice (for Derrida) and happiness (for Nietzsche)? To understand
this we need to meditate on how forgetting as a ghostly reality might
become a political possibility.

Justice can only be an im-possibility because it is "not yet *there*";
if it is not yet *there*, one can only think justice. In the way I conceive
it, thinking bears a particular relation to possibility. As Adorno once
said, "thinking is not the intellectual reproduction of what already exists any way. . . . Thinking has a secure hold on possibility."[21] But, for
Derrida, as it must be clear, possibility cannot be separated from im-
possibility. It is in this sense that I conceive of forgetting as a political possibility. In other words, the possibility of forgetting is the im-
possibility of the nonjuridical (or "justice"), for lack of a better word.
That is to say, if Derrida speaks of the "im-possibility of justice," not
only to note the limitations of the state apparatuses of justice but also
to note how justice remains deferred, as a promise, always "to come,"
then I am thinking of a nonjuridical possibility. To think of this nonjuridical possibility is to think of the question of the other, the other
we do not know or recognize as the other in advance, one who is not
there under a sign of presence. To get at the relations among the trio
of forgetting, justice, and other, I turn, once again, to Sri Lanka. I
want to think briefly about active forgetting in relation to two vastly
disjointed "incidents" in 1983 and 2001. (For the sake of clarity here,
I use the word *incidents*. It will be evident soon that it is better to call
them dates.) *To stress the obvious, such incidents do not at all constitute*

for me empirical examples of how forgetting ought to be done. Rather, the way I read these two incidents, to conceptualize an immeasurable disjunction between them and thereby contemplate the possibility of active forgetting, will be very different from an empirical account of "why" they happened.

The Im-possibility of "Non-presence" Without Explanation

July 23, 1983, Sri Lanka. The date is synonymous with the riots that put Sri Lanka on the map as a danger zone of pulverizing "ethnic" violence and political instability. The riots undoubtedly created a black hole, interrupting postcolonial Sri Lanka's self-proclaimed capitalist march toward its political modernity and multiculturalism, inaugurated by the postcolonial politics of the Jayewardene state, which at once privileged a romantic version of Buddhism and de-privileged the role of Buddhist monks in politics. Coordinated and anticipated, the July riots are often thought to have "erupted" in the wake of the ambush and decapitation of some thirteen members of the Sri Lankan armed forces by the LTTE, which would wage, for almost two decades, a devastating guerrilla campaign for a separate state in northern Sri Lanka. During the riots, which lasted for several days, arguably with tacit approval from government officials, gangs of armed Sinhalese men systematically and brutally killed more than three thousand Tamil civilians and looted and destroyed their property and businesses worth billions, eventually displacing about one hundred thousand others throughout the country. Literature on the pogrom is vast and has gained almost canonical status. I need not rehearse the arguments of that literature here, except to note that they offer varying "explanations," with pronounced emphasis on the "causes" of the riots. Such causal explanations boil down to equations such as: LTTE ambush = > July riots or Sinhala Buddhist hegemony = > LTTE ambush = > July riots.[22] Such causal explanations are neither impossible nor unhelpful ways of making sense of what happened, but I am not interested in such causal explanations here because I do not necessarily want to make sense of the riots in terms of the task at hand. I do not want to make sense of the riots because doing so would make it easy for me to make sense of the next incident/

date to which I will allude. In other words, explaining the July riots of 1983 by way of the above formulas will make readily available an explanation of a later incident that is disjointed from the former. I am not interested in explaining the second incident either, because I am interested in thinking of an im-possibility. Explanation cannot make im-possibility available; explanation kills im-possibility. Explanation kills the ghostly present where im-possibility or chance of its future is thinkable. In the universe of explanation, there cannot be ghosts; they all remain fully exposed, apprehended, located, and mapped. The traces of the ghosts and *arrivants*—where they have come from and where they will go—are all known and knowable in the universe of explanation. In the universe of explanation, all things are "human-ized," giving the chance of the im-possibility of the nonknowledge of the ghosts or the *arrivants* no chance.[23]

July 23, 2001. The second incident also "occurs" in the month of July, but it is separated by a gap of almost eighteen years from the riots of 1983. On July 23, 2001, around three o'clock in the morn-ing, a suicide squad of the LTTE penetrated and attacked Sri Lanka's tightly guarded international airport at Katunayake. There were only a few casualties: five Sri Lankan soldiers and thirteen Tamil rebels were killed in the exchange of gunfire. But the attack caused colossal damage to Sri Lanka's already crippled economy and military. Using shoulder-fired missiles, the rebels destroyed eight military aircraft and five commercial airplanes parked on the tarmac. The airport shut down for fourteen hours. International flights to Sri Lanka were di-verted to other countries, and subsequently major western airlines refused to resume flights to the island. The attack on the airport sharpened the internationalized image of Sri Lanka as a war zone. Commentary by local and international political pundits offered vary-ing explanations "why" the attack took place: The attack was yet an-other indication of the seriousness of the LTTE's persistent demand for a separate state in the Northeast;[24] it was a retaliation against the Sri Lankan military, which refused to suspend its aerial bombings on rebel positions, despite a unilaterally declared LTTE cease-fire and a request for peace talks almost eight months prior to the attack, or it was merely another effort to further weaken the island's largely spent military force, and so on.

These explanations may all be on the mark. What is noteworthy is that however differently cast their explanations were, many of the commentaries on the attack included a distinct reference to the incident/date of the July riots of 1983. At first sight this reference seems inevitable, since the date of the airport attack corresponded to that of the July riots. But this reference was not just to the correspondence in the dates of the two incidents. For some commentators, to write about the airport attack was not only to allude to the brutality of the July riots but also to recall briefly *the entire history* of conflict between the LTTE and the Sri Lankan state, albeit with a certain sense of supposed objectivity. It seems that an LTTE attack of any proportion today can hardly be reported without some reference to the "leading" event of the 1983 July riots. (This is rather like U.S. secularists finding it difficult to speak of any contemporary issue concerning religion and public sphere without mentioning the First Amendment.) It is as if there must always be some connection between the past and the present, the old and the new, the leading and the following, the preceding and the subsequent. The question I want to ask regarding the two incidents/dates is this: why is establishing a connection between them critical? Is it because the connection seems self-evident? Can one write about a potential present/future LTTE attack with no reference to the supposedly leading event of 1983 so that a present/future attack may be seen in relation to its own domain of occurrence? In other words, can one forget the leading and the original? If so, at which point may one forget it?

It seems that the journalistic desire to establish a connection between July 23, 1983, and July 23, 2001, was premature at best, and untenable at worst, since the airport attack and its aftermath lacked a major feature that to date defines the leading event of July 1983. There were no riots on or after July 23, 2001. There were no marauding mobs of Sinhalese men rampaging through the streets and looting Tamil businesses and killing Tamil civilians, either in the vicinity of the airport or elsewhere in Sri Lanka. (Indeed there had been no such Sinhala riots—certainly not of the egregious ilk of the 1983 July riots—notwithstanding numerous LTTE suicidal attacks on Sinhalese civilians and the state targets.) If there were no riots on July 23, 2001, what other constituent features make the connection between the two dates conceivable? Is it the name *LTTE*? That is to say, is the LTTE that ambushed and killed the thirteen soldiers, triggering the riots of 1983, the same as the LTTE that attacked the Katunayake airport? If this connection between the airport attack and the July riots is based on the self-evident identity of the LTTE, it is more than a connection between two dates. That connection represents a particular distinction between two people: Sinhalese and Tamils. After all, the LTTE claims to be fighting for a separate state for Sri Lankan Tamils. I think it safe to say that today it is all but impossible for political commentators to talk about the LTTE and the Tamils without talking about the Sinhalese. So my point here is that to draw a connection between July 23, 2001, and July 23, 1983, is to point to the *difference* between the Sinhalese and the Tamils. Seen in this way, an attack on the state (e.g., the airport and the military base) becomes (for the journalists and perhaps for the LTTE as well) an extension of the conflict between the Sinhalese majority and the Tamil minority. At the end of establishing this connection between the two dates, between the leading and the following, explaining the following with a reference to the leading, the Sinhalese and the Tamils come to stand as they did in 1983, if not prior to that year. They remain the same; nothing has changed; there are no altered views of the relations between them, no altered ethos toward the separatist war on the part of the Sinhalese and the Tamils who might have no direct stakes in the politics of the Sri Lankan state or the LTTE. The LTTE just continues to attack its designated targets, the government continues to retaliate, and vice versa.

I would wager here that the supposed connection between the two dates/incidents can be sustained *only by explaining* them, accounting for "why" they happened. To explain one incident is to explain the other; to explain the two incidents is to establish a connection between them. But to explain these two dates and establish a connection between them, as must be evident so far, is to leave one striking aspect unexplained and unaccounted for: the absence/"non-presence" of riots on July 23, 2001. Why is that? This absence or non-presence has to be left unexplained because it inevitably threatens to disconnect July 23, 2001, from July 23, 1983. The unavoidable question that one must pose here is this: can this absence be explained? My answer is that it can be, but only at the risk of explanation itself—that is, if we understand explanation as a task of establishing connections between disjointed dates in this case. But explaining this absence will not be easy. If explanation of an event is about establishing connections, then it is about accounting for what has already happened, connecting the dots between the reality of one incident and the reality of another. They can be explained because they have happened; they are actualities; they belong to history; they have agents, subjects, names, and dates (LTTE, Tamils, Sinhalese, July 1983, July 2001, and so on). But can one explain that which has not happened, that which is non-presence, that which is absence? Put differently, can one establish a connection between that which has happened and that which has not happened, between the presence of riots in 1983 and the non-presence of riots in 2001? I suppose one can. But, to do that, one will have to privilege the leading event. In other words, one cannot ask why no riots took place on July 23, 2001, without asking why the riots took place on July 23, 1983. So long as one asks the question of why no riots took place on July 23, 2001, one cannot ever disconnect it from July 23, 1983. So long as one asks the question why (or why not), one always remembers the leading event or the date. For this reason, perhaps, Nietzsche once remarked that the question why (or why not) always presupposes a master subject. Slightly amending this, I would say that the question why always presupposes a leading, master, original event.

Now, of course, the journalists never bothered to notice the absence of riots on July 23, 2001, let alone ask the question why not. Had they even noticed this absence, it is clear they would not have been able to *account for* it, at least not that easily. What I want to point out is not the journalistic inability to account for this absence. Indeed, I want to suggest that we forgo precisely this question of why riots never happened if we are to think about this non-presence of riots as a particular kind of possibility (or im-possibility). In other words, I am suggesting that if one disconnects the leading event from the following event, one will have to notice this absence. But one will have to refuse the temptation to ask the question why not. The moment we refuse this why not, we refuse to yield to the temptation of explanation. The moment we are bereft of the temptation of explanation, a new way of thinking about this seemingly hollow moment marked by absence/non-presence may open up.

I would gamble that the absence/non-presence of riots on July 23, 2001, could be imagined and constituted as the space in which a certain kind of forgetting was possible. The absence of riots constitutes, for me, something of the Nietzschean dying moment or the Derridean ghostly present that is out of joint with itself; it is the moment that remains disconnected from the leading event of 1983. This hollow, empty moment of absence/non-presence cannot be grasped or apprehended in relation to a prior moment or event. It has no *visible* traces pointing to a location where it came from. It has no identifiable subject that engineered it. The absence is not necessarily a *result* of anything; it is not *conditioned by* anything; it had no cause; it did not even emerge; it was just absence; it was non-presence. If we need a name for this empty moment of absence/non-presence, we may call it the moment of forgetting. If absence/non-presence was conditioned by anything, it was conditioned only by forgetting. *But forgetting has no actor(s) or agent(s) behind it—not in the way I seek to think about it.* There is no group of people—call them Sinhalese—who are responsible for forgetting. Nobody did it. In other words, riots did not happen because the Sinhalese people had just forgotten, actively or not, their past sour relations with the imagined Tamil others and hence did not riot. Even if this is "why" no riots took place—a fact I suspect could not be easily verified by empirical-ethnographical data—I refuse to think it, because it runs the risk of equating forgetting with an action. Forgetting is not an action that belongs to a people. I do not want to think of it as something that the Sinhalese did for themselves or for the Tamils or even for "peace." If forgetting is such an action of doing by a people, it can never be a nonjuridical possibility; it can only be a form of distributive justice.

Now what I want to emphasize here is that the moment of this forgetting, the moment of the non-presence of riots—has a certain active sense. For me it is active in the sense that "we"—the Tamils and the Sinhalese—cannot forget or allow ourselves to forget the carnage of the riots of 1983. But that carnage cannot be a condition of the absence of the riots on July 23, 2001. It cannot be a condition of the absence, because the possibility of the absence is located in the disjunctive, ghostly present that is out of joint and non-contemporaneous with itself. What is crucial to note is that though it is located in the disjointed present, we cannot talk about the absence of riots without some sense of the presence of riots somewhere—call this somewhere July 1983. Doing so is logically impossible: one cannot talk about non-presence without some sense of presence; one cannot talk about death without some sense of life. Simply put, for something to be absent/non-present, something other must be or had to be present. Hence the non-presence of riots/active forgetfulness is not an obliteration or denying of the presence of the July riots of 1983. The July riots of 1983 may be remembered. Or, better yet, they may haunt us. We may be haunted by those killed and those who died in the riots. (To that extent, 1983 will always survive as a ghost that cannot and must not be exorcized). Yet they have no bearing on the disjunctive present marked by the non-presence of riots. They cannot determine the outcome of July 23, 2001, because that very "outcome"—if you call non-presence an outcome—immediately disconnects it from the riots of 1983. The importance of seeing this non-presence as made possible by the disjunctive moment of active forgetting—without a master engineer—is that it can become the space in which the very distinction between Tamils and Sinhalese would be un-inherited, producing a radical alterity. This space might be the place where Tamils and Sinhalese become irreducible, wholly others. Indeed the space demands this insofar as it is constituted by non-presence, by a sense of radical alterity, by active forgetting; to belong within it, one cannot just *be* Sinhalese or *be* Tamil. In other words, one cannot merely belong in it. To "belong" in this space is indeed to "constitute" this space that demands an alterity, a sense of unheard-of otherness and singularity. Any belonging in it demands the im-possibility of *un-inheriting* the very names *Sinhalese* or *Tamils,* which are deeply implicated in the 1983 riots; the same names continue to be implicated in the ongoing battle between the LTTE fascists and the nationalist Sinhalese state. Those who constitute the non-presence of riots in 2001 cannot simply bear those names. They are the un-inheritors of the names. In other words, in the non-presence of forgetting, one cannot be simply *Sinhalese without being Sinhalese* or *Tamil without being Tamil.*

This space of non-presence, of course, is rapidly dying; perhaps it is already dead. If this space is already dead, the "Tamils" and "Sinhalese" already met each other there. Yet, at the same time, as they meet each other, they constituted an alterity irreducible to a Sinhaleseness or Tamilness. But what is this otherness? Can we define it? Do we understand it yet? Surely it cannot be merely Sinhalese and Tamil. If it is, it cannot constitute this space of active forgetting. Perhaps this otherness that emerged is not recognizable to us now, today, immediately, in our present, which loves time, which remains loyal to history and dating where time always remains connected, connecting the name *Sinhalese* or *Tamil* here (in the present) to the name *Sinhalese* or *Tamil* over there (in the past). As long as such a sense of connected time remains, perhaps this otherness will remain unrecognizable.

More important, perhaps, this otherness will remain unrecognizable to the state. The state will not be able to count it. Perhaps, then, the unrecognizability of this otherness is not such a bad thing. The state is unable to count this otherness, perhaps because when these *others met each other* in this space of non-presence, they did so without law or its vengeance, without demands for apologies or forgiveness for what one people did to the other in the past. The others could not demand and accuse each other because they met without the aid of history or state; they met without a third party intervening to negotiate political settlements. They met in an active forgetting of history; they met in the absence, in the non-presence, of riots. They met in the moment of disconnection, in the non-contemporaneity with itself of the living present. This moment of meeting without history, law, and state is, perhaps, the moment of the im-possibility of justice, "justice" for those who are already dead, those who are living, and those who are yet to be born. But it is no transcendental justice. It does not cut across generations. Rather, the possibility of that justice is the possibility of a hollow moment in which its uncountable otherness may "live on" and survive just as 1983 may live on.[25] Such justice, in the words of Wendy Brown, does not remain "detached from futurity, or confined to a self-identical present. But not only must justice have futurity—it is what *makes* futurity, in so far as it generates the future's relationship to the present as a 'living on' of present efforts and aims. Justice entails the present generation's responsibility for crafting continuity, as well as the limits of that responsibility and that continuity."[26] To put it in my own terms, the irreducible otherness that emerged within the hollow moment will have to be reckoned with by those who continue to bear the name *Sinhalese* or *Tamil*. The hollow moment is a threat to the name *Sinhalese* or *Tamil;* it will survive and haunt all those who will bear the names *Sinhalese* and *Tamil* in the future.

The next time an LTTE attack or a state offensive against the LTTE or a riot takes place, those "Tamils" and "Sinhalese" who met in active forgetfulness in the hollow moment of the absence of riots on July 23, 2001, will have no relation to them; they will stand disconnected and disjointed from them. Data-mongering journalists, anthropologists, historians, and political pundits who continue to write about Sri Lankan history and politics cannot afford to forget the dead, ghostly present of July 23, 2001. Nor can they link it to possible future attacks, counterattacks, and riots involving the names *Tamil* and

Sinhalese. Nor can they include the moment of non-presence on lists tracing the "history" of the conflict between the Sri Lankan state and the LTTE, returning to the leading event of the July riots of 1983.[27] That moment of absence is dead-alive. The ghosts of the Sinhalese and the Tamils who met in that absence will haunt any attempt either to link July 23, 2001, facilely to July 23, 1983, or to conveniently forget them for the sake of the future.

Now what is the significance of such a space of non-presence, made possible by active forgetting, to the question of democracy? Surely, it must be obvious by now that democracy and law cannot account for, let alone create, this space of non-presence and the otherness that emerged therein. Democracy/law cannot because it relies too much on history, on accountability, accounting for/counting (majority) identities and (minority) differences. Democracy depends on this practice of (ac)countability. Can democracy ever learn to live without this practice? Can democracy ever be removed from the "fatality" of history and (ac)countability? Democracy cannot take into account and hence cannot account for such a space of non-presence because democracy loves "presence" too much. Democracy always works in relation to that "sign of presence" which is justice/law. Yes, democracy and its justice are promises, and they remain deferred; yet they always exist as signs of presence, to be reached one day. The sign/presence may be distant and deferred. Nonetheless, democracy teaches us to think that the sign of justice will be accessible one day. In that sense, democracy is a "progress" toward that sign. But democracy can never guarantee when we will all reach it or if we will all have rights and wishes completely obtained. That is why justice will always remain deferred. So when Derrida says that democracy or justice is a promise, the word *promise* is a name for the powerful irony/contradiction inscribed within democracy.

As we know, in many of his writings, over more than four decades, Derrida has argued that much of the history/philosophy of western metaphysics has been concerned with sign/presence. This sign/presence appears in different guises: Being, God, language, truth, life, and so on. [28] Such a notion of sign/presence functions in opposition to its *difference:* non-Being, non-God, absence, nontruth, death. In other words, the western history of the metaphysics of presence/sign is a history of oppositional binaries. One could easily argue that today democracy functions as the most powerful heir to this history of the metaphysics of presence. Democracy is founded upon the logic of binaries such as majority and minority, self and other, truth and non-truth, lawful and unlawful, interior and exterior, western and non-western, foreigner and citizen, Sinhalese and Tamil, and so on. Today nobody would be asinine enough to imply that such distinctions are simply *wrong*. Rather, the point here is that such distinctions remain determined and sustained by and in relation to (a) "history" (of what such distinctions mean). Today, law, of course, functions as the most powerful representative of that history. Put differently, even distinctions such as "right" and "wrong" are not self-evident. It is the history of law that determines such distinctions and not a specific case of injury, suffering, or crime. That is why law always remains unable to attend to the specificity of injury. Nietzsche, well before Foucault, noted this when he said: "'right' and 'wrong' exit from the moment law is established . . . and *not* . . . from the moment of injury" (*Genealogy*, 56). I need not belabor this point. We have already seen how law and history animate each other. My point here is that so long as democracy remains animated by its commitment to dualities *determined by history/law*, it cannot even entertain the im-possibility of a space of non-presence as something of "political" significance. Indeed, the space of non-presence/active forgetting that I discussed threatens the very notion of democracy itself: The space produces a radical otherness that flies in the face of any attempts at sustaining familiar binaries. Democracy cannot understand this space because those who are within it cannot be counted as Sinhalese or Tamils. Here, then, is a challenge to the future of democracy: can democracy ever learn to fold into itself that which it cannot count/account for? As I have already suggested, we do not yet know how to speak of the irreducible otherness that emerges in the space of the active forgetting of history. Perhaps we cannot recognize this otherness because we are still too "democratic." That is to say, we still love history too much. But can we be democratic without history? Can democracy live without history? What would a future of democracy be without history/genealogy? How would we think such anti-genealogical futures? These are the questions that I take up in the next chapter.

Democracy remains to come; this is its essence in so far as it remains: not only will it remain indefinitely perfectible, hence always insufficient and future, but, belonging to the time of the promise, it will always remain, in each of its future times, to come: even when there is democracy, it never exists.

There would be no future without chance.

—Jacques Derrida, Politics of Friendship

7 Politics of "Postsecular" Ethics, Futures of Anti-genealogy

Community Without Community?

The Postcolonial "Problem" of *Ayubowan*

"*Ayubowan!*" This is a particular kind of greeting that has its uses in particular sociocultural domains of differently textured lives of Sinhalese communities, both within and beyond the shores of the island of Sri Lanka. But it is not just any particular greeting. Its particularity, I suspect, assumes a certain generality today. Put differently, the specifically Sinhalese, if not entirely Buddhist, discourse of welcome and hospitality has come to occupy an authorized "national" status in postcolonial Sri Lanka. The status of the greeting resulted not from the frequency or ubiquity of its use. Rather, I think, it acquired such status precisely because of its use in particular places by particular persons. As one transnational discourse—if one may so call a Web site—promoting tourism on the island puts it, "*Ayubowan* is the customary greeting of the Sri Lankans and [it] means 'May You Live Long.' With palms of the two hands held close together against the chest, this is a greeting that denotes welcome, goodbye, respect, devotion or loyalty to suit the occasion." [1]

Obviously, this statement hardly alludes to the specific uses of the greeting. Although the greeting arguably sounds stilted in "ordinary" parlance, even when it is extended (in the manner described above) to guests and visitors on private yet formalized occasions such as funerals, weddings, and (*pirit*-chanting) Buddhist ceremonies, let us assume (as does the statement quoted from the Web site) that this gesture of welcome is a "customary" practice. Nevertheless, it does not follow from this assumption that the greeting custom remains a possessed cultural quality or the property *of* the nation (i.e., "Sri Lankans"). Simply put, it is not clear at all how this supposed greeting custom equals the identity of the nation. At first glance the statement seems grossly unsettling and wholly essentialist, as it obviously—and we might say violently—alienates the ethical-political voices, narratives, and lives of other varying communities (such as Muslims, Tamils, Burghers) in postcolonial Sri Lanka who have their own traditions of greeting and hospitality. One could write a genealogical history of *Ayubowan* and hope that a certain "problematization" or even a deconstruction attained thereby would undermine the easily discernible *problem* of the normalized relation between the customariness of the greeting and the nation. That is to say, to write a history of how it was used by whom, in what contexts, and in what ways would show the various (agentive or agentless) transformations of its meanings as simply irreducible to a single national identity. Even if the statement is so self-evidently disturbing, I doubt that merely writing a history of *Ayubowan* so as to denationalize it, to put a dent in its supposed national hegemony, to show its reality as a fabrication, so to speak, would in itself produce a new politics, a politics of rethinking the questions of postsecular citizenship, community, and pluralism. As flagrant as the attempt to produce an equation between the custom of the greeting and the national identity may seem, the equation cannot be understood or dismissed as something *merely* fabricated or imagined. It seems to me that the possibility of the equation lies in spaces in which the greeting does have its particular uses, however stilted, formal, and "uncommon" they might seem or sound in contemporary Sri Lanka.

Obviously, then, my interest is not in the particularity of the uses of this greeting. Rather, by meditating on such a particular space of this discourse of *Ayubowan*, now assumed to be so customary, I am concerned with the question of imagining a new politics by way of thinking through contemporary postcolonial questions of community and citizenship. Put differently and succinctly, my concern here is not with this discourse of *Ayubowan* itself. Rather, to think about the domains in which *Ayubowan* operates is to conceive of an ethical-political domain that demands thinking about of the questions of difference and community in a new way that seeks to un-inherit the very distinction of minority/majority. Gambling here with Derrida and Nietzsche, I want to find out to what extent thinking of what I call anti-genealogical futures (that is, a radically new future of the political irreducible to democracy) might help us to un-inherit the idea of the community/common altogether. Put more simply but less precisely, to think about the problem of *Ayubowan* is to think of an anti-genealogical future of the political. But such a notion of the political cannot be one that already exists; nor is it one to be fashioned based on the anthropologized *examples* of the day before yesterday's humanist politics of multicultural coexistence in some political "community" out there. As I have noted and will spell out in my reading of Derrida's *Politics of Friendship,* such a future has to be thought in relation, if not in opposition, to that democratic logic of *to come.* It is a future of the political divested of any relation to the category of enmity—a relation defined (and embodied?) by the writings of, among others, Carl Schmitt, the "crown jurist" of the Third Reich—a relation that at times powerfully shaped the global landscape of twentieth-century international politics. The anti-genealogical future(s) will un-inherit the distinction between friend and enemy. Such a future of the political will have no tie to "number," that is, to "history" itself, history understood in terms of determinable connections. It will be less tied to a seamless history of a "fraternity" or a place of origin. It will be tied even less to a history of a given "community," arguably one of the most numerically mappable and statistically organizable properties of state qua citizenship. Such a future will have a radical relationship to "democracy," that is to say, to justice itself. In such a future of the political, neither justice nor democracy will belong merely to the state. Might such a future be what some call a "community without community?" [2] Does such a notion of community without community still retain something of the "common"? Is such a future, which Derrida says is "just beyond law," just beyond the preposition *without*? Put differently, might the future of the political merely lie at the end of "transforming" or "enriching" the already available critiques of democracy and community? Thinking about these sorts of questions will, I suggest, produce a new understanding of whether or not the futures of the political we aspire to imagine will still be secular-democratic or "postsecular."

If justice and democracy today are increasingly and intimately tied, and often defined in proximity, to the concepts of the human and human rights, humanity and humanitarianism, an anti-genealogical future of the political will have less of a proximity to that (more often than not) "fraternal," phallogocentric history of the "human." Thinking about anti-genealogical futures, even though they remain only imaginable and hence seem almost impossible at our contemporary juncture—how can that which is impossible possibly "seem"?—becomes important because what those futures aspire to, at least in my view, are the spaces where we cannot simply appeal to ideas of the human as equivalents to the political. The domains where we cannot appeal to such humanism are the domains where we might begin at least to imagine the possibility of those seemingly impossible futures. Meditating on the seeming problem of *Ayubowan*, in my view, enables us to locate a domain where we can at least begin to extricate ourselves from the allure of humanism. It seems to me that the point where the prospect of the extrication of the political from humanism becomes available to us is the point where we may imagine such antigenealogical futures. That is, if the future of the antigenealogical is about distancing ourselves from the possibility of invoking the human, that future also has something to do with mourning and uninheriting the promise of the secular democracy we have now inherited. Doing so will involve thinking the limits of contemporary political sovereignty itself, which, in its relation to the ideas of democracy, human rights, and all other variant democratic features, depends so much on secularism. To anticipate what this future looks like—if one can ever say this about the future—is to give up the appeal to humanism. To give up that appeal to humanism is to think at the limits of political sovereignty and its relation to secularist principles.

It is in this way that I want to ponder the discourse of *Ayubowan*. To do this I want to turn to a site where we can locate the ways in which *Ayubowan* has a distinctively postcolonial, and if not a *subaltern*, cry to it, a cry in the senses of announcement and lamentation and indeed mourning. But this announcement or mourning does not reflect so much some kind of loss as it does a certain sense of "un-loss" (if you will). This un-loss is not some essential being or burden that a person carries within herself. It is that which enables this cry. This cry has a particular relation to politics. This cry is a cry for a politics of un-inheriting the very problem of *Ayubowan*, which we will identify below. Yet this cry does not aim at securing some knowledge about when, where, and how such a politics of un-inheriting might come into being. This postcolonial cry does not come from the hollow depths of a bygone past, requiring a feat of clairaudience. The cry comes from the shadow of our contemporary present, which demands a new way of engaging the question of the other. Yet the cry is not associated with an individual agent who utters it. Put alternatively, it is not the cry of an individual agent who is doing the conscious work of lamenting or mourning to be heard. As we will see later, this way of thinking about this problem (which, as I suggest later, should be understood as an aporia) will also provide an important corrective to the humanist politics of multiculturalism. So, in a nutshell, the cry is not the voice of a person. Rather, the cry is the voice of *Ayubowan* itself. It is this voice of *Ayubowan* that speaks, through the body, name, gestures, and signs of a person. But the person is not just any person.

To be sure, of course, there are many persons who utter this *Ayubowan* as a form of "greeting." Just to point to one instance—apart from the above statement, which alludes to the conventional (not to mention nationalist) deployment of it, yet echoes its sentiments in a interesting way—I want to delineate a particular site to distinguish between (the third-person) utterance of *Ayubowan* as a *greeting* and *Ayubowan*'s cry of itself. The site that I have in mind is one that negotiates and transcends the differences between the grounded and the ungrounded, the anchored and the aerial, the bordered and the borderless, and the "national" and the "transnational." This site is, to put it in terribly oxymoronic terms, an "invariably" shifting site. It is the site of the airplane.

The particular instance I have in mind is Sri Lanka's national airline. Recently named Sri Lankan, but formally called Air Ceylon and Air Lanka, the airline produces and normalizes a certain Sri Lankan/ Sinhalese nationalness. But, even as it promotes this national identity, the airline is largely owned and operated by the Middle Eastern airline Emirates.[3] This should come as no surprise to most of us, who know something about the international financing of the very idea of nation in many countries—including the United States (which, as I write, borrows more money from China to hold steady the declining value of the U.S. dollar against that of the Euro while simultaneously

fighting the war of "liberation" in Iraq). Given the easily identifiable
paradoxes or contradictions that underwrite the identity of Sri Lanka's
"national" airline, the use onboard of *Ayubowan* seems only to render
paradoxes more visible and more easily elicit a humanist critique of
them. But they are not just paradoxes. They become normalized realities at the point that passengers get on the airline at the port of em-
barkation. When they get on, they are greeted by a flight attendant—
often by a woman wearing the airline's official attire, the green sari
with red peacock feather design. The way in which the passengers
are greeted is described in the airline's official magazine *Serendib* and
on its official Web site. The site's description (in 2004) is remarkable
because of the way it constructs a truly modernist, multiculturalist
relation between the greeting *Ayubowan* and the "serendipity" of the
"magical island":

> A kaleidoscopic experience of vivid intensity, where colourful
> sights and brash sounds intermingle with confusions of aromatic
> spices, friendly smiling faces, cultures that reflect peace and toler-
> ance, and religions that promote total harmony. Lifting the veil on
> this magical island reveals a country where ancient customs and
> traditions blend perfectly with modern life. For many centuries,
> past travelers to Sri Lanka have enjoyed its tranquil hospitality, its
> spellbinding history, and its outright friendliness. *Today nothing
> has changed* and its traditional welcome, *"Ayubowan"*—may you live
> long—is extended to each and every visitor.[4]

One cannot help but be struck by the prose of this description—
not necessarily for the images of beauty and enchantment, of the island's histories and mysteries—but for the diversity of cultures that it
alludes to. The description attempts to navigate, at once, between the
desire to celebrate the (Buddhist?) past and the desire to confront the
reality of the diversity of cultures promoting "peace" and harmony."
There is a double desire here. The celebration of the past, marked by
a desire to recover an *unchanging* identity within that past, is simultaneously guarded by the recognition of the kaleidoscopic religious and
cultural diversity on the island. In many ways, then, this seems as
generous a multiculturalist position as the postcolonial nation-state
could take. This multiculturalist position echoes the seeming contradiction that perhaps inheres in the very modernity of the postcolonial

nation-state. It must recognize and promote a certain national identity, yet it must not (and cannot) overlook its counterpart: diversity and difference. There is nothing new in this formulation, I suppose. But the question that I want to ask to complicate this formulation is this: if the voice of the flight attendant uttering *Ayubowan* is meant to capture something of the complexity of this evocation in the Web description, how does its privileging of *Ayubowan* as a feature of Sri Lankan national life reconcile with the other (acknowledged) matter of the changing identities and cultures of the nation, found in the "confusions of aromatic spices, friendly smiling faces, cultures that reflect peace and tolerance, and religions that promote total harmony"?

Given the allusion to the "confusion of . . . cultures" and "religions" and the specific mention of how they promote "peace," "tolerance," and "total "harmony," one can but surmise that in Sri Lanka there ought to be other racial, ethnic, and cultural forms of greetings, gestures of welcome, signs of distinction. Yes, without a doubt, such social and cultural distinctions do exist in Sri Lanka. But, of course, they cannot be *national,* at least in the way that *Ayubowan* is; they can only be *cultural* distinctions of the other. Indeed, on the airplane itself, one gets a brief exposure to something of such "cultural" distinctions when the in-flight greetings and announcements are made in three languages, Sinhalese (*Ayubowan*), Tamil (*Vanakkam*), and English (*Welcome*). Yet the announcements in two other languages in no way nullify the priority granted to the Sinhalese *Ayubowan*. In fact, in the order of their use onboard, the Tamil and English greetings authorize the priority of *Ayubowan* as *the* national greeting. Tamil and English greetings exist, but in the shadow of the Sinhalese national identity. Seen this way, the postcolonial nation-state does not need multiculturalist theorists to explain how multiculturalism should be applied. The nation—and its national (airline) crew—have already begun the work of multiculturalism. It has been doing its utmost task of *recognizing* the multiculturalist makeup of the nation—perhaps even before theorists like Charles Taylor urged the practice as a political virtue. The nation-state cultivates this recognition while exalting its own national identity. If this indicates the predicament of the modern nation-state as much as it does the poverty of the multiculturalism of our secularist modernity, it ought to send the theorists back to their desks, if not put them out of business.

From a Critique of "Democracy" Toward a Politics of Mourning

My point here partly is this: it will be easy for us to level a humanist criticism at the seeming contradiction or hypocrisy that we see in the practice of multiculturalist politics of the postcolonial nation-state. However valid such a criticism might be in terms of exposing the problem of the nationalist privileging of one language/culture over others, I suspect that such a criticism would accomplish nothing new politically. More pointedly, what would criticism demand of this nationalist (racist, if you will) practice onboard Sri Lankan Airlines? Can it produce a new politics? What would that politics amount to? Does that politics merely amount to a rearrangement of the order of the languages/greetings used onboard Sri Lankan Airlines? Or does it involve abandoning them altogether in place of an entirely new form of common greeting that all groups can equally share and invest in? As a way of seeking answers to some of these seemingly cynical questions, we can cast the overtly Sri Lankan "case" of *Ayubowan* in light of recent debates about the questions of liberalism, minority rights, and justice. To put it differently, we could ask what one of the foremost defenders of minority-ethnic-national rights in liberal political theory today, Will Kymlicka, might have to say about the problem of *Ayubowan*.

I think that it would not be hard for Kymlicka to find a profound ethical-political problem in this national promotion of one language/culture over another, not so much because it negates the other culture or denies its identity, but because it orders a hierarchical, asymmetrical relationship of power between the majority and minority groups. This relationship would worry him despite his concern with endorsing what he calls "societal culture" in ethnically (and religiously) diverse nation-states. After all, in his formulation, a societal culture is a place where minorities and majorities find politically acceptable spaces of belonging. As Kymlicka says, a societal culture is

> a territorially-concentrated culture, centered on a shared language which is used in a wide range of societal institutions, in both public and private life (schools, media, law, economy, government, etc.). I call it a *societal* culture to emphasize that it involves a common language and social institutions, rather than common religious beliefs,

family customs, or personal lifestyles. Societal cultures within a modern liberal democracy are inevitably pluralistic, containing Christians as well as Muslims, Jews, and atheists; heterosexuals as well as gays, urban professionals as well as rural farmers; conservatives as well as socialists. Such diversity is the inevitable result of the rights and freedoms guaranteed to liberal citizens, particularly when combined with an ethnically diverse population. This diversity, however, is balanced and constrained by linguistic and institutional cohesion; cohesion that has not emerged on its own but rather, is the result of deliberate state policies.[5]

Here there is undoubtedly a secularist conception in the imagination of this societal culture. My task is not to mock it but to unmask the kind of conceptual limitation of the liberal multiculturalism that Kymlicka seems to advance. The circumscribed notion of secularism that informs this societal culture is evident when he says (responding to one of his interlocutors, Bhikhu Parekh) that

> some people try to recast Muslim immigrants as the modern-day equivalent of the turn-of-the-century Hassidic Jews—i.e., as a group which rejects the norms of liberal democracy, and so retreats into a self-contained world where these norms are rejected. But this is a fantasy. The overwhelming majority of Muslims in Western countries want to participate in the larger societal culture, and accept its constitutional principles. The majority of their demands are simply requests that their religious beliefs be given the same kind of accommodation that liberal democracies have historically given to Christian beliefs. (61–62)

Now critics like Parekh claim that if minorities ("ethnonationalist groups") ended up accepting liberal principles, there would be no need for a theory of multiculturalism.[6] In response to Parekh, Kymlicka says that even though majorities and minorities might share the same liberal principles, they would not (and perhaps should not?) have a consensus on how minority differences are to accommodated. Hence the presumption here is that we will always need some sort of a multiculturalist theory, because, as Kymlicka says, there will always be differences in how liberal principles ought to be applied (60–61). This is so because "it is by no means clear or self-evident what liberal principles entail" (63). One way to reconcile the difference between what liberal values entail and how "ethnonationalist" minorities should apply them is to sustain a "dialogue" between them (62, 63). This dialogue can supposedly take place in a "societal culture." In response to Parekh's alleged misinterpretation of his arguments, Kymlicka reiterates that the societal culture he proposes does not deprive individual groups of claims to the sacredness of their traditions, cultures, and religions. But, at the same time, "it doesn't allow the group to restrict the civil liberties of its members in the name of the 'sacredness' of a particular cultural tradition or practice" (62, 63).

Even though this argument may not strike us as a groundbreaking theoretical intervention (vis-à-vis the Habermasian conception of public space or the Rawlsian conception of the secular), it would be unfair to accuse Kymlicka of simply invoking an updated notion of human rights or respect or tolerance for minorities. In fact, Kymlicka concedes that the idea of mere respect or tolerance for minorities is not a very helpful political idea these days, perhaps because the idea of tolerance is a close ally of the notion of human rights. It is certainly why he thinks the notion of human rights is inadequate to deal with questions of minority justice. To begin with, "few minorities are merely satisfied with respect for their individual human rights" and in most cases "individual rights do not adequately protect their interests" (72). Hence human rights must be supplemented with a conception of minority rights. As he puts it succinctly and candidly, "the aim of a liberal theory of minority rights is to define fair terms of integration for immigrants, and to enable national minorities to maintain themselves as distinct societies" (55). Here Kymlicka is attempting to straddle a position between integration of minorities into the societal culture on the one hand and creation of spaces (within that society) for maintaining their distinctiveness on the other. Doing so is hardly an easy task, and Kymlicka recognizes the difficulty. Thus he does not think it is in the best interest of some immigrant groups—he calls them "cultural" minorities—to aspire to a public cultural existence distinct from the majority in a given nation. The danger of such an aspiration is that the political interests of the majority can easily eclipse those of such minority groups. Such groups ought even be "pressured" (by liberals) to integrate into the mainstream culture, he says; this is the "only way to achieve equality and freedom" for them, which is, of course, not the case for "national" minorities, who have distinctive languages, cultural histories, and political institutions. They defy easy integration and demand a careful consideration of the distinctiveness of their minority identities. In some ways they constitute a fundamental challenge to liberalism insofar as their demands keep liberalism and its very identity in check. And, if I may liberally paraphrase Kymlicka, liberalism always has work to do when it comes to national minorities.

There is a host of presumptions in these sets of arguments, the least important of which is not the privileged status he accords to "number" and "tradition" in arriving at distinctions between "cultural" minorities and "national" minorities. But I want to leave aside a critique of them for the sake of posing a different question. Given this "liberal theory of minority rights," what would Kymlicka say about the problem of *Ayubowan* in relation to one of the most sizable "minority" communities of Sri Lanka, the Tamils (if not Tamil-speaking Muslims, who have perhaps recently begun refusing to identify themselves as/with Tamils)? The Sri Lankan Tamils would constitute a test case for Kymlicka's definition of a "national" minority. They have distinct cultural, religious, and linguistic differences. They are distinct to the extent that particular Tamil nationalist groups (like the LTTE) have invoked such differences to constitute a "Tamil national identity" and have waged a bloody war in an effort to defend such differences. If such a nationalist group cannot possibly conform to any state integration and is (politically and culturally) overshadowed by the majority Sinhalese identity (as the LTTE contends), how would Kymlicka treat this crucial instance of majority precedence over minority? I suspect he might give a couple of responses. He could simply say that his theory does not provide an answer in every case. Or he could say more carefully that the difficulty of such a case defies easy (constitutional or legal) answers. Of course, to say this is to assume that any facile suggestion of Tamil "self-government" in terms of a separate state is not a politically or ethically safe option, largely because of the bloody politics vis-à-vis competing claims for and against the LTTE demand by various ideological factions in Sinhalese and Tamil communities.[7] Granted this difficulty, Kymlicka could propose that we look to history with a view toward producing a *truthful* account of injustices against the minority communities. In fact, Kymlicka believes that such a study of history, which involves accepting both good and bad pasts, itself could produce almost a redemptive sense of justice.

In a different context of how students should be taught to approach history in schools, he writes that they "should view the nation's history as their history and hence take pride in its accomplishments, as well as shame in its injustices. This sense of identification with the nation's history is one of the few means available to maintain social unity in a pluralistic state, and may be needed if citizens are to embrace their responsibilities for upholding just institutions, and rectifying historical injustices" (315).

If this *liberal investment in history* seems inadequate today, it does so not solely because it supposes in a less than theoretically defensible way that history has something new to offer us beyond an overhauled notion of justice. Surely, it seems inadequate because it cannot precisely gauge the relation between knowledge and justice it takes for granted—the assumption that the more knowledge we have of history and its embedded injustices, the better we can serve (and receive) justice. This position should rouse the ghosts of Nietzsche, Arendt, and Foucault. In this correlation between knowledge and justice, history embodies a redeeming quality, and justice can only be obtained through knowledge of history. Such "knowledge" is posited as a virtue itself. It is this virtue that Kymlicka wants to safeguard. Liberals like Kymlicka, I suspect, will not apologize for privileging that virtue of knowledge because they believe too much in its liberal promise to abandon it for the sake of what is called an abstract conception of justice that "postliberal," "postmodern," and "postcolonial" strands of thinking offer. These liberals tell us that our juridical notion of justice has still much work to do and accomplish. Liberalism still lies on the side of the modern state. It still believes in the secular possibility, and indeed the "promise" of, the modern state's fostering a more just and equitable citizenship that encompasses, recognizes, and honors the rights of minorities. No radical, postmodernist questioning can easily rule out the importance of the norm of justice. As Kymlicka writes:

> A more radical kind of pluralization of citizenship . . . rejects not only the republican commitment to a unitary citizenship, but also the liberal insistence that group-specific rights be constrained by liberal principles of individual freedom, social equality, and political democracy. This sort of position draws on a variety of authors (William Connolly, Jacques Derrida, Julia Kristeva, Judith Butler,

etc.), and can be given a variety of labels: postliberal, postmodernist, postcolonial. What all of these versions of a politics of difference share is that they do not seek to contain differences within
the constraints of liberal justice. After all, they argue, liberal justice is itself just one amongst many cultural norms, none of which
should be privileged, all of which must be politicized and contested
in a multicultural society. *One difficulty with this approach is that it
operates at a more abstract or metatheoretical level than liberal culturalism,* and so finding the exact points of debate is not always easy. It
is sound advice that theorists in a multicultural society should not
take "our" liberal norms for granted, and should instead be willing to consider the objections and alternatives raised by non-liberal
groups. But to say that we should consider such objections and alternatives is not yet to say that we should accept them. We should
not exempt liberal culturalism from contestation, but nor should
we rule out the possibility that it will emerge from the contest as
the most *promising approach* to issues of ethnocultural justice. In
any event, I do not think that postmodernists have provided any
compelling reasons for ruling this out. (44; emphasis added)

We have to append the term *postsecular* to the list of labels against
which Kymlicka contrasts his liberal culturalism as the most "promising" alternative to the problem of our contemporary political landscape. If all liberalism can do today is urge us to seek comfort in the
promise of the possibility of (the revamped notions of state and citizenship being more attentive and responsible to) ethnonationalist justice, this *promise* is no more conceptually sound than the "abstract,"
"metatheoretical," imaginations of new political futures and justice
irreducible to either citizenship or law that Derrida and Connolly are
claimed to be engaged in. My point here is not that (Kymlicka) liberalism's "promising approach" is masqueraded as a real alternative.
Rather, it is that this promise, at least in its attempt to convince us of
its capacity to create a better future, some day, is merely a deferral,
having no answer to the ethical-political predicament that the modernity of the nation-state has found itself in. That predicament, as
we know, is this: the modern nation-state must promote its national
identity and yet must recognize the cultural and religious differences
of its citizens. However, these cultural differences bring into question
the very nationalness the nation-state wants to construct. The crucial

point here is that today liberalism can have no (or can only defer an) answer to this predicament because it is comforted by the belief that our best future hopes can be pinned on fashioning a more thorough, more vigorous, more forceful critique of the nation-state's supposed hegemony, demanding that it be more pluralistic, more inclusive, and more democratic. In this respect, liberalism of this sort might, with reservations, even congratulate a postcolonial nation like Sri Lanka for the "progress" it is making in recognizing the plurality of its culture. Nonetheless, the postcolonial nation-state itself is unsure about what it can possibly do, other than what it is already doing –i.e., the recognition of multiculturalist presence—in terms of public acknowledgment of it or constitutional reforms (undertaken recently in Sri Lanka) to put in the additional safeguards that would make such recognition a permanent part of the nation's identity.

Here the problem, it seems to me, is that if liberalism has no answer to the predicament, it is not so much because it has yet to produce a sharper critique of the nation-state. Rather, liberalism has been taking the very idea of the nation-state and its apparatus to be a self-evidently reachable goal, to fulfill the unfulfilled promise that lies just beyond the corner after exposing its contradictions and paradoxes. *What I am suggesting is that if we are to think the question of the political—and I mean here "think" and not simply write about or prescribe politics—we have to jettison this relentless critique of the nation-state and citizenship as consisting of too easily visible ideological underpinnings.* Critics like Balibar have already alluded to something of the political inefficacy of such a critique. He writes:

> The question of whether nationalism [or nation-state] is in itself an ideology of domination or exclusion is thus (at least in my eyes) a pointless one. Nationalism is the organic ideology that corresponds to the national institution, and this institution rests upon the formulation of *a rule of exclusion, of visible or invisible "borders,"* materialized in laws and practices. Exclusion—or at least unequal ("preferential") access to particular goods and rights depending on whether one is a national or a foreigner, belongs to the community or not—is thus the very essence of the nation-form.[8]

To add to this, I would say that a criticism of the nation-state and its nationalism could only point to its domains of exclusion. This, as

Balibar remarks, is nothing but "the illusion of believing that the nation-state could exist without nationalism, or with respect to the acceptance or rejection of foreigners, that some national traditions are open, tolerant, and 'universalist' by 'nature' or on account of their 'exceptionality,' whereas others still by virtue of their nature or historical specificity, are intolerant and 'particularistic'" (24–25). To put it slightly differently, so long as liberalism continues down the path of seeking to keep the nation-state in check, so to speak, by pointing to its contradictions to prevent it from developing into a regime of total intolerance and exclusion of minorities, it can never envision new futures of the political. The only course of politics that it can recommend, and indeed demand, of the nation-state is to remain true to its democratic identity by never forfeiting the task of recognizing its multiculturalist constituency.

If liberalism remains characterized by a certain conceptual incapacitation, what sort of new politics might it imagine? To do so, it must give up or un-inherit its criticism of the nation-state and democracy as a self-evident ideology. This giving up will involve believing in the most cynical and comical sense possible—and I want to stress the *cynical* aspect of it—that our modern nation-state and its democratic principles, in the wake of the collapse of the hopes of communism and anticolonialism—is not easily vulnerable to its demise or death (as some like Jeffrey Stout might fear). That is, as Nietzsche might have put it comically, our democratic present is now capable of its own "progress." Perhaps this statement is no more true today than ever, when we are bombarded with rallying calls (emanating from the pulpits of powerful nation-states) for our fellowship with the global dissemination of liberty and democracy as a panacea for all political and moral ills. In this cynical sense, democracy is capable of safeguarding itself without liberal critics seeking to prevent perils to it, whether from itself or from the outside. Let me put this matter in a somewhat different way. Take our discussion of the problem of *Ayubowan* as practiced onboard Sri Lankan Airlines. Liberalism that is committed to ethnonationalist justice obviously does not have a response to it, except to point to a humanist engagement of history. This engagement takes us nowhere, as we now know. What if it turns back and says that investing in the problem is no longer politically efficacious? What if it says that it is not politically efficacious because the problem is too easy a target? That is, liberalism detects and dissects too easily the hegemony of the postcolonial nation's (and the airline's) deploy-ment of *Ayubowan* as a constitutive part of the national identity of Sri Lanka. The postcolonial nation (and the "national" airline) itself remain(s) aware of the problem of exclusion that it produces. That is why it goes to the extent of not only recognizing but also celebrating its multicultural differences. Since the nation-state is already obliging what liberalism has been demanding of it, liberalism will then have to find a different target.

This new target is not (and cannot be) easily identifiable and per-haps cannot be an easy object of criticism. That is because, as Derrida might say—perhaps strangely echoing Foucault—the new target does not remain under a sign of "exclusion" or "domination." Rather, this target is less apprehensible. It is almost absent, yet it has a ghostly presence. This ghostly target beckons. It beckons to be seen and heard, not as a sign of exclusion soliciting our humanist care for it, but as a site of mourning toward an im-possible future that is almost upon us. More important, perhaps, this new target would not be easily *problem-atizable*, because it is not an easily *perceptible* effect of an "ideology." Even for Marx, "the theory of ideology depends in many of its features . . . on [the] theory of the ghost" (*Specters*, 127). If ideology is such a ghost, then it needs a body ("a prosthetic body") to make its ghostly presence/absence visible. This is because there can never be a ghost, "never any becoming-specter of the spirit, without at least an appear-ance of flesh, in a space of invisible visibility, like the dis-appearing of an apparition. For there to be ghost, there must be a return to the body that is more abstract than ever" (126). The specter does not return to a "living body." Rather, it is an *"artifactual body,* a *"prosthetic body,* a ghost of spirit, one might say a ghost of the ghost" (126). The fetish is this body, the ghost of the ghost. It is the "borrowed body, the second incarnation conferred on an initial idealization, the incorporation in a body that is, to be sure, neither perceptible nor invisible, but remains flesh, in a body without nature, in *a-physical* body that could be called . . . a technical body or an institutional body" (127). The fetish needs "even a visible-invisible body, sensous-non-sensous, and always un-der the tough institutional or cultural protection of some artifact: the helmet of the ideologem or the fetish under armor" (127). This (as we have already noted in some detail) is partly Derrida's theory of ghosts as he develops it based on his selective reading of Marx. What Derrida is saying—I simplify at the risk of falsifying it—is that if ideology is a kind of ghost, it needs a body to make itself visible. That body is the fetish. But the fetish itself is not so easily visible, either. It, too, has a ghostly presence/absence and is thus "visible-invisible."

I argue that, if liberalism wants to think of new spaces of politics, it has to locate new targets. But such targets must be approached as not so easily apprehensible, ghostly targets that are visible-invisible. To put it differently, it has to locate and think of such targets as those that do not merely await "problematization" (and "historicization"), those that cannot be done away with by way of explanations, which we discussed earlier. If liberalism approaches its targets in this way, it can assess radically its relation to democracy itself, not necessarily to discard democracy—I hope that I have not given this impression in any of these chapters—but to be concerned with mourning and un-inheriting the heritage of democracy. In the rest of this last chapter, I want to attempt to locate an ethical-political target that demands such thinking.

This target is related to what I have been calling the postcolonial problem of *Ayubowan* itself. So far my argument has been that liberal/leftist theories, of whatever disciplinary hue, remain unable to say anything politically worthwhile about the problem of *Ayubowan*. The problem of *Ayubowan*, as we meet up with it onboard Sri Lankan airlines, is not merely a challenge to liberal multiculturalist theory. Rather, it is itself an embodiment of the problem of liberal multi-culturalism! Solving this problem, I have argued—if it is possible at all—requires more than an updating of the old multiculturalist theo-ries and terminology. In other words, a mere "criticism" of the prob-lem of *Ayubowan* as a hegemonic, nationalist discourse authorized by a pluralist postcolonial nation is not going to produce anything new. The problem is a product of the making of multiculturalist politics itself. It has to be approached from a radically new vantage. And this involves giving up thinking of the problem of *Ayubowan* (and the postcolonial politics of the secular nation-state in which it is located) as a self-evident site that can be *improved* by a sharper critique that would lead to the formation of a new policy or law or "conscience." Now a political scientist like Amy Gutmann who still finds hope in our justice system and law claims that conscience has a direct relation to policy making. Gutmann contends that personal "conscientious convictions" can play a major part in shaping our democratic futures. According to her, even though the idea of conscience may have been linked to religion at one time, today it has a secular sense.[9] "Conscience has a special relevance for democratic politics because it can be ignored only at the expense of respect for persons which is a fundamental tenet of democratic justice" (172). I am sympathetic to this suggestion, and I do not want to gainsay many of the social and political achievements that conscientious convictions are said to have made possible. But I doubt (after Nietzsche, Freud, and Heidegger and now in the wake of the problem of *Ayubowan*) that an appeal to conscience is going to yield anything other than what we already have: "respect for persons."[10] (One may argue that this "respect for persons" is respect for law.) Put bluntly, the problem of *Ayubowan* already embodies this conscience. The problem of *Ayubowan* certainly violates no law. Indeed, it abides by law. And, in a sense, it performs and enacts a certain kind of justice. It embodies and practices the democratic principle of "respect" for others. That is, it recognizes others, their cultures, and their languages. It embodies the hopes and aspirations of the multiculturalist project that promotes the conscience of "respect" for others/persons. In a nutshell, the problem of *Ayubowan* embodies the problem of our "secular conscience," which is also the very problem of law and justice.

Here we have reached a critical impasse: we are in need of turning this secular problem of the postcolonial liberal nation-state, this problem of *Ayubowan,* into something else that it may cease to be what its apparent "name" suggests. That is, how might we turn this easily translatable noun/name (*Ayubowan*), which we know so well as the "national" greeting, into something that it is not—a cry? How would *Ayubowan's* "transition" from a greeting to a cry alter its name/meaning? As Derrida might say, if a "name" isassigned to that which we do not know or understand—not yet, at least—then can *Ayubowan* retain its name and mean something different in its transition from a greeting to cry? This transition seems im-possible, however, because the transition—I am deliberately using this word—has the potential violence of the carryover of its former name (*Ayubowan*) and meaning (Welcome!), if not the vestiges of its relation to the nation-state ("*Ayubowan* is the national greeting"). Can we overcome the violence of the possibility of this carryover? I am not sure that I am erudite enough to promise to overcome this im-possibility. Yet I am interested in exploring the im-possibility. It is in this way, then, that I approach this target. The target can be best described as a ghostly target. The target is perhaps not present today. It is vanishing or has already vanished. Hence the target cannot be apprehended or anthropologized or historicized (Again, one may historicize it, and I do not want to deny this possibility, but I am simply imagining that it cannot be done any more only to think of wholly another option.) Yet the specter of this target, the ghost of its ghost, demands thinking, "thinking justice," thinking the future of the irreducible political. Surely this ghostly, spectral target cannot be an "example" of anything. Yet this vanishing/vanished target can perhaps be called upon, as all ghosts can be called upon, to come back, to let us, perhaps, glimpse its fleeting presence, hear the waning sound of its cry in the way I have already tersely described it.

Something of the vanishing possibility of this target may be found in *Ayubowan*'s transition from a greeting to a cry. For me, something of this transition took place during one of my visits to Sri Lanka's up-country, to Nuwara Eliya, the "City of Lights," which rises 5,906 feet above sea level sixty-two miles south of Kandy. Famous for its cool climate, which attracts visitors escaping the scorching heat of the low country, Nuwara Eliya, which the British planters created as a vacation spot in the nineteenth-century, is sometimes referred to as Little England. The sharply winding, bumpy road that leads up to Nuwara Eliya is narrow, making it hazardous for two vehicles on the road to pass each other. In a car (or bus), one is constantly rocked to the left and the right at each hairpin turn, but the breathtaking scenery, the lush hillsides covered with cascading waterfalls and tea plantations, and the fresh misty air all render the discomfort worthwhile. Less than twenty miles before the town of Nuwara Eliya, a sign near the entrance to a tea factory in Uda Pussellawa invites weary travelers to have a cup of tea. In June of 2002, en route to Nuwara Eliya, I found this invitation too welcoming to bypass. My taxi driver-companion, Sirisena, and I pulled onto the factory premises, parked the car, and walked up to the tea shop. The tall, middle-aged woman of slender frame who stood at the entrance placed her palms together and uttered the word *Ayubowan* to invite us into the shop. She bore some distinct signs. She wore a sari on which was pinned an official name tag that gave her name (Kamalam) and her position (manager).[11] She also wore a *pottu* on her forehead and spoke with a distinctive accent. Some of these signs—the name, the *pottu* on the forehead, and the accent—*gave away* her identity as a "Tamil," an identity she herself confirmed in our subsequent conversations. It would not be contro-versial to say that Kamalam's Tamil identity—however differently she may understand it—is connected with my assuming it to be so. Yet this identity also has as much to do with a (Sinhalese) culture that seeks to sustain a relation between such signs and Tamilness in Sri Lanka. Needless to say, Tamilness, and all of its variations, can hardly be reduced to these signs alone. But this brief qualification does not rid the Tamil identity of the problematic politics of its production that makes it available for identification and representation. Nor would a more detailed anthropological account of its identity, of the politics of its history, of its fashionings and contestations in Sri Lanka, do very much.

As we were ushered into an open and airy hall to be seated with a few other guests, Kamalam and I exchanged a few words of cour-tesy. Sirisena and I ordered a pot of tea with milk and some sweet *talaguli* and bananas. A few minutes later, as we were sipping our tea, Kamalam approached to inquire how we liked our drinks and sweets. Sirisena finished his tea and, nodding at me, scooted out for a smoke. Kamalam and I began to talk casually. I asked her how long she had been working at the shop and where she was from. As she responded to my questions and questioned me in turn about where I was head-ing and whatnot, I asked pointedly and perhaps rudely: "Are you Tamil?"[12] When she answered in the affirmative, I followed with the question "Why did you greet us with *Ayubowan* and not *Vanakkam* when we walked in?" "Well, that's how we always greet our custom-ers," Kamalam responded. I, then, asked if the use of *Ayubowan* trou-bled her at all, not merely because it was a Sinhalese form of greet-ing but also because the Sinhalese rarely use *Vanakkam* as a form of official (national) greeting (as Tamils are obliged to use the for-mer). Behind the counter Gauri, the cashier, a Tamil woman herself, overheard our conversation and readily joined in to echo Kamalam's response. They both insisted that "there is no problem" in their us-ing *Ayubowan,* despite my efforts to persuade them otherwise. Gauri went on to add that any greeting is a greeting, be it in Sinhalese or Tamil. There was no difference between *Vanakkam* and *Ayubowan.* Both greetings serve the same purpose. Kamalam nodded her head as if to validate Gauri's remarks.

What does one make of Kamalam's and Gauri's refusal to see any problem with a Tamil being obliged to use *Ayubowan* in a public

setting like the Uda Pussellawa tea factory? One could provide different explanations, if one wants to problematize it. One could see this
as an instance of informants –if you can call these two women that—
refusing to see the use of *Ayubowan* the same way as I—a fellow Sri
Lankan, a Sinhalese, a pseudo-anthropologist, a scholar of religion, a
postcolonial critic, or just a customer at the tea factory—saw it, at an
unexpected ("quasi-ethnographic"?) moment. One could also see their
refusal as a kind of strategy on their part. That is, they responded the
way they did because of the possible danger of losing their jobs by
speaking their minds. One could (following this logic) also argue that
this presents one more example of a postcolonial nation's betrayal of
its secular promise of "equal" citizenship to all its citizens, in one of
the most conspicuous of formerly state-monitored public spaces. That
is, granting in the most liberal sense possible that although most tea
plantations in Sri Lanka are no longer operated by the (Sinhalese)
state today, and hence those (mostly Tamil laborers) who work for
them are no longer state employees, the former national practices still
operate in the hands of their private owners/leasers.[13] Seen this way,
the modern economy, haunted by the former state policies, is engaged
in perpetrating epistemic violence against its minorities by obliging
them to endorse a "national" practice of political-moral import.

But what do these explanations, problematizations, and elabora-
tions accomplish? Is it anything other than producing a mere *criticism* of how our modern nation-state has yet to fulfill its democratic
pledge of, and indeed its "responsibility" for, creating a just community of multiculturalist coexistence? By now, it must be evident that
such a criticism can only appeal to law, to demand that it recognize
that "minorities" like Tamils are full citizens with equal rights. I do
not want to entirely gainsay the validity of such an appeal to the extent that it has already yielded what possibly it has (such as minority
rights). But to think that it can deliver more than what it has already
delivered is to continue believing in the illusion of our liberal ethic of
responsibility, the responsibility of reminding democracy of its unfulfilled promise of responsibility toward, and justice for, all its citizens.
As we have discussed in detail, what we need today is not so much
an exhausted notion of *responsibility* as an ethos of hearing the cry, a
hearing that looks toward un-inheriting the very heritage of the practice *Ayubowan*, which, by extension, would be the heritage of the very
opposition between the Sinhalese and the Tamils in Sri Lanka. *Thus*

the use of Ayubowan is not an isolated cultural practice that anthropologists and historians can simply write about. It mirrors the very history of the distinction between the Sinhalese and their (excluded) others. Hence to think about un-inheriting this problem is to think about un-inheriting the very history of that distinction, a history (of violent racisms and even genocides) that we know quite well today. To that extent, then, writing an alternative history of Ayubowan—if such a history exists "out there"—is not going to change the history of the Sinhala/Tamil distinction. But the demand for this un-inheriting cannot come from an appeal to state/law/justice. As we know now, what law demands is responsibility. On the contrary, a form of hearing the cry of *Ayubowan* that demands its un-inheriting has to come from elsewhere. What I want to suggest is that this un-inheriting can be demanded by the (waning) cry of *Ayubowan* itself. (This is like the aporia of the name that demands its own un-inheriting; see chapter 1.) Put differently, what if we pause for a minute to think that Kamalam's use of *Ayubowan* is irreducible to any further deconstruction. (Just like the aporia of the name, *Ayubowan* is perhaps already deconstructed.) That is to say, imagine that Kamalam's use of *Ayubowan* is beyond scholarly explanations of it as an instance of the state's violation of the rights of minorities. Or imagine that it is beyond the state's ability to fix the problem by some legislative act. This is to assume in turn that the state's forming one more "law" that would allow "Tamil" minorities to use their own form of ethnic-cultural greeting or merely adopt the English version would solve the problem. But this would amount to nothing but multiculturalism. We must *suppose* then that this "problem" cannot necessarily be solved or corrected, at least not by the available multiculturalist, legalist, modernist terms. The problem of *Ayubowan* is the problem of our multiculturalist modernity and democracy. The problem cannot be solved by the problem. The problem is perhaps not deconstructible any more. It can no longer be problematized. Aporia!

The Ghostly Call of *Ayubowan* and the Future of the Political

It is in this sense that I want to think of the problem of *Ayubowan* as a ghostly target or as an aporia. From this ghostly aporia emanates a cry or call. But the call comes not from a person (e.g.,

Kamalam); it is not the call of (an)other. At least, this is not how I want to think of it. It comes from itself. It is the call of itself. This notion of the call cannot "call out" because there is no caller behind it. As Heidegger says, "calling out already presupposes discourse." For Heidegger, this call is not necessarily an "utterance." It "can factically never be found. . . . The call comes from afar to afar" (*Being*, 251).[14] It may be the call of the ghost—the ghost of *Ayubowan*. What this call demands is a certain kind of responsiveness to its ghostly "problem." Call it a demand for being heard. One cannot respond to it, or hear it, just because one feels responsible for or toward it. This is partly because this call is the apparition of responsibility. Already the work of responsibility has been performed on it, so to speak. That is to say, it is the apparition of the problem of multiculturalism and law itself. If there is any "responsible" responsiveness to the call of this aporia, it must do the work of mourning its heritage. But one cannot mourn this problem to get rid of it, to exorcise it, to cast it away. Nor can one mourn this problem because it symbolized something we have lost. Rather, we must mourn it because it haunts us. If the call of *Ayubowan* is a ghostly call, and if this ghost haunts us, this ghost is both visible-invisible, present-absent, dead-alive. This ghost has returned from the past to haunt us. Yet ghosts do not return in the same shapes or forms; ghosts take different shapes. The returned ghost cannot be sent back to the same past because the ghost now inhabits our disconnected present, which does not remain linked to a clearly visible past. This returned ghost is a remnant of a certain problem that has *survived*. If this is so, then this ghost "lives on." As we have already noted in chapters 1 and 6, that which lives on "is reducible to neither living nor dead." (This is why Derrida speaks of "living-dead ghosts [*Specters*, 169].) Simply put, if the problem of *Ayubowan* reflects the past problem of multiculturalist democracy, that past has come back as a ghost to haunt us: it has refused to go away. We are haunted to imagine a future in which we will un-inherit the legacy of the very modernist distinction between self and other, Sinhalese and Tamil, friend and enemy. Thinking of such a future, a future that is absent-present, then, is made possible by this haunting. This sense of mourning the un-inheritable legacy is critical because it does not aim at coming to terms with the loss or death of a subject/object. Rather, haunted by ghosts, one can only think of the absence-presence of the future. But this thinking cannot be done out of obligation or responsibility, that is to say, out of responsibility for the future. One cannot do so, because mourning the problem of *Ayubowan* is made possible by haunting. If those who haunt us are ghosts, there is really no identifiable haunter as such, to the extent that ghosts are present-absent, visible-invisible. If ghosts are not identifiable, one cannot do it for the sake of, out of responsibility for, ghosts. Ghosts are not individuals. Ghosts do not demand accountability or rights. They cannot be placated with an offering of "justice." One cannot be responsible to them because they are not present: they are absent-present. The idea of responsibility, like that of justice, then operates in the domains of the "now," in the present, the time that is not disjointed. Responsibility belongs to the seamless time where the horizons of the past and the future can always be anticipated. Responsibility seeks to repair the cracks that threaten to tear apart the seemingly seamless continuity of the present. Yet ghosts do not belong to a seamless time. Ghosts become visible—if they do become visible at all—in a time that is out of joint with itself. In such a time the future can never be merely anticipated, but only "remains to come." So long as one operates with responsibility, one cannot hear the call of the absent-present ghosts. One may hear the call of a present-contemporary individual demanding justice and accountability. One may even hear the call of an individual like Kamalam—assuming that her open refusal to call for anything itself is a certain call and that this refusal itself constitutes a "sign" of oppression. One may attend to this call by devising a law or policy or program to correct the seeming problem of *Ayubowan*. Surely, this way of hearing the call of the other, of coming face-to-face with the other, encountering and even confronting the other's oppression—this is a Levinasian sense of justice—is important. We cannot and must not discard this kind of care for the other. But this care for the other still remains founded on a belief in an unfulfilled promise of law, justice, and responsibility. This sort of care cannot think the absent-present future. A future of such un-inheriting, I want to contend, is a future of anti-genealogy.

In the remainder of this chapter I want to show what sort of relationship we might imagine between a future of anti-genealogy and an irreducible politics. I want to do so by undertaking a reading of Derrida's *Politics of Friendship*. The text has already gained some notoriety.[15] Those who appreciate this text point to it as one more example of Derrida's interest in the question of the political, whereas others see it as another example of the lack of politics in Derrida's work. Needless to say, I agree with the former claim and wholly disagree with the latter.[16] At any rate, what interests me is how we may read the text to construct a particular relation between the political and anti-genealogy, mourning and future, a theme that has received little attention. For me this text, then, is as much a work of anti-genealogy as it is a work of mourning. What I want to show is that the way in which the text conceives of the relation between anti-genealogy and mourning enables us to think of the question of the political in relation to that of the future. This future, which Derrida claims has to be thought in relation to the democratic logic of *to come*, has a subtle relation to what he calls friendship. Friendship, as I want to read it, is not necessarily a delimitable domain of friendship as such. For Derrida, the question of friendship is inseparable from the question of the future and its relation to the political—that is to say, the future of an anti-genealogical politics.

The jacket description announces that at the heart of *Politics of Friendship* (henceforth referred to as *Politics*) is the issue of "anti-genealogy, upsetting the genealogical motive itself" (and this aspect of it often has been overlooked in largely passing comments on this text). But, at first glance, *Politics* may seem as though it furnishes us with a genealogical history of the problem of friendship in politico-philosophical traditions of the West, because the text begins with a dissection of the history of the address "O my friends, there is no friend," allegedly attributed to Aristotle, and goes on to examine how a generation of modernist critics such as Montaigne, Nietzsche, and Carl Schmitt have commented on it. But Derrida does not dissect that history merely to inform us of the way(s) in which the idea of friendship has come to be, or *emerged*—to use that Nietzsche-Foucauldian term—as a problem. Rather, Derrida meditates on such a history to point to what one may call the "interruptions," "inversions," and "overturnings" of the meanings of the address. Yet the point of this meditation is not to demonstrate how these meanings have *changed over time,* or become subject to the "whips and scorns of time"—as Shakespeare might have preferred to say.[17] Rather, the point of this exercise is to raise the question(s) of un-inheriting and mourning the problem of friendship, which is the very problem of democracy.[18] That is, if friendship has a history of how it came to be understood and contested over time, one cannot easily inherit it. One cannot easily inherit it, appeal to, it, gain access to it, refer to it, or cite it quite simply because it is not available to us in the senses in which it has been rendered. One cannot inherit it because it belongs to disjointed times of its many inversions and innterruptions, if you will. If it belongs to disjointed times, and if it is not merely available to us, to our time, to our disjointed time, the thinking about friendship involves being haunted by it, haunted by its unavailability now, in the present, in the disjointedness of time. To be hunted by the unavailability of friendship in the present is to mourn it, to mourn its unavailability in the present, to mourn inheriting it. Mourning the unavailability of this friendship is to mourn the present itself. Mourning the present this way, then, involves thinking of the future in which an "unheard-of" future of friendship and the political might become an im-possibility. It is in this way that I want to read the relation between friendship, mourning, and time.

A Future of Democracy?
"It will last as Long as It Has"

For Derrida, mourning the heritage of "friendship" has a distinct relation to the future of politics, that is to say, of democracy itself. This is partly because the Aristotelian address, "O my friends, there is no friend," itself echoes a kind of mourning, in the sense of a complaint, an injustice, or a grievance. "It is perhaps a complaint, and a grievance, the complaint of one who complains, to oneself, of oneself, or complains of the other, to others" (ix). This address is "an almost impossible declaration" (1). It is an impossible declaration perhaps because it at once addresses friends and denies them friendship. Or, it is so perhaps because the friends to whom the complaint is lodged "are not there present and living" to receive the complaint or to consider it warranted. (It is in a similar way that I want to think of the cry or complaint of *Ayubowan* itself.) Seen this way, this declaration is as much a complaint as it is an act of mourning. It (or its ghost today) mourns those friends not present and living, not yet, and indeed absent. (The ghost of *Ayubowan* too complains, by itself, not to be heard by any individual/agent present. It calls for thinking and mourning its own un-loss.) And mourning the non-present friends has a distinct relation to the future of "politics" or "democracy," which Derrida clearly separates from that of a regime or a party. The figure of the friend who is also the "[humanist] brother . . . seems spontaneously to belong to a *familial, fraternalist* and thus *androcentric* configuration of politics" (viii). For Derrida, to "dream" of a new friendship that goes beyond this familial, fraternalist, humanist model is at the same time to dream of a new "democracy" or politics. Such a democracy, then, is one of antihumanism as well. Our current notion of democracy itself belongs to a fraternalistic, humanistic politics to the extent that the "concept of politics rarely announces itself without some sort of adherence of the State to the family, without what we call a *schematic* of affiliation: stock, genus or species, sex (*Geschlecht*), blood, birth, nature, nation—autochthonal or not, tellurian or not" (viii).

In my view, this is Derrida's brief (and not so celebratory) definition of our contemporary democracy. This definition of democracy with the emphasis on its "schematic of affiliation" should come as no surprise to those who have read Foucault, if not Nietzsche. They would know that our democratic notions of belonging and affiliation qua private domains and institutions like marriage, family, and community, which seemingly occupy a threshold of distance from civil society and the state, are indeed counted, observed, legislated, regulated, and controlled by the power apparatuses of the state. This is partly why Derrida wonders whether the future of friendship he imagines is necessarily a future of democracy or a *radically* new democracy. Democracy seems to have already seen its best days. That is to say, democracy has already realized its future. In a sense, we already live the future of democracy, which is our present. This present is no longer, in the sense that it cannot be improved or reconstructed anew. Lest one accuse Derrida (and me) of antidemocratic sentiments, Derrida writes, "saying that to keep this Greek name, democracy, is an affair of context, of rhetoric and strategy, even of polemics, reaffirming that this name will last as long as it has but not much longer, saying that things are speeding up remarkably in these fast times, is not necessarily giving in to the opportunism or cynicism of the anti-democrat who is not showing his cards" (105). Now for Derrida there can be no democracy without deconstruction, and no deconstruction without democracy (105). Yet the question that haunts Derrida, and the question that should haunt all democratically minded persons is whether at the end of this deconstruction of democracy—those that remain to come, the *arrivants,* the irreducible singularities that democracy "cannot and should not count" (x)—would still have any relation to the name *democracy* and its legacy. As Derrida muses,

> is it still *in the name of democracy* that one will attempt to criticize such and such a determination of democracy or aristo-democracy ... is it still in the name of democracy, of a democracy-to-come, that one will attempt to deconstruct a concept, all the predicates associated with the massively dominant concept of democracy, that in whose heritage one inevitably meets again the law of birth, the natural or "national law," the law of homophilia, or of autochthony. (103–4)

Derrida's concern here is with whether or not we can continue to (re) inherit democracy, *in the name of democracy,* by criticizing and deconstructing the concept, and it is evident in the following questions he poses:

> What remains or resists still in the deconstructed (or deconstructible) concept of democracy which guides us endlessly? Which orders us not only to engage a deconstruction but to keep the old name? And to deconstruct further in the name of *democracy* to come? That is to say, further, which enjoins us still to inherit from what—forgotten, repressed, misunderstood, or unthought in the "old" concept and throughout its history—would still be on the watch, giving off signs or symptoms of a stance of survival coming through all the old and tired features? Would there be . . . in the concept of equality (equality of birth, *isogonia,* and concept of rights, *isonomia*) a double motif that might, interpreted differently, exclude democracy from autochthonous and homophilic rooting? Is there another thought of calculation and of number, another way of apprehending the universality of the singular which, without dooming politics to the incalculable, would still justify the old name of democracy? Would it still make sense to speak of democracy when it would no longer be a question (no longer in question as to what is essential or constitutive) of a country, nation, even of State or citizen—in other words, *if at least one still keeps to the accepted use of this word,* when it would no longer be a political question? (104)

In my view, these are some of the most pressing questions that our democratic present—a dying one at that—urgently needs to ask itself. As must be evident by now, following in the footsteps of either the relentless pursuers and defenders of the yet unfulfilled promises of democracies or the opponents of democracy, we are not going to be able to find answers to these kinds of questions. Both pro-democratic and antidemocratic theories are not yet attuned to the politics of how we might un-inherit and mourn the very idea of democracy. So, in a way, the questions that Derrida asks are not mere questions. Nor are they mere complaints. In my view, these questions are poignant words of mourning. They mourn the aporia that we have reached in our modernity. That is, we are still heirs to a modernity in which we are not yet able to discard entirely the idea of democracy. Yet democracy has almost become "old and tired"; "It will last as long as it has" and "not much longer." (Note here the sense of the future of democracy that has arrived and almost passed.) It has almost reached the end of being deconstructed. Democracy has almost reached a point where it remains no longer a "political question." Aporia! What does this aporia demand? "Perhaps" friendship?[19]

But friendship itself is not merely a solution to the aporia of our democracy. Friendship does not offer itself as a ready-made solution, because friendship as such does not exist. Or, as Derrida would say, even when friendship is present, it never exists. At least it does not exist "yet," because (phallogocentric) friendship, like democracy, is both "deconstructed and deconstructable." It is deconstructed in the sense that what Aristotle might have meant by it is no longer available to, or recoverable in, our present, at least not effortlessly. Its time, and indeed its future, has already passed us, to the extent that generations of claims upon it, multiple interpretations imposed upon it throughout its history, have irrevocably altered whatever (Greek) senses friendship embodied. (But, concerned as Derrida is with the question of [the] inheritance [of legacy], he asks if we are still heirs to Aristotle's conceptualization of friendship, which stands for, among other things, a particular kind of democratic existence. And, as we will see below, the answer Derrida gives to this question is at the same time both "yes" and "no." For him, this is one of the most effective ways to *relate*—if there is any relating—to the legacy of democracy.)

Derrida begins *Politics* with a discussion of how friendship has been defined and understood—albeit rather vaguely—in relation to questions: how many friends should one have? How long should friends/friendships last within/beyond life? Should friendship be preserved in silence/secrecy? Are friends always male/brothers? What is important to me (and perhaps to Derrida himself) is not that we unearth the answers to these kinds of questions, but that the questions and answers are not available to us today because they are already deconstructed. That is to say, the present we inhabit does not have easy access to the Greek or Roman philosophies of friendship because our present is disjunctured or punctuated, and indeed punctured, by other important discourses about friendship. Or, to put it another way, there are "deliberate perversion[s] of the heritage" of (Greek?) friendship (61). Hence we cannot simply inherit the legacy of friendship. It is in the sense of such a history of perversions that friendship remains, to an extent, deconstructed. Out of the many perversions of friendship, at least two are noteworthy perversions that are critical to thinking about the legacy of friendship in relation to thinking the future of the political. These two perversions belonged to a time just within shouting distance of our modernity, just within the vicinity of our democratic present, if you will. Yet they are so scandalous and perhaps so untimely that neither can fully settle and belong within our disjunctive present. The names/figures associated with the two perversions I have in mind are Carl Schmitt and Friedrich Nietzsche.[20] They are important because Derrida is almost haunted in *Politics* by the interventions of these two men in reshaping the relation between friendship and politics. Nietzsche and Schmitt mark the point where *our* culture is both "old and young," where we both are and are not heirs to the past (of the Greek tradition). They mark the point where we cannot totally dispense with, or totally be tied down to, the past. Their interventions in crafting the relation between friendship and politics perhaps constitute (what Derrida sometimes calls) "historical tremors" just beneath our present. We live within these tremors. Obviously this way of thinking of the past vis-à-vis the present is important to Derrida because of his notions of haunting and mourning and because, like Nietzsche, Derrida wants to think of our present as being non-contemporaneous with itself, where we face the difficult task of simultaneously remembering and (actively) forgetting our pasts (185). This is what he is interested in, "a deconstruction *of the* genealogical schema, a paradoxical deconstruction—a deconstruction at once genealogical and a-genealogical, *of the* genealogical" (105).

Needless to say, Derrida has a rather different relation to Nietzsche than he does to Schmitt. Derrida finds it almost impossible to escape the shadow of Nietzsche's thinking. But, of course, there is also the shadow of Schmitt, whose interventions in and perversions of the history of friendship have proven so instrumental to our democratic tradition. For "the first time" in his life, Derrida says, he wants to move away from Nietzsche's shadow by way of thinking against the genealogical notion of history. To do so, Derrida reads and rereads Schmitt in relation to Nietzsche's inversion of the Aristotelian (and the Augustinian) notions of friendship. Derrida almost pits them against each other. Schmitt is less well known than Nietzsche, yet he has had a decisive impact on our modernity, particularly in its relation to questions of democracy and political sovereignty.[21] Nowhere is this impact more critical than in the relation between friendship, enmity, and the concept of the political that Schmitt constructs. Schmitt (1888–1985) lived and wrote much after the time of Nietzsche (1844–1900). In Derrida's view, the tradition of friendship that Schmitt inherits is as much Greek (as well as Augustinian and Christian) as it is Nietzschean. (Note how this move complicates any notion of mere continuity between the Schmittian and the Greek notions of friendship.) Augustine, who "knew his Aristotle," broke with the Greek tradition to Christianize the idea of friendship (*Politics*, 186).[22] He did so partly by inserting the notions of guilt and conscience.[23] But Nietzsche (who declared "Oh enemies, there is no enemy") inverted the Greek tradition and de-Christianized the Augustinian refraternization and Christianization of the idea of friendship. Augustine, in Derrida's typological reading of him, considered (without exactly quoting the Greek master) the vague phrase "one soul in bodies twain" as "Aristotle's apt definition of friendship."[24] The phrase "one soul in twin bodies" could not possibly have been "the apt definition of friendship," since Aristotle offered other definitions of it. But, for Augustine, the phrase was synonymous with what Aristotle considered friendship to be. Yet, precisely because it was vague, Augustine wrestled with the phrase to give his own "inimitable signature and a universal form of revelation," producing a "cunning, profound, and troubling consequence" (*Politics*, 186). Augustine does so by evoking the idea of "double terror." This is the terror of surviving the death of one's friend, living with half one's soul severed, and the terror of not surviving. Derrida quotes Augustine: "Life to me was fearful because I did not want to live with only half a soul. Perhaps (*forte*) this, too, is why I shrank from death, for fear that one whom I had loved so well might then be wholly dead" (186). In Derrida's view, Augustine constructs a paradoxical relation between self and other in terms of the question "Do you desire to survive for yourself or for the person whom you are mourning" (186; Derrida's words). (Here Derrida does not mince words when he claims that what Augustine conceals in his supposed interest in the question of surviving the other is "a narcissism which is never related to itself except in the mourning of the other" [187].) This is the terror or fear that Augustine inserts into the idea of friendship, and this fear is founded upon "guilt." And, for Augustine, this guilt animates friendship. Again, Derrida quotes Augustine: "This is what we cherish in friendship, and we cherish it so clearly that in conscience we feel guilty if we do not return love for love . . . asking no more of our friends than these expressions of goodwill. . . . This is why we mourn their death . . . and life becomes a living death because a friend is lost" (187). Here friendship becomes not only something of exchangeable value ("love for love") but is also tied to the idea of guilt and conscience. This friendship based on love and guilt is fraternal. As Derrida argues, for Augustine this guilt-bound fraternal friendship is found "in the home—that is, in the family or in the filiation of God," in the "dwelling place of *God*" (187). It is not only in this home/ house of God that the "friendship of friends" is found, however. It is also where the "enmity of the enemy" is found. According to this calculation, Augustine suggests that we love both our friends and enemies. But there is a difference. We must love friends *in* God. But we must love enemies *because of* God. (Nietzsche mocked this idea of loving one's enemy by saying: "The love of one's enemies? I think it has been well learned. It happens thousandfold today.")[25] The difference between loving *in* and loving *because of* is this: the former is based on guilt and the latter on a command: a command by God "because of the Cause he is" (188; Derrida's words). Loving one's enemy, not *in* God but *because of* God, then, is another name for a certain kind of responsibility. One loves one's enemy because of God's commandment, because of responsibility toward God's commandment. This commandment can in turn become a certain kind of law, which we discussed in chapter 3. Schmitt, as we shall see, reverses this Christianization of the enemy/friend distinction to make it impossible to love the enemy. The point I want to make is that Derrida's reading of Augustine is not merely to explain how a secular tradition of friendship came to be Christianized. What Derrida wants to point out is that while Augustine continues to make explicit references to Aristotle to speak of friendship qua enmity, he does not merely reproduce the Aristotelian discourse. Augustine produces a "transplantation and uprooting" of the Aristotelian tradition, "something untimely, some non-identity with self" (188).

Anti-genealogical Futures,
"The *Already of the Perhaps*"

Augustine's Christianization of friendship marks only a temporary intervention or uprooting. This intervention is countered by Nietzsche, who uproots not only the Aristotelian but also the Augustinian notion of friendship. For Derrida, Nietzsche's attempt at the "interruption" of the preceding notions of friendship is found in the latter's statement in *Human All Too Human*: "*Perhaps*, to each of us there *will come* the more joyful hour when we exclaim: 'Friends, there are no friends!' thus said the dying sage; 'Foes, there are no foes!' say I, the living fool."[26] This, for Derrida, parodies, reverses, and interrupts—"*for the first time*, so it would seem"—the (Aristotelian) tradition of friendship. What Nietzsche creates is an "upheaval, to upset its [the phrase's] assurance" (27). If Aristotle's contradictory utterance, "O my friends, there is no friend" marks the death of friends because "one should not be able to address friends while telling them that there are no friends" (27), the Nietzschean statement, a "performative contradiction," creates an upheaval, and indeed a revolution against the idea of enmity. To have friends is to have enemies (at least this is how Schmitt interprets friendship). Nietzsche denies enemies. Can you have friends without enemies? As Derrida puts it movingly: "There is indeed something of an upheaval here, and we would like to perceive, as it were, its seismic waves, the geological figure of a political revolution which is more discreet—but no less disruptive—than the revolutions known under that name; it is perhaps a revolution of *the* political. A seismic revolution in the political concept of friendship which we have inherited" (27). But this Nietzschean political revolution in the history of friendship is not timeless, that is, it is not merely available to our democratic present to employ it and to parrot it. Surely Nietzsche's upheaval constitutes an "interruption." Yet it is only an interruption. "It would inscribe in that history [of friend/enemy distinction] the scansion of an unprecedented event; but—hence the upsetting structure of the event—it would interrupt less than recall (and call again for) a rupture already inscribed in the speech it interrupts" (27). Perhaps it is the attempt to interrupt the legacy of friendship one more time, to produce one more rupture, one more interruption, one more deconstruction, that is not available to us today. Derrida seems to think we can no longer be content with continuing to just interrupt the interruptions of the Greek notions of friendship. Can there be another deconstruction of the idea of friendship? Can such a deconstruction produce a new politics? This is why Derrida doubts that there is such a thing as deconstructive politics. (Recall that this is not the same thing as saying that there is no politics or democracy without deconstruction!) As Derrida argues, it seems that Nietzsche's deconstruction or interruption does not readily turn friendship into a political question. It seems that "at the end of the chain" [of interruptions] we still have to "throw up the question of friendship as the question of *the* political" (27–28). The question of *the* political is "not necessarily, nor in advance, political. It is perhaps not yet or no longer thoroughly political" as long as the political is "defined with the features of a dominant tradition" (28).

Of course, to think the question of the political we may still need Nietzsche. Indeed, for Derrida, thinking such a future of the political begins with Nietzsche, at least with his idea of the "perhaps." This "dangerous" of the "perhaps" has an interesting relation to the future. But that future will not necessarily be Nietzschean, in the sense that it will not rest on the same kind of interruption or political revolution that Nietzsche inaugurates. Nietzsche's interruption does not produce a model of the future of the political. It cannot (as Nietzsche himself would have argued) because "the dangerous" task concerning the possibility of *perhapses* (or *maybes*) involves a future (of new philosophers) "different from its predecessors." [27] This is Nietzsche's envisioning of a "community without community of thinkers to come" (62; Derrida's words). Western philosophy has always viewed the idea of the *perhaps* with a certain disdain. This disdain is partly reflected in the German saying that "perhaps is a practical lie." [28] Nietzsche's calling our attention to it flies in the face of a tradition that always equated reality with (empirically and philosophically verifiable) evidence. For Derrida, Nietzsche's call for playing with the idea of the perhaps is a "telephone call" to the future, and it wages "war . . . on lineage" and genealogy (34). To concern ourselves with the *perhaps*, to think about the question of the future of the political with the idea of the perhaps, requires a "certain non-knowledge" of not only lineage but also the future itself (*Politics*, 31). Here Derrida quotes the *subordinate* (this is *not* a sentence) from paragraph 214 in Nietzsche's *Beyond Good and Evil*. (This is where Nietzsche mocks and spurns "We Europeans of the day after tomorrow," who still believe in our own virtue but wear our grandfathers' "pigtail" of "good conscience."): "Alas, if only you knew how soon, very soon—all will be different!" [29] For Derrida, this sentence, which is really not a sentence, which "begins at the end," is "a ploy figure which is neither a question nor an affirmation, not even a hypothesis, since you are going to know very soon, starting at the end of the sentence, that which you would know if you knew, and that therefore you already know: 'Ah, if you only knew'" (*Politics*, 31). The sentence "precipitates and precedes itself, as if its end arrived before the end." What we find here is "instantaneous teledromatics: the race is finished in advance." For Derrida, the sentence—"however impossible it may seem"—is "future-producing" (31–32). Admittedly, this is a complex set of arguments. Otherwise, how on earth could one adequately speak of the seemingly senseless notion of a Nietzschean "telephone call" to the future, whose very im-possibility has to be thought in terms of the *perhaps*, nonknowledge. This is why Derrida says that Nietzsche's perhaps (and its call to the future) should be understood as *teleiopoetics* or better yet *auto-teleiopoetics*. *Auto-teleiopoetics* is concerned with a "poetics of distance." It speaks to the "distance and the far removed" (32). *Perhaps* does not know. It embodies nonknowledge. It is the only thing, so to speak, with which we may think the future. It is not even an idea. If it were an idea, we would already know it. *This perhaps can speak to the chance of the future.* It was, of course, Hegel, if not Augustine or Machiavelli, who wanted to eliminate the idea of chance from history to "look for a general design [purpose] in history: the ultimate end [purpose] of the world . . . bring[ing] to history the belief and conviction that the realm of the will is not at the mercy of contingency." [30] But, for Derrida as for Nietzsche, the future cannot ever evade chance. "There would be no future without chance" (*Politics,* 50). Let me put this more clearly and imprecisely. Nietzsche's interruption of friendship, though it is part of a chain of interruptions, embodies a certain "teleiopoetics." This anti-Hegelian teleiopoetics demands nonknowledge of the future, speaking as it does to its distance. This teleiopoetics, this *perhaps,* this poetics of speaking to distance, this auto-teleiopoetics, this "chance"—outlives "each author, and each specific reader, him, you and me, all of us, all the living, all the living presents" (32). This is why at one critical point Derrida claims that one day, perhaps soon, we may have to stop following and citing Nietzsche himself—Nietzsche could not possibly have demanded such loyalty from anybody—and those following Nietzsche as well.[31] That is, perhaps we may have to stop following Derrida himself in the future. As he says,

> Now we will not follow [Nietzsche] in order to follow him come what may. He never demanded such a thing anyway without freeing us, in the same move, from his very demand, following the well-known paradoxes of any fidelity. We will follow him here to the best of our ability in order, perhaps, to stop following at one particular moment; and to stop following those who follow him—Nietzsche's sons. Or those who still accompany him . . . as his brothers or the brothers of his brothers. But this will be in order to continue, *in his own way again, perhaps,* turning the virtue of virtue against itself; to dig deeper under this "good conscience" of the "last Europeans" that continue to impel Nietzsche's statements. (33)

This is not a just narrow statement about how we may forget or stop following Nietzsche. Rather, it is a statement about how we may relate to our past-present/present-past that is haunted by one critical "name" associated with modernity: *Nietzsche.* Indeed, it is about how "we" may un-inherit the European grandfathers' pigtails of "good conscience" that have been so important to our fraternalist past of modernity and stop following those who wore them and who are still wearing them. (We have no shortage of them around, especially in our liberal disciplines.) It is about waging war on genealogy, on history, on a certain kind of history, making it difficult to belong merely within the chain of interruptions of our modernity, which is often critiqued by brothers and by the followers of those brothers (including Nietzsche and

Derrida himself!). It is about how we may construct anti-genealogical histories of the past-present, if you will, anti-genealogical histories that would enable us to mourn and be haunted by our (fraternalist) past(s). Of course, doing so is easier said than done. The difficulty of it is registered by Derrida when he says that we still belong to a world "split asunder" by the Nietzschean mutation of our modernity, at least by one dominant feature of it, that is, the friend/enemy distinction (80). Seen this way, *Nietzsche* is not just a name behind a corpus of literature. As Derrida puts it, Nietzsche could not possibly be the only "witness" to this mad world of modernity and its disorder.

> we *belong* (and this is what we take the risk of saying here) to the time of this [Nietzschean] mutation, which is precisely a harrowing tremor in the structure of belonging. Therefore of property. Of communal belonging and sharing: religion, family, ethnic groups, nations, homeland, country, state, even humanity, love and friendship, lovence, be they public or private. We belong to this tremor, if that is possible; we tremble within it. It runs through us, stops us dead in tracks. *We belong to it without belonging to it.* Within it we hear the resonant echo of all the great [living-dead] discourses . . . always emitting mad and impossible pleas, almost speechless warnings . . . syntagms [such as] "relation without relation," "community without community" . . . "inoperative community," "unavowable" communism or community, and all the "X without X." (80; second emphasis added)[32]

The assertion that "we belong to it without belonging to it" is critical on two counts at least. On the one hand, if we did not belong to the Nietzschean mutation of modernity, but instead stood outside its confines, the futures of the political we are seeking to think would be unthinkable, because they have become already thinkable to us in the present, which is the present that wants to have one without the other, the name without the name, Christianity without Christianity, to wit, "all the 'X without the X.'" On the other, if we belonged completely to this mutation, if we remained fully engulfed in it, fully seduced by it, we could not possibly dislodge ourselves from it. (But of course there are so many of those who are entirely satisfied with having the "X without the X" today.) What Derrida wants to contemplate is the im-possibility of un-inheriting this present/past, which is also the future of the democratic promise. That is to say, he wants to ask whether we can continue pretending to "belong to it without belonging to it." And this is precisely what Derrida does by deconstructing Schmitt's friend/enemy distinction and its relation to our political sovereignty.

Derrida is able to deconstruct Schmitt's distinction between friend and enemy precisely because he himself belongs to the Nietzschean mutation without belonging to it. More important, this mutation of modernity is not something that Nietzsche was able to inaugurate alone. If Nietzsche's is only a part of the chain of the interruptions of the history of friendship, Schmitt's friend/enemy distinction constitutes one more interruption. So, again, the point that needs emphasizing here is that by interrupting Schmitt's interruption, if you will, Derrida does not hope to return to a Nietzschean future. Such a future has perhaps already passed. Put differently, Nietzsche, who spoke to distance and who envisioned that the community without community of thinkers to come would follow a path "wholly different"[33] from the last Europeans, among whom Nietzsche sought to count himself, could not possibly envision our returning to a Nietzschean future. (That is why Derrida relentlessly pursues the questions of the political in terms of the anti-genealogical.) What Derrida is interested in showing is how Nietzsche's interruption might enable us to think of the *perhaps* as embodying a paradoxical force, which is what Derrida calls the *"already of the perhaps."* It is the future that is upon us but is not yet. I quote Derrida: "The *already* of the *perhaps* has the paradoxical force of a teleiopoetic propulsion. Teleiopoesis makes the arrivants come—or rather, allows them to come—by withdrawing; it produces an event sinking into the darkness of a [future of] of friendship which is not yet" (42–43). So the teleiopoesis that calls to the future does not contain (or remain contained within) the future. Teleiopoesis withdraws from the future even as it speaks to it.

This future is no illusion. Indeed, Derrida says that the arrivants, the future of the already, of the perhaps, has a relation to "truth," perhaps an unverifiable truth. As he says so memorably, "friends of the *perhaps* are the friends of the truth. But the friends of the truth are not, by definition, *in* the truth. They are not installed there as in the padlocked security of a dogma and the stable reality of an opinion" (43). These friends of truth are the friends of democracy because the future of democracy is a future of friendship. These friends will "begin by denouncing a fundamental contradiction, that which no politics will be able to explain or rationalize, simply because it neither can [have] nor has the right to do so. The contradiction inhabits the very concept of the *common* and the *community*" (43). The contradiction is this: the concept of the common is immeasurable, and it should be so. Yet the idea of community, its supposed commonness, as we understand it, always gets measured, mapped, identified. This is as true of community as it is of democracy. Democracy cannot survive without the logic of identifying the very thing that defies measuring, the commonness. This is why Derrida says, "the common is rare" (43). Yet the rare common is easily available, for the reason that the notion of the common is produced through our political practices of counting, counting bodies and citizens. Nobody can deny that this norm of counting/accounting or (ac)countability defines our democratic electoral politics today. I need not press this point any further. Part of what Derrida envisions the futures might be are "incommensurable subjects . . . these subjects without subject and without intersubjectivity." But the question he poses is this: "can a democrat [and democracy] handle this friendship, this truth, this contradiction? And this measurelessness?" (43–44) Can democracy live without counting and measuring? Democracy will find it difficult to handle this truth. It cannot handle it, because it has not yet learned to live with this "contradiction." If it cannot handle it, will democracy belong in the future?

It is this democracy, based on the politics of measuring and identification, that is key to Schmitt's distinction between friend and enemy. Schmitt believes that the health of each political sovereignty depends on an identifiable enemy. Nietzsche's vocative phrase, "Oh enemies, there is no enemy," "turned the friend into an enemy and vice versa" (83), making it difficult to count them, to distinguish them, to identify them. But Schmitt makes possible the opposite: the identifiable enemy. For Schmitt, Derrida says, the identifiable enemy is "one who is *reliable* to the point of treachery, and thereby familiar" (83). As we know now, Schmitt's theory of the exception, sovereignty, and state is informed by this distinction. Let me partly summarize Schmitt's take on the state. For Schmitt, each state and its progress depend upon having an enemy. The death of this enemy is the death of the political. As Schmitt explained his axiom, "the specific political distinction . . . to which political actions and notions can be reduced, is the distinction *between* friend and enemy."[34] A world without this distinction is a world without politics—a depoliticized world. Schmitt would have us believe this distinction to be a natural one, since he says he is drawing on a tradition of distinction that has gone into oblivion.[35] But, for Derrida, what Schmitt creates is "a determined opposition" and not a mere difference. "This determination specifically assumes opposition" (*Politics,* 85).

For Schmitt, the enemy is not a private enemy. The private enemy is useless. What is important is the *public* enemy. The public enemy is part of an "ensemble of grouped individuals" (Schmitt's words; quoted in *Politics,* 86). For Schmitt, the enemy always exists in the present because war between states is both "possible and eventual." To that extent, the enemy always exists in the present. Derrida puts it quite sarcastically, saying that for Schmitt, the present is like a "tank . . . replenished in the present, with presence" (86). The tank is never empty. There is no "abyss." For Derrida, there is a large hole in Schmitt's theory about the possibility of war in such a present. War is possible simply because it is present. And this possible-present always culminates in an eventuality. According to Derrida, Schmitt seems to infer that "as soon as war is possible, it is taking place" (86). Schmitt puts it in the present participle, to stress the real, continuing presence and possibility of war. War does not happen in the future; it happens in the present. Indeed, as Derrida mocks Schmitt, war "begins before it begins" (86).

This is how real the possibility of war is to Schmitt. And this war confronts an enemy that is always present. "As soon as the war is possible-eventual," Derrida notes, "the enemy is there" (86). Schmitt seems to disguise the distinction between friend and enemy as a purely secular matter in terms of a public/private distinction. But this is not as secular as it may appear. For Schmitt, the supposed secularity—indeed the secular justification—of this war depends partially on a distinction between enmity and hostility.[36] Schmitt says that the enemy one combats and kills should not be hated as a *hostis.* Hence one may love in private the very enemy that one kills in public so long as one does not harbor hostility toward the enemy. Indeed, for Schmitt, what ruins friendship is not the "physical killing" (Schmitt's words) of the enemy but the hostility with which one might kill the enemy (*Politics,* 87–88). Here we begin to hear a religious ring in the purportedly secular distinction between friend and enemy. In fact,

Schmitt cites the often quoted (biblical) maxim "Love your enemies" (Matt. 5:44; Luke 6:27), only to complain that it makes no distinction between the private and the public (*The Political*, 29–30; 28–29). Schmitt seems to be saying that to the extent that he is making a distinction between private and public enemies, he is appealing to a secular politics. Derrida sees this as a disguised "post-Christian metaphysics" (249), and it is only part of the problem.[37] The problem is that Schmitt, who was a sharp critic of nineteenth-century liberalism and its core values, such as humanity, individualism, freedom, and tolerance (*neutralization* is Schmitt's word), himself echoes the same tradition.[38] This is clear when he suggests that "even though Islam [for example] remains an enemy" of Europe, the Europeans "must love the Muslims as neighbors."[39] Schmitt might protest that saying so is not liberal, but rather is Christian or European! This is because, for him, Europe stands for Christianity, and the defense of Europe against Islam is part of the political. Loving Muslims is a private matter (*Politics*, 89). One can only wonder how this statement echoes (even though it may not be the same as) the Christian (Augustinian) principle of "love your enemy" that Nietzsche denounced as hollow! Nietzsche considered it hollow not because it was just Christian or religious, but because it demands familiarity, knowing exactly who your enemies are and how many of them there are. This is what Schmitt loves. He loves this *"practical identification"* of the enemy. The practical seems to provide both the conditions and the consequences of knowing the enemy (116; Derrida's words).

What is important to note here is that for Schmitt, knowing who is an enemy is more important than knowing who is a friend. He gives the enemy priority. Without an enemy, we cannot know who is a friend. This question of who a friend is has a certain place in the Greek tradition of friendship. Derrida says that Plato, in *Lysis*, is the one who asked the question, "who is the friend?" (and not the question, "what is friendship").[40] For Derrida, the serious implication of the former question is:

Who is it? Who is he? Who is she? *Who* [be it Aristotle's or Plato's version of the question], from the moment, when . . . all the categories and all the axioms which have constituted the concept of friendship in its history, have let themselves be threatened with ruin: the subject, the person, the ego, presence, the family, and familiarity, affinity, suitability, or proximity, hence a certain truth and certain memory, the parent, the citizen and politics, and man himself— and, of course, the brother who capitalizes on every thing? (294)

All these names have become part of the answer to the question "Who is the friend?" These names all have something to do with the male/brother. (But, as Derrida puts it so poignantly, "The brother is never a fact" [159].) Friendship is always one between two mortal brothers. The woman was always excluded from friendship. This was a *double exclusion:* that is, "the exclusion of friendship between a man and a woman, and the exclusion of friendship *between* women" (290). We see this exclusion in many canonical models of friendship that mourn the loss of a friend. That is, friendship is always remembered or mourned when the male friend in question is absent or dead (290), which does not mean that women had "no chance" in this history of the canonical models of friendship. But women had "less" chance of belonging within these models.

Surely Schmitt participates in this canonical, fraternal tradition of friendship. For Schmitt, friendship is clear and concrete. To have (male) friends is to have enemies. It is that simple. (Later, many years after the publication of *The Concept of the Political,* as he feigned distancing himself from his involvement with the Nazi moment, Schmitt would say that all these distinctions he earlier claimed to be so concrete and real were only theoretical diagnoses [124, 134n10].) Derrida goes on to raise serious misgivings about Schmitt's claims. For example, Derrida argues that Schmitt's notion of the practical identification of the enemy, which the latter says is always a "real possibility," is based on the mere act of *deciding* someone to be an enemy. (This is part of Schmitt's bizarre decisionism, that is, "the decision deciding who the enemy is" [125].) There are other complaints that Derrida registers against Schmitt's friend/enemy distinction, and we cannot possibly include them all here. But one other point worth noting is that what is important for Derrida is not whether Schmitt's undoubtedly warped conception of politics still animates our modernity. (One could multiply examples to show how a similar distinction between friend and enemy informs the contemporary politics of the "war on terror.") Rather, Schmitt's theory of war and politics, grounded as it is on a fraternal, phallogocentric logic of blood and belonging, with no reference to women, who have played so many different roles in so many wars, is founded upon a self-collapsing theory of the present. Schmitt is invested in a present that goes nowhere, all stuck in itself. Schmitt's is a politics of the present, always competing to realize itself, within the present, with the possibility of war, always present in the present. Schmitt's concept of the political is synonymous with the present, where the real possibility of war always exists. There is a certain contemporaneity, a timelessness, to his notion of the political. It always exists to be realized vis-à-vis a continuing, sustaining distinction between friend and enemy. As Derrida says, "war aims at the death of the enemy." But war can never kill the enemy because enemies always exist, and they must exist for the sake of politics. So the presence of enemies never ends. Enemies are always present. On this account, Derrida notes, "war is not good in view of another end, moral, religious, etc., but it has its end in itself" (132). However, it is not a realizable or desirable end because the end of enemies would mean the end of the political.

This is where Nietzsche's "Oh enemies, there is no enemy!" should begin to haunt us anew, haunting us to hear the echo of its call to a new future. Nietzsche's saying should do so, not simply because it interrupts and inverts the Aristotelian heritage or because it neutralizes the distinction between friend and enemy, stranger and foreigner. On the contrary, what is important about Nietzsche's inversion is that it makes it impossible to count and identify friends or enemies. "Oh enemies, there is no enemy"! If there is no enemy, are there only friends? Can these friends be counted? Are there too many of them to count? Must we search for a friend when there are too many of them to calculate? Or are there none at all, neither enemies nor friends? If Nietzsche's saying gives us no easy answer to these sorts of questions, as Derrida seems to suggest, it can only mark an aporia. It is a certain problem or a riddle that cannot be solved, answered, or deconstructed. As Derrida elaborates on both Aristotle's saying and Nietzsche's inversion of it,

> And as if by chance, from the moment they [the enemies and friends] are spoken of instead of being spoken *to*, it is to say that they are no longer, or not yet, there: it is to register their absence, to *record*, after having *called*. They are summoned to be spoken to, *da*,

then dismissed, *fort*, saying to them, speaking of *them*, that they are no longer there. One speaks of *them* only in their absence, *concerning* their absence. (172–73)

Derrida goes on to ask: "when you speak to someone, to a friend or an enemy, does it make any sense to distinguish between his presence and absence. In one respect, I have him come, he is present for me; I *presuppose* his presence, if only at the end of my sentence. . . . But in another respect, my very sentence simultaneously puts him at a distance or retards his arrival" (173). In other words, when Aristotle laments, "Oh friends, there is no friend," and Nietzsche cries, "Oh enemies, there is no enemy," they both *defer* the very possibility of the friend or the enemy. The enemy or the friend is deferred for the future. He is absent now, but might arrive in the future.

Derrida here is interested in how both Aristotle's and Nietzsche's speaking of friends and enemies supposes a future. In this regard, it is also important to note here Derrida's use of the pronouns *he* and *his*. Aristotle and even Nietzsche retained this concern with a fraternal future. This is why, perhaps, we cannot follow Aristotle or Nietzsche, hoping to transform and enrich them, their concepts and ideas. But we certainly cannot follow them, because the future (like the promise of democracy)of which they speak is "deferred." Derrida goes on to say that "in both cases [of aporia], appealing to the other presupposes his advent. By this very gesture the other is made to come, allowed to come, but his coming is *simultaneously* deferred: a chance is left for the future needed for the coming of the other, for the event in general" (173) Perhaps it is deferred because both Aristotle and Nietzsche fear the arrivant. Who might the arrivant(s) be? As is the case with the idea of a coming messiah, the expectation of the arrivant(s) is always fraught with a certain terror. Perhaps Nietzsche feared this terror as well. That is why the future, that community without community, is invoked but deferred. Perhaps we all have a fear of what such an arrivant might be. We might not recognize the arrivant/arriving others of the future. They may not be who we expect them to be. They might not be our familiar neighbors. This is why Nietzsche described the *perhaps* as "dangerous." The very coming of this danger is made "to quicken and infinitely to retard, as the end of the future" (173–74). Thus, what we find in the Nietzschean deferral of the future is a certain kind of aporia, the need to mourn the im-possibility of un-inheriting that which is both anticipated and feared. Derrida goes on to ruminate on how we may begin to think of living with this danger of the im-possibility of the future of the arrivant(s):

> And if the thinkers of the "dangerous perhaps" can be nothing other than dangerous, if they can signify or bring nothing other than threat and chance at one and the same time, how could I desire their coming without simultaneously fearing it, without going to all ends to prevent it from ever taking place. Without going to all ends to skip such a meeting? Like teleiopoesis, the messianic sentence carries with it an irresistible disavowal. In the sentence a structural contradiction converts a priori the called [other] into the repressed, the desired into the undesired, the friend into the enemy. And vice versa. I must, by definition, leave the other to come (the messiah, the thinker of the dangerous "perhaps," the god, *whoever* would come in the form of the event, that is, in the form of the exception and the unique) free in his moment, out of reach of my will or desire, beyond my very intention. (174)

Still Derrida is using here the male pronoun, perhaps only to allude to the deferred state of this Nietzschean future. How might we anticipate (and inherit) the deferred futures? Can we simply undefer them? They cannot be Nietzschean futures, as we have already noted. Nietzsche has to be un-inherited, un-inherited at some time. He intended to be un-inherited in a future where the anticipation of the deferred arrivants is beyond his and our intention and reach, beyond our will. It is a future where one is not *responsible* for the arriving other. That is to say, it is not a future that can be inaugurated or quickened through some law or policy that demands responsibility to the other. It is not a future where the principal sponsor of responsibility and democracy as such remains already present. It cannot have democratic values installed there already. Law, justice, humanity, and humanitarianism— the history of these values is a history of fraternization (272–73). What is more, they are reducible to a genealogy, a genealogical deconstruction. It is a future animated by the irreducible and incalculable political, the anti-genealogical. Indeed, that future is synonymous with friendship. Yet it is not an "event" waiting to happen. This is a crucial point to stress. This is why Derrida says that even when friendship or democracy is present, it always remains to come. I contend that his notion of "to come" is irreducible to any religious sense of the messianic. "Democracy remains to come; this is its essence in so far as it remains: not only will it remain indefinitely perfectible, hence always insufficient and future, but, belonging to the time of the promise, it will always remain, in each of its future times, to come: even when there is democracy, it never exists" (306). This is so because democracy itself is a promise. As we have noted earlier, this idea may sound disturbing to some whose view of democracy remains tied to a time when it is fully realizable, at some time in the future. Yet democracy as such, if we still insist on that Greek name, can never be fully realized. It is a "promise," as Derrida says. If you see it as a promise, the future in which it remains to come will also remain as a promise. The question is this: will we continue to pursue this promise of/in the future? Can the belief in the promise of democracy attend to the problem of *Ayubowan* in the future? Here, I quote at length what I consider to be a critical passage from an interview Derrida gave on the subject of democracy, friendship, and hospitality.

> So when I speak of a "democracy to come," I don't mean a future democracy, a new regime, a new organization of nation-states (although this may be hoped for) but I mean this "to come": the promise of an authentic democracy which is never embodied in what we call democracy. This is a way of going on criticizing what is everywhere given today under the name of democracy in our societies. This doesn't mean that "democracy to come" will be a future democracy correcting or improving the actual conditions of the so-called democracies, it means first of all that this democracy we dream of is linked in its concept to a promise. The idea of a promise is inscribed in the idea of a democracy: equality, freedom, freedom of speech, freedom of the press—all these things are inscribed as promises within democracy. Democracy is a promise. That is why it is a more historical concept of the political—it's the only concept of a regime or a political organization in which history, that is the endless process of improvement and perfectibility, is inscribed in the concept. So, it's a historical concept through and through, and that's why I call it "to come": it is a promise and will remain a promise, but "to come" means also not a future but that it has "to come" as promise, as a duty, that is to come immediately. We don't have to wait for future democracy to happen, to appear,

we have to do right here and now what has to be done for it. That's an injunction, an immediate injunction, no delay. Which doesn't mean that it will take the form of a regime; but if we disassociate democracy from the name of a regime we can then give this name "democracy" to any kind of experience in which there is equality, justice, equity, respect for the singularity of the Other at work, so to speak—then it's democracy here and now; but of course this implies that we do not confine democracy to the political in the classical sense, or to the nation-state, or to citizenship.[41]

We return full circle to the "problem" of *Ayubowan* seemingly embodied in the female figure of Kamalam at the tea factory in Uda Pussellawa, Sri Lanka. It seems to me that there is a very interesting relation between the problem of *Ayubowan* and the problem of friendship. Just as the problem of *Ayubowan* constitutes an aporia (at least in the way I want to read it), so does the problem of friendship. Friendship has a certain (far from a seamless) history—varying from Greek and Roman to Christian and modernist models of friendship. This history is one of speaking of friendship, always in proximity to the fraternal brother, family, familiarity, ego, self, and often in opposition to the enemy (and the woman, the nonbrother). That is to say, the problem of friendship is a problem of constructing the opposition of friend versus enemy. Regardless of its variations within its history, this opposition today "survives" and "lives on"—in that Derridean, spectral notion of survival. We would be foolhardy to think that this opposition is going to disappear soon (certainly not in this time of "war on terror" in which you are commanded to declare: "you're either with us or against us!"). In this sense, friendship is a certain problem, a historical problem at that. Then what about Nietzsche's inversion of this problem? Does it amount to anything at all? Yes and no. Yes, Nietzsche did invert the Aristotelian and later Christian notions of friendship. But no, because the authority of the brother "still dominates all the reversals," the very figure of the brother that Nietzsche himself could not abandon. Thus, the interruption or rupture might be "insufficient words" to capture what happens with Nietzsche. Nietzsche's perhaps is "an unprecedented thought of interruption" (293).

What does Nietzsche's thought of interruption think against? On the one hand, Nietzsche's "Oh my enemies, there is no enemy" does think against the phallogocentric model of friendship. Did Nietzsche—who said "women are not yet capable of friendship: women are cats and birds, or at best cows"—really overcome at least part of the phallogocentric model? Yes, to some extent he did because this comparison of women to cats and cows has a certain "political value." The comparison situates the figure of the woman in opposition to the phallogocentric model of "humanity" (283). This is critical. As we know, all the fraternal models of friendship are based on a humanist conception. The brother, the mortal friend, who is the friend of a brother, is always "human." The brother/friend belongs to humanity. He is the embodiment of the human. In Nietzsche's formulation, the woman does not belong to this fraternal humanity. Women belong to the nonhuman, if you will? They are closer to cats and cows than to the brotherly human. Nietzsche follows upon this by saying further that "women are not yet capable of friendship: but tell me, you men, which of you are yet capable of friendship?" (quoted 283) *Here, then, friendship is certainly denied to men, but it is deferred for women.* Women's time remains to come. Their time is untimely, if you will.

But this is not all. There is another critical way in which Nietzsche's thought of interruption thinks against the humanist-brotherly heritage of friendship. Derrida argues that all the canonical models of friendship are primarily about mourning, mourning "the moment of loss" of a friend, a dead friend (290). This is why, for example, in the heritage of friendship, those who speak *of* (hardly speak *to*) friends always speak of dead friends. Their very speaking of the friends is made possible by the death of their friends. It is possible to speak of dead friends because the one (often a brother) who speaks is the one who survives—almost by contract—the dead (brother). The brother-friend who speaks of the (dead) brother—in Aristotle's terms—is "another oneself." [42] Even when (post)modernists like Blanchot speak *to* friends, remembering friends like Foucault, they speak *to* dead friends. [43] This, then, is part of the conventional experience of "mourning." The point I want to make is that Nietzsche's utterance produces a very different kind of mourning. It, too, mourns. But it does not mourn the loss of a friend. It mourns those who are not present, those who are absent, who are not dead but "not yet." It mourns those who have yet to come. It is a "mourned anticipation" (283). So, Nietzsche's inversion then does not necessarily solve the canonical problem of friendship. It mourns what I have been calling the problem of the unproblematizable. It does not try to merely deal with it or do away or cope with it. It inverts the problem or it reinvents the problem, if you wish, only to mourn it—mourn to un-inherit it. This mourning opens it up to the future, the future of the *perhaps*.

In a similar way, for me the problem of *Ayubowan* constitutes such an im-possibility of mourning and un-inheriting its legacy. This is of course assuming that *Ayubowan* too has a long history, a history that is inseparable from the history of the (more often than not contentious, murderous, and even genocidal) distinction between the Sinhalese and their others today. If one takes that history today to be inseparable from that distinction, then that history, however complicatedly one may tell it, cannot be changed. Yes, yes, if one sees it as a problem, one can improve and neutralize it, by way of improving and neutralizing the relations between the Sinhalese and their others, but even at the end of the improving, the distinction will remain, without any guarantees that it will not, one day, some day, again need some improving. The distinction, then, and by extension *Ayubowan*, must be seen as an aporia. Such an aporia cannot, then, really be improved or neutralized. It can only be mourned because no coping or dealing with it will make it go away. One may attempt to provide it with an immediate resolution—liberal, democratic, legal, humanitarian, or any other—that will not keep it at bay. (One may, of course, do what one can do "right here and now" for it.) The aporia has to be opened up to the future of the perhaps. It can only be opened up to the future because it does not demand responsibility, obligation, or duty toward it. This is what democracy demands, but an aporetic problem like *Ayubowan* does not. It demands mourning, thinking about how we may un-inherit it. That is its call. Yet it calls by itself. It is a spectral call. It is not dead, not quite. Hence one cannot "mourn" its loss in the conventional sense of the word. It is absent in the sense that it is spectrally present. It is present-absent. This call, as I have suggested, is not the call of a caller. It is not the voice of a subject (e.g., Kamalam) intentionally demanding to be heard. (Recall that Kamalam herself does not make such a demand.) The call of the aporia is larger than the voice of an individual or even of a community.

Mourning, thinking about un-inheriting, this aporia is a way of opening it up to the future. It thinks a future of the irreducibly political. This future cannot be a new community, democratic or otherwise. It cannot be, if it will have anything to do with the conventional notion of community. It cannot because Nietzsche did "bear witness" to a rupture of this notion of community and desired a "community without community" to come. Yet there is still a trace of the fraternal in the notion of community that Nietzsche imagined. Indeed, there is even a demand for an "oath" of brotherhood in Nietzsche! Even though Nietzsche, so memorably, asks his brothers to "lose" and forget him, so that he may one day return as a phantom—he speaks of "phantom friends"—he is still calling on "brothers." Yes, Nietzsche says, "my brother, if you have a virtue and it is your own virtue, and you have it in common with no one" (quoted in *Politics,* 276). Still, he calls to brothers. Can he call on brothers and deny them the *common?* Can the brother ever stand a *chance* of standing alone, without the company of the common? This is why Derrida says that we are no longer in "affinity with Nietzsche—with one Nietzsche, in any case (for there is always more than one)" (297). Yes, we tremble within the "tremors" of the Nietzschean critique of democracy. We still need Nietzsche to problematize those democratic norms that remain unproblematized. Yet, once the problems emerge, we may have to "give up pursuing" Nietzsche (289), because the notion of brotherhood that Nietzsche invokes is so tied to the common. It always risks bringing back the brother, indeed the "father of the brother" (who might be the Greek father(s) or the Christian Father). For Derrida, there can be no enriching or improving this tradition and its past, that is, if we "understand enrich by the very thing it is not or which it excludes from within itself. For what else could ever enrich one, if not what one is not, what one does not have, what one can neither have nor have been" (300). Thus, for Derrida, as far as the heritage of *philia* is concerned, there can be no improvement. Any attempt to improve it will always bring the phallogocentric brother and the father of the humanist past ("The Greek model of *philia* could never be enriched otherwise than with that which it has violently and essentially attempted to exclude" [300]). Thus what Derrida is urging is an anti-genealogical thinking, a thinking against a certain kind of memory and knowledge. It is thinking against the bond of memory. Without this thinking, the *perhaps* remains thwarted or repressed by memory. It enables the "obligatory necessity of . . . bond" to one another. (Nietzsche, of course, asked for a bondless bond, but it was still a bond.) The memory of such a bond "inaugurates as much as it recalls or reproduces truth" (100). In this politics of memory, the *perhaps* "could never stand a chance" (100).

You cannot have memory and think the *perhaps*. The *common*, then, is a name for this memory. It brings back the brother, the "obligatory necessity" of remembering the bond to (dead) brothers and fathers. So, for Derrida, even this idea of *community without community* embodies a risk, despite "the aporia requiring the unceasing neutralization of one predicate by another" (298).

The aporia of *Ayubowan* remains in proximity to memory, the memory of the distinction between the Sinhalese and their others. That is why it remains an aporia! This memory thwarts mourning the arrivants of the future. So long as it remains a problem to the naked eye, to the humanitarian eye, to the liberal eye, to the legal eye, it can help us mourn the past (of the Sinhalese nationalizing of postcolonial Sri Lanka, producing many decades of violent exclusions of Tamils, Muslims, and others). Recognizing it as a problem does help us mourn the (at least the known) dead—those Tamils, Sinhalese, and others who have died and are dying in Sri Lanka, either defending one nationalism or contesting it for the sake of another kind of nationalism, as in the case of Eelam. Thus, recognizing the problem of *Ayubowan* itself is important. It helps us remember the ways in which the postcolonial nation was constructed (and sustained). Yet such recognition is not enough, because it only mourns the past or the presence of oppression. As I have noted, such mourning can amount to nothing other than the retaining and even the hardening of (Sinhalese and Tamil) identities that will always demand respect from (and for) one another. This is what many liberal theorists have yet to grasp.

In the way I want to read it, *Ayubowan* is a ghost—a ghostly call. Perhaps, this ghost demands something other than a community without a community, something more than simply neutralizing one predicate by another, something more than assuming the future that is "just beyond law" is just beyond a preposition! It cannot be a democracy without democracy either. A democracy without democracy, like a community without community, or the name without the name, is virtually im-possible. The preposition cannot make democracy anew or change it into something else. The preposition cannot liberate democracy from its phallogocentric history of the human and all other problems associated with it. The preposition cannot improve and enrich it. The preposition's time has already passed. The time of that preposition is the Nietzschean future. This future has already

passed. This is the future of democracy. It is past because we are already living in its future. The end of that democratic future is already
near, just around the corner. The ghost of the problem of *Ayubowan*
demands a wholly other future. In such a future we surely cannot
inherit the Aristotelian tradition ("Oh my friends, there is no friend").
Neither can we inherit the Christian heritage ("Love your enemies!").
Nor can we inherit and merely recite Nietzsche's antidemocratic critique ("Oh my enemies, there is no enemy"!). It should be evident
that merely transforming or enriching any of these traditions and
their interruptions, building on their "ruins"—to use Judith Butler's
phrase—will not accomplish much, at least not anything other than
what has already been accomplished.[44] The difficulty of un-inheriting
these traditions and their interruptions can be captured in the incomplete, elliptical phrase with which Derrida ends *Politics of Friendship:* "O my democratic friends . . . " Is the anti-genealogical future
to come where we seek to complete this phrase? Or shall we simply
leave the ellipses blank, for fear of making them part of the chain of
interruptions in the history of friendship, community, humanity, and
democracy?

Notes

1. Thinking the Un-improvable, Thinking the Un-inheritable

1. This sense of the "deferred" or the delayed and its relation to the future in terms of "to come," is found in Jacques Derrida's well-known (but perhaps still largely unappreciated) essay, "Différance," in his *Margins of Philosophy*, trans. Alan Bass (Chicago: University of Chicago Press, 1982). "Difference," as he said famously, is neither a concept nor a word. It is a way of thinking "what is most-irreducible about our 'era,'" irreducible to presence or absence, to past or future (7). Différance is that which "differs from, and defers, itself," and thinking about this "radical alterity . . . makes us concerned not with horizons of modified—past or future—presents, but with a 'past' that has never been present, and which never will be, whose *future to come* will never be a *production* or a reproduction in the form of presence" (20–21; the first emphasis added). Note how the phrase *to come*, which Derrida used to speak of democratic futures in many of his later works, is already found in this essay, originally published in the 1960s. For more on thinking about the future in terms of the phrase *to come*, see chapter 7.

2. At times I will use phrases such as *think the future* or *think justice* to be faithful to the Derridean tradition of "thinking" itself, which is concerned with thinking the question of the im-possible, irreducible to possibility or impossibility, presence or absence.

3. Jacques Derrida, *Politics of Friendship*, trans. George Collins (New York: Verso, 1997), 306.

4. Elizabeth Rottenberg's very interesting *Inheriting the Future: Legacies of Kant, Freud, and Flaubert* (Stanford: Stanford University Press, 2005) came to my attention just as I was finishing this book. While Rottenberg's attempt to think about the future in terms of inheriting the "inhuman" is important, her thinking about inheriting does not have the irreducible sense that I am trying to capture in my formulation of "un-inheriting."

5. One would of course look in vain for a theory of un-inheritance in Jean-Francois Lyotard, *The Postmodern Condition: A Report on Knowledge* (Minneapolis: University of Minnesota Press, 1999).

6. Paul Gilroy, *Postcolonial Melancholia* (New York: Columbia University Press, 2005), 2.

7. Paul Gilroy, "From a Colonial Past to a New Multiculturalism," *Chronicle of Higher Education,* January 7, 2005.

8. Jeffrey Stout, *Democracy and Tradition* (Princeton: Princeton University Press, 2003).

9. Even though this is not exactly how Amy Gutmann—to cite one more name randomly—conceives democracy, her recent work, *Identity in Democracy* (Princeton: Princeton University Press, 2003) displays a similar concern with retaining the name in terms of having more and more democratic conscience. I take up parts of her work in chapter 7.

10. John Dewey, *The Public and Its Problems* (Athens, OH: Swallow, 1927 [1991]); also see chapter 3, this volume, for more on this view.

11. Maurice Blanchot, *Michel Foucault as I Imagine Him* (New York: Zone, 1987), 108–9; cited in Derrida, *Politics of Friendship*, 299.

12. Jacques Derrida, *Rogues: Two Essays on Reason*, trans. Pascale-Anne Brault and Michael Naas (Stanford: Stanford University Press, 2005), 13. For more on this concept, see chapter 3.

13. Even in my previous work, *Colors of the Robe: Religion, Identity, and Difference* (Columbia: University of South Carolina Press, 2002), I was detained by a strong suspicion about the very concept of change as far as the name *Buddhism* was concerned and hence refused to subscribe to any notion of a Buddhism "transformed," "betrayed," "changed," or "politicized." My aim there was to understand the constitutive relation between Buddhism and difference in terms of the ways in which the questions of what it means to be Buddhist come into view and fade from view in contingent conjunctures. That is to say, nowhere did I simply emphasize difference as a virtue in itself. Difference was not something that was simply "out there," in history, available for anthropological appropriation and canonization. This, for me, was, and still remains, one of the sounder ways of thinking about the concept of difference even though it is ultimately inadequate for thinking the question of the future of the political.

14. See, especially, Slavoj Žižek, *The Fragile Absolute: Or, Why Is the Christian Legacy Worth Fighting For?* (London: Verso, 2000).

15. Following Derrida, I use the word *im-possibility* to avoid the binary between possibility and impossibility. As it will be clear later, the legacy of our modernity and religion must be thought as im-possible inheritances. Thinking

about the im-possibility of such a legacy allows us to think of a future of the political that is not reducible to what we know as politics today. In such futures one
neither forgets nor remembers, receives nor renounces, history/legacy. Rather,
one is always haunted by the specters of it.

16. Gianni Vattimo, *After Christianity*, trans. Luca D'Isanto (New York:
Columbia University Press, 2002).

17. The question of political inheritance itself is rarely theorized, even within
the field of postcolonialism. Semantic attempts at thinking about the postcolonial
can be found in Anthony K. Appiah, "Is the 'Post-' in 'Postcolonial' the 'Post-'
in 'Postmodern?'" in Anne McClintock, Aamir Mufti, and Ella Shohat, eds.,-
Dangerous Liaisons: Gender, Nation, and Postcolonial Perspective (Minneapolis:
University of Minnesota Press, 1997). On the problem of the term, see Anne
McClintock, "The Angel of Progress: The Pifalls of the Term 'Postcolonialism,'"
Social Text 10(2–3): 84–98; Ella Shohat, "Notes on the Postcolonial," *Social
Text* 10(23): 99–113. There are, however, some rare exceptions such as Dipesh
Chakrabarty (see chapter 4).

18. Needless to say, I use the word *postsecular* not to mean the "end" of the
secular but to note something of the political present animated by the aporia of
secularism, as should be evident in the discussion that follows. In this regard I
disagree with Phillip Blond that rescuing religion from the hands of "fascists" as
a corrective to the "liberal erasure of God" can be seen as "the end of the secular." See his introduction in Phillip Blond, ed., *Post-Secular Philosophy: Between
Philosophy and Theology* (London: Routledge, 1998), 54.

19. Jacques Derrida, "Others Are Secret Because They Are Other," in his *Paper
Machine*, trans. Rachel Bowlby (Stanford: Stanford University Press, 2005), 142.

20. In a recent moving attempt at intervening within the anthropologized
name of the country, literary critic Qadri Ismail suggests that Sri Lanka should
be seen as a text. But he does not see the relation between the text and deconstruction in the way I am proposing it here. See Qadri Ismail, *Abiding by Sri
Lanka: On Peace, Place, and Postcoloniality* (Minneapolis: University of Minnesota Press, 2005). I engage Qadri's work in chapter 2.

21. Friedrich Nietzsche, *On the Genealogy of Morals* (1887), trans. Douglas
Smith (Oxford: Oxford University Press, 1998), 119. Man for Marx here is "*the
human world*, the state, society" (53).

22. "And especially, in relation to Heidegger . . . there is a Christian, or more
precisely a Lutheran tradition of what Heidegger calls *Destruktion*. Luther, as I
describe in my book on Jean-Luc Nancy and what Nancy calls the 'deconstruction of Christianity,' was already thinking about *destructio* to designate the need
for a desedimentation of the theological strata hiding the original nakedness of
the evangelical message to be restored. What interests me more and more is to
make out the specificity of a deconstruction that wouldn't necessarily be reducible to this Lutheran-Heideggerian tradition. And that's perhaps what differentiates my work from those who are close to me, in France and abroad. Without
refuting or rejecting anything at all, I would try to make out what separates an
ongoing deconstruction from the memory it inherits, at the very instant when it

is reaffirming and respecting that memory's inheritance." See Derrida, "Others Are Secret," 137–38. Thus deconstruction does not seek to restore the "original nakedness," which is what concerns Heidegger and Luther, nor does it really reject anything, even as it separates itself from the memory it inherits. The book on Jean-Luc Nancy to which Derrida refers is *On Touching—Jean-Luc Nancy*, trans. Christine Irizarry (Stanford: Stanford University Press, 2005).

23. On such concepts as radical democracy and fugitive democracy, see David Trend, ed., *Radical Democracy: Identity, Citizenship, and the State* (London: Routledge, 1995); and Sheldon S. Wolin, "Fugitive Democracy," in Seyla Behabib, ed., *Democracy and Difference* (Princeton: Princeton University Press, 1996).

24. Karl Marx, "Contribution to the Critique of Hegel's *Philosophy of Right*: Introduction," in *Marx-Engels Reader*, ed. Robert C. Tucker (New York: Norton, 1978 [1972]), 60.

25. In this respect, I must mention that my work has nothing whatsoever to do with John D. Caputo's *The Prayers and Tears of Jacques Derrida: Religion Without Religion* (Bloomington: Indiana University Press, 1997). Caputo wants to appropriate Derrida for an unmistakable Christian theological project, desiring to have religion without religion. It will be clear to the reader of my book that Derrida's deconstructive thinking cannot ever be appropriated for such a (Christian or other religiously or politically minded) *reconstructive* project.

26. Talal Asad, *Formations of the Secular: Christianity, Islam, Modernity* (Stanford: Stanford University Press, 2003).

27. David Scott and Charles Hirschkind, eds., *Powers of the Secular: Talal Asad and His Interlocutors* (Stanford: Stanford University Press, 2006).

28. Jose Casanova, *Public Religions in the Modern World* (Chicago: University of Chicago Press, 1994).

29. Jose Casanova, "Secularization Revisited: A Reply to Talal Asad," in Scott and Hirschkind, *Powers of the Secular*, 13.

30. Talal Asad, "Responses," in Scott and Hirschkind, *Powers of the Secular*, 208.

31. On the ways in which Asad's Foucauldian genealogical inquiry sits in tension with his notion of tradition, as understood by Alasdair McIntyre, see David Scott, "The Tragic Sensibility of Talal Asad," in Scott and Hirschkind, *Powers of the Secular*.

32. It would be interesting to think about the relation between catastrophe and necessity. But I doubt that catastrophe or tragedy can ever be understood in terms of *necessity*. On the problem with the term *necessity* in its relation to law, see chapter 4. However, I am not claiming that some aspects of (postcolonial) modernity cannot be viewed in terms of tragedy, for which Scott makes a good argument in his book *Conscripts of Modernity: The Tragedy of Colonial Enlightenment* (Durham: Duke University Press, 2004). Nevertheless, I think that aporia is a more helpful concept.

33. As Derrida explains, "one of the laws that deconstruction responds to, and that it starts off by registering, is that at the origin (thus the origin with no origin), there is nothing simple, but a composition, a contamination, the

possibility of a grafting and a repetition. All that resists analysis even as it sets it going. This is why deconstructive operation is not only *analytical* or *critical* ('critical' meaning capable of deciding between two simple terms), but trans-analytical, ultra-analytical, and more than critical. Critique, the need for critique, for *krinein* [judging] and crisis (*Krisis*) has a history. Deconstruction of this history . . . cannot therefore simply be critical in either the Kantian or Marxist [or, might we add, Foucauldian?] senses of the term, although at the time when I am doing this 'other thing,' I also want to stay faithful to these legacies. A faithful heir should interrogate the inheritance, shouldn't he?" ("Others Are Secret," 138–39). Deconstruction, then, deconstructs the very history of critique, and deconstruction cannot be critical so as to reshape, refashion, and re-inherit the history of critique. As we will see in chapter 7, democracy or secularism itself has such a history of critique, and one cannot critique this history in the hope of re-inheriting it. Deconstruction interrogates the very possibility of this inheritance. This is what we do not see in Asad's genealogical critique. At the end of his critique he does not interrogate the problem of the inheritance of secularism.

34. Asad does not develop the notion of the shadow, but it would be interesting to think of it in contrast to the Derridian idea of haunting that is central to this study.

35. On the distinction between *law* and *laws*, see chapters 4 and 6. It seems to me that Asad takes into account the problem of laws but not of the problem of law. Laws are deconstructable and changeable, but law in its relation to justice, that is, law/justice, cannot be deconstructed.

36. Even in Richard Beardworth's very impressive *Derrida and the Political* (London: Routledge, 1996) there is no discussion of the notion of aporia in terms of the question of un-inheritance. On how the term *aporia* in Derrida's thinking differs from other thinkers such as Levinas and Heidegger, see especially the chapter, "Aporia of Time and Aporia of Law: Heidegger, Levinas, and Derrida," ibid.

37. Jacques Derrida, *Aporias: Dying—Awaiting (One Another at) the "Limits of Truth,"* trans. Thomas Dutoit (Stanford: Stanford University Press, 1993).

38. It is this story by Seneca about the shortness of life that Diderot recognized as his own and encouraged others to read.

39. Martin Heidegger, *Being and Time*, trans. Joan Stambaugh (New York: SUNY Press, 1996), 228. For more on Heidegger's idea of "being-toward-death" and its relation to the notion of "not-yet," see chapter 3.

40. Etienne Balibar, *We, the People of Europe: Reflections on Transnational Citizenship* (Princeton: Princeton University Press, 2004), 109.

41. See Jacques Derrida, "*Ousia* and *Gramme*: Note on a Note from *Being and Time*," in *Margins of Philosophy*, trans. Alan Bass (Chicago: University of Chicago Press, 1982). As Derrida goes on to explain the Aristotelian contradiction in relation to Hegel, "like the point in relation to the line, the now, if it is considered as limit (*peras*), is *accidental* in relation to time. It is not time, but time's accident. . . . The now (*Gegenwart*), the present, therefore, does not define the essence of time. Time is not thought on the basis of the now. It is for this reason that the

mathematization of time *has limits.* Let us take this in all possible senses. It is in the extent to which time requires *limits,* nows analogous to points, and in the extent to which limits are always accidents and potentialities, that time cannot be made perfectly mathematical, that time's mathematization has limits, and remains as concerns its essence, accidental" (61). For more on this, also see note 17 to chapter 4.

42. See also Derrida, ". . . that Dangerous Supplement . . . ," in *Of Grammatology,* trans. Gayatri Chakravorty Spivak (Baltimore: Johns Hopkins University Press, 1974).

43. Maurice Blanchot and Jacques Derrida, *The Instant of My Death/Demeure: Fiction and Testimony,* trans. Elizabeth Rottenberg (Stanford: Stanford University Press, 2000), 46. The book is largely a commentary by Derrida on Blanchot's short essay, "The Instant of My Death."

44. Also see Maurice Blanchot, *The Writing of the Disaster,* trans. Anne Smock (Lincoln: University of Nebraska Press, 1986). There Blanchot writes: "Dying is, speaking absolutely, the incessant imminence whereby life nonetheless endures by desiring. The imminence of what has aways already taken place" (64); cited in Blanchot and Derrida, *The Instant of My Death,* 49–50.

45. The problem of decision or decisionism is one that Derrida takes up in numerous places. On some aspects of how it figures in the notion of (ir)responsibility, see chapter 3.

46. One of the well-known proponents of negative theology is Jean-Luc Marion.

47. Jacques Derrida, "Sauf le nom," in *On the Name,* trans. David Wood, John P. Leavey, Jr., and Ian McLeod (Stanford: Stanford University Press, 1995), 58.

48. I take this phrase from the interview that Derrida gave a couple of months before his death. Jacques Derrida, "I Am at War with Myself," *Le Monde,* August 18, 2004 (*truthout* editorial). Here Derrida speaks of living life with "unfaithful infidelity" to "his" language, French. By *unfaithful fidelity,* he means to think of a way of responding to the language—and, by extension, to the name—that highlights its survival. As he says, "In the same way that I love life, my life, I love what has made me, the essential of which is language, this French language, which was the only one I was taught to cultivate, the only one for which I may call myself more or less responsible. . . . Love in general goes through the love of language, which is neither nationalistic nor conservative, but which demands its struggles, its ordeals, its proofs. One may not do whatever one wants with language. It was there before we were. It will survive us. If one affects the language of anything, it must be done in a refined way, by respecting its secret law through disrespect. That is it, unfaithful fidelity."

49. Jacques Derrida, "Passions," *On the Name,* 17.

50. For Derrida, "living on" is not reducible to living or dying. See his "Living On," in Harold Bloom, Paul Deman, Jacques Derrida, Jeoffrey H. Hartman, J. Hillis Miller, *Deconstruction and Criticism* (New York: Seabury, 1979).

51. For more on the notion of survival, see chapter 6. Also see Derrida, *Politics of Friendship.* Derrida states that his notion of survival, trace, vestige, and the

spectral is in part influenced by Walter Benjamin's "distinction between *uber-leben:* surviving death as a book may survive the death of its author, or a child the death of his parents, and *fortleben:* living on or continuing to live" (Derrida, "I Am at War with Myself"). This living on is irreducible to dying or living. The text that Derrida has in mind here is Benjamin's "The Task of the Translator," in Walter Benjamin, *Illuminations: Essays and Reflections,* ed. Hannah Arendt (New York: Schocken, 1968).

2. Aporias of Secularism

1. Friedrich Nietzsche, *The Gay Science* (New York: Vintage, 1974), sec. 125.

2. For samples of the continuing academic interest in questions about the "Death of God," see Robert B. Pippin, "Nietzsche and the Melancholy of Modernity," *Social Research* 66(2): 495–520; Michael Harr, "Nietzsche and the Metamorphosis of the Divine," in Phillip Blond, ed., *Post-Secular Philosophy: Between Philosophy and Theology* (New York: Routledge, 1988), 158–64; Tyler T. Roberts, *Contesting Spirit: Nietzsche, Affirmation, and Religion* (Princeton: Princeton University Press, 1998), 196–98; Louis A. Ruprecht Jr., "Nietzsche, the Death of God, and Truth, or Why I Still Like Reading Nietzsche," *Journal of the American Academy of Religion* 65(3): 573–86.

3. Literature on this is abundant. My own take on Kant and Rorty is in chapter 5.

4. Steven Bruce, *God Is Dead: Secularization in the West* (London: Blackwell, 2002).

5. Charles Taylor, *Varieties of Religion Today: William James Revisited* (Cambridge: Harvard University Press, 2002), 106–7.

6. Friedrich Nietzsche, *Twilight of the Idols; or, How to Philosophize with a Hammer,* trans. Duncan Large (New York: Oxford University Press, 1998), 21.

7. As mentioned in chapter 1, I do not use the term *postsecular* to mean its end. The possible dangers of "new traditionalist" criticisms of secularism to democracy are the subject of Jeff Stout's *Democracy and Tradition* (Princeton: Princeton University Press, 2004).

8. Michel Foucault, "Politics, Polemics, and Problematization," in *Ethics, Subjectivity, and Truth,* ed. Paul Rabinow (New York: Free, 1997), 112.

9. John Rawls, *A Theory of Justice* (Cambridge: Harvard University Press, 2000 [1971]).

10. If I were contributing one more history of the problem of tolerance here, I could provide a long bibliography. Among those who have thought about tolerance in fruitful ways recently is William Connolly, *The Ethos of Pluralization* (Minneapolis: University of Minnesota Press, 1995). Wendy Brown's *Regulating Aversion: Tolerance in the Age of Identity and Empire* (Princeton: Princeton University Press, 2006) promises to be a classic. It might be useful to note, as Derrida reminds us, that the supposed secularity of the idea of tolerance has a history of "Christian domesticity." Voltaire, who, a little like Kant, believed that

"Christianity is the sole moral religion," defined tolerance as "the prerogative of humanity." This *secular* sense of humanity was profoundly Christian. Voltaire, who accused the "Apostolic Catholic and Roman Religion" of betraying some original Christianity, wrote: "Of all the religions, Christianity is without doubt that which ought to inspire the greatest tolerance, even if until now Christians have been the most intolerant of men." See his article, "Tolerance," in *Philosophical Dictionary*; cited in Derrida, "Faith and Knowledge: Two Sources of Religion at the Limits of Reason Alone," *Acts of Religion*, ed. Gil Anidjar (New York: Routledge, 2002), 59–60. For Derrida, in this respect, the French Enlightenment is "no less essentially Christian than Aufklarung." In a bold move, Derrida goes on to write: "The word 'tolerance' thus conceals a story: it tells above all an intra-Christian history and experience. It delivers the message that Christians address to other Christians. The Christians ('the most intolerant') are reminded, by a co-religionist and in a mode that is essentially co-religionist, of the word of Jesus and of the authentic Christianity at its origins. If one were not fearful of shocking too many people all at once, one could say that by their vehement anti-Christianity, by their opposition above all to the Roman church, as much as their declared pretense, sometimes nostalgic, for primitive Christianity, Voltaire and Heidegger belong to the same tradition: proto-Catholic" (ibid., 60).

11. Talal Asad, *Formations of the Secular: Christianity, Islam, Modernity* (Stanford: Stanford University Press, 2002), 177.

12. The text of Bush's speech can be found at http://www.whitehouse.gov/news/releases/2001/09/20010917-11.html.

13. Rawls, *A Theory of Justice*, 214–20.

14. "'In God We Trust'—Stamping out Religion on National Currency," http://www.atheists.org/flash.line/igwt1.htm.

15. Legal scholars have pointed to the implausibility of trying to figure out the "original intent" of documents like the Constitution. In many instances the interpretations of legislative acts may become legislative acts themselves. See Jeremy Waldron, *Law and Disagreement* (New York: Oxford University Press, 1999), esp. 119–46.

16. Michael Taussig, *Defacement: Public Secrecy and the Labor of the Negative* (Stanford: Stanford University Press, 1999), 2–6.

17. On how publicity works as a secret and how what is public is not necessarily helpful to democratic politics, see Jodi Dean, "Publicity's Secret," *Political Theory* 29(5): 624–50.

18. For sometime now, in different ways, Dipesh Chakrabarty has been reminding us of the nonwestern partnership in the architecture of modernity. More than a decade ago, Chakrabarty argued that "modernity is not the work of Europeans alone; the third-world nationalisms, as modernizing ideologies par excellence, have been equal partners in the process." See his *Provincializing Europe: Postcolonial Thought and Historical Difference* (Princeton: Princeton University Press, 2000), 43. The chapter "Postcoloniality and the Artifice of History" first appeared in *Representations* in 1992.

19. Michael Ondaatje, *Anil's Ghost* (New York: Knopf, 2000).

20. Qadri Ismail, *Abiding by Sri Lanka: On Peace, Place, and Postcoloniality* (Minneapolis: University of Minnesota Press, 2005), 240.

21. Qadri Ismail, "A Flippant Gesture Toward Sri Lanka: A Review of Michael Ondaatje's *Anil's Ghost*," *Pravada* 6(9/10): 24–29.

22. This sort of view of modernity, advanced by Benedict Anderson in *Specters of Comparisons: Nationalism, Southeast Asia and the World* (London: Verso, 1998), is elegantly criticized by Partha Chatterjee. See his *Politics of the Governed: Reflections on Popular Politics in Most of the World* (New York: Columbia University Press, 2004).

23. Ismail, *Abiding by Sri Lanka*.

24. In this regard Qadri seriously misjudges, in my view, the importance of the work of Dipesh Chakrabarty, particularly his *Provincializing Europe*. The idea of *Provincializing Europe* is not merely to "humble" Europe, as Ismail thinks. Though Chakrabarty does not say it explicitly, the idea recognizes something of the aporectic nexus that we inhabit. I will show in chapter 4 that an aspect of Chakrabarty's work, particularly *Habitations of Modernity*, is critical to mourning the aporia of our political sovereignty, which a critique of the idea of Europe cannot help us do.

25. Radhika Coomaraswamy, "In Defense of Humanistic Way of Knowing: A Reply to Qadri Ismail," *Pravada* 6(9/10): 29–30.

26. The literature on the colonial practices of humanism is too numerous. Fanon's criticism of it in *The Wretched of the Earth* (New York: Grove, 1963) is well known and informs many subsequent postcolonial works. Heidegger's critique is found in "Letter on Humanism," in Martin Heidegger, *Basic Writings*, ed. David Farrell Krell (San Francisco: Harper, 1977). Derrida's best treatment of the problem is *Politics of Friendship*, trans. George Collins (New York: Verso, 1997), and see particularly the chapters "In Human Language, Fraternity . . . " and "For the First in the History of Humanity." "For Derrida's criticism of what could be called Heidegger's own humanism without humanism, see "The Ends of Man," in *Margins of Philosophy*, trans. Alan Bass (Chicago: University of Chicago Press, 1982), 111–136.

27. Lila Abu-Lughod, "Writing Against Culture," in Richard G. Cox, ed., *Recapturing Anthropology: Working in the Present* (Santa Fe: School of American Research Press, 1991).

28. Friedrich Nietzsche, *Thus Spoke Zarathustra: A Book for All and None*, trans. Walter Kaufmann (New York: Modern Library, 1995), 60. It would be interesting to compare Nietzsche's criticism of the concept of the neighbor with Freud's. For Freud, the commandment "love thy neighbor" is grounded in a logic of familiarity. "If I love someone, he must deserve it in some way. . . . He deserves it if he is so like me in important ways." Ultimately, he says, it is no different from "'love thine enemies'"; they are both the mere efforts of civilizations "to set limits to man's aggressive instincts." Sigmund Freud, *Civilization and Its Discontents*, trans. James Strachey (New York: Norton, 1989), 66–70, 109.

29. One of Derrida's points here is that Nietzsche produced a rupture with the Christian notion of the neighbor. Nietzsche equated friendship with a "new

justice" (*Gay Science*, sec. 289) but still echoed the Greek notion of the fraternal "friend." After all, Aristotle, who also spoke of a new justice, retained a similar notion of the fraternal friend. Aristotle says, "When men are friends, they have no need of justice, while when they are just, they need friendship as well, and the truest form of justice is thought to be a friendly quality." Aristotle, *Nichomechean Ethics* 7.2.1155a, 25; quoted in Derrida, *Politics of Friendship*, 278, also see 176. In this sense, for Derrida, Nietzsche both belongs and does not belong to the Greek heritage. As we will see, this belonging and not belonging to history/heritage is not an option for our futures.

30. Slavoj Žižek, *The Fragile Absolute: Or, Why Is the Christian Legacy Worth Fighting For?* (New York: Verso, 2000).

31. Similar nonsensical, Orientalist assertions about Buddhism are repeated in Žižek's *The Puppet and the Dwarf: The Perverse Core of Christianity* (Cambridge: MIT Press, 2003). He calls Buddhism an "Oriental spirituality." Never mind his other dubious claims about Zen Buddhism and how the "very force of compassion wields the sword" (27). This, as we will see soon, is how Žižek politicizes or engages the other politically.

32. Terry Eagleton, "In the Gaudy Supermarket," *London Review of Books*, http://www.lrb.co.uk/v21/n10/print/eagl01_.html.

33. Gayatri Chakravorty Spivak, *A Critique of Postcolonial Reason: Toward a History of the Vanishing Present* (Cambridge: Harvard University Press, 1999), 358, 190.

34. Ismail, *Abiding by Sri Lanka*, xxxii–iii.

35. To put it crudely, Žižek might have thought that the *Gita* was available to him simply because he could easily reach for a copy of it on a bookshelf in his study or a library somewhere.

36. *Beyond Good and Evil: Prelude to a Philosophy of the Future*, trans. Walter Kaufmann (New York: Vintage, 1989), 94.

37. Remarkably, Jodi Dean's eager defense of Žižek's supposed challenge to democracy misses these problematic aspects of the latter's work. Jodi Dean, "Žižek Against Democracy," *Law, Culture, and Humanities* 1(2005): 154–77.

38. See note 10 to this chapter.

39. Of course, Žižek will remind us that, after all, he has criticized the problem with multiculturalism and tolerance because they deprive the other of its otherness. See his *Desert of the Real*.

40. Žižek, *The Puppet and the Dwarf*, 32–33.

41. This tradition of wanting to have religion without religion has a certain history. See note 5 to chapter 4.

42. Also see note 20 to chapter 3.

3. Postcolonial Community or Democratic Responsibility?

1. See Friedrich Nietzsche, *Twilight of the Idols*, trans. Duncan Large (New York: Oxford University Press, 1998), 31.

2. Friedrich Nietzsche, *On the Genealogy of Morals*, trans. Douglas Smith (New York: Oxford University Press, 1996), 40.

3. Note that Hannah Arendt also claims that one of the distinctive features of the American Revolution and its succeeding democratic sovereignty is the binding act of promise making between individuals. But, unlike Nietzsche, Arendt believes too much in the virtue of promises. For more on this, see chapter 4.

4. If one is unconvinced by the example of Foucault's *Discipline and Punish*, I need only remind of the postcolonial literature that has discussed the problem of the relations among community, number, and democracy. See, for example, Qadri Ismail, "Majority Rules," in his *Abiding by Sri Lanka: On Peace, Place, and Postcoloniality* (Minneapolis: University of Minnesota Press, 2005); David Scott, "Community, Number, and the Ethos of Democracy," in his *Refashioning Futures: Criticism After Postcoloniality* (Princeton: Princeton University Press, 1999); Dipesh Chakrabarty, "Governmental Roots of Modern Ethnicity," in his *Habitations of Modernity: Essays in the Wake of the Subaltern* (Chicago: University of Chicago Press, 2002); Arjun Appadurai, "Number in the Colonial Imagination," in Carol A Breckenridge and Peter van der Veer, eds., *Orientalism and the Postcolonial Predicament: Perspectives on South Asia* (Philadelphia: University of Pennsylvania Press, 1993).

5. Judith Butler, *Giving an Account of Oneself* (New York: Fordham University Press, 2005), 135.

6. Jacques Derrida, "Others Are Secret Because They Are Other," in his *Paper Machine*, trans. Rachel Bowlby (Stanford: Stanford University Press, 2005), 139.

7. Jacques Derrida, *The Gift of Death*, trans. David Wills (Chicago: University of Chicago Press, 1995), 51.

8. Gayatri Chakravorty Spivak, "Responsibility," *Boundary* 21(3): 19–64.

9. Tomoko Masuzawa, *The Invention of World Religions; Or, How European Universalism Was Preserved in the Language of Pluralism* (Chicago: University of Chicago Press, 2005), 1–2.

10. She writes: "this book takes recourse in history and initiates an investigation with a set of fairly uncomplicated empirical questions posed on relatively uncontroversial grounds, namely, when, and how, this particular mode of counting and mapping religions came about" (13).

11. In a footnote Masuzawa notes that she is following in the footsteps of predecessors like Talal Asad, *Genealogies of Religion: Discipline and Reasons of Power* (Baltimore: Johns Hopkins University Press, 1993). But I do not think that Asad is interested in the same kind of historicization that concerns Masuzawa. At times, in *Genealogies* Asad is too genealogical for my taste. Yet his emerging concern with the relation between genealogy and the political is discernible in that work. The last sentence in the book testifies to this: "It is the secular modern state's awesome potential for cruelty and destruction . . . that deserves our sustained attention—as citizens and anthropologists of modernity" (306). But, as I have argued in chapter 1, Asad does not have anything to say about how we may think the aporia of our democratic modernity and political sovereignty.

12. In fact, when she says that her purpose in writing the book is not to propose a method of how religion should be studied, but because she is "inquisitive about the marvelously loquacious discourses on religions," Masuzawa seems to disavow any interest in the question of politics (Masuzawa, *The Invention of World Religions*, 10).

13. This is perhaps the place to note that David Scott's important work *Refashioning Futures* has made a serious argument for postcolonial criticism to move away from the politics of representation to a theorization of postcolonial politics. Scott contends that representation of colonial discourses and histories itself cannot constitute a politics and the question of the political has to be thought differently. This is a suggestive proposition, but now I think that Scott's understanding of the political in terms of "agonistic respect for pluralizations of subaltern difference" is insufficient (224). On the concept of agonistic respect and its problems, see chapter 5.

14. Donald Lopez, jr., *Prisoners of Shangri-La: Tibetan Buddhism and the West* (Chicago: University of Chicago Press, 1998).

15. It would require a long bibliography to list the far too numerous works in the field of postcolonial studies that assume this relation between historicization, responsibility, and politics. I take *Prisoners of Shangri-La* to be one of the most eloquent representatives of that field. Of course, as will be evident in this book, there are exceptions, such as the works of Dipesh Chakrabarty, David Scott, and Ismail.

16. The book created a (perhaps much needed) controversy within the field of Tibetan Buddhist studies. Some of the Tibetologists took issue with the seeming neutrality of the book and suggested that the unclarity of the "author's own positionality" seems to undermine his arguments. Needless to say, this is not the question of the political that I have in mind. See "Symposium on Donald Lopez's *Prisoners of Shangri-La: Tibetan Buddhism and the West*," *Journal of the American Academy of Religion* 61(1): 165–201.

17. Michel Foucault, *The Archeology of Knowledge and the Discourse on Language* (New York: Pantheon, 1972).

18. Nowhere does Lopez adequately theorize the question of agency. He simply thinks that agency is found in history. One of the most promising attempts to meditate on the problem of agency and its relation to the question of responsibility is Talal Asad's "Thinking about Agency and Pain," in his *Formations of the Secular: Christianity, Islam, Modernity* (Stanford: Stanford University Press, 2003). I take the epigraph to this chapter from p. 94 of his chapter.

19. Richard King, *Orientalism and Religion: Postcolonial Theory, India, and the "Mystic East"* (New York: Routledge, 1999), 187.

20. At the risk of incurring the wrath of anti-essentialists, I should note that today much of the hubris of so-called postcolonial and even postmodern works passes for a seemingly enlightened and responsible recognition that identity/culture is nonessential; it is only an alibi for redeeming the legacy of colonial racism. The recognition does not combat racism, except to produce the disclaimer "we are not all racists." I suppose the anti-essential empiricists and aficionados

of facts would demand evidence and sources to back up this claim. I would remind them that Donald Rumsfeld, who, among other neocons of the second
Bush administration, accused the so-called liberal media of overplaying the civil
war in Iraq, insisted that *all* of the country was not on fire. On the problem of the
critique of essentialism, which today passes for a theory that accomplishes almost nothing, see Gayatri Chakravorty Spivak, *A Critique of Postcolonial Reason:
Toward a History of the Vanishing Present* (Cambridge: Harvard University Press,
1999), 282–93.

21. And this is perhaps why Spivak argues that much of postcolonialism is
"bogus." "Elite postcolonialism [which pretends to give history back to its people
or let "the natives speak"] seems to be a strategy for differentiating oneself from
the racial underclass as it is to speak in its name" (*A Critique of Postcolonial Reason*, 358).

22. Jean-Luc Nancy, *Being Singular Plural*, trans. Robert D. Richardson and
Anne E. O'Byrne (Stanford: Stanford University Press, 2000).

23. Julia Kristeva, *Strangers to Ourselves*, trans. Leon S. Roudiez (New York:
Columbia University Press, 1991), 1. She goes on to write: "The foreigner is
within us. And when we flee from or struggle against the foreigner, we are fighting our unconscious—that 'improper' facet of our impossible 'own and proper'"
(191). Even though it sounds promising at first sight, Kristeva's notion of "strangers to ourselves" works within the binary of self and other. Ultimately, Kristeva
cannot interrogate, much less think beyond, that binary.

24. Ismail, *Abiding by Sri Lanka*, 85. Ismail quotes the following sentence
from *Being Singular Plural*: "What I have in common with another Frenchman
is that I am *not* the same Frenchman as him" (Nancy, *Being Singular*, 155; cited
in *Abiding by Sri Lanka*, 255). But how similar is this statement to (or different from) what Nietzsche said about the "brother"? "My brother, if you have a
virtue and it is your own virtue, you have it in common with no one." Friedrich
Nietzsche, *Thus Spoke Zarathustra*; cited in Derrida, *Politics of Friendship* (New
York: Verso, 1997), 276. The point here is that just as Nietzsche himself wanted
to abandon the idea of the "common," but could not give up the category of the
"brother," Nancy cannot forsake the category of the "Frenchman" while wanting to abandon sameness. The "Frenchman" *remains* without being in common
with another Frenchman. Derrida would say that this desire to be "X without X"
cannot be inherited in our futures. For more on the idea of the "common," see
chapter 7.

25. Jeffrey Stout, *Democracy and Tradition* (Princeton: Princeton University
Press, 2003).

26. Jacques Derrida, *Rogues: Two Essays on Reason*, trans. Pascale-Anne Brault
and Michael Naas (Stanford: Stanford University Press, 2005), 13.

27. Despite Stout's qualification that the book is about American democracy, its total absence of any engagement with certain postcolonial-subaltern
criticisms of democratic modernity is inexplicable, particularly given its wide-
ranging interests. The presumption is that other places may be concerned with
forms of democracy, but they are not American. Is this not the worst kind of

area studies mentality? At times, as he calls for the true embodiment of (responsibility to) the principles of American civic life, making it an *example* for other nations, Stout seems to run the risk of championing a dangerous American exceptionalism. He frequently and unabashedly uses terms like *we* and *us*: "we are already members of such a community," "we are now losing it [the ideological battle against terrorism] very badly," and "we have yet to repent for [our past horrors]." Translation: we are not against them; we are different. Hence behind the seemingly innocent criticisms of the American "arrogant use of massively destructive military power" and advocacy of "the disciplined use of armed forces against terrorists" and a "persuasive argument on behalf of democracy [for other countries to follow]" lies a deeply nationalistic vision. (Need I remind Stout that the mere fact that "we [like other races and ethnicities in Americas] care about succor" and "about how the pizzas and tortillas are made" [302] does not render (white) Americans in power nonracist, but only makes them consumerist?) Had Stout read and engaged works like *Provincializing Europe* (Princeton: Princeton University Press, 2000) by Dipesh Chakrabarty, perhaps he would have at least suspected the fallacy of thinking about democratic modernity and difference in this way. Fredric Jameson has reminded us recently how the talk of "multiple modernities" is itself an attempt to vindicate the problems of capitalism. See his *A Singular Modernity: An Essay on the Ontology of the Present* (New York: Verso, 2002).

28. Another recent example of such works is Amy Gutmann's *Identity in Democracy* (Princeton: Princeton University Press, 2004).

29. In *Conscripts of Modernity: The Tragedy of Colonial Enlightenment* (Durham: Duke University Press, 2004), in a thoughtful reading of C. L. R. James's *The Black Jacobins*, David Scott argues that much of the postcolonial thinking about politics is founded upon a logic of romance, overcoming, and vindicationism. He suggests that postcolonial politics can better be conceived within a narrative frame of tragedy because tragedy casts into doubt the "conventional conceptions about agency, responsibility, and freedom" (206). The sense of the tragic may, I suspect, help us abandon the Enlightenment notions of self-mastery and rationality, creating a space for "contingency and chance," but nowhere does Scott theorize the concept of responsibility vis-à-vis self-mastery (207).

30. The differences between Kristeva and Butler are considerable. See Judith Butler, *Gender Trouble: Feminism and the Subversion of Identity* (New York: Routledge, 1990).

31. Emmanuel Levinas, *Otherwise Than Being; or, Beyond Essence*, trans. Alphonso Lingis (The Hague: Martinus Nijhoff, 1981), 105; cited in Butler, *Giving an Account of Oneself*, 91.

32. Elsewhere she wrote precisely on such a virtue. See Judith Butler, "What Is Critique? On Foucault's Virtue," in David Ingram, ed., *The Political* (London: Blackwell, 2002).

33. Michel Foucault, "What Is Critique?" in *The Politics of Truth*, ed. Sylvère Lotringer and Lysa Hochroth (New York: Semiotext(e), 1997), 25.

34. Foucault noted that the idea of desubjugation of the subject is found in Kant. But "in his attempt to desubjugate the subject . . . Kant set forth critique's primordial responsibility, to know knowledge" (ibid., 36).

35. For a very instructive attempt to think about the relation between genealogy and politics, see Wendy Brown, "Politics Without Banisters: Genealogical Politics in Nietzsche and Foucault," in her *Politics Out of History* (Princeton: Princeton University Press, 2001). She too, like Butler, argues that, given the contingent, fractured history it provides, genealogy does not ask what one can do but what one can become. This distinction aside, as we will see, genealogical problematization fails to account for how we may un-inherit those haunting pasts and identities that cannot be problematized anymore. Brown herself seems to recognize this in a brilliant chapter, titled "Specters and Angels: Benjamin and Derrida," in the same book.

36. Michel Foucault, *Fearless Speech*, ed. Joseph Pearson (New York: Semiotext(e), 2001).

37. I am not sure about the context of Rorty's charge that Foucault has in mind. Rorty takes up this issue of "we" in relation to Foucault in "The Contingency of a Liberal Community," in his *Contingency, Irony, and Solidarity* (Cambridge: Cambridge University Press, 1989).

38. "Polemics, Politics, and Problematization: An Interview with Michel Foucault," in Paul Rabinow, ed., *Foucault, Ethics: Subjectivity and Truth* (New York: New, 1997), 114–15.

39. Rorty is referring to Bernard Yack, *The Longing for Total Revolution: Philosophical Sources of Social Discontent from Rousseau to Marx and Nietzsche* (Princeton: Princeton University Press, 1986).

40. Nietzsche's idea of the new philosophers to come is discussed in chapter 7.

41. Heidegger is thinking of the Da-sein's initial understanding and knowing of itself and failing to recognize itself vis-à-vis its thrownness. As he writes, "As this understanding, it 'knows' *what* is going on, that is, what its potentiality of being is. This 'knowing' does not first come from an immanent self-perception, but belongs to the being of the there which is essentially understanding. And only *because* Da-sein, in understanding its there, *can* go astray and fail to recognize itself. And since understanding is attuned and attunement is existentially surrendered to the thrownness, Da-sein has always already gone astray and failed to recognize itself." See *Being and Time*, trans. Joan Stambaugh (New York: SUNY Press, 1996), 135.

42. See Spivak, *A Critique of Postcolonial Reason*, 354–55, for a sharp criticism of Rorty's patriotism and ethnocentrism.

43. Jacques Derrida, *Specters of Marx: The State of the Debt, the Work of Mourning, and the New International* (New York: Routledge, 1994), 165.

44. Derrida writes: "I say *oblique*, since . . . one cannot speak *directly* about justice, thematize or objectivize justice, say 'this is just,' and even less 'I am just,' without immediately betraying justice, if not law." See Jacques Derrida, "Force of Law: The 'Mystical Foundation of Authority,'" in his *Acts of Religion*,

ed. Gil Anidjar (New York: Routledge, 2002), 237. I address the relation between justice and deconstruction in chapter 6.

45. These are Spivak's words. See "Setting to Work of Deconstruction," in her *A Critique of Postcolonial Reason*. She considers "Force of Law" to mark this decisive ethical turn. But Derrida himself says that there has never been an "ethical" turn as such in his writings. See Derrida, *Rogues*.

46. Derrida's succinct (and perhaps much misunderstood) "definition" of deconstruction is well known: "What deconstruction is not? Everything of course! What is deconstruction? Nothing of course!" See "Letter to a Japanese Friend," cited in Martin MacQuillan, ed., *Deconstruction: A Reader* (New York: Routledge, 2000), 1. Here I agree with Spivak that deconstruction can provide no political models. She writes that "if one wanted to *found* a political project on deconstruction, it would be something like wishy-washy pluralism on the one hand, or a kind of irresponsible hedonism on the other." See Spivak, "Practical Politics of the Open End," ibid., 397–98.

47. Jacques Derrida, "Politics and Friendship: A Discussion with Jacques Derrida," by Geoffrey Bennington, at http://www.sussex.ac.uk/Units/french-thought/derrida.html.

48. Curiously, Butler does not engage this or any other text by Derrida in *Giving an Account of Oneself*. Elsewhere, however, in a brief review article following Derrida's death, she acknowledges his consuming interest in the problem of responsibility. She claims that Derrida considered responsibility an incalculable response that one "owes" to the other. Derrida would say that such a response is better than no response, but it is not that which we ought to hope for in our futures. See Judith Butler, "Jacques Derrida," *London Review of Books,* vol. 26, no. 21, http://www.lrb.co.uk/v26/n21/butl02_.html.

49. Patocka's understanding of responsibility is influenced by Levinas and Heidegger.

50. Derrida, *The Gift of Death,* 28.

51. Eventually, Derrida says, Kierkegaard ends up echoing a Kantian sense of duty. "In spite of the opposition that seems to obtain between *Fear and Trembling* and the Kantian logic of autonomy, Kierkegaard still follows the Kantian tradition of a pure ethics or practical reason that is exceeded by absolute duty as it extends into the realm of sacrifice. Access to pure duty is, in Kant's terms, also 'sacrifice,' the sacrifice of the passions, of the affections, of the so-called 'pathological' interests" (ibid., 92–93).

4. Toward Mourning Political Sovereignty

1. Hannah Arendt, *On Revolution* (New York: Penguin, 1990 [1963]), 205.

2. Arendt's personal and intellectual relationship to Heidegger is fascinating and complex. They were lovers for a brief period, but Arendt later severed relations with Heidegger and began to work with Karl Jaspers. She subsequently criticized Heidegger, calling him a "political idiot." In a note to Jaspers, Arendt

even said that she considered Heidegger a "potential murderer" because he had expelled his own teacher, Edmund Husserl, from the faculty at Freiberg University for being a Jew. On these details, see Dana Villa, "The Anxiety of Influence: On Arendt's Relationship to Heidegger," in Dana Villa, *Politics, Philosophy, Terror: Essays on the Thought of Hannah Arendt* (Princeton: Princeton University Press, 1999).

3. Martin Heidegger, *Being and Time*, trans. Joan Stambaugh (New York: SUNY Press, 1996).

4. As we know, Heidegger is claiming that *being* goes astray because of its thrownness into relations with others, which he calls the Da-sein's losing in the "they." "But because the Da-sein is lost in the 'they,' it must first *find* itself" (ibid., 248).

5. This is no place to enter into a discussion of Heidegger's Christian metaphysics. The relation between Christianity and Heidegger's ideas of authentic being has been well noted. For example, see Gianni Vattimo, *After Christianity* (New York: Columbia University Press, 2000), 123–37. Derrida says that Heidegger belongs to a tradition of Christian ethics that wants to have religion without quite having religion. "Heidegger . . . belongs to this tradition (of Christianity) that consists of proposing a nondogmatic doublet of dogma, a philosophical and metaphysical doublet, in any case a *thinking* that 'repeats' the possibility of religion without religion." Jacques Derrida, *The Gift of Death* (Chicago: University of Chicago Press, 1995), 49. For Derrida, as we will see in chapter 7, just as there can be no "community without community," there can be no religion without religion. Arendt's own criticism of Heidegger's Da-sein as a statement of radical humanism, and that as a reduction to a certain functionalism, is found in her "What Is Existential Philosophy," in *Essays in Understanding, 1930–1954*, ed. Jerome Kohn (New York: Harcourt Brace, 1994). Others, like Levinas, claim the idea of authenticity produces a certain dangerous sense of "mineness." Yet Levinas insists that even though some may read it (wrongly) as an expression of Heidegger's support for the Nazi party, there is no evidence for that in *Being and Time*. See Emmanuel Levinas, *Entre Nous: Essays on Thinking-of-the-Other*, trans. Michael B. Smith and Barbara Harshav (New York: Columbia University Press, 1998), 226.

6. See Jacques Derrida, *Aporias: Dying—Awaiting (One Another at) the "Limits of Truth,"* trans. Thomas Dutoit (Stanford: Stanford University Press, 1993), 22.

7. Magda King, *A Guide to Heidegger's Being and Time*, ed. John Llewelyn (New York: SUNY Press, 2001), 149.

8. See chapter 1 and note 17 below.

9. Here I am following a set of arguments made by Derrida in his *Aporias*.

10. For a criticism of such a view, see Dipesh Chakrabarty, *Provincializing Europe: Postcolonial Thought and Historical Difference* (Chicago: University of Chicago Press, 2000), 250.

11. Even Terry Eagleton cannot resist the lure of the "now." Eagleton writes: "Radical academics, one might have naively imagined, have a certain political responsibility to ensure that their ideas win an audience outside senior common rooms." See Eagleton, "In the Gaudy Supermarket," *London Review of*

Books, http://www.lrb.co.uk/v21/n10/print/eaglo1_.html. Eagleton does not even bother to think that wanting to speak to the public is a dangerous, if not elit- ist, desire, perhaps not due to his own naïveté but because of his belief in the importance of the democratic principle of number, which has been responsible for incalculable atrocities. (This is why I think that modern democracies become so alarmed and moved by news about genocides or catastrophes, which under- mine their supervision of and monopoly over the calculable. We have to aspire to futures in which "one"/the figure/the *arrivant*/whoever will be incalculable, irreducible to being numbered.) I suppose such thinking does not appeal to the Eagletonian liberals, who want academics to aspire to, if not to put out of busi- ness, the far-reaching, radical-public critique pioneered by the John Stuarts (*The Daily Show*) of the world.

12. W. J. T. Mitchell, "Critical Inquiry in the Twenty-First Century: A Call for Statements," *Critical Inquiry* 30(2): 330.

13. Dipesh Chakrabarty, "Where Is the Now," *Critical Inquiry* 30(2): 458.

14. Robert Pippin, "*Critical Inquiry* and Critical Theory: A Short History of Nonbeing," *Critical Inquiry* 30(2): 425.

15. Catharine R. Stimpson, "Texts in the Wind," *Critical Inquiry* 30(2): 436.

16. Teresa de Lauretis, "Statement Due," *Critical Inquiry* 30(2): 365.

17. The problem of the "now" has a long history. Several decades ago, Derrida demonstrated that even Heidegger, who sought to break with not only Hegel's but also with Aristotle's vulgar concept of time, could not really escape the prob- lem of the metaphysics of presence, within which operates the idea of the now. It is Aristotle in *Physics* 4 who "thinks time on the basis of *ousia* as *parousia*, on the basis of the now, on the point, etc." Jacques Derrida, "*Ousia* and *Gramme:* Note on a Note from *Being and Time*," in his *Margins of Philosophy*, trans. Alan Bass (Chicago: University of Chicago Press, 1982), 61. Aristotle's concern was to take into account the multiplicity of nows that mark time in terms of points on a line. Hegel borrows more or less the same concept of time from Aristotle. Heidegger, despite his labors to avoid the problematic now through his critique of the "vul- gar" concept of time, ends up in the same conceptual paralysis. Though Heide- gger's criticism seeks to present a different, *other* concept of time, it cannot avoid the problem: it is situated within the very metaphysical, ontological concept of time. This is because "time in general belongs to metaphysical conceptuality. . . . The extraordinary trembling to which the classical ontology is subjected in *Sein und Zeit* still remains within the grammar and lexicons of metaphysics" (*Ousia,* 63[0]). This is why Derrida coined the term *hauntology,* which cannot be allied with any metaphysical, ontological sense.

18. Michael Hardt and Antonio Negri, *Empire* (Cambridge: Harvard Univer- sity Press, 2000).

19. Jacques Derrida, "Force of Law: The 'Mystical Foundation of Authority,'" in his *Acts of Religion,* ed. Gil Anidjar (New York: Routledge, 2002).

20. Arendt argues that after America had forgotten the revolutionary spirit, what remained "were civil liberties, the individual welfare of the greatest num- ber, and the public opinion as the greatest force ruling an egalitarian, democratic

society" (221). Arendt's argument here should in no way be compared with the contemporary right-wing criticism of "big government." Her criticism is directed at the liberal notion of "compassion."

21. This relation between necessity and sovereignty is absent in recent important commentaries on the concept of modern political sovereignty. See, for example, Hardt and Negri, "Sovereignty of the Nation-State," in *Empire*; William Connolly, "Pluralism and Sovereignty," in his *Pluralism* (Durham: Duke University Press, 2005). Gregory Jusdanis's *The Necessary Nation* (Princeton: Princeton University Press, 2001), an unabashed defense of a certain kind of (nonviolent?) nationalism, curiously has nothing to say about the problem of necessity. Even Foucault's discussions of sovereignty lack any reference to this idea. He uses the word *rationality*. Foucault argues that two sets of doctrine that emerged about a century after Machiavelli were crucial to modern political rationality: "reason of state" and "theory of police." Entirely different from Machiavellian attempts to keep up or reinforce "the link between prince and state," reason of state is concerned with "the very existence and nature of state itself." Reason of state is "to reinforce the state itself." It is "not an art of governing according to divine, natural, or human laws. It doesn't have to respect the general order of the world. It's government according to the state's strength. It's government whose aim is to increase this strength." Michel Foucault, "'Omnes et Singulatim': Toward a Critique of Political Reason," in *Essential Works of Foucault:1954–1984*, ed. James D. Faubion (New York: New, 2000), 316–17.

22. She does not deny that some revolutions had a certain religious origin, as was the case with the Reformation. But "it may turn out ultimately that what we call revolution is precisely that transitory phase which brings about the birth of a new, secular realm" (26).

23. Here Arendt is referring to article 6 of the "Declaration des Droits de l'Homme et du Citoyen" of 1789.

24. Rousseau, in a letter to Marquis de Mirabeau, July 26, 1767; cited in Arendt, *On Revolution*, 312.

25. In an interesting essay, Beatrice Hanssen reminds us that Arendt understands violence to be located outside the domain of politics. Hanssen, "On the Politics of Pure Means: Benjamin, Arendt, and Foucault," in Hent de Vries and Samuel Weber, eds., *Violence, Identity, and Self-Determination* (Stanford: Stanford University Press, 1997), 248. Hanssen is restating a set of arguments Habermas made in his "Hannah Arendt: On the Concept of Power," in *Philosophical-Political Profiles* (Cambridge: MIT Press, 1983). I too think that Arendt runs the risk of producing this instrumentalist conception of violence. But her analysis of violence and its relation to necessity, something not noted by either Habermas or Hanssen, can help us think of a domain of nonpure politics that she herself might not have imagined possible.

26. Hannah Arendt, *The Human Condition* (Chicago: University of Chicago Press, 1998 [1958]), 71.

27. We know now that Arendt's notion of freedom builds on Heidegger's idea of "disclosedness." For more on Arendt's appropriation and critical use of

Heidegger in *The Human Condition*, see Villa, *Politics, Philosophy, and Terror*, 75–81.

28. Jacques Rousseau, *Discourse on the Origin of Inequality*, ed. Donald A. Cress (Indianapolis: Hacket, 1992).

29. Friedrich Nietzsche, *On the Genealogy of Morals*, trans. Douglas Smith (New York: Oxford University Press, 1996), 7.

30. Friedrich Nietzsche, *The Will to Power*, trans. Walter Kaufmann and R. J. Hollingdale (New York: Vintage, 1968), 297.

31. Jacques Derrida, *Specters of Marx: The State of the Debt, the Work of Mourning, and the New International*, trans. Peggy Kamuf (New York: Routledge, 1994), 73. I return to this text in chapter 6.

32. Giorgio Agamben, *State of Exception* (Chicago: University of Chicago Press, 2005), 1.

33. This is precisely the kind of worry that Christian theologians like Stanley Hauerwas have about the just war theory of violence. He and his coauthors write: "At the heart of the just war tradition in theory and practice lies a Christian contradiction. On the one hand its 'realist' defenders maintain that peace is not possible in our fallen, sinful world, on the other hand, they promote war as the only way to defend/achieve a just peace." Stanley Hauerwas, Linda Hogan, and Enda McDonagh, "The Case for the Abolition of War in the Twenty-First Century," Society for Christian Ethics, Miami, 2005, http://www.idst.vt.edu/rel/RSP webpage/AbolitionofWar.pdf.

34. Carl Schmitt, *Political Theology: Four Chapters on the Concept of Sovereignty*, trans. George Schwab (Cambridge: MIT Press, 1985).

35. Étienne Balibar, *We, the People of Europe: Reflections on Transnational Citizenship* (Princeton: Princeton University Press, 2004), 136. Derrida has taken on Schmitt with regard to his distinction between friend and enemy and its relation to the power of the ruler to decide on the state of exception. See Jacques Derrida, *Politics of Friendship* (New York: Verso, 1997), 125–28.

36. Friedrich Nietzsche, "On the New Idol," in *Thus Spoke Zarathustra: A Book for All and None*, trans. Walter Kaufmann (New York: Viking, 1966), 48. The full quotation is: "State is the name of the coldest of all cold monsters. Coldly it tells lies too; and this lie crawls out its mouth: 'I, the state, am the people.' That is a lie. It was creators who created people and hung a faith and love over them."

37. Jean Bodin, *On Sovereignty*, ed. and trans. Julian H. Franklin (Cambridge: Cambridge University Press, 1992); Thomas Hobbes, *Leviathan, or the Matter, Forme, and Power of a Common-wealth, Ecclesiastical and Civill*, ed. Richard Tuck (Cambridge: Cambridge University Press, 1996).

38. Jacques Derrida, "The Deconstruction of Actuality: An Interview with Jacques Derrida," in *Deconstructions: A Reader*, ed. Martin MacQuillan (New York: Routledge, 2000), 528.

39. Arendt, too, spoke of a certain kind of nonviolent, political action to interrupt violence. As she says, "it is the function, however, of all action, as distinguished from mere behavior [by which she strangely means such things as "disruptive student activities"], to interrupt what otherwise would have preceded

automatically and therefore predictably." Arendt, *On Violence* (San Diego: Harcourt Brace), 30–31. Hanssen has raised important doubts about this distinction. See her "On the Politics of Pure Means," 250.

40. I have more to say about the conceptual problem of interruption in chapter 7.

41. Dipesh Chakrabarty, *Habitations of Modernity: Essays in the Wake of Subaltern Studies* (Chicago: University of Chicago Press, 2002). Chakrabarty's best-known work is *Provincializing Europe*.

42. Cited in Talal Asad, "Ethnography, Literature, and Politics," in his *Genealogies of Religion* (Baltimore: Johns Hopkins University Press, 1993), 275.

43. Chakrabarty has in mind, among others, Bruno Latour, *We Have Never Been Modern*, trans. Catherine Porter (New York: Harvester, 1993).

44. Dipesh Chakrabarty, *Provincializing Europe: Postcolonial Thought and Historical Difference* (Princeton: University of Princeton Press, 1998), 108.

45. Søren Kierkegaard, *Fear and Trembling*, trans. Alastair Hannay (Harmondsworth: Penguin, 1985), 60.

46. Eric J. Hobsbawm, "Lecture Given at the Central European University, Budapest," reproduced in *Pravada* 2(2); cited in R. A. L. H. Gunawardana, *Historiography in a Time of Ethnic Conflict: Construction of the Past in Contemporary Sri Lanka* (Colombo: Social Scientists' Association, 1995), 1.

47. Fredric Jameson, *The Political Unconscious: Narrative as a Socially Symbolic Act* (Ithaca: Cornell University Press, 1981), 9.

48. Eric Hobsbawm, *On History* (London: Weidenfeld and Nicholson, 1997), 277.

49. Ashis Nandy's latest statement in this regard is *Time Warps: Silent and Evasive Pasts in Indian Politics and Religion* (New Brunswick: Rutgers University Press, 2002). Part of Nandy's controversial argument is that there exists a form of religious tolerance irreducible to secularism and that it can be *recovered* from the Indian pasts.

50. We know that Heidegger made a distinction between fear and anxiety. Anxiety, for him, unlike fear, cannot come from the "world of things at hand," but must come from oneself. *Being and Time*, 174.

51. *Derrida [at Oxford]* (Princeton: Films for the Humanities and Sciences, 1996), a documentary film.

52. In this regard, I cannot engage here Pheng Cheah's important *Spectral Nationality: Passages of Freedom from Kant to Postcolonial Literatures of Liberation* (New York: Columbia University Press, 2003). But it would be worth considering in detail his argument that, contrary to what many critics claim, the postcolonial nation "is the most apposite figure for freedom today" (395).

53. See William Connolly's fine "A Critique of Pure Politics," in his *Why I Am Not a Secularist* (Minneapolis: University of Minnesota Press, 2000).

54. In the contexts of the inauguration and maintenance of the (post)colonial state, law's limitations in attending to the demands of so many gendered and religious others, as evident in the problems of religious conversion (of women), prostitution, child marriage, and female infanticide, are well documented. For

example, see Gauri Vishwanathan, *Outside the Fold: Conversion, Belief, and Modernity* (Princeton: Princeton University Press, 1998), particularly the chapter "Rights of Passage"; Rajeswari Sunder Rajan, *The Scandal of the State: Women, Law, and Citizenship in Postcolonial India* (Durham: Duke University Press, 2003); Partha Chatterjee, *The Nation and Its Fragments: Colonial and Postcolonial Histories* (Princeton: Princeton University Press, 1993), particularly the chapters "The Nation and Its Women" and "Women and the Nation."

55. Amitav Ghosh, *The Glass Palace* (New York: Random House, 2000), 473.

56. Emmanuel Levinas, *Ethics and Infinity: Conversations with Philippe Nemo*, trans. Richard A. Cohen (Pittsburgh: Duquesne University Press, 1985), 77.

57. Derrida, "The Deconstruction of Actuality," 528.

58. Levinas, *Entre Nous*. Here it is worth recalling Derrida's early criticism of Levinas, particularly with regard to his notion of the "face" of the other and its relation to humanism. Derrida writes: "Levinas simultaneously proposes to us a humanism and a metaphysics. It is a question of attaining, via the royal road of [Judeo-Christian] ethics, the supreme existent, the truly existent ('substance' and 'in-itself' are Levinas's expressions) as other. And this existent is man, determined as face in his essence as man on the basis of his resemblance to God." Derrida, "Violence and Metaphysics," in his *Writing and Difference* (Chicago: University of Chicago Press, 1978), 142.

5. Im-passable Limits of Fugitive Politics

1. Qadri Ismail, *Abiding by Sri Lanka: On Peace, Place, and Postcoloniality* (Minneapolis: University of Minnesota Press, 2005), particularly the chapter "Majority Rules."

2. William Connolly, *The Ethos of Pluralization* (Minneapolis: University of Minnesota Press, 1995), xxiv.

3. Sheldon S. Wolin, "Fugitive Democracy," in Seyla Behabib, ed., *Democracy and Difference: Contesting the Boundaries of the Political* (Princeton: Princeton University Press, 1996), makes an important argument about "the futility of seeking democratic renewal by relying on the powers of the modern state" (43). For Wolin, part of the irony is that "democracy is a rebellious movement that may assume revolutionary, destructive proportions," but the democratic governments have domesticated and tamed democracy. While this argument may not appear as new today, I find his suggestion—"democracy needs to be reconceived as something other than a form of government"—important (ibid.) Whereas Wolin seems to recognize something of the aporetic structure of a fugitive democracy, "conditioned by bitter experience, doomed to succeed only temporarily," I am not ultimately persuaded that fugitive democracy as such can continue to animate the question of democracy. I thank Antonio Y. Vazquez Arroyo for pressing me to engage Wolin.

4. Chantal Mouffe, *The Return of the Political* (London: Verso, 1993), 132.

5. Talal Asad, *Formations of the Secular: Christianity, Islam, Modernity* (Stanford: Stanford University Press, 2003), 185.

6. Bernard Cohn, *An Anthropologist Among the Historians and Other Essays* (Delhi: Oxford University Press, 1987). Again, Ismail's *Abiding by Sri Lanka* is a powerful critique of this sort of anthropological practice that privileges the relation between empiricism and knowledge.

7. Michele Ruth Gamburd, *The Kitchen Spoon's Handle: Transnationalism and Sri Lanka's Migrant Housemaids* (Ithaca: Cornell University Press, 2000), 3.

8. Immanuel Kant, "To Perpetual Peace: A Philosophical Sketch" (1795), in *Perpetual Peace and Other Essays: On Politics, History, and Morals*, ed. Ted Humphrey (Indianapolis: Hackett, 1983), 125.

9. John Gray, "Toleration: A Post-liberal Perspective," in his *Enlightenment's Wake: Politics and Culture at the Close of the Modern Age* (London: Routledge, 1995); Partha Chatterjee, "Secularism and Toleration," *Economic and Political Weekly*, July 1994; David Scott, "Toleration and Historical Traditions of Difference," in Partha Chatterjee and Pradeep Jeganathan, eds., *Community, Gender, and Violence: Subaltern Studies XI* (New York: Columbia University Press, 2001).

10. John Locke, "A Letter Concerning Toleration," in *A Letter Concerning Toleration: Latin and English Texts*, ed. Mario Montouri (The Hague: Marius Nijhoff, 1963 [1689]), 84.

11. John Locke, "An Essay on Toleration," in *Locke: Political Essays*, ed. Mark Goldie (Cambridge: Cambridge University Press, 1997), 140.

12. Jean-Jacques Rousseau, "Social Contract or Principles of Political Right," in his *Basic Political Writings*, ed. and trans. Donald A. Cress (Indianapolis: Hackett, 1987), 155. For a suggestive reading of how Rousseau's ideas of sociability and general will are founded on exclusion and violence, see Pierre Saint-Amand, *The Laws of Hostility: Politics, Violence, and the Enlightenment* (Minneapolis: University of Minnesota Press, 1996).

13. Immanuel Kant, "On the Proverb: That May Be True in Theory, But Is of No Practical Use" (1793), in *Perpetual Peace*, 83.

14. Immanuel Kant, "The Answer to the Question: What Is Enlightenment?" in *Perpetual Peace*, 45.

15. For a sample debate about this, see Stanley Fish, *The Trouble with Principle* (Cambridge: Harvard University Press, 1999), particularly chapter 10; Judd Owen, "Fish, Locke, and Religious Neutrality," in *Religion and the Demise of Liberal Rationalism: The Foundational Crisis of the Separation of Church and State* (Chicago: University of Chicago Press, 2001).

16. For a brilliant criticism of disciplinary attempts at universal definitions of religion, see Talal Asad, *Genealogies of Religion: Discipline and Reasons of Power* (Baltimore: Johns Hopkins University Press, 1993).

17. John Rawls, *The Law of the People* (Cambridge: Harvard University Press, 1999), 149–52, 166–68; Richard Rorty, *Achieving Our Country: The Leftist Thought in Twentieth-Century America* (Cambridge: Harvard University Press, 1998), 15–23, 28–30.

18. Richard Rorty, *Contingency, Irony, and Solidarity* (Cambridge: Cambridge University Press, 1989), 21–22.

19. Thomas Jefferson, *Notes on the State of Virginia* (Chapel Hill: University of North Carolina Press, 1987 [1954]), 161.

20. William Connolly, *Why I Am Not a Secularist* (Minneapolis: University of Minnesota Press, 1999), 36.

21. Amy Gutmann, "Religion and State in the United States: A Defense of a Two-Way Protection," in *Obligations of Citizenship and Demands of Faith: Religious Accommodation in Pluralist Democracies* (Princeton: Princeton University Press, 2000), 143.

22. Nancy Rosenblum, ed., *Obligations of Citizenship and the Demands of Faith* (Princeton: Princeton University Press, 2000).

23. Some of this information is based on interviews I conducted in 1997 with people like Raja Wansundara, Arisen Ahubudu, the late Gamini Jayasuriya, and Piyasena Disanayaka, all of whom remain(ed) at the forefront of these organizations as their major spokespersons.

24. Lack of space prohibits me from citing the many interesting newspaper clippings about this debate. A glance at some of the newspapers roughly between September 20 and October 20 will provide rich insights into this acrimonious dispute.

25. Michel Foucault, "Subject and Power," in his *Power*, ed. James D. Faubion (New York: Free, 1994), 342. As Faubion explains in a footnote, "Foucault's neologism is based on the Greek agonisma meaning 'a combat.' The term would hence imply a physical contest in which the opponents develop a strategy of reaction and mutual taunting, as in a wrestling match" (ibid., 348).

26. For a fine discussion of how Mills's version of freedom in relation to the individual self differs from Foucault's, see Michael Clifford, *Political Genealogy After Foucault* (New York: Routledge, 2001), particularly chapter 4.

27. Michel Foucault, "About the Beginning of the Hermeneutics of the Self," in his *Religion and Culture*, ed. Jeremy R. Carrette (New York: Routledge, 2000), 162.

28. Michel Foucault, *The Care of the Self*, trans. Robert Hurley (New York: Vintage, 1986), 65–68, 238; Michel Foucault, "Ethic of Care for the Self as a Practice of Freedom," *Philosophy and Social Criticism* 12:113–14.

29. Foucault, *The Care of the Self*, 238.

30. Martin Heidegger, *Being and Time*, trans. Joan Stambaugh (New York: SUNY Press, 1996), 118.

31. Friedrich Nietzsche, *The Gay Science* (New York: Vintage, 1974), sec. 304.

6. Active Forgetting of History, the "Im-possibility" of Justice

1. Emmanuel Levinas, *Totality and Infinity: An Essay on Exteriority*, trans. Alphonso Lingis (Pittsburgh: Duquesne University Press, 1969); cited in Jacques

Derrida, *Specters of Marx: The State of the Debt, the Work of Mourning, and the New International* (New York: Routledge, 1994), 23.

2. Levinas, *Totality and Infinity*, 72.

3. I discuss différance and its relation to mourning heritage and aporia in chapter 1.

4. For a clear statement on this, see Jacques Derrida, "As If It Were Possible, 'Within Such Limits,'" in *Paper Machine*, trans. Rachel Bowlby (Stanford: Stanford University Press, 2005), 88.

5. Jacques Derrida, "Not Utopia, the Im-possible," in *Paper Machine*, 131. It is precisely on account of a notion like "the im-possible" that Derrida distinguishes himself from thinkers like Levinas. Derrida has "reservations of every kind" with regard to Levinas's concept of justice, which, he says, is founded on the "perversions of ethics that are always possible" (ibid., 135).

6. Jacques Derrida, "A Discussion with Jacques Derrida," *Theory and Event* 5:1(2001); http://muse.jhu.edu/cgi-bin/access.cgi?uri = /journals/theory_and_ event/v005/5.1derrida.html.

7. Derrida develops this idea of auto-immunity in "Faith and Knowledge: Two Sources of Religion at the Limits of Reason Alone," in his *Acts of religion*, ed. Gil Anidjar (New York: Routledge, 2002).

8. Jacques Derrida, "Force of Law: The 'Mystical Foundation of Authority,'" in his *Acts of Religion*, 270. Derrida has in mind here Franz Kafka, "Before the Law," in *Franz Kafka: The Collected Stories*, ed. Nahum Glatzer, trans. Willa and Edwin Muir (New York: Schocken, 1983), 3–4.

9. Derrida, *Specters of Marx*, 10. Hauntology or the ghost in *Hamlet*, for Derrida, runs in the face of the very Shakespearean opposition "to be or not to be?"

10. The most eloquent statement in this regard is, again, Qadri Ismail, *Abiding by Sri Lanka: Peace, Place, and Postcoloniality* (Minneapolis: University of Minnesota Press, 2005). I suspect that anthropologists and historians (of religion) will snub Ismail's work because they cannot risk losing institutional benefits by breaching the parochial perimeters of area studies manned by those "professional" custodians of pragmatic empiricism who hold the reins of powers at universities, funding agencies, and whatnot, ultimately professionalizing, controlling, and colonizing the terms of what should be funded, written, taught, and published. Again, I suspect that anti-essentialist empiricists will ignore this note as a generalization.

11. David Scott's "Dehistoricizing History" appeared first in Pradeep Jeganathan and Qadri Ismail, ed., *Unmaking the Nation* (Colombo: Social Scientist Association, 1995), 10–24; then in David Scott, *Refashioning Futures: Criticism after Postcoloniality* (Princeton: Princeton University Press, 1999), 93–105. All references to the article are from *Refashioning Futures*. It must be noted that I wrote this chapter before the publication of Qadri Ismail's *Abiding by Sri Lanka*. Ismail, who, as we saw earlier, also calls for "de-authorizing of history," takes up Scott's intervention. Ismail acknowledges the critical significance, and, indeed, the impossibility, of his own work without Scott's intervention. But, ultimately, Ismail

finds Scott's response to the debate "too timid" (ibid., 164). For Ismail, Scott's response does not help us deauthorize history; it merely dehistoricizes it, perhaps makes it less historical. I partly agree with this judgment. But I think that Ismail's notion of deauthorizing history has an inadequate conceptualization of the present, which, I would argue, must be understood to be disconnected not only from the past but also from the present itself.

12. Michel Foucault, "Politics, Polemics, and Problematization," in *Ethics, Subjectivity, and Truth*, ed. Paul Rabinow (New York: Free, 1997), 112–13.

13. Friedrich Nietzsche, "On the Uses and Disadvantages of History for Life," in *Untimely Meditations*, trans. R. J. Hollingdale (Cambridge: Cambridge University Press, 1983), 122.

14. Ludwig Wittgenstein, *Philosophical Investigations*, trans. G. E. M. Anscombe (New York: Macmillan, 1968 [1958]), xiii.

15. For an interesting take on the idea of the future in relation to Heidegger's "not-yet," see Dipesh Chakrabarty, *Provincializing Europe: Postcolonial Thought and Historical Difference* (Princeton: Princeton University Press, 2000), 249–53. But we know that for Derrida this "not-yet" is not adequate to thinking the impossibility of the deferred futures.

16. Friedrich Nietzsche, *On the Genealogy of Morals*, trans. Douglas Smith (New York: Oxford University Press, 1996), 39. Also cited in James Soderholm, "Byron, Nietzsche, and the Mystery of Forgetting," *CLIO* 23(1): 51–63. Soderholm is primarily concerned with Nietzsche's interest in Lord Byron's hero Manfred.

17. Even though I use the word *appear* loosely, ghosts do not even appear; they simply return.

18. Wendy Brown, *Politics Out of History* (Princeton: Princeton University Press, 2001), 151.

19. For Derrida's take on the Truth and Reconciliation Commission, see his "On Forgiveness," in *On Cosmopolitanism and Forgiveness: Thinking in Action*, ed. Simon Critchley and Richard Kearney (New York: Routledge, 2001).

20. We need not go too far to point out that Derrida's idea of "not yet *there*" is very different from Heidegger's "not-yet." Note our discussion in chapter 1.

21. Theodor Adorno, "Resignations," in his *Critical Models: Interventions and Catchwords* (New York: Columbia University Press, 1998), 292.

22. Pradeep Jeganathan's work casts doubt on these sorts of explanations of violence. See "After a Riot: Anthropological Locations of Violence," Ph.D. diss., University of Chicago, 1997.

23. Interestingly, Nietzsche noted something of the problem with explanation. For him, explanation, particularly as science does it in terms of cause and effect, is a way to humanize the world "as faithfully as possible," which is to say, "as we describe things and their one-after-another, we learn how to describe ourselves more and more precisely. Cause and effect: such a duality probably never exists." Friedrich Nietzsche, *The Gay Science* (New York: Vintage, 1974), sec. 112.

24. I have in mind an assortment of articles one can easily find on the web by typing something like "LTTE attack on the Katunayaka Airport in Sri Lanka" into a search engine like Google.

25. Note the discussion in chapter 2.

26. Brown, *Politics Out of History*, 147.

27. Writing about majority-directed violence against minorities in Sri Lanka, Sankaran Krishna argues, "We have to explain *why*, even as they help neighbors to escape or provide succor to victims, significant sections of the majority community feel the violence against minority community is, at a certain level, both understandable and necessary." See his *Postcolonial Insecurities: India, Sri Lanka, and the Question of Nationhood* (Minneapolis: University of Minnesota Press, 1999), 55 (emphasis added). Though there is some merit to this statement, it seems to me, the pursuit of the question why is no longer a worthwhile conceptual strategy.

28. I am thinking of Derrida's early essay"The End of the Book and the Beginning of Writing," in his *Of Grammatology*, trans. Gayatri Chakravorty Spivak (Baltimore: Johns Hopkins University Press, 1974), where he launches a powerful critique of the idea of the "metaphysics of presence." Take this key sentence, for example: "the concept of the sign—which has never existed or functioned outside of the history of (the) philosophy (of presence) remains systematically and genealogically determined by that history" (ibid., 14).

7. Politics of "Postsecular" Ethics, Futures of Anti-genealogy

1. See http://www.trinetratours.com/sri-lanka-tours.html. The same description appears on several other websites.

2. The phrase occurs in Maurice Blanchot, *The Unallowable Community* (New York: Station Hill, 1988). Blanchot borrows the phrase from Georges Bataille. Derrida does not name that source. Blanchot's work has been important to Jean-Luc Nancy's *The Inoperative Community* (Minneapolis: University of Minnesota Press, 1991). Derrida, who salutes Bataille, Blanchot, and Nancy "as friends," says that "there is still perhaps some brotherhood" in their work. See Jacques Derrida, *Politics of Friendship*, trans. George Collins (New York: Verso, 1997), 47–49. We will return to the relation between brotherhood and friendship later.

3. The merger between Sri Lankan Airlines and Emirates Airlines took place after the LTTE attack on the Katunayake International Airport and the destruction of more than ten commercial airplanes parked on the tarmac in June of 2001. For more on this, see chapter 6.

4. http://www.srilankan.aero/aboutus/about_srilanka.shtml (emphasis added). In that sense, the airline seems to be heeding the call of scholars who emphasize the importance of seeing culture/religion in kaleidoscopic terms and promote "respect" for others even as they criticize multiculturalism. See Bruce Lawrence, *New Faiths, Old Fears: Muslims and Other Asian Immigrants in American Religious Life* (New York: Columbia University Press, 2002).

5. Will Kymlicka, *Politics in the Vernacular: Nationalism, Multiculturalism, and Citizenship* (New York: Oxford University Press, 2001), 25.

6. Bhikhu Parekh, "Dilemmas of Multicultural Theory of Citizenship," *Constellations* 4(1): 54–62.

7. Kymlicka advocates self-government for groups of "national minorities who have been involuntarily incorporated into a larger state through conquest or colonization or the imperial cession of territory" (*Politics in the Vernacular*, 314).

8. Étienne Balibar, *We, The People of Europe: Reflections on Transnational Citizenship*, trans. James Swenson (Princeton: Princeton University Press, 2003), 23.

9. Amy Gutmann, *Identity in Democracy* (Princeton: Princeton University Press, 2003), 168.

10. Here there is no need to engage Nietzsche's *Genealogy of Morals* and Freud's *Civilization and Its Discontents*, both of which are famous for mocking the idea of conscience. As for Heidegger, even though he speaks of what is called the "call of conscience," his use of the term lacks the sense of "guilt" (*schuld*) or "debt" that Gutmann's use of the term seems to embody. See Martin Heidegger, *Being and Time*, trans. Joan Stambaugh (New York: SUNY Press, 1996), 147–72. The term *schuld* is usually translated as "guilt," but it can, as Dreyfus uses it, also mean "responsibility" and "indebtedness." See Hubert L. Dreyfus, *Being in the World: A Commentary on Heidegger's "Being and Time"* (Cambridge: MIT Press, 1991), 305.

11. I am using pseudonyms here.

12. Now most of our conversation, including this question itself, took place in English. Hence a word about the language. As Pradeep Jeganathan reminds us, in everyday parlance the English word *Tamil* can have a different sense than its counterpart *demala* has in Sinhalese. Consider, for example, the question "oya 'Tamil' da?" (are you Tamil?), as opposed to "oya 'demala' da?" Replacing the word *demala* with the word *Tamil* in this question makes one feel welcome and accepted, as someone who would possibly be a friend and not a total stranger or an enemy. See Pradeep Jeganathan, *At the Water's Edge* (New York: South Focus, 2004), 13–14. I confess that, when I asked Kamalam the question, I was not thinking of that difference between the two words.

13. This is, of course, following the early 1990s privatization of the previously government-owned tea estates. My thinking about some aspects of economic transformations of the tea plantation sector was enriched by conversations with Kanchana N. Ruwanpura. For a brief ethnographic history of Tamil plantation workers, see E.V. Daniel, *Charred Lullabies: Chapters in an Anthropography of Violence* (Princeton: Princeton University Press, 1996), 74–76.

14. Heidegger is referring to his notion of the "call of conscience." As we know now, Heidegger wants to liberate this notion of conscience from its usual sense of guilt and whatnot.

15. For example, see Anne Orford, "Critical Intimacy: Jacques Derrida and the Politics of Friendship," *German Law Journal* 6(1): 31–42. Chris Farrands, "Touching Friendship Beyond Friendship: Friendship and Citizenship in Global Politics," *Alternatives* 26(2): 143–74; Peter Fenves, "Politics of Friendship—Once Again," *Eighteenth Century Studies* 32(2): 133–55.

16. Those who question the political relevance of Derrida's work range from Edward Said to Terry Eagleton. Mark Lilla's slapdash essay "The Politics of Jacques Derrida," in the *New York Review of Books*, June 25, 1998, is an example of such a customer service–based criticism vis-à-vis *Politics of Friendship*. While I would say that this debate yields very little political capital today, I think no serious reader or thinker of Derrida work would claim (as Lilla does) that Derrida is merely interested in a "messianic dream" or "repoliticization."

17. This phrase is from Shakespeare's *Hamlet*.

18. In many ways this is very similar to the question of inheritance that Derrida raised in *Specters of Marx*.

19. The adverb *perhaps* is placed by Derrida in quotation marks to emphasize the Nietzschean sense of it, which I take up below.

20. There are noteworthy names/figures synonymous with other perversions of the Greek tradition of friendship, such as Augustine and Montaigne. Derrida discusses them in terms of texts like (Augustine's) *Confessions* and *Retractions* and (Montaigne's) "On Friendship." For Derrida, both these names mark a very interesting relationship to the Greek tradition. They both "knew Aristotle" (*Politics*, 186). Yet Derrida is careful to suggest that, although they understood friendship differently, from one another and from Greek culture, each nurtured the idea of brotherhood so central to the Aristotelian tradition of friendship. Hence they and "we" mark a culture both old and young. Europe does not inhabit a culture that marks a total rupture with the Greek tradition, at least not yet. "We are here in the vicinity of a generative graft in the body of our culture. 'Our' 'culture' is such an old body, but such a young one too" (*Politics*, 185). As an aside, I would say that here Derrida shows—perhaps intentionally—that he is still too Eurocentric. Of course, I argue, we will have to "un-inherit" Derrida, too, if we are to inherit an anti-genealogical future, in order that he, like Nietzsche, may return as a phantom. Derrida himself demands this of the future.

21. See chapter 4 for more on this.

22. Augustine was indebted to the Aristotelian vocabulary. For example, Augustine defined friendship in terms of the phrase "one soul in twin bodies," and this was the answer that Aristotle sometimes gave to the question: "What is a friend?" Aristotle, *Eudemian Ethics* 7, 1240b, 2–15; cited in Derrida, *Politics*, 177, 190.

23. Derrida quotes a passage from the Gospel according to St. Matthew (vv. 43–48), part of which reads: "love your enemies, pray for your persecutors" (*Politics*, 285). This, of course, is the Christian tradition that Augustine participates in, a tradition Schmitt reinvents by configuring the idea of the enemy as being essential to democracy.

24. Now, as Derrida says clearly elsewhere, Aristotle at least had in mind three kinds of friendship: 1. friendship between two virtuous men, 2. useful, political friendship, and 3. friendship based on pleasure. Now these kinds of friendship hardly conform to one definition but generate various kinds of questions and problems. Should one have a friend who is a political opponent? Should one find friends in political groups? Do politics and friendship belong together at all?

As Derrida writes, "in Aristotle again you have this idea that the quest for justice has nothing to do with politics, you have to go beyond or sometimes betray friendship in the name of friendship. So, there are a number of problems in which you see love—not love, but *philia* or friendship playing an organizing role in the definition of the political experience." Derrida, "Politics and Friendship: A Discussion," http://www.sussex.ac.uk/Units/frenchthought/derrida.html.

25. Friedrich Nietzsche, *Human, All Too Human: A Book for Free Spirits* (Cambridge: Cambridge University Press, 1986) 1, 531; cited in *Politics*, 26.

26. Ibid., 28.

27. Friedrich Nietzsche, *Beyond Good and Evil: Prelude to a Philosophy of the Future*, trans. Walter Kaufmann (New York: Vintage 1966), part 1, "On the Prejudices of Philosophers," para. 2. The edition I am referring to uses the word *maybes*.

28. Rodolphe Gasche, "Perhaps—A Modality? On the Way with Heidegger to Language," *Graduate Philosophy Journal* 16(2); cited in *Politics*, 46.

29. Nietzsche, *Beyond Good and Evil*, para. 214. The "sentence" that Derrida quotes from another edition is slightly different.

30. Georg Wilhelm Friedrich Hegel, *Lectures on the Philosophy of World History*, trans. H. B. Nisbet (Cambridge: Cambridge University Press, 1975), 28. As Koselleck reminds us, Augustine wanted to see all chance "as the singular work of God," while ridiculing the Roman goddess Fortuna. See Reinhart Koselleck, "Chance as Motivational Trace in Historical Writing," in his *Futures Past: On the Semantics of Historical Time*, trans. Keith Tribe (New York: Columbia University Press, 2004). Machiavelli's opposition to the notion of fortune in *The Prince* is, I think, widely known. For more on the history of the concept, see Ian Hacking, *The Taming of Chance* (Cambridge: Cambridge University Press, 1990). Needless to say, although a history of the *concept* of chance may be written, chance is never reducible to any concept of history/time.

31. Recall how Nietzsche warned one against following him down his path instead of "'proceeding on one's own path'" where one "encounters no one." *Daybreak: Thoughts on the Prejudices of Morality* (Cambridge: Cambridge University Press, 1997), 1.

32. Here again Derrida is thinking of figures such as Blanchot, Batialle, and Nancy, who continue to invoke those syntagmas as alternatives to our democratic problems.

33. Nietzsche, *The Gay Science*, 1, 8; cited in Derrida, *Politics*, 62.

34. Carl Schmitt, *The Concept of the Political* (New Brunswick: Rutgers University Press, 1976 [1932]), 26; hereafter referred to as *The Political*; quoted in *Politics*, 109.

35. Schmitt appeals to Plato to justify his distinctions. Schmitt says that the Greeks waged war between themselves and the barbarians. They fought among themselves but never waged war on each other. On this account, Schmitt does not believe in "civil war," because "a people cannot wage war on itself." Derrida questions the accuracy of Schmitt's reading of Plato and the Greek tradition (*Politics*, 90).

36. At the very beginning of *The Political*, Schmitt says: "democracy must do away with all the typical distinctions and depoliticalizations characteristic of the liberal nineteenth century . . . [including] antitheses and divisions pertaining to the state-society." One such liberal division is seeing "religion as the antithesis of the political." (23). I refer here to the 1996 Chicago edition.

37. Now Derrida reminds us that after his conviction and imprisonment for involvement with the Nazi state, Schmitt sought to distance himself from a theologically grounded approach to politics. He claimed that "the theologians tend to define the enemy as something which must be annihilated. But I am a jurist, and not a theologian." Since this claim directly contradicts his emphasis on the "physical killing" of the enemy, Derrida says that Schmitt should be the first one to laugh at his distinction between friend and enemy (*Politics*, 161–62). For more on Schmitt and his relation to Christianity and the notion of utopia, see Gopal Balakrishnan, *The Enemy: An Intellectual Portrait of Carl Schmitt* (New York: Verso, 2000), particularly chapter 17.

38. Briefly, for Schmitt, liberalism is the antithesis of the state and politics. Liberalism seeks to negate politics because of its neutral, "all-embracing" "doctrines." These doctrines would make "impossible" the friend/enemy distinction. The triumph of liberalism means the end of such distinctions and the end of the political itself. See *The Political*.

39. Schmitt's hostility to the liberal tradition perhaps shows more clearly through the odium in which he held the Hague Agreement of 1907 and the Geneva Convention of 1949. In *Theory of the Partisan*, Schmitt says that they undermine the "system of essential distinctions"; cited in *Politics*, 143.

40. The text *Lysis* records a conversation that takes place between Socrates, Lysis, and Menexenus. At the end of the text, the question of what friendship means is never answered. As Socrates says, "we conceive ourselves to be friends with each other—you see I class myself with you—we have not as yet been able to discover what we mean by a friend." This text echoes the structure of the Aristotelian saying, "O my friends, there is no friend"; quoted in *Politics*, 155.

41. "Politics and Friendship: A Discussion," 6.

42. *Nicomachean Ethics*, 9, 4, 1116a 32; cited in *Politics*, 276.

43. Derrida has in mind Maurice Blanchot's *Michel Foucault as I Imagine Him* (New York: Zone, 1987); *Politics*, 299–30. On the other hand, Derrida finds much that is important in Blanchot's other works, such as *The Writing of the Disaster*, trans. Anne Smock (Lincoln: University of Nebraska Press, 1986), where he had sought not to receive the heritage of the Greek tradition. Blanchot attempts to think of friendship and political responsibility in terms of "the proximity of the most distant . . . the contact of what does not reach us . . . the unpresence of the unknown" (ibid.; quoted in *Politics* 196). Yet this thinking of the "unknown" is grounded in a belief in "transforming," always with a view toward "enriching" early Aristotelian notions of friendship (*Politics*, 300). Derrida does not put much stock in this idea of "enriching" a heritage founded upon the violence of the exclusion of the other (*Politics*, 300).

44. I can appreciate Butler's argument that "if identities were no longer fixed

as the premises of a political syllogism, and politics no longer understood as a set of practices derived from the alleged interests that belong to a set of ready-made subjects, *a new configuration of politics would surely emerge from the ruins of the old.*" See her *Gender Trouble: Feminism and the Subversions of Identity* (New York: Routledge 1990), 189–90 (emphasis added). But I wonder if the idea of "a new . . . politics . . . from the ruins of the old" might still run the risk of subscribing to the notion of transforming and enriching of pasts that Derrida distrusts.

Index